Teaching Language Arts Creatively

SECOND EDITION

Teaching Language Arts Creatively

SECOND EDITION

MIMI BRODSKY CHENFELD

HARCOURT BRACE JOVANOVICH, PUBLISHERS
San Diego   New York   Chicago   Austin   Washington, D.C.
London   Sydney   Tokyo   Toronto

To my parents Iris and Joe Kaplan
To my in-laws Rose and Charles Chenfeld
To my kids Cliff, Cara, and Dan and their new families
To my husband Howard, always my safest place

To all the kids and all the teachers and all the families ready for the celebration of learning!

Preface

I wish that we could meet and talk, compare notes and ideas, experiment with old and new approaches, remember the smart and wise and wonderful things we know and have forgotten, discover new nuggets of truth and insight. But that is not possible: Life is too short, our journey is too pressing, and the kids are waiting. So I give you this book.

Teaching Language Arts Creatively, Second Edition, is a textbook of creative and practical ways to teach language arts to students of all ages and all grades. Every page is filled with a passion for learning and a commitment to teaching in life-affirming, success-centered, integrated ways.

I believe more than ever that we must help students make connections. With our students, we must continuously see the relationships among ideas. By considering all ways of learning valid, by respecting the materials, resources, and lives of our students, and by offering numerous and rich approaches to learning and knowing, we help them make meaning out of the world. These experiences happen in *a safe place,* where respect, joy, success, and affirmation define the climate. You can create such a safe place, whether you teach in a school that has an open environment or in one that is more formal and tightly structured. *Teaching Language Arts Creatively,* Second Edition, will help you see how.

Part One is all about YOU—a creative person, a member of a creative tribe. This section asks "How are YOU? What attitudes, beliefs, experiences make up YOU? As the most important component of a child's formal education, how do you feel about language? What is your approach to the curriculum? How do you see your students?" This section is filled with mirrors.

Part Two is all about the language arts currriculum—listening, talking, movement and drama, literature, reading, writing, and skills. Each chapter addresses one of these language arts through activities that are practical, accessible, and classroom-tested. To be usable, the chapters must present the topics separately, but *they are always interrelated:* studying literature through dance, writing to music, practicing skills by writing a class newspaper are activities designed to spark your students' interest in the language arts.

In this Second Edition, such new developments in education as reading recovery, Marie Clay's early intervention theory, Dorothy Heathcote's drama in the classroom, Jeanne Chall's update of reading in America, and Donald Graves' and Lucy Calkin's work on writing conferences are discussed. Increased attention is given to ideas and resources that enrich multicultural understanding, family and community involvement in the schools, computers, movement education, and English as a Second Language. The lists of resources, organizations, periodicals, and bibliographies offered throughout will add to your ever-growing cache of teaching ideas. As in the first edition, each chapter ends with checklists that will help you measure your awareness in the classroom and your students' responses to the curriculum.

In my travels around the country, I have been privileged to work with thousands of kids and teachers in hundreds of schools. They shared their light with me and now I pass it on to you. Many contributed experiences and ideas to this book but did not contribute their names. I am indebted to them as well as to the special people (see pages 407–408) who talked to me, showed me, and wrote to me.

I could write a Yellow Pages of thanks, but special acknowledgments go to the following: John E. Davis of Purdue University, David Moore of the University of Northern Iowa, and Shari Hatch for their careful reviews of the Second Edition manuscript; the Greater Columbus Arts Council's "Artists in the Schools" program; the teachers and students at the Leo Yassenoff Jewish Center's Early Childhood Program; the Johnson Park Middle School Footsteps; the "Days of Creation" Arts Program; the OSU Hillel International Folkdancers; the late Frayda Turkel; Barbara and Phil Newman; Marvin and Nona Rosen; Mark Svede; Anna Grace; Michael Rosen; the "Berwick gang"; Jerb Miller; and the Kaplan, Chenfeld, Cohen, Walcher, Frankel, Bloom, Jacobson, Selinger, Rappaport, and Berger clans. Thanks also to my new families—Jim and the Wilbats, Elaine and the Trabouts, and Chana and the Gandals—and to all my friends, family, and neighbors who did not give up on me.

Special love to my sister, Laura Walcher, and my brother, Mike Kaplan, and their families.

Lastly, I have been fortunate to work with outstanding people at Harcourt Brace Jovanovich. Thank you to Julia Berrisford and Cate Safranek, who supervised and edited with dedication and sensitivity. Thanks also to the other HBJ employees who worked on this book: Ruth Cornell, Susan Holtz, Merilyn Britt, Schamber Richardson, and Ramona Rodger.

MIMI BRODSKY CHENFELD

Contents

9 Write? Of Course Write!   316

10 Smile When You Say Skills   370

EPILOGUE   397

Just the Beginning   398

Special Acknowledgments   407

Index   410

PART
ONE

Before teaching
anyone else,
I must teach
myself . . .

SYLVIA ASHTON-WARNER[1]

1

The Unique You

Every day, the sun; and, after sunset, Night and her stars.
Ever the winds blow; ever the grass grows.
Every day, men and women, conversing—
beholding and beholden—

RALPH WALDO EMERSON[2]

Start with yourself. Did you know that there is only one of you in all of time? Never before, since the beginning of human history, has there existed a person exactly like you! You are unique; you are special. The way you see is peculiar to your own eyesight and your own viewpoint. The way you do things is a reflection of your own particular personality. You and I may walk arm and arm, may share the same park bench, may look at the same scene, and yet come away with very different observations, feelings, and conclusions.

You might see children playing, people talking, crowds bustling in shops and street. *I* might see the loneliness of people passing without speaking, the alienation of the individual lost in the vastness of urban chaos. Marcel Proust said, "The universe is true for all of us and different for each of us."

A Look at You

Who are you? A student? A teacher? A parent? A taxpayer? An athlete? A citizen? You cannot really be labeled, categorized, or filed away. You are not that simple. You are full of surprises. Maybe you just lost thirty pounds and started lessons in yoga. Maybe you just decided to learn to play soccer or to revive an old interest in archeology. Maybe today you feel wonderful, alive and energetic, while yesterday you were dragging around, feeling off-key. One person may think of you as shy and retiring, while another breaks into laughter at the thought of your unusual sense of humor.

Be Yourself

Even if I wanted to, I couldn't *be* exactly like you nor could you *be* exactly like me. We could inspire each other with qualities of personality or behavior to emulate, but there is no way to carbon copy human beings. I once had an outstanding teacher in a graduate education course. Her name was Bess Haile, and she spoke in a soft, relaxed manner. When she instructed children she was very firm in her quiet, unassuming way. She said to them: "I want you to listen very closely to these directions. I am going to tell them to you three times. By the third time, I know you are going to understand our activity." Then she would slowly and deliberately repeat the explanation three times. The children were totally attentive, straining to catch every word. You could almost see their minds working as they listened and remembered her words.

I was so impressed with Bess's approach that I wanted to be like her. I tried her technique of explaining things when I faced my fourth graders the following autumn. It was a failure! Deep down, I'm not the kind of person who can limit the number of times I will give an explanation. I will go on trying to explain something until the very last person in the very last row says "All right! I understand it! Enough!" Even though I loved and admired Bess, I couldn't be like her. I could only be like me. *And you can only be like you.*

There is an old story, attributed to the philosopher Martin Buber, which establishes the belief in the uniqueness of every individual. Every person born into the world represents something new, something that never before existed, something original. The story is about a Rabbi Susya, who said a short while before his death, "In the world to come I shall not be asked, 'Why were you not Moses?' I shall be asked, 'Why were you not Susya?'"

Throughout this book, you will be encouraged to be only one person—*yourself!*

A Knapsack on Your Back

Whoever you are, you have an invisible knapsack attached to your back. It has been part of you since your birth. Everything goes into your knapsack: impressions, sounds, words, songs, sensory images, people, places, things, dreams, fears, good times, bad times. You carry it with you everywhere you go and add to it all of your life.[3]

Your knapsack can never be detached from you. It provides you with a continuing source of material to tap when you want it, when you need it. Such writers as Hermann Hesse, Ray Bradbury, and Madeleine L'Engle strengthen the knapsack image. Hesse's character Steppenwolf muses over his life:

> These pictures—there were hundreds of them, with names and without—all came back . . . they were my life's possession and all its worth. Indestructible and abiding as the stars, these experiences though forgotten could never be erased. Their series was the story of my life, their starry light the undying value of my being. . . .[4]

Ray Bradbury sees all human beings as

> stuffing ourselves with sounds, sights, smells, tastes and textures of people, animals, landscapes, events, large and small. We stuff ourselves with those impressions and experiences and our reaction to them. Into our subconscious goes not only factual data but reactive data, our movement toward or away from the sensed events . . . a fantastic storehouse, our complete being. . . . All that is original lies waiting for us to summon it forth. . . .[5]

Madeleine L'Engle writes about herself (and all of us):

> I am part of every place I have been: the path to the brook, the New York streets, and my "short cut" through the Metropolitan Museum. All the places I have ever walked, talked, slept, have changed and formed me. I am part of all the people I have known. . . . I am still every age that I have been. Because I was once a child, I am always a child. Because I was once a searching adolescent, given to moods and ecstasies, these are still part of me, and always will be. . . .[6]

If you look carefully, you will see the knapsacks on the backs of even the youngest children in school. The material in your knapsack and in those of your students is priceless. It is a resource that never runs out! Dip into your knapsack. Rummage through the layers of words and images that symbolize all your expe-

riences and impressions. Reach for those items that have become important in your life. A common expression today is "get yourself together." We all must get in touch with our deepest feelings and concerns, our strengths and weaknesses, and cut through the layers of inhibition, programmed responses, and stereo-typed answers. Ask yourself questions, such as

What makes me laugh?

What moves me?

What hits me?

What am I enthusiastic about? Curious about? Interested in?

What kind of experiences evoke sensitive responses?

When do I accomplish the most with the least feeling of effort?

In what direction does my energy flow most easily?

Where, in what I'm doing, do I experience myself as most alive?

When does my life sing for me?

What color does air smell like?

Do I know that when I breathe I feed the trees?

In what areas do I feel most competent?

In what areas do I get my best ideas?

When do I get my best ideas?

What things do I want to do, but never get around to doing?

What is the most boring part of what I'm doing? the most exciting?

Am I willing to experiment with new ideas at the risk of their failing?

Does a door keep me in some-where or out of somewhere?

What do I value?

What do I want to do?

What am I doing?

Who am I?

" 'How are you this morning?' The eternal question . . ."[7]

These questions are pertinent to all members of the human family. The process of self-discovery is fascinating and often yields important revelations. After provocative group discussions about ourselves and our lives, children respond enthusiastically to the assignment "What hits you?" "What do you care about?" "Who are you?"

What Hits Me

Beautiful music hits me and excites me.
The thought of suffering hits me and makes me fearful and afraid of it.
A thought expressed in eloquent words thrills me.
Injustice hits me and angers me.
Man's cruelty to his fellow man hits me and infuriates me.
Poverty and ignorance hits me and saddens me.
An honor given to someone I love hits me and makes me joyous.
People indifferent to their surroundings and to events in their lives hit me and frustrate me.
The poisoning of the minds of the younger generation by the older one with the passing on of old hatreds and prejudices hits me and saddens me.
My loneliness in a world of many millions of people hits me and gives me a sense of individuality and oneness.
The knowledge I possess in relation to all the knowledge to be had in the world today affects me, for no matter how knowledgeable I become I will never obtain even one tenth of it.

Esther K.
Age 12

Me

I like the smell of the air.
I love my mom and dad.
I'm afraid of while loins. (wild lions)
The best thing in the world is baceball.
I want a bike.
The best time of day is noon.
The most beautiful sight is Pali Lookout.

Scott
Age 8

Feelings

I like the world.
I love my mother and father.
I'm afraid of robbers.
The best thing in the world is friendship.
I want more friends.
I don't like selfish people.
The best fun is fairs.
It is very hard to tell lies.

Andy
Age 9

When I work with children, I always wear T-shirts with messages. One of my favorite shirts reads I CARE ABOUT THE PUBLIC SCHOOLS. This serves as a launching pad for a collective gathering of words answering the question "What do YOU care about?" In no time, the chalkboard is running over with "care" words. Some samples from a third-grade gathering:

We Care About

families	school	our teacher	our president
pets	friends	our bodies	peace
houses	food	money	god
spring	birthdays	learning	the world

What care words will you write on *your* T-shirt?

Stop, Look, Listen   You, with your bulging knapsack, your unique perceptions and personalities, are a marvelous piece of work. No machine or computer can equal your capabilities or powers. You are probably not even aware of all of your powers. Do you think you come close to functioning at the peak of your abilities?

Think back to a vacation you enjoyed. Were your senses sharp? Did you turn your bright lights on everything? Did you notice the shapes of houses, the types of trees and flowers, stone designs on streets, the contour of hills, sky hues, the smells of food and flowers, the sounds of language and music, old buildings and sculptures? Were you interested, curious, attentive? Did you collect vivid experiences for your knapsack? Did you write lively postcards, jot notes in a journal, make sketches, take photos?

Now, contrast that experience with your day-to-day existence. How observant are you? How much of the day do you catch? What details do you gather? How curious are you about your surroundings? Most of us will admit that our usual everyday visibility is close to zero. We keep our headlights at dim.

George Bernard Shaw wrote:

When I went to those great cities I saw wonders I had never seen in Ireland. But when I came back to Ireland, I found all the wonders there waiting for me. You see, they had been there all the time; but my eyes had never been opened to them. I did not know what my own house was like, because I had never been outside it. . . .[8]

Stop reading this page.

Look around you.

What do you see? Where are you? What is the season? What is the weather outside of your window? What is *your* inner season and weather?

Listen to the sounds around you.

What do you hear? Write down all the sounds that you hear in two minutes. Just as your body needs exercise to grow in a healthy way, so your mind needs exercise to sharpen your imagination and develop your sensory machinery.

Children, too, enjoy a few minutes during a busy school day to appreciate the sights and sounds around them.

> I hear sounds everywhere.
> I hear birds chirping.
> I hear wind blowing.
> I hear dogs barking.
> I hear cars spinning the motor.
> I hear something snapping.
> I hear everything I can.
> I live in a world of sound.
>
> Dan
> Grade 4

> I see chalkboard, chalk, desks, chairs, books, shelves, people, TV, globe, turkey bones, insects, ruler, pencil, paper, me . . .
>
> Jeff
> Grade 6

Take a few minutes out of every day to *stop*, *look*, and *listen*. Record your findings in a journal. The more easily you learn to write, the more effective you will be in guiding youngsters to write more fluently, more freely.

The Focus Is on You

Self-searching is not easy. Sometimes it's a great struggle to marshal the courage to look clearly at yourself, and sometimes it can be fun. Whether painful or pleasurable, the process is important in developing a creative way of teaching. Before you extend your energies into the classroom, you must be in touch with yourself, with your own energies. Emerson wrote, "As I am, so I see." Let me amend that to "As I am, so I teach." Everything you do in life is caught up in the kind of person you are. Your teaching will be an extension and a reflection of yourself.

The amazing thing about focusing on yourself is that there is no end to the search. The more you discover about yourself, the more there will be to discover. You are a never-ending source of information and wonder.

An enjoyable way of finding out a little more about yourself (remembering things you may have forgotten) is to write a collage. There are many variations of this activity, but here is one of the most effective. First write down your name and your nicknames. Under the names, write the words "I am" followed by your present address and any other places you have lived. Then write "I am" again and follow it with your responses to such questions as

What *times of day* most reflect my spirit?

What *kinds of clothing* most represent me?

What *seasons* am I? *colors? textures? holidays?*

What are my favorite *places? objects? foods?*

Who are my *heroes? heroines?*

What *myths, folk tales, legends* most intrigue me?

What are my favorite *books? stories? works of art?*

What *sounds* would I record on a tape to describe myself?

Here are a few examples by elementary school and university students who responded to collage writing with enthusiasm.

I am saddle shoes, sandals, tennis shoes . . .
I am pizza, cookies, cheese, cupcakes . . .

Marianne C.
Grade 3

I am a bird . . . blue jay, cardinal, seagull . . .
I am a time of day; noon, 8:05 A.M.

Lisa K.
Grade 5

I am an animal lover . . . dogs, cats, Polar Bear, birds, horses . . .
I am trees . . . redwood, pine cone, oak, maple. . . .

Michelle C.
Grade 5

I am golden! I am blue! I am bouncy . . .
I am spring—unpredictable?
One day a calm and serene May day?
Another time, I can be a stormy, dark,
threatening April thunderhead racing
across the sky ready to dip down and
destroy . . .
I am an egg ready to hatch. . . .

Nancy Lee
University

I'm a buckwheat pancake, grapefruit with maraschino cherry, scrambled egg, whole wheat toast with fresh strawberry jam BIG BREAKFAST EATER from a country-type childhood on an Illinois farm . . . I'm a Colorado, not a Florida Vacation, a Maine-rather-than-ever-live-in-California type person; a Vista dome train rather than a plane. . . .

Marg Hoskins
University

> I'm faded denim jeans,
> rustic furniture. Old country
> homes and kerosene lamps.
> I'm ancestors, memories,
> old tintypes, musty records
> and family legends. . . .
>   Nancy Siders
>   University

Inside/Outside Bags   One dramatic way to encourage self-discovery begins with a simple paper bag. Gather magazines and newspapers and cut out words that you think describe the YOU the outside world sees. Paste those words on the outside of the bag. Now find words that describe the YOU known only to those who know you well—your friends and family. These are the qualities not so easily seen by most people. Paste or tape those inside words to the inside of your bag.

The outside words can be clearly seen by all, just as your more public qualities are readily recognized. But if people want to discover your deeper qualities they must look inside.

This activity is especially successful with middle-graders, who need a variety of challenging ways to express themselves.

Remember to *share*! Sharing is an important part of the experience. It makes us aware of both our individual uniqueness and our common bonds.

How Old Are You?

What are *your* statistics? The fourth/fifth grade group hushed in concentration as pencils scratched figures. It was Kira's tenth birthday that day. This is what she discovered:

> Today is my 10th birthday.
> I am 10 years old.
> I am 120 months old.
> I am 520 weeks old.
> I am 3,650 days old.
> I am 87,600 hours old.
> I am 5,256,000 minutes old.
> I am 315,360,000 seconds old.

Is a minute a long or short period of time? How many solid minutes of your life can you remember? How many hours? Are your statistics changing as you read this page?

I share these questions with children of all ages, and they immediately respond to the challenge of facing their own time. Apathetic kids, slumped with folded arms and half-mast "show-me" eyes, sit bolt upright and open their minds' eyes at the revelation of their statistics. A feeling of self-worth invigorates them. A new urgency catches them. We talk about the uniqueness of every single person. We share the idea of the knapsack and the wealth of experiences that are part of us all. We write, creating new patterns, discovering new avenues of communication. We take one minute of our time and write. The world may keep spinning for centuries, but never again will there be another minute *exactly* like this one.

One Minute

Boy One Minute
Yicky! Yoummy! EEk!
Google! Oh! Yea!
Slurp! Helping! One!
Slop! Super! Lee!

Lee C.
Grade 5

One Minute

A dog running. Pencils writing.
A girl going to a party.
The teacher turning pages.
People breathing. Little pieces of
dust flying around the room.
Erasers erasing.

Barb G.
Grade 5

One Minute

I can't think of nothing right now
only I'm happy on this spring day.

Grade 4

8:48 A.M.

I am writing. I'm on the floor.
There is a plane going over. I'm
in school. It is now about 12 till 9.
It is up. Time is up.

Connie H.
Grade 5

Write for one minute. This minute. In a minute your mind can travel across miles and through years. When you write down the feelings, images, memories, and thoughts of any given minute of your time, you are recording the journey of your mind on the map of your life. Writing is like marking your time. Your written words will hold those recorded moments as vividly as photographs catch people and events. Share your "minutes" by reading them aloud.

Your Powers of Awareness

People like the writer Jesse Stuart's father see the world with special eyesight.

My father didn't have to travel over the country like other people searching for something very beautiful to see. Not until very late in life was he ever 100 miles away from home. He found beauty everywhere around him. He had eyes to find it. He had a mind to know it. He had a heart to appreciate it. He was an uneducated poet of this earth.[9]

Theodore Roethke said, "I wish I could find an event that meant as much as simple seeing."[10]

Walt Whitman wrote, "I think I will do nothing now but listen."[11]

tune up your equipment

What do you see when you turn on all your lights? Commit yourself to a way of life that keeps your senses and mind alive and working. Rediscover how exciting the most ordinary scenes can become under close observation. Catch the special flavor of every day. Do you take life for granted? Cast your special lights on everything around you. Be a person on whom nothing is ever lost. You are in control of your machinery. Would you tolerate a slurry-sounding tape recording, a blurry television picture, or a stereo crackling with static? So, tune up your own amazing equipment. *As you are, so you teach!*

My knapsack is packed with shining examples of kids using their special powers. For example, one day the fifth graders and I were in the gym/multi-purpose room/cafeteria. We were celebrating the idea of Peace through movement, music, words, song, design. Just as we really began to touch the theme, the cafeteria staff began setting up tables, clinking dishes, and readying half the space for lunch. Early lunch classes formed lines and scraped trays. The fifth graders were lost to the theme of Peace. All eyes followed the action of *lunch*. I drew the children closer to me and talked to them about their ability *to select from everything around them what they wanted to pay attention to*. They had the power to make choices and to concentrate their attention on whatever place or idea they chose. I asked them to try to shut out all the distracting activities around them and shine their "brights" on our small area and on what we were doing. They agreed, and our celebration of Peace turned out to be one of the most moving and effective I have ever experienced.

You Are Creative

If someone asked you if you were a creative person, what do you think you would say? Would you answer, "Me? I'm not at all creative! I can't play an instrument, dance, or sing a note." "Creative? No way. I can't draw a straight line."

Creativity is getting to be one of those overused but greatly misunderstood words, because it is usually associated with the making of some sort of artistic product—a symphony, a ballet, a picture, or a sculpture. There is a far broader approach to the concept of creativity than to tie it solely to a specific artistic achievement. Creativity is a process, a way of thinking, a way of living.

Stretch your mind and try to answer these questions.

Have you ever rearranged or revised a plan, room, or project?

Have you ever exhibited adventurous thinking or tried something unfamiliar that took you away from the main track?

Have you ever explored a new idea or experimented with a different way of doing something, even at the risk of failing?

Have you ever made up a song or a story or improvised a game?

I'm referring to the widespread kind of creativeness that stamps all people. Observe children making games from air, constructing toys from junk, building sculptures from popsicle sticks, making houses out of cardboard boxes. See city kids turn a crowded, traffic-jammed street into a playing field, change a tin can into a ball, and play a new game. Think about the many ways we improvise, rearrange, and change the elements of our environment to make something new, something meaningful to us, something we want or need.

The Creative Response   People express creativeness in their response to their existence and environment. Such scholars as E. Paul Torrance and Abraham Maslow focus their studies of creativity on those qualities of personality that cluster under the label "creativity"[12]: people are curious, spontaneous creatures, willing to go out on a limb to find answers, courageous in their attempts to solve problems, adventurous in their exploration of new ideas, flexible in their approach to life. They synthesize—link things together—to make something new. They are capable of demonstrating originality and inventiveness, the fruits of imaginative thinking. They are aware and sensitive and have the ability to respond to life situations and stimuli in a positive way— creating rather than simply reacting—which separates them from all other species on earth.

People hate emptiness. They cover empty paper and canvas with words and colors. They pour sounds into empty air. They build shapes to fill empty spaces. They design movement to occupy empty time. People want to leave ,more of themselves on earth than their bones. They splash graffiti on New York City subways, carve initials in the bark of trees and on the backs of old park benches. They paint "Kilroy was here" on the peaks of mountains and stamp their footprints in newly poured concrete sidewalks. "The universe resounds with the joyful cry—I am!"[13]

If you have ever arranged or rearranged, acted spontaneously in response to an immediate challenge, experienced a moment to its fullest, or followed an unfamiliar path, then you have expressed what we are talking about—creativity that goes far beyond drawing a straight line or playing a musical instrument.

We Belong to a Creative Family

Robins sing robins' songs and build robins' nests. Robins don't play around with bluebirds' songs or wrens' nests. Only human beings "play around"—experiment, make new sounds and shapes.

Jog to the woods on a snowy day and follow an animal's tracks. Deer, rabbits, horses all leave easily identifiable ones. But never has one deer whispered mischievously to another, "I'm sick of making deer tracks. Let's pretend to be rabbits today and leave rabbit tracks!" Only humans have this *gift*, this ability to imagine, to pretend, to experiment with new ideas, to make something different, to change, to rearrange.

We think of young children as being especially creative. They have refreshing ways of expressing feelings and observations; they are filled with a free, imaginative playfulness, an extraordinary ability to pretend. Thoreau said, "Every child begins the world again."

Two-and-a-half-year-old Emmy found her grandmother's worn yellow house slippers.

"Grammy," she called, running to her grandmother, "Are these the golden slippers you wore when you were a prince?"

I asked the four-year-olds in preschool if they knew what caterpillars turned into. Without hesitation, Jordan answered,

"Caterpillars turn into butterflowers."

Dan added the question, "Do you think the butterfly remembers being a caterpillar?"

"Want to meet my two make-believe friends?" Gregory, four years old, asks me.

"Sure, what are their names?"

"Amy and Deena. They're outside. Want me to get them?"

"Any friends of yours, Gregory, are friends of mine. Bring them in."

"I've had them since I was little," he says, running to open the door.

We were all born with creative abilities and lived by those abilities as we groped and crawled our way through new discoveries and challenges. No one sat next to our cribs twenty-four hours a day giving instructions on how to turn over or find our toes. Perhaps someone in your family remembers the joy on your face when you suddenly understood a puzzle, whether it was your own hands, how to ring a bell, or how to say a first word.

How are you now? Are you still a person who knows the joy and the excitement of discovering and exploring new ways, new experiences?

Do you still celebrate learning?

Creativity: Encouraged or Discouraged?

As strong and universal as are the qualities of creativeness in all people, so these same qualities are fragile and easily destroyed. Before we talk about the strength and persistence of creativity in society and throughout history, it is essential that you try to remember your own history. Did your family, teachers, and friends respond positively to your creative efforts or were such efforts criticized or ridiculed? Did your brothers, sisters, and friends accept and respect your creative activities and products or were your efforts met with apathy and indifference? Were you trapped by rigid sex roles? Were you afraid to experiment with more original endeavors because they might be considered "sissy" or different? Did you learn at home and at school to be afraid to try new ideas because of possible failure? Were you afraid of making a fool of yourself? Were you discouraged or encouraged in your creative development? How can you encourage the creative growth of your students if you don't get in touch with your own creative process and experiences?

CAREFUL

Katy, a merry first grader, jumped into her assignment. "Make a clock and be sure all the numbers on your clock are clearly printed."

Katy, always enthusiastic, carefully wrote the twelve numbers of the clock on a round paper plate. They were perfect. So beautiful that she was inspired to decorate each number with a tiny flower around it. She hurried to school with her colorful clock held in her hands like an offering.

A different child returned home from school that day. Back slumped, head bent, eyes down, she opened the door.

"Did your teacher like your clock, Katy?" her mother asked anxiously.

Without a word, Katy dropped the clock on the floor. Her mother picked it up. Across the face of the clock, scratched so deeply that it tore the paper, was a huge X and, in angry handwriting, the teacher's message:

"Did not follow instructions."[14]

What happened to the celebration of learning?

I'm Worried about Our Kids

The eighties have been turbulent years for American education. One of the most disturbing developments has been the push for educators to start very young children in highly formalized, tightly structured, adult-directed learning experiences. Once familiar images of children playing in sand boxes, humming to themselves as they discover the wonders of the world, have been largely pushed aside. Anxious parents, already worried about their children's ability to compete in the job market of the decades to come, are demanding a rigid "back to basics" curriculum to ensure their success. In such a system, the freedom of spirit, the imagination, curiosity, and courage to explore that we associate with young children, must diminish.

This movement has inspired reaction in such strongly written books as Marie Winn's *Children Without Childhood* (Pantheon, 1983) and David Elkind's *The Hurried Child: Growing Too Fast, Too Soon* (Addison-Wesley, 1981) and *The Miseducation of Children: Superkids at Risk* (Knopf, 1986). A new term was introduced to America when *Newsweek* Magazine's cover story of March 28, 1983, carried the title "Bringing Up Superbaby" and the subtitle "Parents Are Pushing Their Kids to Learn Earlier Than Ever. Does It Help or Hurt?" The article featured the accomplishments of infants and toddlers and gave accounts of how some programs and materials have succeeded in teaching babies to read, to do math, to learn to play musical instruments. Some of the programs offered educational flash cards to be introduced soon after birth! (Before or after we cut the cord?)

Does such pressure and high expectation coming from families and schools encourage or discourage creativity in young children? *What do you think?*

I'm worried about our kids! I'm afraid that many of these "superbabies" are learning how NOT to be children. They are learning—before they need to, more than they need to—about tension, competition, failure, disappointment, and frustration. Most important, they might be learning that love is somehow connected to how successfully they can perform for their parents and teachers.

Children who lose their spirit of adventure, their willingness to risk in new experiences, their ability to play with ideas and concepts, can be considered "deprived," even "handicapped." In this unnatural, high-anxiety setting, there is no room for questions, no slot reserved for spontaneous discovery and the excitement of learning. In this scheme of things, it's the product that is emphasized. The process is devalued.

Plato believed that "the only beginning of learning is wonder." Where does wonder fit into this accelerated, pressure-cooker scheme?[15]

In an article in *Phi Delta Kappan*, David Elkind reminds us that young children do not learn in the same way that older children and adults do. "They learn best through direct encounters with their world rather than through formal education involving the inculcation of symbolic rules." He believes that sound early childhood education encourages children's self-directed learning by providing an environment that is rich in materials to explore, manipulate, and talk about.[16]

What Elkind describes is quite a contrast to the new kindergarten found in too many schools: no longer a "garden of children" but a mini-model of first grade where play is downplayed, free time is no time, and reading for pleasure has turned into mastering reading skills under pressure.

Mary K. Willert and Constance Kamii discuss this push "back to basics." They describe how many kindergartens teach phonics to prepare children for first grade and how some child-care centers give worksheets to four-year-olds. The authors believe that this kind of early direct instruction is employed based on the "erroneous assumption that children are like empty glasses who learn by having bits of knowledge poured into them, and that the sooner we start to fill the glasses, the sooner the process will be completed."[17] Willert and Kamii have found that such dry and solitary activities as phonics lessons and worksheets do not encourage the exchange of ideas among children. Yet in traditional instruction children are generally told to do their own work and not to help others. We must ask ourselves—what is the purpose of education? Is it only to achieve high test scores, or is it to "enhance children's *desire* to read, to write well, to acquire more knowledge, to think critically about what they read and to communicate effectively with other people?"[18]

Craig Ramey, quoted in the "Bringing Up Superbaby" issue of *Newsweek*, warns us that

A sure prescription for trouble is making learning stressful. Scientists don't exactly know how much information gets into the brain but there are hints that experiences infused with unpleasant emotions never reach the memory banks. If an hour with cue cards makes the child anxious, the lesson may never be learned—and future lessons will be less effective. [19]

Consider the most terrible possible outcome: The suicide rate among our young people has escalated frighteningly. Many of those young suicides indicated that anxiety over academic achievement and fear of academic failure caused them to choose death.

If our youngest children are already being introduced to anxiety and failure, what is in store for them as they grow toward adolescence?

I'm worried about our kids!

Examine Your Attitudes

Do you know people whose spark has been dimmed, whose song has been stilled in their throats? People who stay on familiar ground and don't venture beyond, who are closed to new ideas, inflexible in their thinking, afraid of what others may think of them? *Have you ever felt that way yourself?* If all humans are born with courage, spontaneity, flexibility, curiosity, and awareness—the stuff of creativity—why do so many of them lose touch with that vital part of themselves?

Many of our most outstanding thinkers have explored this subject and have identified the factors that discourage the healthy, natural development of creativity in individuals and groups. Some of these destructive agents are undue criticism, ridicule, overemphasis on "right answers" and on doing things the "correct way." All these things lead to a fear of failure, a fear of taking a risk, and a cautious, repressed approach to life and learning and foster a stereotyped attitude toward sex roles.

Do you think that most put-downs of originality and self-expression are deliberate—or thoughtless? Have you ever, unwittingly, discouraged the original self-expression of another person? Jot down a list of behaviors that discourage creativity. From now on, become more aware of negative attitudes in others. Sometimes a sarcastic word or a giggle of ridicule can freeze the flow of ideas and expression in a person or a group. Children are experts in put-downs. "That's stupid!" "How dumb can you be?" "What a weird thing to do!" are commonly heard. They are arrows that pierce people's hearts, silencing their words and paralyzing their plans.

Even more important, become aware of your own attitudes and behavior toward your own creativity as well as that of others. Sometimes we are our own worst enemy. We block ourselves more effectively than does anyone else. We say, "Oh, I can't do *that!* I'm no good at *that!* I never did *that* before and I don't want to make a fool of myself!" As a result, we stop ourselves from trying something new.

Similarly, do you put down others who are exploring and experimenting with new methods and materials? Consider how easily we give up our freedom of expression and range of movement and activity when we hold ourselves back, reading STOP when we should read GO. There are no guarantees that any idea or activity will succeed absolutely. The safest, most familiar paths have their own risks. Living life to the fullest, reaching out to new experiences, expanding your own range of interests and ideas, developing your own abilities to search, explore, and experiment are qualities of creativity.

"Before I teach others, I must teach myself."

Leo Buscaglia said,

> If you want the people in your life space to become, then you must become. . . . If you want them to be free, then you must be free. . . . I have never known a dead teacher to teach life. A dead teacher can only teach death.[20]

Metaphors help shape my life. Here is one of my most vivid images: The minute we wake in the morning, a voting booth is waiting for us. Only two issues are on the ballot: LIFE and DEATH. If we vote for DEATH, we choose all the negatives: discouragement, frustration, anxiety, disappointment, bitterness, jealousy, fear, disillusionment, anger, "don't," "can't", "won't." If we vote for LIFE, we choose the positives: affirmation, appreciation, wonder, anticipation, enthusiasm, optimism, encouragement, serendipity, trust, courage, faith, "will," "can," "do."

The best thing about this voting process is that we can vote anytime, not just every four years! If we vote DEATH at 7 A.M., we can turn around at 7:15 A.M. and vote again, this time for LIFE. Our vote counts. It affects our words, thoughts, and feelings, our actions and reactions. It shapes our time.

How did you vote this morning? This afternoon? Five minutes ago? Did this page catch you in the middle of deciding?

Hector Babenco, a Brazilian film director, shared a bit of his philosophy in a *New York Times* interview: "I prefer to say Yes instead of No. I am from the Culture of Yes."[21] *Are you from the "Culture of Yes" or from the "Culture of No"?*

Preserving your own natural, healthy energies and those of others is a matter of life and death. It is not a curriculum item that can be cut from a school budget or relegated to a specific time slot. *It is no less than a way of life, a way of living, a way of teaching.*

Perhaps you feel, as we all do at times, that you are not capable of originality or inventiveness, that education is a painful process yielding little satisfaction. You have *both* forces within you vying for your attention, your vote. You can *choose*. (Remember, on those uninventive days, your knapsack, packed with memories of explorations, joyous moments, amazing discoveries. Remember within you the flames of curiosity and adventure.) The voting booth is waiting for you.

First we must nurture our own spirits, our own wellspring of unique resources. Then we will be able to ensure the health and safety of children's spirits. With us, they can learn that life holds many wonders; our journey together can be one of discovery and appreciation. Together, we can enrich the quality of our experiences.

We can ask open-ended questions that encourage creativity and original-ity—questions such as

How does a rainy day make you feel?

If you were as tiny as Thumbelina how would your life change? What would you see? Hear? Think? Touch?

There are so many interesting ways to travel from New York to California. How would you go?

Or we can ask questions like these:

How long was the Six Day War?

When was the War of 1812?

What flower was the Wars of the Roses named after?

If you were making a list of all the antonyms for *creative*, you might start with words such as *flat, tight, frightened, closed, rigid, overly cautious, inflex-ible, apathetic, overly critical.* What others can you think of? People who have lost touch with their creative energies are, according to Maslow, "people who can't laugh or play or love or be silly or trusting or childish . . . people whose imagination, intuitions, softness and emotionality seem to be strangulated or distorted . . ."[22] People who live in the "Culture of NO!"

Starting with ourselves (you, me), we need to work toward becoming peo-ple who do not cling to the familiar; who do not have an unbending need for certainty, safety, definition, and order; who are not afraid of what other people will say or demand or laugh at. We need to free our imaginations, spirits, and bodies so that we can become more spontaneous, less controlled, less rigid— less compartmentalized! We must learn to synthesize—to unify our lives. [23]

We need to practice saying YES to LIFE. How are you voting today?

We Can Develop Our Creative Powers

Creativity is not a static quality. We can develop our own creative powers as well as provide an environment that will nourish and strengthen those of our students. Pledge yourself fiercely to these goals. Begin with yourself. Your own creativity can grow and expand. Just as your body can be developed with exercise and healthy eating, so your powers of self-expression, spontaneity, courage, flexibility, awareness, and willingness to try new methods can be strengthened.

Alex Osborn, a writer as well as a student of creativity, suggests that

> the highest form of imagination is the truly creative. Through this we seek new slants on old facts. We reach beyond the facts at hand in search of facts not yet known. . . . We use imagination as a searchlight. . . . We beam it hither and thither, into the known and the unknown. Thus we "discover."
>
> We use creative imagination to combine known elements in order to produce the unknown. By changing combinations, we turn out still more ideas. Ideas which otherwise would not come to us. Thus, we "invent"— whether it be a new plot, a new mousetrap or a better way of living our lives. . . . [24]

Heed Goethe, who wrote, "We must always change, renew, rejuvenate ourselves; otherwise we harden."

Open your mind! Open your eyes! Open yourself to new experiences, ideas, materials. Buscaglia speaks of creativity as our ability to

> see the continual wonder and joy of being alive! I am sure that God meant for us to be happy because he put so many beautiful things in our lives—trees and birds and faces. There are not two things alike. How can you get bored? There has never been the same sunset twice. Look at everybody's face. It's different. Everybody has his own beauty. There have never been two flowers alike. Nature abhors sameness. Two blades of grass are different. . . . When you are teaching, teach. When you are now talking with someone, talk. When you are looking at a flower, look. Catch the beauty of the moment! [25]

The philosopher Martin Buber believed that everything is waiting to be hallowed by you. For this, your beginning, God created the world. What do you hallow?

I know a man who decided to spend an entire week of his life being "creative." On the first day, he wrote a poem. On the second, he painted a picture. On the third, he composed a song. On the fourth, he built a sculpture. On the fifth, he made up a dance. On the sixth, he invented something. On the seventh, he rested. He claims he hasn't done anything "creative" since!

I don't recommend that method as a way of exercising your creative potential! That smacks of our American instant remedies. The ninety-eight-pound weakling who works on developing his muscles doesn't turn into Mr. Universe overnight. It takes time and effort. And even after he achieves Mr. Universe status, he must keep a daily schedule of exercise and healthy habits or he will dissolve into Mr. Flab. Developing your imaginative powers, widening your vision, flexing your flexibility, tuning up your sensitivity and awareness are daily commitments to a bold, new way of living your life. Mauree Applegate reflects: "Creativeness cannot be taught; it can only be released and guided."[26]

All your statistics are changing. This day will never come again. Unless you believe in reincarnation, *this is your life*. How you live it is up to you. What can you do with your days to make each of them wonder-full? How can you strengthen your own creative abilities? Here are some starters.

Keep a Journal   Write in a journal every day, even if your writing amounts to "I can't think of anything to write today." Keep notes on your existence for your own eyes, for your own sake. It's a good discipline as well as a valuable exercise in creative expression. How many times has a fleeting idea or intriguing thought flown into and out of your mind? Jot down those wandering observations, random mind-notes, and surprise yourself with what is churning inside of you waiting to be expressed.

Gather Sense Impressions   Write impressions in your journal. Out of all the sights, sounds, smells, tastes, and touches you experience each day, train your mind to note at least *one* for each sense, then move on to two . . .

Turn On Your Bright Lights   Your vast, intricate machinery is waiting for you to turn it to its highest level. Choose *something* to focus on each week— it can be humorous, like mustaches, or scientific, like signs of electricity, or humanistic, like the ways people speak or laugh. Choose your topic. Pay attention to it. Jot down your observations in your journal, the way an art student does quick sketches. You will be astonished at your powers of observation and awareness.

Make a New Day's Resolution   Professor Herb Sandberg gave his students a simple assignment: "Do something you never did before and write about it." It turned out to be the most enthusiastically received assignment of the school year.

There are so many possibilities for launching into a new experience that the list could fill this book. Just for starters, why don't you

Walk on a street you've never walked on.

Listen to a new record.

Order something different from a menu.

Read a book by an author you don't know.

See a movie without reading a review of it beforehand.

Try walking in a new style.

See how many shapes you can make with your hands.

Listen to the sounds you can create.

Collect a pile of junk and make something out of it.

Learn a new word.

Make up a new word.

Make a funny face.

Take a chance.

Do all of the above.

Do none of the above.

Add your own ideas.

Get Ready for a Journey

This book is a journey through the language arts curriculum in which we emphasize originality and joyfulness—creative ways of teaching language arts, of celebrating learning. Just as muscles must be warmed up in order to swim the lake or ride a bike, so imaginations have to be exercised and creative energies revived for that other, larger journey—a trip that really lasts a lifetime.

Can you think of other ways to prepare yourself for living a more creative life?

Take a Look at the World Outside

So far, the focus has been on *you*, a unique individual with your own wealth of experiences, your own special interests and attitudes, your own creative potential.

However, you do not exist in a vacuum. You are not a neutral being dangling in empty space but part of a greater community in which you live and learn and teach, which you affect and by which you are affected.

In modern American society, scientific and technological achievements have exceeded the expectations of all except science-fiction writers and dreamers. We have put human beings on the moon. We dial telephones and speak to people continents away. We press buttons that start numerous swirling, pounding machines that wash our clothes, dry our dishes, sort our papers, and massage our faces. We can flip on television and see football games, soap operas, or assassinations. Our children hardly blink at violence, fear, hatred, or chaos as these images are flashed to them between advertisements for beer, bras, and bikes. *Or do they?*

Our technology brings events and personalities to our immediate attention. We see them at the moment of their happening. We see leaders elected, governments toppled, natural and man-made disasters and triumphs on screens in our living rooms. Daily, the mass media report stories of divorce, suicide, runaways, alcoholism, mental illness, and drug addiction. We listen to political leaders speak of integrity and morality and know their words can cover deception and betrayal. We applaud our scientists' search for cures for cancer, while we release pollutants into our already dangerously polluted air. We search for roots as we uproot, changing jobs, schools, and homes with unprecedented frequency. We cannot keep up with all the headlines, all the events, all the catastrophes and celebrations. The speed of their happening mixed with the immediacy of our knowing often dulls our feelings and shrinks our capacity for compassion. Perhaps *numbness* is the word to describe the feeling that can overtake the individual caught in the vortex of our rapidly changing society.

We met an acquaintance at the airport. He told of being a passenger on a hijacked plane.

"What was it like? How did you feel?"

He shrugged. "I guess we read so much about hijacking and see it so much on television that it didn't seem real. No one really believed it was happening."

What can happen to our children who spend hours watching television or listening to a stereo blare? According to Sylvia Ashton-Warner, the cause for concern is not that the channel outward is blocked to this imagery; it is that a defenseless human mind, the frail, unique marvel of a child's living feelings, is being bombarded into sedation or even extinction by overstimulation. She warns that our children no longer feel with love or with hatred; they do not feel at all. With the third dimension muted or erased, we have people with only two dimensions—and that's how they stay for life.[27] Even the words our children hear and read can cause a kind of existential numbness, a feeling of disbelief, a loss of sensitivity and responsiveness. The words once cherished by the great writers and carefully chosen for song, poem, and story have been captured by modern advertising: *joy* has turned into a dishwashing liquid, *total* into a cereal, *white cloud* into toilet paper, *all* into a laundry detergent, and *time* into a magazine.*

Play the game yourself. Browse through any magazine or newspaper and see how many words that once inspired readers now label a product. When you are exhausted from this assignment, you can lie down in beauty and rest, which is a mattress, until dawn, another dishwashing liquid, and for breakfast have toast made from wonder, which is a bread.

As we grow accustomed to the hype of advertising, we also get used to the familiar topics of hostility and destruction shouted at us from the daily headlines and nightly news. *Or do we?*

Our children are exhibiting a new fear—the fear of nuclear holocaust, the fear of no future. In 1983, one TV network presented a special program about nuclear war called *The Day After*. Kim Morrison, then a high school junior, wrote a poem that captures the emotions of many children.

---

*Eve Merriam's poem "Checklist," from *The Nixon Papers* (New York: Atheneum, 1970), reflects this same concern.

from the journal of Kim Morrison   11-83

Don't want my mother dying in some old nuclear war.
Don't want my brother or sister dying in a nuclear war.

Somewhere an adult is getting a new toy.
I hear him saying,
"Hey friends, I split an atom. Can you help me
clear Detroit? I made a bomb and I
let them have it. There's millions dying still.
I'm awful sorry about all our babies
but, see, they got in the way."
(Come back, kids, now we have time to play.)
"Hey, friends, I split an atom. Can you help me
clear Detroit? I made a bomb and I
let them have it. There's millions dying still."
You say, "What about the younger generation?"
Well, look around, There's millions dying still.

We killed them all. Yes, we let them have it
'cause they got in the way.
(Come back, kids, now we have time to play.)
I see a baby in a cradle.
She didn't even get a chance to live.
I'm awfully sorry. But, see,
they got in the way
with all their talk of Peace and Freedom—
and they would change it to *their* way
with no nuclear play.
I know someday we'll all be released
and at ease because kids have something
that adults don't need to lose.

We are the future
but it seems like we have nothing
in common.
Visions of yesterday—how fast
they slip away.
Every life is meant for living,
it's the same for everyone.
Though the world is run by dreamers,
we kids are part of that dream.

If the world was made for dreamers,
let the kids have a chance to dream.

Tie a Knot in Your Belt/Build a House Made of Bricks

Here in the midst of the churning—in the center of the storm of words, images and events—is the individual. Here we stand, trying to find some meaning, some order; trying to make sense out of the cacophony of contemporary existence. This is the world in which we live. This is the world into which our children are born. This is the world in which you will teach.

An old Chassidic story expresses the challenge to the individual caught in the winds of society. It goes something like this:

> Two men who lived in ancient times had the same dream. They dreamed that the wheat, which was soon to be harvested, had some kind of potion in it, and everyone who ate it would go crazy. The next day, they met, talked a while, and discovered their similar experience.
>
> "It must be true!" They wrung their hands. "Oh dear, what shall we do?"
>
> They pondered the situation and finally came up with a solution.
>
> "I know," the first man said, "When the new wheat is ready and everyone eats it, we won't. Then they'll be crazy and we won't!"
>
> That sounded like a good idea for a while. But suddenly, the second man realized: "No, we can't do that. If everybody else goes crazy and we don't, they'll think *we're* crazy!"
>
> They slumped down again, bewildered. Finally, they saw there was only one possible solution.
>
> "When everyone eats the wheat and goes crazy, we'll eat it and go crazy, too. But—*let's tie a knot in our belts. When we touch the knot, we'll remember who we really are and what we really believe!*"
>
> And they did.

I think we have all eaten the poisoned wheat. We've all felt the craziness, the insanity. Many people did NOT tie the knots in their belts to remember who they really are and what they really believe. *Have you?*

We must start with beliefs. If our beliefs, our commitments, our values are as flimsy as the Three Little Pigs' houses of straw or sticks, we will be blown away by any wolf. Our beliefs must be as solid as the house made of bricks. The knot in our belts must be tight and strong so when we touch the knot we will get back in touch with who we really are, with what we really believe, even if everyone around us is lost and confused from eating the poisoned wheat.

Take a Look at the World Inside

How do you feel about this whirling, spinning planet of ours? How do you respond to some of the aspects of our society? How do you feel about the forces throbbing around us? Are you puzzled, confused, angry, afraid, indifferent, calm, involved, or uninvolved? Do you think it is important for you to know how you feel about things, what you believe, what you value? Do you think your feelings and beliefs have anything to do with the way you will teach? In the *Bhagavad-Gita* is a line that reads: "Man is made by his belief. As he believes, so he is."

Edmund Fuller writes grimly about loss of belief:

> The new gullibility of our particular time is not that of the person who believes too much, but that of the person who believes too little—the person who has

lost a sense of the miracle—who is capable of believing that Creation is in some way an automatic or commonplace thing, or even that human beings, physically and psychically, can be dissected into neat packages susceptible to complete explanation.

When awe and wonder depart from our awareness, depression sets in, and after its blanket has lain smotheringly upon us for a while, despair may ensue, or the quest for kicks may begin. The loss of wonder, of awe, of the sense of the sublime, is a condition leading to the death of the soul. There is no more withering state than that which takes all things for granted, whether with respect to human beings or the rest of the natural order. The blasé attitude means spiritual, emotional, intellectual and creative death. . . .[28]

Sometimes I think we are protected from outside stimuli by a feeling-proof vest and a shock-proof seat as we make the voyage of every day with its jolts, unknowns, and hidden dangers. Sometimes our minds turn off. Often our senses shrivel. Our ability to respond or to be touched is almost destroyed. "Alienated" and "detached" describe too many people.

What Do You Believe?

Before you inspire and guide your students, you must get in touch with your own wellsprings of inspiration; you must build your own philosophical framework for creative teaching.

No one can tell you what to believe or which values to choose for your life. I can only share some ideas that are important to me, that I remember as I touch the knot in my belt, that give me direction and purpose.

I believe that the desire for self-expression is basic to human existence. Despite the strains and pressures of society and history, people want and need to make their mark while expressing something about their lives.

My Wishes for the World

I wish people were all supplied with food and water.
I wish everybody loved everybody else.
I wish there was no such thing as a war.
I wish nobody said, "I can't."

> Leslie
> Grade 4

My Wishes for the World

I wish my fish won't die.
I hope I don't flunk.
I hope I'm going to be an officer in the navy.
I wish all the children never feel sorry.
I wish they never get in trouble unless I'm mad at them.
I wish that nobody is going to be poor.

> Greg
> Grade 4

My Wishes for the World

I wish there would be no war.
I wish freedom was everywhere.
I hope there will be no hunger.

Cliff
Grade 3

The time
1982
Peace happened.
It was nice.
A lion and a mouse
played.

Clarissa
Grade 2[29]

I believe that human beings' persistent urge for creative self-expression is a powerful force in human history. From the beginning, dictators, kings, tyrants, and haters have tried to extinguish the light. Artists have been punished; writers have been exiled; books and paintings have been burned; music has been silenced; dancers have been stopped. But still the songs, dances, poems, and pictures keep flaming, reminding us that the human spirit is an eternal light that cannot be snuffed out.

Can you call to mind the names of people who persisted in their creative expression through pain and fury, devastation and destruction, exile and alienation?

In Hawaii there is a forest of lava where Ohia trees once bloomed green and strong. Now, lava covers the ground, the bare corpses of the trees, the roads, and the hills. If you go there, you will learn that the name of this place is Devastation Trail. But if you look carefully as you walk through the bleak reminder of volcanic fury, you will see tiny wildflowers pushing up through hard lava earth. They are Thimbleberry, Swordfern, Creeping Dayflower, and Nutgrass. These sturdy little plants, bright and green with hope, grow through lava, through burned earth, through charred roots. I was heartened by the flowers because to me they symbolized the persistence of beauty, of spirit, and of gentleness in a devastated world. To me, they represented the indomitable human spirit that pushes through destruction and grows and brightens with feelings of hope and faith. It will bloom, despite volcanic eruptions.

I believe that creative expression is a universal language that links people together and is the heritage of us all.

The Language of Creative Expression

The marks we make to carve some meaning into our lives—to put something of ourselves in stone, musical notes, dance, words, wood, canvas, or walls—are part of a universal language. The language of poetry, folklore, dance, art, music— all the creative arts—cuts through political, geographic, racial, economic, and religious differences. It is a language that bridges the gap between generations, cultures, and countries. It is a language that *all* people can understand and respond to. It is a communication that will not change despite all the catastrophic changes of our times. It fosters in people a loyalty to the human spirit, calling to the deeper places within us, enriching us and nourishing us.

Just as our modern images persist in hammering away at our senses, jamming our ability to respond, so our human heritage—the wealth of songs, legends, pictures, plays, sculptures, dances—provides a continuous counterpoint. This treasure chest of creative expression is always available to us and waiting to be opened. If we add another gear to our machinery, one that will move us into the music, dance, art, and great literature of the world, we will be strengthened and nourished. We will find beauty and pleasure in experiencing a language that moves all people. We will be able to pass such knowledge and appreciation on to our students, who need to be encouraged to live as unique individuals in the chaos that is their world. They can learn from the many individuals who have enriched the world.

So the arts, our first ways of knowing and experiencing, our oldest ways of communicating and expressing ourselves, are *basic* to human life. I think of the arts as the BASICS; when schools boast that they have "gone back to the basics," I clap my tambourine joyfully, thinking how fortunate those students are to learn through such life-affirming ways. Do you think those schools are defining the *arts* as the *basics?*

I have heard that in some African languages there is no word for *art*. In those cultures, the arts are PART OF everything, not APART from. Let us cherish the arts as part of all aspects of our lives and learning, as basic ways of knowing.

Martha Graham, whose creative imagination has extended the vocabulary of dance and theater to new dimensions, writes in her notebooks:

I am a thief—and I am not ashamed. I steal from the best wherever it happens to be—Plato, Picasso, Bertram Ross. I am a thief—and I glory in it—I steal from the present and the glorious past—and I stand in the dark of the future as a glorying and joyous thief—There are so many wonderful things of the imagination to pilfer—so I stand accused—I am a thief—but with this reservation—I think I know the value of what I steal and I treasure it for all time—not as a possession but as a heritage and a legacy. . . .[30]

The Legacy of Creative Expression

We hope that our children will be able to reach beyond themselves to touch others, affect situations, search for solutions, seek new answers to old questions. We hope that they will have a sense of history and a sense of the cultural and creative heritage that is part of their human birthright. Every child is born with a limitless reservoir of creative potential. Every child is born into a world of legends, poems, songs, dances. Children are truly deprived if their avenues

of creative expression are blocked. They are truly disadvantaged if they are not put in touch with their cultural legacy.

Do you believe that you, as a teacher, have a sacred responsibility to help children grow into healthy human beings by strengthening their creative abilities and teaching them to enjoy and appreciate the creative endeavors of all human beings?

Gathering the Materials of Creativity

Frederick is a wonderful picture-book mouse created by Leo Lionni. While the rest of his family of field mice worked hard gathering nuts and corn to store for the winter, Frederick sat off by himself gathering warm sun rays for cold winter days. While the other mice worked night and day, Frederick gathered colors to brighten the gray winter days and gathered words for the time when the mice would run out of things to say.

The winter came and the mice took to their hideout. After a while, they had just about run out of food and stories. They called on Frederick to share his words of warmth and color, his gatherings of observations. The mice were heartened by Frederick's beautiful speech. They told him, "You are a poet!" and Frederick "blushed, took a bow, and said shyly, 'I know it!' "[31]

Frederick is an example of that precious, irreverent nonconformist so needed by human society. He is the poet or the musician, the artist or the novelist, likened by Kurt Vonnegut to the canary in a coal mine. The canary is more sensitive than the miners to changes in the air. As long as the canary is singing, everything is fine. But if any poison seeps into the coal mine, however slowly and imperceptibly, the canary will sense it first and die. And this is so with creative people: as long as their works go on, as long as they are singing or doing, we have not been overcome with poison.

Do you believe that your personal expression, in whatever form you choose, is important? Do you believe that your students' personal expression is important? Do you believe that the personal expression of all people who ever lived and left some positive mark is important? How do you feel about the place of creative expression in a society? Do we need Frederick?

We Are All Creative

Let me go a step beyond. *I believe that we are all Frederick*. I think Frederick lives inside all of us. We are all capable of gathering colors and warmth for cold, dull days. We are all capable of gathering words. We do not need to delegate such assignments to a special person.

Many cultures encourage all their members to express themselves creatively. Pick up any collection of Native American poetry or African poetry. The chances are good that you will not see an individual taking credit for any of the poems. Instead you will note, after each poem, Hopi or Navajo or Cherokee. The name of the tribe. In these cultures, everyone was Frederick. It was the responsibility of all the people to make up songs, stories, and poems. African children are not given the words and music of a song to learn by rote. They make their own. They change what they hear and add something of their own to it. Native American and African people are not afraid of rejection or humiliation, of being judged and graded. Their poems are given to the tribe. Their poems become the poems of the tribe.

Bess "Chee Chee" Haile is a princess of the Shinnecock tribe. She talks of the Indian custom of giving, as a gift, not a department store gift certificate, not a box of candy, or a bottle of wine, but a song, a poem, or a dance. "This is a good day. I am happy today. We enjoyed our time together. I will make a poem about it. Here is my poem. It is my gift to you. I give you my song."

In less technically advanced cultures, poetry, song, story, dance, jewelry, and paintings are all integral parts of everyday existence. No one is off meditating and daydreaming while others work, but as they all work, they all daydream, meditate, and make songs, because those activities belong to all people. They belong to us, as well, and especially need to be revived in these dissonant times.

Tapping Our Creativity

There are songs and poems in all of us, waiting to be shaped. There are stories and myths and dances in all of us, waiting to be expressed. So many unwritten words, unspoken words, and unsung songs in our knapsacks waiting to be released. Poetry, song, story, myth, and dance are part of a language we know. We may

have forgotten that we know it, but it is somewhere in our individual and collective memories. The students we teach will become stronger and healthier human beings if we help them to express that language.

As we walk through lava hills of devastated forest, let us not miss the Thimbleberry, Swordfern, Creeping Dayflower, and Nutgrass. Let us not ignore Frederick gathering colors. Let us not hesitate to sit down and join him in his gathering. Let us remember that we are all members of a single human tribe, and we can respond to the prayers and chants, the pictures and dances, of all people.

Back to You

You will note that this is, most of all, a chapter of questions. A popular myth holds that teachers know all the answers. But any thinking person knows the truth: *nobody has all the answers!* It takes courage to stop and ask, "Where am I going? Who am I really? What do I believe? Is my house made of straw or of bricks?" Don't be afraid of puzzles and mysteries. Ask your questions—how else will you be able to encourage the children you share time with to ask *their* questions.

You may be thinking, "How can I, with half-formed ideas and hundreds of blank spaces, ever teach children in a creative and meaningful way?"

L'Engle responds:

We can surely no longer pretend that our children are growing up into a peaceful, secure and civilized world. We've come to the point where it's irresponsible to try to protect them from the irrational world they will have to live in when they grow up. . . .

What do we do when words fail us? . . . Often they fail me entirely, as when young people ask me ultimate and unanswerable questions. It has been very helpful to remember that quite a few reputable scholars, including one Socrates, made a point, when asked such a question, of saying, "I don't know."

But children want to know, and perhaps it is our desire not to let them down that has led us into the mistake of teaching only the answerables. This *is* a mistake and we mustn't refuse to allow them to ask the unanswerables just because we can't provide tidy little answers. . . .[32]

Rainer Maria Rilke, in a letter to a young poet, has another inspiring response:

Be patient toward all that is unsolved in your heart . . . try to love the *questions themselves* like locked rooms and like books that are written in a very foreign tongue. Do not now seek the answers, which cannot be given you because you would not be able to live them. And the point is, to live everything. *Live* the questions now. Perhaps you will then gradually, without noticing it, live along some distant day into the answer.[33]

We are not talking about lesson plans or formulas. We are talking about a way of life to which teaching in creative ways is as natural as breathing, a wonderfull journey with questions at every step. At least you care enough to question. That in itself is a commitment.

Exercise Your Imagination

Sometimes we don't know how we feel about a thing unless we trigger some kind of expression that reveals an attitude or belief of which we were unaware. Self-discovery is a major component of our adventure together.

Ten Important Words   If you could choose only ten words as the most important words in your vocabulary, the most important words to you, what would they be? Write these ten words. Discuss them, share them with your classmates. What do they reveal about your value scheme?

Theme Synthesis   Many stories and ideas have persisted through the centuries, crossed many languages, and been expressed in diverse forms. Part of the excitement and dynamism of the creative process is that different people are inspired to respond to the same idea in different unique ways. For example, the story of David and Goliath inspired both Donatello and Michelangelo to carve their own Davids. David has also been celebrated in song and dance, as well as on canvas.

Discover how many variations of Cinderella have been recorded. Begin a research project that will be a continuous gathering for your entire teaching career. Focus on some basic themes in your favorite ballads, legends, or fairy tales and discover the different ways they have been expressed throughout history. Not only is this an exercise in developing your own awareness and appreciation of the human creative process, but it will also enrich your teaching. Children love synthesis, and their understanding will deepen if you help them see relationships among ideas and the different ways human beings have responded to those ideas over the centuries.

Myths   This is an extension of the preceding activity. Choose a mythological or legendary character or story and express your feelings about it in any form you choose—through any of the arts, music, movement, or words. Share your work with others.

Creative People   Many people in all fields have, through personal courage, faith in themselves, and belief in their work, continued expressing themselves despite great social and physical obstacles. All human beings are affected by such unquenchable flames: Solzhenitsyn, Beethoven, Renoir, Monet, Helen Keller, Anne Frank, and Leo Tolstoy come to mind. Who can you add to the list? Keep your eyes and ears open for such people. Learn their stories. Courage is contagious.

The Power of Repetition   This is a writing exercise to add to the suggestions throughout the book. Read a book of Native American or African poetry. Copy some of your favorite poems in your journal. You will notice how repetitive most of them are. Repetition, found in almost all tribal poetry, is a quality that is aesthetically powerful as well as helpful in learning language. Choose a repeating phrase or stanza from one of the poems and continue on, writing your own poem and using the repeating lines as a refrain whenever you want to. The simplicity and directness of this kind of poetry helps thoughts and feelings turn easily into words. Enjoy these examples of traditional Native American poems followed by the original poems of university students who continued the themes.

> Our father, the Whirlwind,
> Our father, the Whirlwind—
> By its aid I am running swiftly,
> By its aid I am running swiftly.
> By which means I saw our father,
> By which means I saw our father.
>
> Arapaho

> You have no right to trouble me,
>   Depart, I am becoming stronger;
> You are now departing from me,
> You who would devour me;
> I am becoming stronger, stronger.
> Mighty medicine is now within me,
> You cannot now subdue me—
>   I am becoming stronger,
> I am stronger, stronger, stronger.
>
> Iroquois

Depart

Depart, I am becoming stronger.
I know I can leave you now
With only one tear or two.
Depart, I am becoming stronger.
I know I can leave you now.

With only remembering you
Once or twice every moment of my life.
Depart, I am becoming stronger.
I have stored you in my memory bank.
I know I can leave you now
With only one tear or two.
Depart, I am becoming stronger.
Depart.

Marie Smith

Our Father, the Whirlwind

Our father, the whirlwind,
Whirling the wind around,
My heart and soul.
Let me stand strong
When the whirlwind departs.

Jack Snyder

ENDNOTES

[1] Sylvia Ashton-Warner, *Spearpoint* (New York: Vintage, 1974) 17.

[2] Ralph Waldo Emerson, "The American Scholar," *The Complete Essays and Other Writings*, ed. Brooks Atkinson (New York: Modern Library, 1950) 47.

[3] I heard about the knapsack image from Dr. Howard Banchefsky.

[4] Hermann Hesse, *Steppenwolf* (New York: Bantam, 1969) 161.

[5] Ray Bradbury, "How to Keep and Feed a Muse," *The Writer* (July 1961).

[6] Madeleine L'Engle, *A Circle of Quiet* (New York: Farrar, 1972) 199–200.

[7] Theodore Roethke, *Straw for the Fire* (Garden City: Doubleday, 1974) 183.

[8] George Bernard Shaw, *John Bull's Other Island* (New York: Harper, 1942) 209.

[9] Jesse Stuart, *To Teach, To Love* (New York: Penguin, 1973) 17.

[10] Roethke, *Straw for the Fire* 184.

[11] Walt Whitman, from "Song of Myself," *The Illustrated Leaves of Grass* (New York: Madison Square/ Grosset, 1971) 48.

[12] E. Paul Torrance, *Education and the Creative Potential* (Minneapolis: U of Minnesota P, 1963); Abraham Maslow, *Toward a Psychology of Being*, 2nd ed. (New York: Van Nostrand, 1968). You will find all of Torrance's work of great interest. I especially enjoyed reading the book cited here. Maslow's book is very influential.

[13] Caption from Edward Steichen, ed., *The Family of Man* (New York: NAL).

[14]Mimi Brodsky Chenfeld, "Words of Praise: Honey on the Page," *Language Arts* 62.3 (1985): 266–69.

[15]Mimi Brodsky Chenfeld, "I'm Worried about our Kids!" *Day Care and Early Education* Fall 1984: 34–35.

[16]David Elkind, "Formal Education and Early Childhood Education: An Essential Difference," *Phi Delta Kappan* May 1986: 631–36.

[17]Mary K. Willert and Constance Kamii, "Reading in Kindergarten: Direct vs. Indirect Teaching," *Young Children* May 1985.

[18]Willert and Kamii.

[19]"Bringing Up Superbaby: Parents Are Pushing Their Kids to Learn Earlier Than Ever. Does It Help or Hurt?" *Newsweek* 28 Mar. 1983.

[20]From a speech by Leo Buscaglia. See also Buscaglia's book *Love* (Thorofare: Slack, 1972).

[21]*New York Times* 21 July 1981: sec. 2: 19.

[22]Maslow, *Toward a Psychology of Being* 142.

[23]Maslow.

[24]Alex Osborn, *How to Become More Creative* (New York: Scribner's, 1952).

[25]From a speech by Leo Buscaglia.

[26]Mauree Applegate, *Helping Children Write*, 3rd ed. (Evanston: Row, Peterson, 1961).

[27]Ashton-Warner, *Spearpoint* 86.

[28]Edmund Fuller, *Man in Modern Fiction* (New York: Random, 1958) 163–64.

[29]Clarissa Boiarski's piece was published in *The Kids' Connection* Spring 1983.

[30]Martha Graham, *The Notebooks of Martha Graham* (New York: Harcourt, 1973) xi.

[31]Condensed from Leo Lionni, *Frederick* (New York: Pantheon, 1967).

[32]L'Engle, *A Circle of Quiet* 204.

[33]Rainer Maria Rilke, *Letters to a Young Poet*, rev. ed. (New York: Norton, 1963).

2

You: A Creative Teacher

Don't you see my rainbow, teacher?
Don't you see all the colors?
I know that you're mad at me.
I know that you said to color the cherries red
    and the leaves green.
I guess I shouldn't have done it backwards.
But, teacher, don't you see my rainbow?
Don't you see all the colors?
<u>Don't you see me?</u>

ALBERT CULLUM[1]

A magic store is a wonderful place. Playing cards, colored scarves, and disappearing doves line the shelves. Top hats, capes, and magic wands are modeled on mannequins. But just putting on a hat and cape and waving a wand won't cause magic to fill the air. You have to have skill, knowledge, a special knack, showmanship, and, most important, an understanding of the mystery of magic and an ability to translate that understanding into an unforgettable experience for your audience.

One gifted magician, Doug Henning, believes that *reality is the greatest magic of all: the wonder of everyday life is more incredible than the most dazzling trick*. He believes that many people grow blasé and apathetic about the miracle of life and lose their ability to feel surprise and delight. Henning says the real purpose of magicians is to rekindle those feelings of amazement in people who have long felt nothing. He thinks that once these people enjoy experiences of surprise, they may apply those feelings to the reality they live in and thus enrich their own lives.

What does all this have to do with teaching?

The Magic of Creative Teaching

Imagine you are in a vast convention hall filled with an immense display of the latest, brightest, and best educational materials: film strips, tapes, videos, computers, cassettes, movies, magazines, workbooks, photographs, craft kits, cutouts, stencils, and textbooks. Except for these items spread in colorful array, the room is empty. Until one human being enters the scene, walks, stops, looks, and touches, all the materials are nothing but inert matter, just as the magician's props are nothing but objects until used by the individual who can change them into something wonderful.

Creative teachers transform ordinary learning into magical moments. They translate routine lesson plans into memorable experiences. They present facts in such original ways that the information fuses with other, deeper understandings and results in exciting discoveries for students.

Two incidents come to mind that vividly demonstrate the ability of creative teachers to transform the ordinary into the extraordinary.

At one reading workshop a first grade teacher shared this delightful story.

Most creative teachers are scroungers. She had scrounged her local ice cream store for a big cylindrical ice cream tub to use in her classroom. This particular time, she decided to do something a little different with the container. She painted it, cut a little hole near the bottom for a door, and called it a "Mouse House." Every day, the mouse left little notes in the "Mouse House" for the children. The teacher had to reach her fingers into the "House" to pull the notes out. The children were very excited about the "Mouse House" and waited eagerly each day to discover who would receive letters.

One morning, around 6:30 A.M., a local family heard a stirring in their front hallway. Alarmed, the husband and wife tiptoed down the stairs to find the source of the noise. There, just inside the front door, stood their first grader, fully dressed, with coat and mittens and lunch box in hand!

"Why are you up so early?" they asked, relieved to find their six-year-old and NOT an intruder.

"I've got to get to school early today," she told them, practically bouncing with excitement. "I have a feeling I have a letter from the Mouse!"

Sometimes, the most successful, memorable experiences creative teachers share with their students are also the simplest and depend the most on serendipity, on the teachers' instincts for turning ordinary into special!

The other incident occurred during a creative writing session in a third grade.

We had finished the talking–sharing–doing part of our session, and now there was the marvelous hum of children enthusiastically concentrating on their individual writing activities. Suddenly, in the midst of the quiet writing sounds—a shout! A yelp! We all jumped. What had happened?

This third grade had a secret I didn't know about. In each child's pocket was a special packet. A few days before our writing session, their teacher, always full of surprises, had given each of them a bean seed and a sheet of paper towel. The children had folded their paper towels into small squares, wet them, and placed their seeds carefully in the center of the squares. Then they each received a little plastic bag. The beans on their wet towel beds were placed in the bags. Each child put the bag in a pocket—"pocket gardens." The moisture plus body heat would cause the seeds to sprout. On the day that we were writing together, one of the boys peeked into his "pocket garden" and there—before his very eyes—was the first sprout from his seed! Of course, the seeds pre-empted our writing lesson for a while as all the kids pulled their "gardens" from their pockets to see if their seeds had sprouted! Such a time!

We talked about it and wrote about it. Afterward, the seeds were replanted in soil.

Creative teachers have seeds of ideas in all their pockets. And creative teachers are *flexible!* One never knows when a seed will decide to sprout!

Some Creative Teachers

Jack Snyder was a septuagenarian when he started teaching. He never had any children of his own and, as a freelance writer, spent most of his time communicating with adults. Crusty, sarcastic, opinionated, he was *not* a "grandfatherly" type. In the city where he lived, the school system relied heavily on volunteers to share skills, hobbies, travel or work experiences, and other valuable enrichments not otherwise available or possible in the classroom.

Jack was taking a writing course at the university when the call went out for volunteers to come into the schools and work with classes in creative writing. Jack was asked, but dismissed the idea instantly. He had hardly talked to a child in sixty years!

Midwest winters are bleak, and retirement schedules leave a lot of time for leisure, so Jack finally decided to volunteer. He didn't sleep the night before his first class—a fourth grade in an inner-city school. He went through the nightmares and jitters that all beginning and many experienced teachers suffer "the night before." He awoke to a snowstorm that snarled traffic, paralyzed the city, and postponed his first class until the next day. Two straight days and nights with no rest; he could hardly eat; his head swam with fears and fantasies. He had no experience to draw from, no education courses, no guidebooks in his library to inspire him. Dread overcame anticipation. He finally dragged himself into that fourth-grade class, was introduced, and stood in front of the room with all those quizzical, "show me" children's eyes staring at him.

"To tell you the truth, I'm scared," he admitted to the class. "I'm not used to talking to kids so it may take me a little while. Be patient with me, please."

Silence.

He picked up a piece of chalk with shaking fingers. He wrote across the top of the board:

RULES

The class moaned.

He wrote:

1. No loitering
2. No trespassing
3. No drinking
4. No smoking
5. No writing in Greek or Latin

By this time, the class was delighted. They relaxed and smiled at each other in merriment.

6. No rules except . . .

The class stiffened. What now?

Jack took the eraser and erased the entire board except for Rule 6, to which he added: everyone must write.

And they did! Stories, poems, plays, books, comics, and songs flew from their pencils. They have written assembly programs, television shows, and holiday plays. In one term he taught six classes in creative writing in various schools and was invited to many more. He was asked for help by teachers who felt a lack of confidence in initiating and motivating creative activities themselves but who wanted their students to have such experiences. Jack enriched the lives of all the children he taught. When he was out sick for a week, he received many original poems, stories, pictures, and cards—an outpouring of the love and concern that the children felt for him.

"An ideal teacher is nice and loving. An ideal teacher works hard. An ideal teacher is considerate. . . ." Following a recent inservice workshop, a teacher came up and shared an experience with me which she labeled one of the most important in her teaching career. She taught third and fourth graders in a Special Education class. The file of one of the boys was full of negative evaluations of his behavior and attitudes. He was a "problem child" and had been for all of his school life. One day he walked up to the teacher and handed her a piece of paper on which he had written in big, bold letters a common obscene word. The teacher related that she froze inside but managed to say calmly, "That's pretty good spelling, Johnny. What other words can you spell correctly?"

The boy stared at her, then walked back to his seat. A few minutes later, she saw him rip up the paper. At the end of the day, he gave her a paper that had these words written clearly across the top:

I LOVE YOU

Johnny lost his "problem child" reputation, because for the rest of the year his behavior in the room was commendable.

A university education major, doing his student teaching at a nearby school, tutored individual students a few times a week. He was doing multiplication problems with a nine-year-old boy. The boy was tense. He took forever to multiply a group of examples using one number as the multiplier. The university student put down his pencil and leaned back in his chair after the boy had finished the first exercise.

"Do you play baseball?" he asked the boy.

The boy nodded.

"What position?"

"Outfield."

"Who's your favorite team?" the student continued. "Mine's the Dodgers."

The two spent the next few minutes exchanging baseball talk. When they returned to the math, the boy did the entire page of multiplication problems using the two-number multipliers without any hesitation or signs of tension.

At the time this happened, the student teacher did not consciously realize what he had done, how he had contributed to the boy's feeling of safety and well-being. Only weeks later, when the topic of the creative teacher was discussed in a seminar, did he gain insight into his encounter.

I visited Brenda Sims' third-grade class. Brenda and her kids greeted me with an enormous group hug. Brenda told me proudly, "Mimi, these are the most talented, imaginative, interesting writers I have ever met. You'll really enjoy working with them."

The third graders glowed with pride. Brenda walked over to one of the boys, put her arm around his shoulder and twinkled, "Now, Mark is such a gifted writer. Sometimes, though, he has to translate his work from the original!"

Mark smilingly agreed, then voluntarily pulled two sheets of writing from his desk. The first sheet was totally illegible, the kind of stuff many teachers would reject immediately. But not Brenda Sims! The second sheet was much neater. Not championship neat, but no comparison with the first copy. Written boldly at the bottom of the second paper was Mark's name and the explanation, "Translated from the original by Mark."

One Saturday afternoon, I took two of my middle school folk dance kids, Tim and Kim, on an outing. Tim—tall, skinny, blond, tough; Kim—short, stocky, dark-skinned, a cool kid. We wandered in and out of shops until we came to one of the large bookstores. There we met Paul Hammock, a dynamic, fun-filled teacher then teaching language arts at a local middle school. Paul gave me a big bear hug. Kim and Tim raised their eyebrows, watching from a safe distance.

Paul shared his feeling of being bored with giving spelling tests to his seventh and eighth graders. He explained, "Yesterday I just got sick and tired of giving the weekly spelling tests so I had a puppet do it for me!" He then imitated his puppet's voice giving the spelling test. I listened to Paul intently and enjoyed his story, but my attention also fell on Kim and Tim, whose eyes narrowed with fascination as Paul talked.

We said our goodbyes and then walked a while in silence. About a street later, both kids stopped and, almost with one voice, said, "Wow, we wish we had a teacher who let a puppet give his spelling test!"

All of the creative teachers I know have outstandingly good *instincts!* They come from the "culture of Yes." They vote LIFE. They have positive, healthy intuitions about what children will respond to best.

Jack Snyder was loyal to himself, shared his feelings and humor.

The Special Education teacher could have scolded the child for writing the obscene word. But her instincts told her to go with the positive.

The student teacher recognized the tension the child was feeling. His gut reaction was to be reassuring, to help the boy relax.

Brenda could have put pressure on Mark for writing illegibly. She could have voted DEATH and rejected or humiliated him. Instead, she found a fun way to encourage him to improve.

Paul decided that, if *he* was getting bored with spelling tests, imagine how his students felt! So, to amuse himself and to wake up his kids, he played around with a new approach. Even cool middle-school toughies like Tim and Kim responded with enthusiasm.

Who Are Creative Teachers?

Clark Moustakas writes eloquently about "the authentic teacher":

> The authentic teacher recognizes the uniqueness of the learner and confirms him as an individual self; makes the classroom a place for open, genuine, human relations; presents material which is vital to his growing self and in the process initiates new experience, awareness and sensitivity for himself and the child; . . .[2]

Do you think creative teachers have to sing, dance, paint, carve, or compose to be creative? The creative teachers I know are open, flexible, willing to try new ways and risk failing; they are honest, responsive, curious, enthusiastic, and welcoming of new experiences. Creative teachers have adventurous minds and spirits and are deeply committed to the minds and spirits of their students. They aren't satisfied with teaching the same content the same way all the time. Last year's lesson plans may act as guides for this year's but not as blueprints. There are always new ideas, new approaches to explore, new challenges to meet, and, of course, a *new* class of students.

One of the many outstanding teachers I have known was Shraga Arian, who was remembered eloquently by one of his colleagues.

> He combined the rare attributes of creativity, curiosity and sensitivity. He had a genius for "capturing the moment"—or seizing upon an event, a thing, a personality to fashion a dramatic object lesson. This was the secret of how his teaching was able to penetrate so deeply. He brought his lessons from the real world of living experiences. He had an uncanny knack for using the individuals around him, searching out their uniqueness and exposing these worthy personalities to his students for their edification and pleasure. He did not think in clichés. He intuitively knew that there is a vast, untapped human treasure always present all around us that we so often waste, and he endeavored to make this treasure available. He related in a similar way to his students, in whom he would always seek to find—and magnify—something special, thereby helping to increase their sense of self-worth. Through his persistence and loving way one could expect, sooner or later, to be summoned by him to share one of his enterprises. Knowing, living and working with him was a constant stream of surprises.[3]

Alice Miel writes,

> Teaching is a non-repetitive process. No two groups of learners are ever the same, nor is one class the same from day to day. The world around the classroom changes constantly. The teacher himself changes. The teacher has abun-

dant opportunities to be "creative" in the way he deals with all of these changing conditions. The product of the teacher's creativity is opportunities for the individuals and groups to experience and learn.[4]

If ten teachers were handed the same lesson plan, materials, time limitations, and class, do you think the learning experiences would be exactly the same for each? Teaching is an individual matter, an art that constantly eludes scientific definition or categorization, although attempts are constantly being made to label and quantify it.

Here is a collection of the late Theodore Roethke's words about teaching, gathered from his book *Straw for the Fire*.

Teaching is one of the few professions that permits love.

Teaching is an act of love, a spiritual cohabitation. . . .

Are there dangers? Of course, there are dangers every time I open my mouth. Hence at times when I keep it shut, I try to teach by grunts, signs, shrugs.

To be less than you are is so easy: even a child needs no lessons in this.

Those students get the highest grades who take their responsibilities of educating me most seriously.

Our ignorance is so colossal that it gives me a positive pleasure to contemplate it.

I dream of a culture where it is thought a crime to be dull.

I ask you: I beg you: Bring to this task all the sweetness of spirit you possess. . . .

I trust all joy.[5]

We All Learn Differently

When the book *Drawing on the Right Side of the Brain* [by Betty Edwards (Tarcher, 1979)] was published in the late 1970s, the country was launched into research and discussion based on the finding that the brain is made up of two very distinct hemispheres. People tossed terms like "left-brained" and "right-brained" around in everyday speech. The two hemispheres, researchers reported, process information in two distinct ways; they yield different ways of knowing and experiencing. On the left-hemisphere side, the way of knowing features analyzing, abstraction, counting, measuring, sequential learning, logic, verbal communication. On the right-hemisphere side, more nonverbal communication reigns—movement, drama, gesture. This is the more imaginative side, the side of metaphors and images, of spatial relationships and intuition. The results of the studies on the hemispheres of the brain are revolutionary: we all learn differently; no two people are alike; we all have different combinations of right- and left-brain influences.

Yet all the creative teachers I have ever known already *knew* this. It was their "given." Human beings are unique individuals. What works immediately for you may be a total dud for me! All the creative teachers I have ever met are always looking for, experimenting with, ways of communicating ideas that will reach all of their students. Not all methods will work with all students. Creative teachers are eclectic. They are not fanatically loyal to ONE system or ONE method, no matter how outstanding its reputation. They know that, with some students, that method will NOT work. If they keep insisting on trying, over and over again, something that doesn't work, then who is the slow learner?

Some students defy all methods. Nothing seems to reach or touch them. Creative teachers may be exhausted but they never exhaust their ideas or their attempts to make connections. They try everything—old, new, borrowed, blue. They may not know Edwin Markham's little poem, but they live it:

> He drew a circle that shut me out,
> Heretic, rebel, a thing to flout.
> But LOVE and I had the wit to win:
> We drew a circle that took him in.[6]

Creative teachers realize that some combinations of hemispheres, heredity, environment, geography, history, sociology block learning in some people. They know they are not miracle-makers (although I know many teachers who have performed miracles!), but their faith is strong and their stubbornness legendary. They do not give up! They keep drawing circles and taking children in.

Kids Describe Their Favorite Teachers*

Children have valuable ideas to share about teachers. A group discussion in a fourth grade on the "ideal teacher" yielded these points, reprinted in their original form.

1. Be strict but nice
2. That understands you
3. That gives you a break to talk
4. That knows what she's doing
5. By caring how we learn
6. That lets you make things
7. Help us when we don't know something
8. One that helps you learn
9. Be honest to the children
10. Treat everyone equal
11. Be patient and understanding

Cara's English teacher in junior high school engenders enthusiasm. She prods her students to contribute ideas, to think, question, respond. She gives

---

*I am very grateful to the many teachers, principals, and parent volunteers who have assisted me in gathering the children's papers. All the samples of "ideal teacher" ideas in this chapter come from children in Franklin County and Columbus schools in Ohio.

open-ended assignments that encourage originality. She asks questions that may have a variety of answers or no answer. She is always springing surprises—and I don't mean surprise tests. She uses newspapers, art materials, and magazine illustrations for projects. Her students are excited about English.

A group of boys and girls, seven to thirteen years old, took a break from some art activities to talk about their favorite teachers. I wrote their comments. Here are excerpts:

> *He makes learning fun.*
> *She is caring and very nice.*
> *She wants to help you learn and she cares a lot about you.*
> *He is forgiving and helpful and funny. He's the whiz of the school!*
> *He's always fair and explains things good to the class.*
> *We do neat things and she doesn't yell at you. She knows how to take care of the kids who are bad.*
> *He makes things interesting. He understands me. And, sometimes, he's mighty funny.*

Some Characteristics of Creative Teachers

Torrance describes creative teachers as having "a breadth of vision; they see relationships between seemingly remote things and bring them together in meaningful ways. . . . The creative teacher is an unpredictable, independent spirit. . . .[7]

Children in elementary grades through junior high school have important things to say about teaching and their teachers. Almost always, their comments and observations pinpoint qualities emphasized in numerous studies of quality teachers. In the following "mix and match" sampling, enjoy the children's opinions as they parallel the Columbia University Teachers College "indicators of quality" findings.[8] Although more recent reports include such terms as "time on task" and "monitoring learning," I want to focus on these more personal and social characteristics:

Demeanor: The teacher is relaxed, good-natured, cheerful, courteous, and, if using humor, is always inoffensive, rather than yelling, shouting, frowning, glaring, insulting or being sarcastic. Pupils reflect similar demeanor.

I think a teacher should be nice, friendly and considerate. She should be able to explain our work and take it seriously. And she should let us have fun sometimes.

> Sally
> Age 10

Patience: Both teacher and pupil take time to listen and accept one another, rather than press, hurry, interrupt, or give rigidly directive orders.

I think an ideal teacher would be someone who is fair, honest, impartial. . . . A teacher has to be patient and want to listen when you want to talk. . . .

> Maribeth
> Age 12

Pupil Involvement: Pupils are eager, prompt, willing, show initiative, or make voluntary contributions, instead of being apathetic, reluctant, or slow to respond.

I think a teacher should discuss a lot. Should ask the kids what they want to study, like maybe read a chapter of a book and maybe play a game and ask questions about the chapter or draw a picture of something after you read the story. What I hate about a teacher is when he or she says do this and that and never tells you what to do or discusses it. Just says work and work and is just lazy to answer your questions.

Patty
Age 11

Respect: There is mutual respect among pupils and teacher as evidenced by commending, accepting, helping, rather than rejecting or ignoring.

I think an ideal teacher is willing to help you with your work and if you have a problem they would help you so you will feel better than you did.

Sam
Age 10

Evaluation as Encouragement: Positive, encouraging, and supportive criticism, which pupils accept, is used rather than discouragement, disapproval, admonishment, blame, or shame, which pupils ignore or reject.

A person who doesn't discourage curiosity by putting down question-askers. Likes kids.

Ron
Age 12

If a child is having trouble the teacher shouldn't put the child in more trouble but should try to help the child and give the child more attention so he improves.

Sean
Age 10

Error Behavior: Both pupils and teacher openly and naturally accept and recognize each other's errors, rather than trying to cover up, losing face, or showing guilt.

I don't like some teachers because if you do one thing wrong they yell at you or if you walk around the room they yell. I like some teachers because they discuss things and don't yell at you when you do something wrong.

Julian
Age 11

Question and Answer Technique: The teacher uses open-ended questions rather than questions with a "right" answer, presents unsolved problems

I think it's wrong when my teacher tells me that I have the wrong idea about *Up a Road Slowly.* I read it and that was the idea I had about

rather than a lecture with "correct" information filled in; pupils test and challenge rather than attempt to key in on the wanted correct answer, and are encouraged to consider questions for which they do not have the answer.

it. I think it's wrong for my teacher to make me change to her idea.

Susan
Age 10

Testing Ideas: The examination, comparison, and testing of divergent ideas are encouraged, as opposed to referring to authority.

I like a teacher that lets you check your own math, spelling and health papers and has a big reading group and lets the group talk about the stories and doesn't test all the time. I like a teacher that lets you share on Fridays and lets you give things out to the class and bring things in.

Jeannette
Age 10

Unusual Ideas: Unusual ideas are entertained without anxiety or tension and unusual questions are considered with respect.

I think an ideal teacher is one that is friends with the students and learning is fun. If you think of something way out, she doesn't make you feel stupid and if someone asks a dumb question she won't let anyone make fun of them. School would be a place where children would want to go and I mean fun for all children.

Robert
Age 12

Time for Thinking: Time is allowed for students to think and discover, play with ideas, manipulate objects, experiment, without pressure to get "the answer" or get it "right."

I like a teacher who reads good books to the class but doesn't give tests on them. Just reads for the story. I like a teacher who lets children use their imagination. I like a teacher who lets children do things on their own sometimes.

Julian
Age 11

Abundance of Materials: Pupils have the stimulation of materials and other resources in great richness and variety.

I like teachers who let you do art and hang pictures on the walls. They should show films and slides and let you listen to music once in a while and give you time to build things and make things too.

Mark
Age 10

Skills of Thinking: A variety of skills used in creative thinking is practiced: inquiring, searching, manipulating, questioning, abstracting, analyzing, summarizing, outlining, generalizing, evaluating, and the like.

My ideal teacher is understanding of children's questions. She does not scold when you want to discuss something or say we have no time now. She is friendly and fair to all.

Cindy
Age 11

Pupil Problems: Personal problems or handicaps are accepted with consideration, understanding, and sympathy, rather than with ridicule or embarrassment.

I like an ideal teacher that doesn't have a bad temper. And someone who doesn't have a best student and likes everyone in the class, even the dumb kids. Someone who can be trustable and fair.

Pam
Age 10

Atmosphere of Agreement: Pupils and teacher respect opinions of others and come to agreements without external coercion; conflict and hostility are not characteristic of problem solving.

I think an ideal teacher is a teacher that has time for her students and has the time after school to talk to the ones with problems. An ideal teacher is a teacher with the knowledge to explain things, play games once in a while. A teacher that has no favorites and treats some better than others. A teacher that has a

*nice warming, understanding smile
and wants to help you learn.*

> Rita
> Age 11

Teacher–Pupil Identification: Teacher meets pupils on their level as one of them and is not withdrawn, aloof, or superior.

*A good teacher is a person who is
understanding, will let you ask
questions and discuss, has time for
the individual, has some creativity
in doing things. Does not wreck a
person's high hopes. Someone who
doesn't put down. Someone who
can relate to students, who doesn't
seem like they're in a different
world than you're in.*

> Cliff
> Age 13

Self-Initiated Activity: Pupils take the responsibility for self-initiated learning, extend the limits of the topic; the teacher encourages and credits pupil efforts to go beyond the lesson plan, assignment, or question.

*I would like to have a teacher that
made me laugh and would teach
me a lot of stuff but also let me do
my own projects and think up interesting things to find out about
myself.*

> Stan
> Age 11

Evaluation as Motivation: Original-ity is rewarded with recognition, pupils' ideas are treated as having value, unusual questions and diverse contributions are recognized and creative effort is rewarded with praise, while formal evaluation and marking are delayed.

*I wish my teacher wouldn't mark
my poem. She gave me a C on a
picture I drew of a farm. My ideal
teacher would just put the picture
on the bulletin board with all the
others and no marks. And just read
the poems and no marks.*

> Charlene
> Age 9

In "The Influence of Teachers," Mihaly Csikszentmihalyi and Jane McCormack talked with high school students about their feelings about teachers. The older children echoed the spirit, the direction of thinking, of the younger students.

> Most often, the teenagers described influential teachers in terms of their ability to generate enthusiasm for learning through personal involvement with the subject matter and skill in teaching it. The students respond to teachers who communicate a sense of excitement, a contagious intellectual thrill. When excitement is present, learning becomes a pleasure instead of a chore. . .[9]

Influential teachers the students see as being "easy to talk to," "ready to listen," when students have difficulties.

Caring about students and caring about the subjects taught are qualities of influential teachers. In addition, the kids describe such teachers as taking the trouble to express their messages in unusual and memorable ways, engaging their students' attention by presenting material in original ways. With such teachers, students not only enjoy the class but also learn to enjoy the subject matter. Only after a student has *learned to love learning* does education truly begin.

The authors continue to emphasize that enthusiasm, a sense of humor, and the ability to make learning enjoyable are NOT gimmicks. They remind us that young people don't need just information. They need meaningful information. They need knowledge that makes sense and inspires belief. They need knowledge that helps them understand why learning and living are worthwhile.

> How can young people believe that the information they are receiving is worth having, when their teachers seem bored, detached or indifferent? Why should teenagers trust knowledge that brings no joy?[10]

How Important Are You, Teacher?

The importance of you, the teacher, in the lives of children is immeasurable. Your power to affect what children learn, how they learn, and how they feel about themselves while they are learning is humbling. Theodore Roethke wrote, "What we forget is the effect we have on the young: that we are their lives in a way that is no longer quite realizable to us."[11]

Sometimes you, as a teacher, may be a child's only friend. Sometimes you, as a teacher, may be the only source of encouragement, praise, positive motivation in a child's life.

A thoughtless word, an abrupt rejection, a nonverbal expression of disapproval, an indifferent response if a child is put down by others, humiliates children and teaches them to be afraid to share, afraid to be open.

Last year, a young friend of mine in the fourth grade had a teacher who believed in strict discipline, harsh criticism, rare encouragement, and silence. My friend, along with others in the class, was sick almost every morning. She had stomach cramps, nausea, and feelings of dread. This year, she has an easygoing, relaxed teacher who enjoys the children, cares about them, and thinks of education as a shared learning process. My friend hasn't missed a day. She feels great! She has a teacher who votes LIFE!

Do you remember how your teachers affected *you?*

In the midst of the crush and rush of everyday pressures on teachers from parents, administrators, the demands of a diverse group of children, and the constant attempt to meet time and curriculum goals, it is easy for you to forget the importance of your role, your place in the life of your students. When you realize the strength of your influence on your students, you will become aware that you can have a part in your students' lives that goes beyond three o'clock on Fridays, beyond the end of the school year—a part that could last a lifetime. You can turn students' gray days into bright ones, help direct the values that will affect the quality of their lives. In *A Tree Grows in Brooklyn,* the young heroine is aware of the power of good teachers: "School days went along. Some were made up of meanness, brutality and heartbreak; others were bright and beautiful because of Miss Bernstein and Mr. Morton. And always, there was the magic of learning things."[12]

Do you feel the influence of the outstanding teachers in your life? Do you remember the "magic of learning things"? One of Marysue Garlinger's favorite letters is from a child who wrote her, "Thank you for coming to our school today. You made me happy for the rest of my life." Did you ever have a teacher who made YOU happy for the rest of your life?

Margalit Ovid, a dancer and teacher, said at a recent lecture-demonstration, "There is no technique in the universe to equal the technique in the human heart." Reflect on the stories of the writer Jack Snyder, the teacher with the "problem" boy who wrote the obscene word, the student teacher who took a "baseball break," and Shraga Arian. You will become aware of the part that simple instinct and spontaneity played in each situation. That is why the emphasis is first on *you* as a person, a person in touch with your own strengths, weaknesses, areas of enjoyment, goals, and values. If you have a healthy respect for yourself, a sense of dignity and self-worth, and an openness to whatever life has in store for you, then you will be able to trust your instincts in responding to difficult situations. You will enjoy relationships with adults and children that are characterized by honesty and mutual respect. These characteristics are necessary because you cannot always plan your next action or your next bit of dialogue. The moment changes. A situation turns around. New elements are introduced that you are not prepared to meet. Jack Snyder's basic honesty touched the skeptical fourth graders immediately, and he was able to develop a rapport with them. The teacher with the "problem child" who wrote the obscene word is basically a kind, patient person who responded immediately out of these feelings. She is not a punishing person. Ask yourself how you would have reacted to a similar situation. The student teacher could have ignored his pupil's tenseness and lack of self-confidence and gone on to the second exercise. But his sensitivity was basic to his personality. He was a caring person who responded to the nonverbal messages the boy was sending him. Would you have stopped in the middle of the exercises to relax and calm the child before you continued?

And How Will You Teach?

"As I am, so I teach." How *are* you and how will you teach? How *do* you teach? Do you teach "with all the sweetness of spirit you possess?" With the knowledge of skills, materials, content curriculum, and unit plans, will you also keep your eye on the knapsacks on the backs of your students, as well as delving into your own? Will you truly respect each student, accept his or her strengths and weaknesses as you do your own, and build from there with warmth and compassion? In honest relationships marked by acceptance and mutuality, there's room for

errors and there's room for mistakes—both are parts of the learning process. If you have an unreachable child will you give up, or will you consider that child to be a person as yet unreached and try to find new ways to communicate? Will you practice all the tricks, wares, and techniques at your disposal, never forgetting the magical, undefined quality that turns teaching into an art and learning into an adventure? Will you

appreciate children being children, see purpose and beauty in their noise and movement, and understand how wide open their senses are to receive meanings from everywhere? Will you appreciate corny jokes, tough guy swaggers? Will you have respect for their ways of telling us about themselves and respect for their relationships with others outside of school? Will you be able to respond with sensitivity to children and sense the meaning of what they are trying to tell you, not just through the literal meaning of their words but through their bodily movements and facial expression, their noises and their fantasies, their picture making, their playing and even their silences?[13]

I think an ideal teacher likes children, helps you to understand and explains things thoroughly. He gives examples of how to do things, and if you don't understand he'll help you in recess and after lunch and doesn't yell unless needed and listens to your problems and gives you plenty of time to do your work and read and do projects. He helps you learn to spell words right and gives credit for extra things you do on your own. He gives you jobs to do in the classroom and saves time for sharing. He lets you have singing every day and some field trips to make things interesting.

Karen
Grade 6

I was teaching creative writing and creative movement to tough teenage Upward Bounders in Hawaii years ago when rock music first soared to popularity. At that time, young people had discovered that part of their body called the pelvis, and they danced with gyrations that few adults could relate to. The Hawaiian youngsters added a kind of rhythmic head movement to their dance, which I found an exciting dimension. I tried and tried. I practiced loosening my neck, jerking my head around, but to no avail. Finally, I asked the kids: "Help me with this head. It doesn't want to move when I dance. These muscles don't know how to do that." They laughed and, in pidgin English, gave me this answer:

"Hey, Meem, you gotta shake your head *yes*. Keep shaking your head *yes* and you'll get it. But you a teacher. Teachers nevah shake their head *yes*, only *no*. You no get it!"

How are you? How will you teach? Will you shake your head *yes*?

Miss Wilson, a third-grade teacher, finished her lunch early and went outdoors to playground duty a few minutes before the children arrived. It was a beautiful day and she felt wonderful. The swings looked so inviting that she sat on one of them and rocked gently back and forth. A small first grader walked over to her, watched her with serious eyes, and finally asked, "Who are you?"

"I'm Miss Wilson."

"You're not a teacher," the child stated.

"Yes, I am. I teach third grade."

"No. You're not a teacher," the little girl insisted. "You swing!"

How will you teach? Will you be a person who laughs, cries, tries, gets angry, forgives, inspires, perspires? Will you be a teacher who touches students with your humor, warmth, and wisdom? Will you swing?

Dawn Heyman is a third-grade teacher who has touched the lives of many children in many positive ways. One of her students asked her, "Miss Heyman, do you want to know the four things I love best in the world?"

Dawn did. These are the four things:

"Number one is school.

Number two is school.

Number three is school.

Number four is school."

Suggested Activities

Dig into Your Knapsack

Think back through your own school years. Can you remember any outstanding teachers who affected you and influenced you? What kind of people were they? What characteristics do you recall about them? What kind of experiences and activities did you share with them? Write a brief character sketch or memory of an outstanding teacher you had. Be as specific as possible. If you cannot remember ever having had such a teacher, create one and write a character sketch for your "ideal teacher." Share your outstanding or ideal teacher with the class.

Now try to remember the teachers who had a profoundly negative effect on your life. Try to remember details about your experience in their classes. Write a brief character sketch of a teacher who had a negative effect on your life. Be as specific as possible. If you cannot remember ever having had such a teacher, create one and write a description. Share with the class.

Learn from the Experiences of Others

Many excellent books have been written by a diverse group of articulate, deeply committed teachers. Read some of these: *Spinster* and *Teacher*, both by Sylvia Ashton-Warner; *Thirty-six Children* and *Growing Minds: On Becoming a Teacher*, both by Herbert Kohl; *The Water Is Wide* by Pat Conroy; *Death at an Early Age* by Jonathan Kozol; *The Lives of Children* by George Dennison; *What Do I Do Monday?* by John Holt; *Being with Children* by Phillip Lopate; *Twenty Teachers*, edited by Ken Macrorie.*

Share at least two episodes or situations from these books which especially moved you to a deeper understanding of creative teaching.

Characteristics of a Creative Teacher

In your journal, note some characteristics that you believe are important in the development of a successful creative teacher. Honestly examine your strengths and weaknesses and note how you assess your own potential for creative teaching. How do you think you can strengthen areas of weakness? For example, *flexibility* might be one of the characteristics that you write, and you note that you are basically rigid in regard to many areas of life. How do you think you can learn to become more flexible? Are there any specific things that you can do to become a more open person?

Spinster and *Teacher* by Sylvia Ashton-Warner (both, Simon & Schuster, 1971); *Thirty-six Children* (Norton, 1968) and *Growing Minds: On Becoming a Teacher* (Harper & Row, 1984), both by Herbert Kohl; *The Water Is Wide* by Pat Conroy (Dell, 1974); *Death at an Early Age* by Jonathan Kozol (Bantam, 1970); *The Lives of Children* by George Dennison (Random House, 1970); *What Do I Do Monday?* by John Holt (Dell, 1974); *Being with Children* by Phillip Lopate (Doubleday, 1975); *Twenty Teachers*, Ken Macrorie, ed. (Oxford Univ. Press, 1984).

Some Improvisations   With your class, role play various situations. Choose different individuals to take turns being the teacher. The rest of the class will play the role of children. Add your own suggestions to this brief list of situations.

1. The teacher is explaining a lesson. One or two children don't understand. They keep raising their hands and telling the teacher that they don't understand.

2. Children are reading their original poems. One child begins to read his poem, and the rest of the class giggles and makes fun of him.

3. "Sharing Time" is on Friday. Today is Wednesday. The children have seen *The Wizard of Oz* on television and want to talk about it *today*.

4. The teacher reads a poem to the class. The teacher writes on the board the meaning of the poem. One of the children disagrees with that meaning.

5. The class is responsible for an assembly program. The teacher meets with the class to discuss and decide the program.

6. There has been a fire in the school. All the books and materials were burned. Without books and materials, the teacher is introducing a lesson on proper nouns.

7. The teacher gives a book report assignment. One child raises her hand and asks if she can do the book report in a way different from the usual procedure.

8. The teacher is about to start a math lesson. One eager child jumps up to show a letter from a relative in South America.

9. A new child hesitantly, fearfully enters the classroom. How does the teacher respond?

10. Add your own ideas for improvised situations.

Questions! Questions! Questions!

A workshop wouldn't be a REAL workshop without a handout, would it? This questionnaire was written for workshops in creative education. I enjoyed writing it. Read it, respond to it, think about it, enjoy it.

TO: You, my fellow teacher

FROM: Mimi Brodsky Chenfeld

WHAT: True–False statements

WHERE: Wherever you are on the spinning planet Earth

WHEN: Today and always

WHY: Why not?

This is for your knapsack. It will not be marked, spindled, or mutilated. It is for you.

Answer True or False

I think teaching is one of the few professions that permits love.

I believe that all human beings are born with creative potential.

I am not creative. I can't sing, dance, write, or draw.

I am creative because I have some original ideas; I'm inventive, curious, open to new ways and materials, and I like to rearrange old patterns of thinking and teaching.

I'm pretty inflexible. I don't like to deviate from my preplanned lessons.

I don't like to teach the same thing in the same way all the time.

I have a way of teaching that has worked all right for years and I don't want to change.

I'm open to using or adapting other people's suggestions and ideas.

I believe school is hard work. Fun is for after school.

I share many of my experiences with my students and welcome sharing on their part. I'm interested in their ideas and responses.

I grade *everything:* neatness, handwriting, grammar, and punctuation always count on all written work.

I never grade any creative projects, such as poems, stories, pictures, plays, except to give credit for participation and to give lots of encouragement and praise.

I enjoy my students. I remember the FUN in Fundamentals!

I know that sometimes my plans don't work out, but I keep trying.

I try to plan successful experiences for each student in my room. I think that having many chances to succeed is very important for the healthy self-image, feeling of self-worth, and dignity of every person.

This is a competitive world. The sooner the children find that out, the better they'll be able to cope. It's survival of the fittest!

I like kids even when they don't listen, ask too many questions, mess up the room, don't follow instructions, get off the subject, argue, talk back, don't learn what I'm trying to teach. I still like kids.

I can't cope with the disorganization that often accompanies creative activities.

I encourage questions. Even though I may not know the answers, I enjoy exchanging and discussing ideas and opinions.

I try to find the time and the occasion to praise each student. A pat on the back goes a long way.

With a few exceptions, I will use almost any material (from baseball cards to popular songs, from creative movement to road signs) that will add to learning and make it more interesting.

There are always kids who are picked on by others. You can't baby them. They have to work out problems for themselves. It's not my job.

I won't stand for any person being put down in my room, and I will grow more aware of my own behavior so that I don't, consciously or unconsciously, put anyone down.

I'm not comfortable with people from backgrounds different from my own.

I think I can communicate with and find points of common interest and concern with almost anyone.

I believe traditional teaching methods are the best and I will continue to use them rather than experiment with other, less tried techniques.

I hope to encourage independent thinking in my students and I try to provide many opportunities for self-starting, original projects.

I know there are some students who can't be reached.

I think every student is reachable. Some haven't been reached as yet, but I'll keep trying.

I am still learning.

I am an expert.

Some of my best lessons have often been spur-of-the-moment happenings. I believe in serendipity.

It's too late for me to become more creative. I'm already set in my ways.

I have a lot going for me. My own experiences and knowledge are a great resource for teaching.

I know I can strengthen my own creativity by opening myself to new experiences and rekindling interests and talents that I've neglected for years.

I see where I can introduce some simple, enjoyable experiences to liven up my classroom. Sometimes, I guess, I'm too predictable and inflexible.

I think people learn more when they learn in a happy environment.

There is no end to this quest. Write your own list.

Schools and Their "Weather"

You are a weather report. Sometimes you are sunny. Sometimes you are stormy. Your climate may be consistently mild and warm or harsh and cold. You not only affect the children you teach, but the environment in which they learn. That immediate environment depends largely on you, the kind of person you are, your values, interests, and beliefs. Before our zoom lens focuses on one room, perhaps your room, let's direct a wide-angle lens to whole school buildings. They have climates, too.

The Footsteps is a group of middle school boys and girls who perform folk dances in their city school system.* They are invited to many elementary schools to present programs and assemblies. Without academic training or background in education and psychology, largely ignorant of research and data in related sociological fields, the Footsteps have become expert at sensing the climate of the school they are visiting. Within minutes, they sense the environment of the school and articulate their responses in no uncertain terms.

After an hour at School A, they finish their dances, rush to the parking lot with shoes untied and buttons undone and jump into the bus as if they are being chased.

"Wow!" they exclaim with relief. "Really couldn't wait to get out of *there!* Those poor kids were even afraid to do the Follow-the-Leader dance with us. And those teachers—they sat with their arms folded and stared at us as if they had never seen people before! Let's sneak out and rescue those kids before it's too late!"

*The group is from Johnson Park Middle School, Columbus, Ohio.

In contrast, listen to the Footsteps' conversation after a program at School B. The audience is bouncing out of the auditorium, kindergarten through sixth grade students are dancing up to the Footsteps, cheering, talking to them; teachers stop to compliment them. The dancers and the audience are all smiles.

"Let's come back to this school!" the dancers plan as they hear the final bell ring. "It's really a sharp place! Even the teachers danced with us, and everyone clapped so hard in the Rumanian dance we could hardly hear the music. This school is really together!"

They are not talking about physical beauty or extraordinary facilities. School A might be a shining new building of modern architecture and innovative lights and colors. School B might be an old, shabby, about-to-be-demolished structure with generations of footprints marked on its corridor floors. The point is, *what is the climate?* What is the atmosphere, the spirit of a place, of a school?

I visited a small city school system to work with its teachers and students. The superintendent of the system picked me up at the airport and we had a chance to talk for a few hours before my program began. His school system was in the process of "evaluation." One of the unique features of the evaluation method was the taking of numerous random, candid photos in all of his schools: shots of hallways, lunchrooms, classrooms, playgrounds, auditoriums, and school grounds. When the photographs were developed and displayed to the staff, they told very clear stories. The superintendent shared his concern about one particular school in the city that was known for its rigidity, its flat, strict, more narrow approach to education. His problem, he said, was that all the inservice programs in the world couldn't reach the faculty of that school: no matter what the communication or program, they sat smugly with arms folded and said, "We do these things already. We already know this. So what?"

When the photos taken in that school were shown, there was nothing ambiguous about the situation there. Hundreds of photos—no smiling kids; hundreds of photos—no smiling teachers. Not one photo showed children working together informally, talking together or in close, warm contact with each other or their teachers. Grim-faced children walked in silent lines, sat at separate desks, hunched over their own work under a teacher's stern eye.

If anonymous photographers took candid shots of your school, your classroom, what would those pictures show?

What About Your Weather?

Are there places in your life that inhibit you? Make you feel tense? Make you clam up or shrivel down? Are there places that reduce your voice to a hesitant whisper and unnerve you so that you forget even your own name and telephone number? Are there places in your life that warm you? Relax you? Invite you to stretch out, smile, make yourself at home? Do you have places where you feel open and trusting and in touch with everything around you and within you?

Your Classroom's Weather?*

There are classrooms and schools throughout this country that freeze children, contribute to their insecurity, anxiety, and fear, and sap their confidence, self-worth, and pride. Silence and order are high on the list of values. Obedience and strict discipline are the rules. There is no hum of activity in the corridors, and the walls do not brag about the specialness of the children who are within them. In such hostile places, the climate is frigid. The color is gray. The music is flat. Children's spirits shrink. Their bodies droop. Their minds contract. How are they feeling about themselves and what they are learning?

Then there are schools in our country that provide a warm, bright climate where children can grow and learn in wholesome and healthy ways. Teachers' magazines like *The Instructor* feature such schools in every issue. They call them A+ Schools and highlight a different school each month to serve as an inspiration and example of what is possible. No matter the size, location, or style, you will find top-notch, involved, caring, imaginative teachers working with a supportive, encouraging administration in close communication with the community. In such schools, look for lively, colorful bulletin boards and walls proudly displaying the works of the children. Note scenes that say "Education is hard work. It's challenging. It's exciting. We don't have time to waste!" Some of the ingredients that make the mix of A+ Schools are kids working alone, in

---

*During the eighties, a great number of studies and books analyzing and evaluating schools in the United States were widely circulated and discussed. Such studies as the National Commission on Excellence in Education's *A Nation at Risk: The Imperative for Educational Reform* (USGPO, 1983); such books as John Goodlad's *A Place Called School* (McGraw-Hill, 1983); and such educational journals as *Educational Leadership,* devoting its March 1985 issue to "Excellence: School by School"; and *Phi Delta Kappan* devoting its June 1985 issue to "Reaching For Excellence: Now Comes the Hard Part," are just a few samples of the challenging, controversial materials vying for the attention of educators.

groups, in twos, one to one; the murmur, the buzz of ideas exchanged, plans made, learning shared; the easy way children walk through the halls and greet you with a smile that says "Welcome to our school"; the pride on the faces of the kids as they show you their work or explain the activity of the moment (They know what they're doing. They know why they're there!). In such schools, kids, teachers, administration, families, and custodial staff are celebrated. Each is a V.I.P. The contributions of all to the enrichment of the school are valued. The school is like a family. Everyone is needed. Everyone is wanted. LIFE is the party in power.

There are many schools in every state that reflect this kind of warmth and encouragement, that strengthen the spirit of the children and spark the flames of curiosity, imagination, and a feeling of self-worth. In these schools, friendliness, cooperation, trust, pride, and enthusiasm rain like confetti in the lobbies, hallways, classrooms, offices, and playgrounds. Children are proud of their work, respect their own ideas and products and those of others, and welcome new experiences with enthusiasm. All of these schools reflect Warner's idea that "energy and curiosity make good desk mates."[14]

But what if the school you teach in is the opposite? What if the general discipline is rigid, order and obedience are the most important criteria, competition is the rule, and originality and curiosity are discouraged? How can a creative teacher survive in an atmosphere where children are frightened and suppressed, where their self-worth and self-confidence are diminished each day, and their faith in themselves and trust in others disappears? The creative teacher must, as John Holt says, "push the walls out or they will push you in." Or, as one teacher suggested at a workshop, "Our little rooms are sanctuaries. Once the children make it to our classrooms and the door closes behind them, they're safe. Home free!"

These are the truly courageous, dedicated teachers who believe in children as fellow human beings and in education as a shared, continuous life-adventure. Such outstanding teachers can truly be called "lifesavers" because they reach out, in the life and death struggle for the spirits of drowning children, and rescue them. A young, vital teacher in an uptight Michigan school confessed that "whenever we're doing something special—something that's fun—I put a sign on my door that reads "Testing—Do Not Disturb." Just as monks kept the lights of learning kindled during the Dark Ages, so creative, authentic teachers keep the joyfulness and excitement of education alive in their bright rooms within grim schools.

Close-up of a Classroom's Climate

Lexa, age nine, recalls her first day in a new class:

> When I walked into the room that day, I was kind of scared. Most of the kids I hadn't met. But, there were so many things I wanted to do—like there was a Science Center with bottles like a mad scientist would use, a lot of art and some signs in French. I liked the games and books that were there. Just the setup of the room was interesting—a great library corner with lots of good

books like mysteries and biographies. The teacher had bright, springy, colorful posters like yellow, light blue, and orange, and that makes you have cheerful feelings. There was one section with little cubbyholes for each child with our names on them—I loved that. It made you feel at home.

I visited a delightful third grade. Busy, happy, involved, the kids took time to welcome me. I jotted notes about their room. Some of the things I saw were

Butterfly and folk-tale mobiles

A wall about birds. "Feed the Birds" was the title. Each child had created an individual bird.

A celebration of Winnie the Pooh characters

An incubator with chicks hatching

Self-portraits

A space featuring April showers. Rabbits carried umbrellas. Each child had created an individual rabbit and umbrella.

Displayed on a "Reading Fun" wall were the books the kids were reading: *Prehistoric Animals, Ogres and Trolls, Green Is for Growing, Play with Seeds,* and *Red Fairy Book.* "These books we read together," one of the children explained.

A humorous chart named different "Handwriting Diseases" with demonstrated examples. The diseases listed were

Slantritis

Giant Writingitis

Tiny Writingitis

Loopitis

Frillyosis

The Class Rules were printed on a colorful board:

1. Follow directions.
2. Raise hands and wait to be called.
3. Use time wisely.
4. Make no negative comments or use abusive language.
5. Keep hands and feet to ourselves.

The kids told me that the whole class had decided on these rules.

Penny Sanecki is a teacher who happens to love animals. Kids and animals are free spirits in her bustling third-grade room. When I visited, I toured her animal kingdom with her students, who easily and competently explained, showed, demonstrated as we moved around the room. We inventoried the pets in the room and wrote their names on a chart which now became part of the classroom design. Here's some of that gathering:

Animals in Our Room

Our Mice: Guest Star, Mighty, Danger, Crocket and Tubbs,
   Mickey, Minnie, Walt, Tommy, Karen, Annette, Bobby,
   Sharon, Cubby, Dianne
Our Rabbit: Bugs Bunny
Our Guinea Pigs: Baskin and Robin, Squeaker
Our Fish: too many to list
Our Hamster: Springsteen
Our Turtle: Cousteau
Note: We have six new baby mice we will soon name.

What will your room express of your special personality, your beliefs, and interests? What messages will your students receive as they enter your room for the first time? The climate of a classroom is almost totally dependent on the values, attitudes, commitments, and personality of the teacher. You, the teacher, caught in the crosswinds of societal conflicts and crisis, with divorce, drugs, runaways, unemployment on the increase and signs of peace on earth and brotherly and sisterly love on the decrease, will try to blaze some path through this chaos so that the children can follow. You, the teacher, alone, can't solve the colossal problems challenging modern men and women, but there is one basic power teachers have that is unique to the profession. *You can do something about your time and space with the students entrusted to your care.* The whole world may be crashing around outside, but in *that* room, *your* room, kids may feel safe. In your room, students may learn that their opinions, ideas, and feelings have value. In your room, children may learn to trust their own responses and abilities and to respect those of others. In your room, they may learn that education is a joyful adventure and that discovering, exploring, sharing, searching, and creating are healthy, nourishing experiences.

Dawn Heyman started back to work in the fall teaching a new group of third graders in an inner-city school. We have no trouble seeing what she values, what's in her heart. Here is what she told her third graders this first day:

"I know that some of you have problems at home, things that you're worried about.

"I can't take you out of your home or change that situation. But together we can make this room—our classroom—a warm and happy place where everyone is affirmed and accepted.

"We have 181 days together to discover the gifts that everybody brings to this classroom. The important thing is to grow from wherever you are. You know what a garden is. In April, tulips and daffodils bloom. Later, peonies and roses bloom. We don't embarrass or humiliate roses because they bloom later. We know each flower comes up in its own time and season.

"In our room, nobody will ever be humiliated because of where they are at a given point. We're all different and we all learn and grow in our own way. I remember a boy who couldn't spell *one word* at the beginning of the year and would never participate in spelling games or spelling bees. By the end of the year, not only did he join the spelling bee but he stayed up for seven rounds.

When he missed his word, the children applauded. Not because he missed, but because he stayed up for so long. They recognized the mountain he had climbed.

"This year, we're all going to climb our own mountains and help each other up.

"What this class is about is growing and becoming. Don't be afraid to make mistakes. Mistakes are how we direct our learning. The only foolish questions are the ones that aren't asked. Now—let's put on our hiking boots and start our journey."

In Dawn's class, children bloom. She doesn't think of herself as being removed from the children in some lofty role of Teacher. She thinks of herself, often, as a fellow learner.

"My kids have seen me laugh, have seen me cry. They know I make mistakes, goof up, lose my temper.

"But they know I share myself with them: what I'm reading, my yoga, my travels, my feelings. We just share our human-beingness. They have to know grown-ups are not infallible. We have REAL lives."

One day, one of Dawn's students, Channelle, had a bad day.

Dawn offered, "You sure look like you could use a hug, Channelle."

Later that day, Channelle told Dawn, "Miss Heyman, that hug did a lot of good."

About six months later, Dawn was having a bad day. Channelle stopped on the way to recess and offered, "You sure look like you could use a hug, Miss Heyman."

And it did a lot of good.

What happens to children when they learn in a harsh climate, empty of warmth, trust, and joy and full of rigidity, competition, and anxiety? What would happen to you if you learned in such an atmosphere? Would you grow afraid? Would you distrust your own instincts and responses? Would you grow insecure about your worth and lose self-respect in your work? Would you lose interest in learning?

"I have never seen such a dramatic change in a class," the art teacher says sadly as she leaves a fifth grade room. "Last year they were bubbling with enthusiasm, so responsive, full of original projects and ideas. Now, here they are, the same kids—different room, different teacher—and they are unrecognizable. Even their posture is different. They have no life! They're afraid. They're cowed!"

That story can be repeated hundreds of thousands of times and will always, tragically, be true.

Ask yourself how successful the best list of creative activities will be in a negative, hostile climate? How effective will the swimming instructions be when there's no water in the pool? How will your seeds grow if there's no dirt, sun, or water to bless them? When you are tense, your body tightens. If you are asked to touch your toes, you may be so stiff from anxiety that you might not even be able to bend to your waist. When you relax, that same body can do cartwheels and somersaults.

A third grader stands in the doorway of the remedial reading room looking longingly back at his reading teacher. He finally says, "How come I do everything right in here with you and when I go back to my own room I'm stupid again?"

In classrooms where they breathe stultified air, where the message of the teacher and the room is the same—"stifle yourself," where there are absolute rights and absolute wrongs and very little in the middle, where they are humiliated if their work isn't "up to par," where negatives and weaknesses are highlighted and rigid competition is the rule, what do you expect to happen to the children? In such a climate, you can burn this book of creative experiences and let it join the ashes of all broken dreams.

A Warm, Safe Climate

Many years ago, I taught fourth grade in a small, cramped school not far from Albany, New York, in miles but very far from Albany in worldly knowledge and experience. We took a class trip to the State Education Building in the heart of the city—into the vast main hall, over to the elevators, up to the museum floor. In our class, qualities such as independence, trust, and self-direction were highly emphasized. Consistent with our way, we gathered in the lobby in front of the elevators and agreed on a plan. "The Indians are there," I pointed. "The rocks and fossils, there. The animals and birds, there. Go in whatever direction you want, see as much as you can, and we'll all meet back here in two hours. All right, synchronize watches."

We separated. Two hours later, when I went back to the lobby, there was Wayne, sitting on the bench facing the elevators. "You're punctual," I praised him as the group met. Later, back at school, we talked about our trip—what we had seen, what we had liked. We wrote words on the board and shared observations. When it was Wayne's turn, he responded to the question, "What did you like best about the museum?" with one word, "Elevators!"

Wayne had never left that bench during that whole field trip. He sat in front of the elevators the entire two hours, watching the lights flash, the doors open, the people appearing and disappearing. He had never seen elevators before. Because the climate in our room was one of acceptance and trust, Wayne knew that he would never be put down for sharing his favorite sight. He knew that he would be accepted and respected for his interest, whatever it was. What would you have done? Would you have flunked him in museum or given him a D in field trip?

Everything in your room—everything spoken and unspoken, everything shared and planned and dreamed—goes into the making of a warm, safe place where children learn in healthy, positive, life-affirming ways. The language of the room—your words, the way you respond to questions, problems, and everyday situations, the interchanges and exchanges among your students—contributes to the spirit of your space. Are you consistent? Do you *say* that you believe in sharing ideas, that you welcome suggestions from the kids? *Do you mean it?* Here is a fragment from a conversation I heard while eavesdropping.

CAREFUL

A teacher said, "Boys and girls, here's where I want YOUR ideas, your opinions. We've been discussing the idea of 'Celebrating Becoming.' Now, what does that mean to you? What does 'celebrating becoming' mean to you?"

After a little pause, one hesitant student offered, "Um . . . well . . . like celebrating learning?"

"Wrong!" the teacher snapped. "Really, I thought you could come up with a more original idea than that. I guess I just expected more from you!"

Kids have extrasensory awareness to pick up on whether your proclamations of belief match your behavior. One such incident demonstrates to the entire group that there is no room in this class for individual opinions or guesses. This is NOT a SAFE place!

Remember, everything you say or do reflects your philosophy, shows the LIFE or DEATH of your beliefs and values.

How can you translate your beliefs about education, your feelings about children, and your own interests and unique qualities into a reality—a classroom? In your room, will children have opportunities to see for themselves, do for themselves, discover and explore by themselves, make mistakes and correct them by themselves? When children are denied that important closer look, when they must not touch, when they are given no real chance to encounter the many exciting things in their environment, creative learning disappears.

Torrance describes a healthy classroom climate as one that encourages cooperation, helping, working together, organizing, praising one another, consideration, communication, and consulting with one another in a congenial, interested, questioning, and curious way. He looks for clues that reveal a classroom climate where positive, enjoyable learning takes place.

Are the students' questions treated with respect?

Are imaginative and unusual ideas treated with respect?

Are pupils shown that their ideas have value?

Are opportunities provided for practice and experimentation without evaluation?

Is self-initiated learning encouraged and evaluated?[15]

An important element in the building of a positive climate is your personal input into the space, into the place. Are you interested in sports? Will you share that interest with your class? Are you fascinated by animals? Do you love poetry? Are you a science-fiction fan? Sharing is an essential quality of a "warm, safe place." If the uniqueness of each person is to be valued and appreciated, individuals must share with each other in an open and trusting way. You, as a teacher, set an example, consciously and unconsciously, of an attitude, of a value system, of a way of life. How do you share this with your students?

Think about your room. What special corners will you plan? What interest centers will you offer? What topics and focus will you choose for the different bulletin boards and wall spaces? What colors do you like? In what ways will your students know that yours is a caring and friendly place, an interesting and stimulating environment, with plenty of room for their own works and ideas?

Ronni Hochman, who teaches Special Education in a way so special that kids in *regular* classes ask to go into Ronni's class, always has a wall devoted to the works of every student. Each child has a designated space with room to display any work he or she chooses to share. Not only are the kids reaffirmed daily by Ronni's words and actions, but the walls of her room celebrate their achievements.

When your students walk into your room for the first time, they are introduced to a new person in a new place. Both person and place tell something about the climate, the weather. When your students walk into your room for the first time, what do you want the message of the room to be? What will be their environment for the school year? What kinds of values do you want to see reflected in your room? How can these be translated into tangible elements?

Teacher/consultants Chick Moorman and Dee Dishon have spent years developing practical, effective ways for teachers and students to transform their room and time into a cooperative, nurturing environment where children learn to succeed and to value themselves, others, and the wonder of education. Their book *Our Classroom: We Can Learn Together** is packed with excellent sug-

---

*Chick Moorman and Dee Dishon, *Our Classroom: We Can Learn Together* (Prentice-Hall, 1983). Chick and Dee do national consulting work through their Institute for Personal Power, P.O. Box 68, Portage, Michigan 49081, (616) 327–2761.

gestions for activities and projects aimed at contributing to a cohesive, caring group.

Just as you are being asked to seriously commit yourself to living a more creative life and extending that flexibility, openness, warmth, and enjoyment into your teaching, so you are being challenged to commit yourself to the building of a healthy positive classroom climate. Can you consciously plan ways for your values and beliefs to take form and action so that they become the "way" of your place, the "why" of your space, the "how" of your time?

"With trust you will find ways that glisten, lead to gladness, companioned by many who love. The pathways are for choosing. Walk in awareness."[16]

Activities for a Warm, Safe Place

Names, Symbols, and Signals

Name your class! With your students, choose a name. Isn't Stars or Wizards more exciting than Ms. Reedy's Fourth Grade in Room 6?

What's your *symbol?* What's your *class motto?* Special way of *greeting?* Choose *hand or visual signals* for such messages as "Please be quiet," "Let's take a break," "I've got a problem," "Welcome." In many classes, such special ways of communicating are immensely successful. The ancient hand signals of thumbs up (Life) and thumbs down (Death) are excellent examples of immediate communication.

I know teachers who give each student a set of three color cards at the very beginning of school. The green card means "Great, I've got it!" The red card means "Help! I don't get it." The yellow card means "I'm not sure. I'm still shaky." This is a safe way for a child to say "I don't know."

All through the school year, you and your class celebrate yourselves!

No Put-downs!

Ridicule and humiliation are the enemies of creative growth. In a classroom in which kids are put down, made fun of, laughed at, or teased by either the teacher or the other students, the chance that any one of the suggestions in this book will succeed is doubtful.

Teachers MUST respond immediately to put downs, setting a tone of safety and trust, urging the children to work together on this problem so that everyone feels safe and hallowed. Think of put-downs as *bad habits* we are trying to break. Avoid humiliating the child who puts others down. Help the child become aware of how such behavior is hurtful. Also explain that if anyone tried to put down *that* child, you would be equally as distressed.

Creative teachers have some tangible ways to encourage positive behavior. Here are a few variations.

The Good-Deed Box   When a person puts down another, he or she picks a good deed from the Good-Deed Box (all of the good-deed suggestions are made up by the class). The person keeps the deed a secret and then, sometime during the next day, cancels out the put-down by doing that good deed for the victim of the put-down.

Bean, Popcorn, or Pebble Jars   One kindergarten teacher found a very simple way to emphasize positive behavior. Required: an empty jar, beans, popcorn kernels, or pebbles, a class discussion. The plan:

"Whenever I see people being kind, considerate, helpful . . . I'll just add a pebble (bean, popcorn kernel) to the jar. When it's filled to the top, we'll celebrate!" (pizza party? popcorn party? afternoon of games? puppet day?)

In one situation, using this jar really helped turn around a group of children who were often very mean and hostile to one another. Such consistent comments by the teacher as "I like the way you helped Bobby pick up his spilled-out desk." or "When Jeff shared his new book today, you all listened with such fine attention and respect. Let's add a bean to the jar!" encourage the children to think, speak, and behave in more positive ways.

Ronni Hochman uses a huge jar and labels different levels of it. If it fills to level one, a colorful label reads: "Free Time for All." When the jar is filled to the second level, the children enjoy "A Game of Your Choice," and when the jar is filled completely, it's time for a "Popcorn Party with Favorite Music."

Find your own variations. Beg, borrow, steal, improvise. Experiment.

In the course of your readings, observations, and discussions, gather ideas for handling ridicule and humiliation in the classroom, and jot them in your notebook. Do not rely on memory as an absolute resource. Become aware of your own behavior. Do you put people down unconsciously? When you are tired or frustrated, do you resort to angry sarcasm or ridicule? As you are, so will you teach. How are you? Discuss and share these ideas in your class.

You're Special

Another basic requirement in the building of a positive classroom climate is the acceptance, respect, and appreciation of each person in the room as a unique and special individual who has much to contribute and share with other students.

When you visit the rooms of creative teachers, you'll note that walls and bulletin boards feature the *names* of the children, their photos, portraits, pictures, papers. There are places to "sign in," to add individual contributions to a whole (create YOUR animal for the zoo, and YOUR balloon to the circus, plant YOUR flower in the garden). This is not a once-a-year activity, but an ongoing component of the class' life.*

Start your own variations of the ideas that follow, used successfully by many teachers throughout the country.

Salute to a Child   Leave a space on a bulletin board or a wall in the room. The heading on the space is "We Spotlight" or "We Salute" or "Child of the Week," and the subject is one of the children in the class. Each child gets a turn

---

*My book *Creative Activities for Young Children* (San Diego: Harcourt, 1983) features numerous activities for celebrating children in special ways.

Darren Brooks

Kindergarten 1986
AM Playmate of the Week

Darren has brown eyes, blonde hair, and freckles. He is _____ and weighs 51 pounds. Darren is 6 years old, and he has 1 eight-year old brother, Dwayne. His mom is _____ ,and his dad is Howard. They have a dog named Ingrid.

Darren's favorite color is (blue) ,and his favorite shape is a triangle. He likes to eat spaghetti and corn-on-the-cob. "Family Feud" is Darren's favorite T.V. show, and he liked _____ at the movies. In school, he likes to paint, and, at home, he likes to play with trucks. Darren's best friends are Todd and April. Someday, he wants to be a dentist !!

to be spotlighted and can share photos, pictures, hobbies, words, poems, stories, collages—anything to brighten up the room space that will belong entirely to that child for a few days or a week.

Don't feel you must be bound by strict alphabetical order in selecting the child. Sneaky teachers pick names out of a grab bag of children who need special attention earlier in the year.

Good News Notes   Many teachers send Good News Notes home to families. On a small sheet of paper with a happy design in the corner and the words "Good News Note," the teacher fills in the lines after "I Am Happy to Report That . . ." A note should be written for each child at least once during the school year and, if possible, more often. We all respond to praise and encouragement and such growth-sustaining behavior is often absent from our classrooms.

Here are two examples of Good News Notes.

I AM HAPPY TO REPORT THAT   Kevin found the gerbil that we have been looking for since Monday. We are happy to have such a good gerbil-finder in our class.

I AM HAPPY TO REPORT THAT   Mindy's Spring Word was the one the class picked as their favorite. We are all drawing pictures about her wonderful word, "life."

The notes are sent home to the family with the child. They are a positive way to dispel the belief that all the notes that teachers send home are negative.

Share your findings with your class so all can benefit from the exchange.

Open-ended Experiences

Providing successful experiences for all the children in your class is vital if you are to have a climate where ideas and creative learning can flourish. There are many activities that you, as a teacher, can plan that will guarantee success for students in your class, whatever the level of intellectual development. Begin a section in your journal or notebook that will also be a continuing assignment to last through your teaching career. In this section, gather learning experiences that yield success to all who participate in them. As you are thinking, let me hint to you that all of the ARTS afford numerous success experiences.

CAREFUL

No subject or material is immune from destructive criticism by a teacher. I have personally witnessed children learn to hate Tom Sawyer and caterpillars. I have listened to children complain about looking for "Signs of Spring." There is no curriculum area immune to destruction if the teacher's attitude is negative, rigid, uptight, inflexible, without warmth, interest, life, or joy. A lesson plan with dialogue and procedures on the subject of "love" can be presented in such a way that the class, in its entirety, will vote against "love."

This is a true example of how easy it is to kill interesting and meaningful material.

Jody: "My grandma brought me this Eskimo jacket from Alaska. May I show it to the class?"

Teacher: "I'm sorry, Jody, but you know that Thursday is our Sharing Day. You'll have to wait until then. Besides, we don't study Eskimos till March!"

Providing open-ended experiences that have no absolute right or wrong answer but many possible responses is one way to ensure success for all your students. Here are two examples.

Mystery Box   Inside your mystery box, you might place a piece of fabric dipped in pine-scented lotion or a clump of cotton or peanut shells. Pass the box around and ask each child to guess what it is he or she is feeling, touching, smelling. Everyone succeeds because everyone has a response. If the children are not afraid of being *wrong*, then they will enjoy the diversity of the answers and the interesting responses of their classmates.

Sharing   Use this activity to spark your students' curiosity. What are some of the things we have seen today? Let's go around the room and tell one thing.

The child in the slowest reading group may have seen something more interesting than the best student, but all their words go on the board. Everyone succeeds in the experience. Or ask each person

What's your favorite food? TV program? song? game?

What's your favorite animal? holiday? color?

What's your lucky number?

This activity has double value! Not only do all the children feel successful in making important contributions to the class discussion, but also, if you write down their ideas, you have gathered a wealth of language material for stories, pictures, poems, and projects!

CAREFUL

When you ask students to share poems, stories, pictures, works of creative personal expression, don't mark or grade them! On creative works, find ways to stamp acceptance or approval that say "Thank you for sharing this with us." Grade spelling tests, grammar exercises, skill development sheets, paragraph writing drills, but not the creative works! Giving a child a 75 or a C− on a poem is a betrayal of the invitation to share feelings and personal impressions.

Now, if those works are to be celebrated—displayed on the bulletin board, included in a class poetry book, sent home to families, used for illustrations—then, of course, they will need editing. *That's just a matter of courtesy, isn't it—to be sure our works are clearly written and spelled so everyone can read and enjoy them?* Help children "rejoice in all their works."

Take Field Trips

This is such a dynamic time to be teaching! There are so many new and old methods to try and new approaches to explore that the beginning teacher can easily grow dizzy from the choices. If possible, visit a diversity of schools. Many school systems are experimenting with "magnet" or "alternative" schools that feature the arts or science or patriotism as the core of their curriculum. Others follow Montessori or Piaget. No matter the type of school, observe how such important qualities as respect, appreciation, trust, communication, flexibility, sharing, involvement, independence, and enjoyment are reflected. Don't be surprised if you find a very open, free-spirited atmosphere within four traditional walls and a more authoritarian, rigid climate in one of the "pods" of an open school.

Note your observations as you "sniff the climate." Share and discuss your experiences with your class when you return.

All ways work and don't work. It's almost totally up to . . . who else? THE TEACHER! YOU—A V.I.P.!

ENDNOTES

[1] Albert Cullum, *The Geranium on the Window Sill Just Died But Teacher You Went Right On* (New York: Harlin Quist, 1971) 34.

[2]Clark Moustakas, *The Authentic Teacher* (Cambridge: Doyle, 1966) 17.

[3]Chaim Picker, ed., *He Kindled a Light: From the Speeches and Writings of Shraga Arian* (New York: United Synagogue Commission on Jewish Education, 1976) xviii.

[4]Alice Miel, "Teaching as a Creative Process," *Creativity in Teaching: Invitations and Instances* (Belmont: Wadsworth, 1961) 8.

[5]Theodore Roethke, *Straw for the Fire* (Garden City: Doubleday, 1974).

[6]Edwin Markham, *Poems* (New York: AMS, 1950).

[7]E. Paul Torrance, "Creative Potential of School Children," *Education and the Creative Potential* (Minneapolis: U of Minnesota P, 1963) 13.

[8]*Indicators of Quality (Signs of Good Teaching)*, Institute of Administrative Research, Teachers College, Columbia University.

[9]Mihaly Csikszentmihalyi and Jane McCormack, "The Influence of Teachers," *Phi Delta Kappan* Feb. 1986: 415–19. See the whole issue. Its theme is The Influence of Teachers.

[10]Csikszentmihalyi and McCormack.

[11]Roethke, *Straw for the Fire* 201.

[12]Betty Smith, *A Tree Grows in Brooklyn* (New York: Harper, 1943) 141.

[13]Evelyn Wenzel, "Finding Meaning in Education," *Creativity in Teaching: Invitations and Instances* (Belmont: Wadsworth, 1961) 60.

[14]Sylvia Ashton-Warner, *Spearpoint* (New York: Vintage, 1974) 101.

[15]Torrance, "A Climate to Think and Learn Creatively," *Education and the Creative Potential* 58.

[16]Paraphrased from the Dedication to the Ohio Association for Children with Learning Disabilities Conference, Sept. 1974.

3

You and the Language Arts Curriculum

As the cool water gushed over one hand, she spelled into the other, the word, water, first slowly, then rapidly. . . .
I knew then that "w-a-t-e-r" meant the wonderful cool something that was flowing over my hand. That living word awakened my soul, gave it light, hope, joy, set it free. . . .

HELEN KELLER[1]

The underlying focus throughout this book is on *you*, a creative, unique individual, committed to teaching, who understands the absolute necessity of developing a positive classroom climate where you and your students can share the exciting adventure of learning.

In this chapter on the language arts curriculum, a course of study that generally includes the major communication skills of listening, speaking, reading, and writing, the focus remains on you. Think of the three *u*'s in the word "curriculum": one to represent *you*, the individual; one to represent *you*, the student (we are always learning); one to represent *you*, the teacher.

What Is Language?

The word "language" is provocative. To some people it conjures up fears of failing grammar tests and oral reports, while to others it means memorizing vocabulary lists and filling in the blanks of incomplete sentences. One person may imagine the word "language" taking flight and carrying meanings, ideas, feelings, and thoughts from one mind to another. To a pragmatist, language is a school subject assigned to a specific slot in a regular schedule. Yet for others language is so all-encompassing a human medium of expression and communication that no curriculum can confine it to a box in a plan book.

My own feelings about language reflect the broadest, most universal outlook. I agree with Morton Bloomfield, who conceives of language as "central to and pervasive in the realm of all human thought." He sees language as forming the basis of whatever social cohesion we can attain and determining in large measure the way we look at the world. He believes that language intimately links the past with the present and makes possible continuity from the present to the future. Bloomfield looks with awe at language, acknowledging its magic and its hypnotic power to elevate or depress. We cannot escape its influence, even by silence. Human beings need language to grasp things intellectually and to get others to do so. In its broadest sense, language defines our very humanity.[2]

Dwight Bolinger describes the whole process of language learning as "one of bringing our personal ways of talking and comprehending in line first with those of other individuals at close range and then with expanding circles of speech communities outward to the limits of our reach in society."[3]

I think of language as being at the core of our thinking and learning. It is doubtful that an individual could attain success in academics, science, business, commerce or trade, the arts—any field of endeavor in our modern world—without a strong, stable language foundation. In our society, people who can't read or write are truly handicapped. I think of language as being connected with LIFE, with our lives and the quality of our lives.

Language is one of the unique characteristics of the human family. People use language on different levels, communicating basic physical needs as well as expressing complicated abstract ideas. In the biblical story of creation, one of Adam's first assignments was to *name* the animals (language). Human beings are gifted and talented in naming the objects and inhabitants of their world.

They are also brilliant symbolizers—inventing metaphors and similes, imagery and symbols to enrich the naming. They are askers of questions and explorers searching for answers. They are playful, making jokes and riddles and puns. They are actors—expressing words they may not mean, hiding feelings behind a camouflage vocabulary. They give words to their deepest dreams and try to find words to comfort them through darkest times.

I think of language as being at the core of our thinking, learning, and living.

How Do You Feel about Language?

How do *you* feel about language? How aware, curious, and knowledgeable are you about language? Your attitudes toward the various components of the language arts curriculum and toward your students' language experiences are as important as the subject itself. This may sound corny, but you really *are* the curriculum. Otherwise, books like this would not be necessary; the subject would teach itself. Because the language arts are so intrinsically fascinating, all children should love the subject. No child should ever say, "I hate English!" or "Poetry? How dull!" The success or failure of the curriculum depends on you, the teacher.

As you read, think about what language means to you. What place does it have in your life? How has language affected your own behavior and beliefs? Have there been times in your life when your thoughts were misinterpreted because of the way you communicated them or the way they were received by others? Can you recall instances when the meanings of others and the words they chose to convey them, as well as the meanings you interpreted in them, caused you grief, laughter or tears? Think beyond your own experiences to the incredible power of language over the destiny of peoples and nations. Life or death, war or peace, love or hate—which we choose may depend on whether language is understood, misunderstood, or misinterpreted.

If we do not have a complete grasp of a subject, or if we have ambiguous feelings about it, we may unconsciously perpetuate a destructive, fragmented kind of learning. Our teaching of that subject area will be splintered. It will lack cohesion. Moustakas warns us that

> the shattering of unity or wholeness is taken for granted in a compartmentalized world . . . where the emphasis is so extreme that spontaneity, spirit, feeling, wonder and other aesthetic and moral dimensions of the self are repressed or harnessed or controlled in order to accumulate more and more facts. . . . [4]

But, if your mind is filled with the wonders, the mysteries, the incredible complexities and achievements of language, then your curriculum and the ways you interpret and teach it will reflect that excitement, that continuous discovery and searching for knowledge and meaning. Take time now to develop a framework, a philosophical and attitudinal base for teaching the language arts, that will help your students to develop as whole persons, vivacious, alive, authentic, with new attitudes, awarenesses, skills and knowledge. . . . [Where] genuine meaning exists between the person and the world, meaning emerges which forms a bridge between the self and others, between subject and object, between the known and the knowers. Then, there is mutuality; there is genuine connection with life.[5]

Language: A Human Phenomenon

Have you ever traveled to a different country or to a specific cultural community in the United States like "Little Russia" in Brooklyn or the Arabic community in Detroit or Chinatown in San Francisco? Were you astonished at how fluently the children there spoke Russian or Arabic or Chinese? Have you ever stopped to think that you might have been born in another country or another culture and so learned to speak another language as naturally as you speak English?

We visited relatives of my mother who left Rumania after World War I and settled on a Moshav (cooperative community) in Israel. These were the languages spoken at that emotional event: The older couple, my mother's cousins, spoke Rumanian, Russian, Hebrew, and Yiddish; their children spoke Rumanian, Russian, Hebrew, Yiddish, French, a little Arabic, and English; we spoke only English.

The frustration my mother's cousin felt was tragic/comic: "We have finally met," he moaned. "Now, how will we speak to each other?"

Working out that important communication was an achievement of mammoth proportions as each sentence was translated many different times. Each idea took a long time to make the rounds of connection. But the effort was worth it!

How important is language?

The prize-winning author Isaac Bashevis Singer was asked on a radio interview, "Why did you choose Yiddish to write in?" He answered, "I did not choose Yiddish. Yiddish chose me!"

Peter Farb continues the image of a person chosen by a language:

Linguistically speaking, man is not born free. He inherits a language full of quaint sayings, archaisms, and a ponderous grammar; even more important, he inherits certain fixed ways of expression that may shackle his thoughts. Language becomes man's shaper of ideas rather than simply his tool for reporting ideas.[6]

Although there are approximately 3,000 major languages spoken on this planet today (not including dialects), most of *you* were chosen by American English, and it is that national language that you might call (in a moment of sentimentality) your "mother tongue." You might speak English with a southern drawl or a Bostonian twang. Your English may be Brooklynese or Texan, but despite your dialect, you join over 300,000,000 English-speaking people around the world. Only Chinese, with its complicated dialects, is spoken by more people.

The reality of America is that we are not only an English-speaking country. We are a nation of immigrants and our people speak numerous languages in addition to English. This "fact" was vividly demonstrated at a recent teachers' workshop. One of the participants, who taught at a nearby high school, brought in a copy of a computer print-out giving information on "Languages at Lincoln." The list is dramatic. At this typical American high school in a suburb of Chicago, the students speak over thirty different languages. Some of them: Rumanian, Russian, Serbo-Croatian, Spanish, Tagalog, Korean, Mandarin, Polish, Pakistani, Taiwanese, Tamil, Turkish, Urdu, Vietnamese, Slovene, Hebrew, Italian, Japanese, Indian, Hindi, Greek, Gujarati, Armenian, Assyrian, Cantonese, Chinese, French, German, and Panjabi. Some of these students will be multilingual, speaking English as well as another language. Some will need help in learning English. English itself reflects the contributions of many other languages. Just as our country is enriched by the interactions of all our diverse citizens, so our language is enriched by its integrating of many other languages.

And our lives are enriched as we learn about and learn from children of different cultures, different languages.

The challenge to classroom teachers, ESL (English as a Second Language) teachers, and LES (Limited English Speaking) teachers is clear: Show that you respect, appreciate, value, and are interested in the cultures and languages of the minority students while helping those students learn the new language and the world which that language represents!

Those children who do not understand the workings and phonics of their own language will have difficulty learning the systems of their new language. Those who have already mastered metalinguistic skills will be more able to apply those skills to their new language. *Both kinds* of students need the kind, encouraging, accepting, warm support of teachers who will act as role-models of positive behavior for the rest of the students.

Successful teachers are eclectic in their approach. They don't rely on any one method or technique; they don't depend on one kind of material. They use a variety of printed matter: stories, songs, poems, charts, posters, lists, magazines, newspapers. *As often as possible, they choose themes and topics familiar to the minority children.* They share many holistic language experiences with their students: story-telling, discussions, dramatizations, games, songs, science experiments, cooking activities. They know that formal instruction in specifically needed skills is necessary but not to the exclusion of informal communication where students have opportunities to interact one-to-one, in small groups, in larger groups.

They encourage their students to write from their own experiences, from their own special knowledge, so that those works become the material of the class and have intrinsic value. As they help children make meaning out of their new world and the new words, they provide concrete experiences: touching, tasting, seeing, listening, building, making. Every context cue is provided. We don't learn on one level in one narrow lane. We need repetition, different ways of approaching the same idea, a variety of questions and ways of questioning, ample opportunities to explore answers.

The same exciting, dynamic, integrative, supportive, language-rich environment is good for our English-speaking students as well!

Is English a Simple Language?

Think of the influences and changes that have affected the English language throughout the centuries. Roman troops came to Great Britain in 50 A.D. and conquered the Celtic population, which spoke a language similar to modern Welsh. They were followed by a Danish invasion in 800 A.D. that enriched the already changed language. In 1066, William the Conqueror's victory at the Battle of Hastings introduced a Norman French influence that lasted for several hundred years, until the Renaissance rekindled Latin's effect on the polyglot language. Early British colonists brought their language with them to the New World and all the following waves of immigrants added their languages to the ever-changing "mother tongue." The English vocabulary is rich with words contributed by other languages. Consider these few examples:

Italian: broccoli, opera, confetti

Dutch: yacht, cruiser, and toy

Arabic: algebra, orange, and alcohol

Hebrew: camel, ebony, and cherub

Spanish: alligator, cocoa, and rodeo

American Indian: woodchuck, raccoon, and tobacco

Japanese: karate, kimono, hibachi

African: yam, safari, chimpanzee

Chinese: tea, silk, yen[7]

I enjoyed reading a newspaper survey reporting the favorite foods of American children. The list included:

pizza, tacos, hamburgers, hot dogs, French fries,
bagels, popcorn, chili, chow mein

I thought: What a way to turn kids ON to American history! At a social studies conference, I asked teachers to play with the idea of using the kids' favorite foods to launch American history: Where did those foods come from? How did we get them? The kids who looked up the history of pizza would also find the story of the journeys made to America by Italian immigrants. Some of the teachers experimented with this approach and reported that it was one of their most successful "projects."

American English is noted for its adaptability and flexibility. It is a living, growing, dynamic organism, not a dead, dull, limited vehicle for limited communication. You can personally attest to the flexibility of the language when you think of the word "whom," which is rapidly declining in use, and the acceptability of using the expression "It's me" rather than "It is I." The catch-all word "whatever" is used by everyone and may soon work its way into dictionaries with its new meaning. Middle-class white children use black-American English "soul" expressions, such as "That's bad!" to mean good and "bro" to mean brother. Some years ago when I taught in Hawaii, I didn't know whether to laugh or cry when my high school students told me that my dress was "bitchin'." It was actually a compliment. Social-critic humorists, such as Lenny Bruce and George Carlin, have used the English language itself as the subject of monologues. A few decades ago, Lenny Bruce was punished by society for his blunt, satirical use of taboo words. Yet today George Carlin enjoys widespread popularity and acclaim for his comedy sketches using some of the very same expressions.

A Japanese exchange student, puzzled by the mysteries of the English language, finally asked his host family questions that had been bothering him over the weeks:

> How can you "love" a banana?
>
> What do you mean, "You cut school"?
>
> What is a "round trip"?
>
> Please explain this headline: COUPLES PLIGHT THEIR TROTHS
>
> I don't understand "You dig me!"
>
> Please translate "That flick turned me off."
>
> It's so warm out, why do you say "That's cool"?
>
> Why does the word psalm start with a *p* and not an *s*?

Large doses of humor and imagination are a big help to our understanding and appreciation of language. For example, Fred Gwynne's delightful picture book, *The King Who Rained* (Windmill/Dutton, 1970), and Norton Juster's *The Phantom Tollbooth* (Random House, 1964) are children's books that encourage a playful, joyful look at the idiosyncrasies of our mother tongue. As the Japanese exchange student's confusion reminds us, English is often a "weird" language! But it's OUR language, and we need it to survive and to succeed.

If you have traveled abroad, you are familiar with the change of languages, customs, foods, and currency as you cross the different borders of the world. Mario Pei, who writes eloquently about language, compares your language to your money, which is worthless in another country unless you get it changed, or, in the case of language, unless you can translate it.[8]

Unspoken Language

Of course, when words fail you or your oral language is useless, you can still communicate with your eyes, hands, or other parts of your body. You have a language of gestures, facial expressions, and body movements. Have you ever felt like an amateur Marcel Marceau as you use the universal language of pantomime to convey your message? Think of all the borders that can be crossed by a friendly smile. Nonverbal communication is a new label for an old phenomenon: bodies express thoughts and feelings as clearly as words do. My words

can say "Pleased to meet you," but my body may communicate the opposite. Martha Graham, the multigifted American dancer-choreographer, considers the body the true conveyor of meaning. She believes that words can lie but bodies cannot.

Your own students will communicate in this language-without-words. They will "tell" you whether they are interested in what you are saying, whether they are excited about a project, whether they are afraid of an assignment, or whether they are glad to be in your classroom.

Your words, their pitch, tone, stress, and rhythm, reinforced by your gestures, body movements, and facial expressions make up the major part of your language process. Your speech is unique. It has its own peculiarities, which distinguish it from the speech of other people. Those who know you can identify you unseen, by your speech.[9] Your language is as integral a part of you as your breathing and your thinking.

But don't you really have more than one language? Don't you speak one way with your family? Another way when you're being interviewed for a job? And yet another when you participate in a formal meeting or when you're just relaxing with your friends? Do you have a citizens band radio in your car? Do you speak CB lingo? Can you tune in to the language of the "drug cult," with its own exclusive vocabulary? Are you a sky diver? Do you fish? Are you a student of ballet? A break-dancer? Every subgroup has its own language, its own jargon. Even *education* has its unique vocabulary, recognized by its membership but foreign-sounding to those not in the field. My own children spoke fluent pidgin on the playgrounds of Honolulu before I even realized that they had acquired that second language.

A black friend of mine speaks excellent standard English to his university classes. When he relaxes with some of his close friends and family, he communicates perfectly in black English. When he visits his hometown in the South, he converses fluently in the dialect and rhythms of that region.

Aren't we all multilingual?

How many languages do YOU speak?

What Your Language Says about You

If an American counterpart of George Bernard Shaw's Henry Higgins heard you speak, he could immediately tell you which broad speech community you fit into. He would not stop at such a general description of your speech patterns, but might trace them to the city, town, or village in which you grew up. It is very likely that he could specifically describe your speech by your dialect plus the colloquialisms, vulgarisms, jargon, and slang that contribute to your unique speech, your idiolect.

Despite the fact that I have lived in a variety of places (Albany, New York; Boston, Massachusetts; Honolulu, Hawaii; Columbus, Ohio), Henry Higgins would have no trouble identifying my hometown as that section of New York City known as the Bronx. The sounds of the Bronx are grooved into my tongue and no amount of geographic mobility has erased them. My gestures are a mix of Eastern European–American Jewish (from my family) and Italian (from the neighbors of my childhood). If you tie my hands, you tie my tongue! Add a generous variety of facial expressions gathered from years of mimicking friends, movie stars, singers, politicians, teachers, and students; add remnants of movement adopted from hundreds of dance classes and folk dance festivals—and you'll begin to have a good picture of my nonverbal language.

When we first moved from Albany to Columbus we learned that soda was "pop," that a grocery bag was a "sack," and that people stood not *on* line but *in* line. We, native New Yorkers, spoke in rapid-fire rhythms, while most of our new neighbors (probably influenced by more relaxed, Southern speech habits) spoke comparatively slowly. In one classroom, a curious fourth grader asked me, "What country are you from?" He had never heard a New York City accent before.*

And listening to many people in Columbus, Ohio, was like listening to people speaking a different language. Mike Harden, a gifted columnist for the *Columbus Dispatch*, has an ear for language and a sense of humor. In two delightful columns, he presents "A Newcomer's Guide to Columbusese and the Central Ohio Twang, or Ahm OK, Yer OK."[10] These are some of the words heard in Columbus and their translations:

---

*For a hilarious study of the speech habits of New York natives, see Deborah Tannen's "Talking New York: It's Not What You Say, It's the Way That You Say It," *New York* Mar. 1981: 30–33.

Melk: The juice of uncontented cows.

Hunnert: The number that follows 99.

Uhfeeshul: Official.

Gwover: A contraction of the words "go over."

Uhtall: At all. "I loaned him a hunnert dollars; now I haven't seen or heard from him uhtall."

Aigs: Small oval spheroids laid by domestic poultry.

Well, you get the idea . . .

And what about my children, born in Albany and reared in Columbus, grandchildren of Polish, Russian, and Rumanian immigrants? Cara, a natural mimic, is in the retail business in Chicago and SOUNDS as if she was born in that windy city. Dan, running a skydiving business in Xenia, Ohio, SOUNDS as authentically Appalachian as if he had rolled off the mountains. Cliff, a lawyer in New York City, has the urban, intellectual SOUNDS of the "Big Apple" in the music of his speech.

Many different elements contribute to the uniqueness of your own language. What geographic and cultural characteristics do you express in your speech and gestures? What messages do you convey with your nonverbal language? What is your language story?

Often you are judged by your language. Doors are opened or closed to you

on the basis of how you communicate. Your success or failure at work, in school, and in your interpersonal relationships is based largely on the way you use language.

Literature is rich with examples of the importance of language. E. B. White's spider, Charlotte, saves Wilbur's life by spinning wonderful words in her web; George Bernard Shaw's Liza Doolittle rises from the slums of London to the closed circles of the aristocracy because she learns to speak well; and Edmond Rostand's Roxanne falls in love with the beautiful words of Cyrano de Bergerac.

You can use your language to communicate your feelings and ideas to others. Conversely, you can use it to obscure your meaning and to keep people from you. The way you use language reflects your view of yourself and the world.

For the same reasons, you are drawn to or repelled by people because of their language. Verbal and nonverbal messages from others can profoundly affect your sense of well-being and self-confidence. The wrong word, a grimace, a shrug, or a turned-down mouth can convey a universe of meaning that can please you or distress you. Language is an index of

> culture, breeding, upbringing, personality, sometimes even of intelligence, decency, and integrity. Language is something more than a system of communicating; it is also a social convention which one must observe under penalty of being misjudged. Ignorance or improper use of language can easily interfere with your success or advancement.[11]

How closely our language reflects our personalities and behavior was imaginatively demonstrated to me by my six-year-old cousin, Debbie, who was complaining about her oldest brother, Douglas, and praising her next-to-oldest brother, Jeffrey. This is what she said:

"Douglas is bossy. He's mean. Do you know, Douglas has . . ." She stopped, thought a moment, then continued, "He has *Douglas Words!*"

"Douglas Words?" I asked. "What are Douglas Words?"

"Douglas Words are, hmmmm, well, they're bossy words. Mean words. Yukky words."

"What about Jeffrey?" I prodded.

Debbie's face brightened. "Oh, Jeffrey has *Jeffrey Words*. Jeffrey Words are, let's see, ummmm, Jeffrey Words are . . . *funny* words! Playful words!"

"And what about Debbie?" I asked.

Debbie's eyes twinkled, and without pausing for a second, she reported, "Debbie Words are all the NICE words!"

(I promise that, by the time you read this, Douglas Words will be off Debbie's "bossy" list!)

Language is a strong reflector of different social attitudes and behaviors. Racial and religious prejudice, sexism, bigotry toward people in different cultures or economic groups, have language components that cause as much tension, resentment, and hatred as actions. Derogatory terms based on race, sex, religion, or cultural background, stereotyped labeling, derisive name-calling are as destructive and cruel as weapons and, often, are even more effective. Tragically, when adults in responsible positions, such as parents, teachers, or members of the clergy or government, are guilty of such abusive language they convey confusion, betrayal, and anxiety to children who are watching them as models. *In other words, teacher, be aware of your language.*

Language Affects Your View of the World

The linguists Edward Sapir and Benjamin Lee Whorf theorize that your language is intimately linked with your culture. Not only does language reveal the way people in your culture view the universe, but it shapes your perceptions, feelings, thoughts, and actions. Psycholinguistics, the study of the relationship between language and perception and behavior, is involved in finding out how deeply language affects our thought processes, our experiences, our ideas. If we don't have a word for something, do we still perceive it or think about it? If we don't have a word for the color orange, do we *see* orange?

Clyde Kluckhohn points out that every language has a special way of looking at the world and interpreting experience. One sees and hears what the grammatical system of one's language has made one sensitive to, has trained one to look for in experience. This bias is insidious because we are unconscious of our native language as a system.[12]

We English speakers were born into a language that categorizes outside reality into nouns and verbs. We see the world as separated into things and categories of substance. We even categorize time into a mass to be divided into sections such as hours, days, years. Not all people perceive reality this way.

The Hopi Indians have a very different view of the universe, and their language reflects and influences their perceptions. They have a subjective set of verbs that includes not only an indefinite indication of the future, but also psychological factors "existing in the heart," such as hope and fear. This set of verbs also implies the heart of all living things, all of which are part of the Great Spirit.[13]

How does language reveal and define *your* world?

If you are a Hopi, if you are a Navaho, water is very important, and you have learned the many Hopi words for various kinds and quantities of water. If you are an Eskimo, seals and snow play large parts in your life, and you have many separate words in your vocabulary to describe the various types of each. If you are a Navaho Indian, you learn chants and prayers by which you endeavor to influence the universe and to strengthen the failing power of supernatural beings. Your chants could cause crops to grow and rain to fall. Your words are powerful and magical and link you with the great, mysterious forces in the universe.[14]

Language affects every aspect of your life. You, like S. I. Hayakawa's Mr. Mits, are profoundly involved in the words you absorb daily and the words you use daily.

Words in the newspaper make him pound his fist on the breakfast table. Words his superiors speak to him puff him out with pride, or send him scurrying to work harder. Words about himself, which he has overheard being spoken behind his back, worry him sick. Words which he spoke before a clergyman some years ago have tied him to one woman for life. Words written down on pieces of paper keep him at his job or bring bills in his mail every month which keep him paying and paying. Words written down by other people . . . keep them paying him month after month. With words woven into almost every detail of his life, it seems amazing that Mr. Mits' thinking on the subject of language should be so limited.[15]

Language: Some Unanswered Questions

Have you ever wondered how language started? What its origins are? Linguists have accomplished remarkable breakthroughs in understanding the process of language, its various components, how it changes from place to place, but they have not yet discovered how language started. Many fascinating theories have been suggested, among them

1. The *bow-wow* theory: Language first came about as an imitation of sounds heard in nature, such as the barking of a dog or the falling of a tree.
2. The *pooh-pooh* theory: Language is an extension of exclamations indicating surprise, pain, pleasure, or other sudden emotion.
3. The *yo-heave-ho* theory: Language developed from grunts and wheezes accompanying physical exertion.
4. The *singsong* theory: Language evolved from inarticulate, primitive chants, much like a small child's original song of sounds.
5. The *gift* theory: The numerous religious beliefs that language is a gift to man from a god.[16]

Although linguists have been puzzled by this mystery, they have discovered a great deal of information about the history and process of language. Our ancestors have used speech as a means of communication for from five hundred thousand to a million years. They spoke for many more years before they experimented with making "permanent marks and scratches which stood for language on clay tablets, bits of wood or stone, skins of animals and paper—in other words, used written language.[17]

And before the spoken and the written word was nonverbal language—the language of gesture, the language of sign.

The desire for communication and self-expression is so basic to human life that language develops even when there is no sight, no sound. Sign language is an intricate, rich language. Observe deaf or mute people "talking" together and you will catch the immediate meanings, moods, ideas, and plans ping-ponging back and forth. Braille opens the opportunities for written language to those who cannot see.

What Does Language Mean?

On every page of this book, you will be encouraged to develop qualities of openness and flexibility toward yourself, your students, and the curriculum. In this focus on language, let us think about it in its broadest meaning. We have referred to oral and written speech and to nonverbal communication. Do you think that is all there is to language? Consider Mario Pei's definition of the purpose of language: "the transfer of meaning from one human mind to another."[18]

Language involves understanding and agreement. People must agree on meanings and symbols. There must be a community of understanding so that "for the time being you and I think in the same terms. If this fails to happen, we may as well 'save our breath.' "[19]

Consider viewing language as a human phenomenon that touches every activity of life, is linked with all areas of existence, serves as a vehicle for thought, and is an indispensable tool in the development of human civilization—linking people together, enabling one generation to learn from another and to look into the future and the past.[20]

S. I. Hayakawa credits language with making progress possible and with developing independence in human beings. A person

> is never dependent on his own experience alone for his own information.
>
> Even in a primitive culture, he can make use of the experience of his neighbors, friends, and relatives, which they communicate to him by means of language. Therefore, instead of remaining helpless because of the limitations of his own experience and knowledge, instead of having to discover what others have already discovered, instead of exploring the false trails they explored and repeating their errors, he can *go on from where they left off.*[21]

Can you imagine how your life would be without language? All the meanings that exist in your mind, all the explanations for your existence, all the infinite questions puzzling you, are directly linked to language. Piaget considers language a system of signs, a socialization of meaning, and believes that, without language, true concepts are not even possible.[22]

How Did You Learn Your Language?

Many brilliant linguists, educators, and social scientists have spent their lifetimes probing the mysteries of language acquisition. Their studies are fascinating. There is not always agreement among their findings. There are still unanswered questions, choices of theories. I urge you to read some of their works to broaden your own appreciation of this uniquely human phenomenon.[23] As you read, you will discover that this field is as complex and controversial as any scientific arena. You will discover stimulating explanations for language development.

Nativistic philosophers, such as Ervin, Miller, and Lenneberg, view language as rooted in the biological makeup of human beings and closely linked with the maturation process.

Behaviorists, such as Skinner, Pavlov, and Watson, see language emerging as a result of environmental conditioning. They believe that language learning occurs when imitative behavior is reinforced.

Psycholinguistic scholars, such as Chomsky, McNeill, and Slobin, see the child possessing at birth innate, inherited language abilities which develop as the child interacts with his or her environment and constructs a system, an understanding of the way the language works.

Cognitivists, such as Piaget, Inhelder, and Sinclair-de-Zwart, take a more interdisciplinary approach, giving weight to various elements in human development: biological, sociological, psychological, and so on. Just as bodies and minds mature, so language goes through a maturation process.

Whether language begins with muscles in the tongue, sounds in the ear, or pictures in the mind is still a mystery. Enjoy the exploration!

Ours will be a simpler language story.

Take a few minutes break from your reading and experiment with sounds. Discover how many different sounds you can make that you have never made before. You were born with body parts shaped as much for sound production as for nourishment.[24]

Any sound made by the human vocal apparatus and given a meaning that is agreed on by a group of people could conceivably become part of a language. All languages are made up of specific sounds, called *phonemes*. Combined with other sounds in various arrangements, they become meaningful units of language—words or parts of words called *morphemes*.

As a baby, you had the ability to learn any possible group of sounds you heard. No matter what the language, the process of learning it is basically the same. In separate and distinct studies of children, linguists and psychologists have discovered many common occurrences in the development of the individual. You would not be reading this book right now or engaging in most of the other activities that fill your days if you yourself had not gone through this developmental process that took you from birth as an inarticulate newborn to the knowledgeable, articulate individual you are today.

A baby is born. It could be you. Even though you are tiny, you are not helpless or passive. From birth, you are moving, listening, crying, reaching out to the world around you, trying to make order out of the confusion of sensory impressions bombarding you. At first, you do not even realize that you are separate from your surrounding environment—blanket, crib, bottle, parents are all extensions of yourself.

After the first few months of your life, your random, uncoordinated body movements evolve into more deliberate patterns as you discover interesting objects such as your own toes, fingers, and arms, as you interact with your environment.

Now you are imitating sounds and gestures. Your babbling begins to sound like conversation in rhythm, stress, and intonation. Somewhere toward the end of your first year, you probably say your first word. Let's say the word is "dog." You say it repeatedly, delighted with your achievement. If you have experiences with various types of dogs, you will soon differentiate between them and perhaps say "big dog" or "puppy dog" rather than just "dog."

You recognize most of the people and objects in your world, but you are easily confused if something about them is changed or if they appear or reappear quickly. If your sister wears glasses for the first time, you may not recognize her. Even though you do not say many words, you understand most things that people say to you and you respond to simple commands and instructions. Each day you are adding words to your growing vocabulary. You love the words and say them over and over to yourself, enjoying the sound of them and the positive response from your family as they recognize your new words. Genesis relates how "man gave names to all cattle, to the birds of heaven and to every wild animal." You, too, give names to all the things and beings surrounding you. Gradually, as you distinguish one thing from another by recognizing identifying characteristics, you find that you begin to see relationships between them and you begin to manipulate them. You learn many words and put them together in short sentences. Your movements are no longer trial-and-error accidents but deliberate experiments. Although you have accidents and setbacks time after time, you become more successful in learning to control your body and your environment. You are interested in everything and, to you, everything has a reason, a purpose, and a cause. Your own perspective is absolute. The world is your oyster. It was created for you. If you reach out your hand, you can hide the sun. If you close your eyes, you'll make the rain go away. If you fall down, you spank the floor for hurting you, and the glass is naughty because it spilled milk on you. Words and sentences tumble out of your mouth as you talk to yourself or other children. You drive adults to distraction asking questions endlessly. At this stage, you don't want a long involved answer. A simple response will do.

You think about the relationships among objects, time, and space, and language provides the main foundation for your developing thought processes. Your learning is cumulative. Each new level is a base from which to move on to another level. Fantasy and imagination enable you to play different roles and experience different situations. You practice life through your play and grow into a more social person, exchanging ideas, taking turns with other children, answering and asking questions, and verbalizing commands, requests, threats, and criticism. By the time you are three years old, it is possible that you can produce all the major varieties of simple English in ten- or eleven-word sentences. By the age of four or five, according to Piaget, you have performed miracles of real learning. By the time you start school, you already know over seven thousand five hundred morphemes, as well as the basic structure of the language you learned at home.

Early Influences

In this dynamic process, two influences have an extremely important effect on your early language development: *The language you heard spoken in your immediate environment and the way your family responded to you as you experimented with words are of equal importance to you in learning your language.* Most of the basic structure of your language came from imitating the sounds and rhythms around you. You mimicked these sounds until you were able to initiate them yourself. Imagine how your language development would have been affected if the people around you spoke infrequently or if, when you tried to speak, you were ignored or scolded. If you were praised for being silent and called troublesome when you asked questions, it is likely that you were left behind in the language process. The belief that children should be seen and not heard is absurd in the light of what we know today about language learning.

The more language experiences a child has, the greater the opportunities for developing a rich vocabulary. These experiences go into a child's knapsack and turn into words and meanings. All babies should shout "don't forget about me" to remind their families to stimulate them, to introduce them to new things and activities, to respond to their language efforts with enthusiasm and encouragement, to invite their participation in the process of celebrating language.

Yet with all that we know about the process of language acquisitions, mysteries remain. Who can fully explain why one two-year-old child talks in complete sentences while another, a three-year-old, hardly speaks? Who can analyze completely why, of twin brothers, one has a book in his hands from the time he is an infant and the other refuses to even listen to a story? What reasons do social scientists give that explain why Piaget, at ten years old, published his first scholarly paper on his observations of a partly albino sparrow, while a normally intelligent ten-year-old struggles with a simple paragraph?

There is awe in the realization that

> a child can extract from the finite sample of speech he happens to hear a latent
> structure that will enable him to construct indefinitely numerous new sen-

tences, sentences he has never heard and which even may never have been spoken by anyone.[25]

Building a Language Framework

We have been discussing the *subject* of language with your experiences, your knowledge, and your attitudes about language as our primary focus. It is vital that you find your own philosophy of language and the language arts curriculum so that the framework you build will be strong enough to withstand the huffs and puffs of any attempts to blow it down. Before we go on to the specific components of the language arts curriculum and share practical methods of teaching them effectively, you should be certain of your own feelings about language, understand your students and their languages, and believe in the need to adopt a universal approach to the language arts curriculum.

Examine Your Attitudes

Only when you begin to confront your own likes, dislikes, fears, weaknesses, and strengths can you begin to recognize, accept, value, and encourage your students' exploration and expressions of their own uniqueness through language.

1. Are you aware of how your own and other people's words affect you? Are you sensitive to the verbal and nonverbal messages you receive and transmit? To what degree are your prejudices influenced or revealed by your language? Are you aware of how language has been used as a means of subjugating and humiliating minorities?

2. How do you feel about your own language? Are you aware of your own dialect, pronunciation, syntax? How many languages do you have? (See page 84.)

3. Do you think certain kinds of speech are superior to other kinds of speech? In what way? How often do you judge people by their speech?

4. How do you feel about written language and the theory of some linguists that writing is becoming obsolete because technology provides other means of conveying ideas? These linguists believe that we no longer need to emphasize writing because the tape recorder, computer, radio, television, and motion pictures now preserve speech for future generations. Should writing, then, be relegated to a minor position in the language arts curriculum or do you feel that the written word is still a necessary and valuable tool for children? Why?

5. Do you think of language as a sacred body of inflexible rules or as a dynamic process that reflects a constantly changing society? How do you think your attitude will affect your teaching of the language arts?

6. Can you recall language arts experiences from your own schooling that stand out in your memory as significant? In what areas did they occur: speaking, listening, reading, writing, grammar, or a combination of all of these?

7. What aspects of your own language arts education did you most enjoy and what aspects did you least enjoy?

8. Which aspects of the language arts curriculum are you most enthusiastic about teaching and about which you are least enthusiastic?

9. What are your goals in teaching language arts to children?

10. Do you believe that the more competently children learn to use language in our society, the greater will be the opportunities afforded them and the greater their chances for success in life?

11. Do you believe that effective teaching of the language arts can go beyond the practical goals to a broader realm, one in which your students will be enriched because they are enabled to "learn to profit by and take part in the greatest of human achievements—that which makes all other achievements possible—namely, the pooling of our experiences in great cooperative stores of knowledge. . . ."?[26]

Understanding Your Students' Languages

By kindergarten, almost every child, through trial and error, has learned the basic structure and sounds of a personal language. It may not be the standard language, but it is one in which the child is relatively competent. *Since language is intimately bound up with one's concept of self, accepting a child means accepting his or her language even if it is different from your own. I cannot emphasize enough the importance of treating children with respect and dignity, and this includes accepting their languages.*

Controversy rages in our country over language. Is black English a legitimate language? Should Spanish-speaking children be provided with bilingual education? Opinions are strong and clashing. But when you reject a person's language, aren't you really rejecting the person as well? James Baldwin reminds us that children cannot be taught by teachers who demand that they repudiate their experience and all that gives them substance.[27]

Thus, acceptance is the basic ingredient necessary to building an authentic and successful relationship with your students. If you believe that competency in the language arts will provide your students with more choices and opportunities in life, then you must begin at their level and work toward a more standard English. Think of this endeavor as introducing them to another language rather than replacing their own.

Listen to your students. Keep your ears open to their language as they play on the playground, walk through the halls, have "free time" to visit informally in the classroom. The child who cannot finish the ditto page from the reading workbook on rhyme and meter may have mastered numerous intricate jump-rope songs and chants. Children's sub-rosa skills demonstrate a wide variety of language competencies that go unrecognized by teachers and so are never used to enrich the curriculum.[28]

In a moving interview, Paulo Freire, a widely acclaimed Brazilian educator, shared his feelings about the life of teachers and children in the classroom. Here are a few excerpts from that interview:

> Humility is an important virtue for a teacher . . . humility implies understanding the pain of others, the feelings of others. . . . We teachers must learn to make a life together with our students who may be different from us. . . . Kids should come full of spontaneity—with their feelings, with their questions, with their creativity, with their risk to create, getting their own words "into their own hands" in order to do beautiful things with them. . . . Teachers must be able to play with children, to dream with them. They must wet their bodies in the waters of childrens' culture first. . . . The spoken word is our reading of the world. . . .[29]

A Universal Approach to the Language Arts Curriculum

Listening, speaking, reading, and writing, the major components of the language arts curriculum, cannot be relegated to a specific time on a certain day, but are in evidence all day, in all subject areas, and all classroom experiences. Every minute of your school day is saturated with language arts—from giving assignments to scolding, from planning field trips to playing a game, from explaining the words in the new science unit to writing the rules for fire drills.

Sometimes you may schedule specific learning experiences and activities related to the language arts, and even call it "language arts time," but under no circumstances must you believe that your teaching of language arts is limited to that particular time. Children learn language through all the language experiences they have, such as discussions, conversations, lectures, scoldings, stories read, reports given, field trips, parties, songs, and games. *They learn by participating in the language process itself*. Piaget reminds us that "children do not learn by sitting passively in their seats, listening to the teacher, any more than they learn to swim by sitting in rows on a wharf and watching grown-up swimmers in the water."[30]

The language arts are vitally linked to other subject areas. If you cannot communicate in some way (through speech, sign language, writing), you cannot share your experiences, ask questions, or exchange ideas. If you cannot read, you cannot read a book, a newspaper, a magazine, or the warning label on a medicine bottle. If you cannot write, you cannot write down your findings for a science experiment or send a friend happy news in a letter. If you cannot comprehend (listen and understand), you cannot follow a simple arithmetic problem or develop thoughtful responses to situations in your environment that demand sound solutions.

It is only for the purpose of clarity and practicality that the various components of the curriculum are handled in separate chapters in this text. In reality, *all parts of the curriculum overlap and intertwine. They are bound together in one process*. For example, when you speak, I listen and when I speak, you listen. These are interactions between the distinct language arts skills of communication. We teachers spend most of our time with the material of the language arts: words spoken, words heard, words read, words written, words thought about, words dreamed, words feared. Words define us and our lives. Our feelings about words, our fluency and competency with words, can determine the quality of our lives. Your classroom should be filled with words: written, spoken, listened to, read. Your students should be fascinated by words, appreciating with you their power and magic. If you infuse your teaching of this curriculum with a feeling of awe and excitement, your students will reflect your enthusiasm.

In a curriculum she prepared, Frayda Turkel included a section she called "A Word to Teachers":

> The constraints of a written curriculum are such that it conveys the more or less cognitive or intellectual side of what we teach, yet it is the concepts underlying all of these themes that are of utmost importance. A teacher should always ask oneself: Why is this important? What does it really mean?
>
> We would like to urge you to use as much imagination as possible. Please try to use experiential methods. . . . Let the students get into the fray as much as possible. . . . Let there be ferment, excitement and grappling with issues in your classroom. . . .
>
> The curriculum has been designed to give as much latitude as possible to teachers, so each can use his or her strengths. Do you have wonderful photographs pertinent to your subject matter? Are you musical? Can you use dance or movement to teach? What about drama? What personal experiences can you share?
>
> The students will benefit most from your enthusiasm and the excitement you generate in the classroom.

As we turn to the language arts curriculum, think of it as the dry bones in the valley. Only when Ezekiel breathed a special spirit into the bones did they

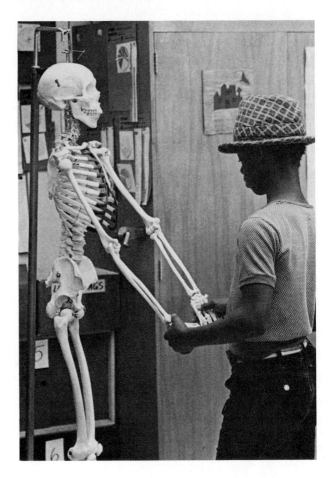

live. So, the curriculum is nothing but dry bones waiting to be infused with YOUR spirit and the spirits of your students. Only then will the curriculum come alive.

The Goals of Education

Our kids do not need a miscellany of meaningless, unrelated, soon-to-be-forgotten facts pushed into their minds. Torrance frames some questions that I recommend you write over every lesson plan in order to keep in touch with the real goals of education.[31]

1. What kind of children are they becoming?
2. What kind of thinking are they doing?
3. How resourceful are they?
4. How responsible are they?

5. Are they learning to give thoughtful explanations for the things they do and observe?

6. Do they believe their own ideas are valuable?

7. Are they able to share ideas and opinions with others?

8. Do they see relationships between similar experiences and draw conclusions?

9. Do they think for themselves?

Plato believed that the only real beginning of learning is *wonder*. David McCord ends his poem "Take Sky" with the same idea:

> Put not asunder
> Man's *first* word: wonder . . . wonder . . .[32]

With those inspiring reminders, I close this part of the book with one word:

BEGIN

For Your Knapsack

Teachers' associations and organizations such as the following publish excellent journals and materials on language in the classroom. They are worthy of your investigation and membership.

National Council of Teachers of English
    1111 Kenyon Road,
    Urbana, Illinois 61801

International Reading Association
    800 Barksdale Road
    P.O. Box 8139
    Newark, Delaware 19714

National Association for the Education of Young Children
    1834 Connecticut Ave. N.W.
    Washington, D.C.
    20009–5786

ERIC Clearinghouse on Languages and Linguistics
    Center for Applied Linguistics
    3520 Prospect Street N.W.
    Washington, D.C. 20007

Integrated Education Association
    School of Education
    Northwestern University
    2003 Sheridan Road
    Evanston, Illinois 60201

Association of Childhood Education International
    11141 Georgia Ave., Suite 200
    Wheaton, Maryland 20902

Some excellent materials for teaching English as a Second Language and/or teaching in the multicultural classroom are
    Language Arts 63.1 (Jan. 1986) (the whole issue)
    Ruth A. Hough, Joanne R. Nurss, and D. Scott Enright, "Story-reading

with Limited English-speaking Children in the Regular Classroom," *The Reading Teacher* 39.6 (Feb. 1986): 510–16.

J. A. Fishman, "Language and Ethnicity in Bilingual Education," *Culture, Ethnicity, and Identity: Current Issues in Research*, ed. W. C. McCready (New York: Academic, 1983).

D. W. Hicks, *Minorities: A Teacher's Resource Book for the Multiethnic Classroom* (London: Heinemann, 1981).

A. Tosi, *Immigration and Bilingual Education* (Oxford: Pergamon, 1984).

Marge Scherer, "The Caring Fields," *The Instructor* Sept. 1985: 43–50.

Phi Delta Kappan Apr. 1983. (the whole issue)

Olivia N. Saracho and Bernard Spodek, eds., *Understanding the Multicultural Experience in Early Childhood Education* (Washington, D.C.: National Association for Education of Young Children, 1983).

M. J. Gold, C. A. Grant, and H. N. Rivlin, eds., *In Praise of Diversity: A Resource Book for Multicultural Education* (Washington, D.C.: Teacher Corps/Association of Teacher Educators, 1977).

J. Huang and E. Hatch, "A Chinese Child's Acquisition of English," *Second Language Acquisition* (Rowley: Newbury, 1979).

G. Zamora, "When Spanish Is the Native Language," *Proceedings of the First Inter-American Conference on Bilingual Education*, ed. R. Troike and N. Modiano (Arlington: Center for Applied Linguistics, 1975).

J. C. Stone, ed., *Five Heritages: Teaching Multi-Cultural Populations* (New York: Van Nostrand, 1971).

B. E. Cullinan, A. M. Jaggar, and D. Strickland, "Language Expansion for Black Children in the Primary Grades: A Research Report," *Young Children* 29 (Jan. 1974): 98–112.

E. B. Freeman, "The Ann Arbor Decision: The Importance of Teachers' Attitudes Toward Language," *Elementary School Journal* 83 (Sept. 1982): 41–47.

Joseph Leibowicz, "Classrooms, Teachers and Nonstandard Speakers," *Language Arts* 61.1 (Jan. 1984): 88–91.

John U. Ogbu, "Cultural–Ecological Influences on Minority School Learning," *Language Arts* 62.8 (Dec. 1985): 860–69.

Language Arts Sept. 1986. (the whole issue)

ENDNOTES

[1] Helen Keller, *The Story of My Life* (New York: Grosset, 1905) 23.

[2] Morton Bloomfield, "The Study of Language," *Daedalus: Journal of the American Academy of Arts and Sciences* Summer 1973: 5.

[3] Dwight Bolinger, *Aspects of Language*, 2nd ed. (New York: Harcourt, 1975) 421.

[4] Clark Moustakas, *The Authentic Teacher* (Cambridge: Doyle, 1966) 3–13.

[5] Moustakas, *The Authentic Teacher* 7–9.

[6] Peter Farb, "Man at the Mercy of His Language," *A Return to Vision*, ed. Richard L. Cherry, 2nd ed. (Boston: Houghton, 1974) 86.

[7] An enjoyable resource on the richness of our language is *Success with Words: A Guide to the American Language* (Pleasantville: Reader's Digest, 1983).

[8]Mario Pei, *Voices of Man* (New York: Harper, 1962) 24–25.

[9]Mario Pei, *Invitation to Linguistics* (Garden City: Doubleday, 1965) 33.

[10]Mike Harden, "An Uhfeeshul Lingo Bingo," *Columbus Dispatch* 18 Nov. 1983; "Tips Hit Heart of Local English," *Columbus Dispatch* 28 Nov. 1983.

[11]Mario Pei, *Language for Everybody* (New York: Devin-Adair, 1956) 4–5.

[12]Clyde Kluckhohn, *Mirror for Man* (New York: McGraw, 1949) 159.

[13]Dwight Bolinger, *Aspects of Language*, 2nd ed. (New York: Harcourt, 1975) 240–43; Fred West, *The Way of Language* (New York: Harcourt, 1975) 155–60.

[14]Margot Astrov, "The Magic Creativeness of the Word," *A Return to Vision* 70–71.

[15]S. I. Hayakawa, "Language and Survival," *A Return to Vision* 66.

[16]Pei, *Invitation to Linguistics* 4.

[17]S. I. Hayakawa, *Language in Thought and Action*, 3rd ed. (New York: Harcourt, 1972) 11.

[18]Pei, *Voices of Man* 109.

[19]Pei, *Voices of Man* 109–13.

[20]Pei, *Invitation to Linguistics* 8–9.

[21]Hayakawa, "Language and Survival," *A Return to Vision* 62. Italics are from the original.

[22]Mary Ann Spencer Pulaski, *Understanding Piaget* (Garden City: Doubleday, 1971) 122.

[23]There are excellent books available in the fields of linguistics and language. Here are a few that I have enjoyed and learned much from.

Jean Piaget, *The Language and Thought of the Child* (New York: Meridian, 1955).

D. McNeil, *The Acquisition of Language: The Study of Development Psycholinguistics* (New York: Harper, 1970).

Roger Brown, *A First Language: The Early Stages* (Cambridge: Harvard UP, 1973).

Noam Chomsky, *Language and Mind* (New York: Harcourt, 1972).

Susanna Pflaum-Connor, *The Development of Language and Reading in Young Children*, 2nd ed. (Columbus: Charles E. Merrill, 1978).

Fred West, *The Way of Language* (New York: Harcourt, 1975).

L. S. Vygotsky, *Thought and Language*, ed. and trans. E. Haufman and G. Vakar (Cambridge: MIT P, 1962).

Dwight Bolinger, *Aspects of Language*, 2nd ed. (New York: Harcourt, 1975).

[24]Dwight Bolinger, *Aspects of Language* (New York: Harcourt, 1975) 3.

[25]A speech given by Noam Chomsky at the Massachusetts Institute of Technology inspired this comment by Roger Brown.

[26]Hayakawa, "Language and Survival," *A Return to Vision* 63.

[27]James Baldwin, "If Black English Isn't a Language, Then Tell Me What Is," *The Essay*, ed. M. Shugrue (New York: Macmillan, 1981) 51–54.

[28]Perry Gilmore, "Assessing Sub-rosa Skills in Children's Language," *Language Arts* 61.4 (Apr. 1984): 384–91.

[29]"Reading the World and Reading the Word: An Interview with Paulo Freire," *Language Arts* 62.1 (Jan. 1985): 15–21.

[30]Pulaski, *Understanding Piaget* 192–93.

[31]E. Paul Torrance, "Conditions for Creative Growth," *Education and the Creative Potential* (Minneapolis: U of Minnesota P, 1963) 17.

[32]David McCord, "Take Sky," *Take Sky* (New York: Dell, 1971) 5.

Behold,

I do not give lectures

or a little charity.

When I give,

I give myself.

WALT WHITMAN[1]

Notes for the Journey

Unless you teach in a school where textbooks are considered obsolete, you will probably be expected to use a set of basic texts for all the curriculum areas. Experienced teachers appreciate the attractiveness, realism, and relevancy of contemporary texts, but no matter how outstanding the texts, they cannot be relied on to provide *all* teaching ideas and materials. Texts are standardized in order to serve millions of children in schools across the country. Certainly your students will have much in common with other children, but they will also have needs that cannot always be fulfilled by any one book or group of books. If the poems in a textbook don't really touch your students, *you* will have to find poems that are meaningful to them. Paragraph exercises using topics that are irrelevant to your class will not hold their attention. *You* will have to draw on an array of sources if education in your classroom is to be an ongoing process. The education field abounds with excellent, practical materials that can be helpful to you. The number of journals and magazines is truly impressive and will provide a constant flow of ideas and new materials for your knapsack. Records, learning kits, cassettes, computers, and films will also prove effective in the classroom. Yet, despite the availability of these commercial devices, your own original or adopted ideas are the best basis for learning.

Be a Scrounger   Creative teachers are always on the lookout for "found" materials. Scrounge and gather newspapers, magazines, greeting cards, posters, catalogues, gift-wrap remnants, pipe cleaners, wallpaper samples, all the different "throw-away" containers that fast foods come in, buttons, ribbons, hats, shoes. Keep a scrounge box handy at all times, filled with materials for a thousand uses—from original collages to puppets, from "junk" self-portraits to shoebox scenes.

Yours—A Language-Rich Environment   Whatever your space, it is lively, dynamic, filled with the works of your students, filled with the sounds of work and play, planning and dreaming, learning and teaching. It is a place where you and your students find success and excitement in the process of education. Stimulating words, pictures, poems, riddles, questions, posters, charts are always on the walls. The children whisper, talk, discuss, question, exchange ideas, take turns, listen attentively, laugh easily, and appreciate stillness. The environment is rich with language experiences.

Only in such a life-affirming environment will ideas take root and blossom.

Ideas! Ideas! Ideas!

Part Two takes you on a journey through the language arts curriculum and encourages you to take the scenic route, to teach in creative and imaginative ways.

The ideas suggested in the following chapters are for you to consider. Remember, an idea is only a *good* idea if YOU like it! Unless an idea evokes enthusiasm and interest, it will not be effective. YOUR response to ideas—YOUR interpretations of them, what YOU bring to them, how YOU shape them to meet YOUR own particular situation—greatly determines their success or failure. If you are a flexible, open person, you will find ideas everywhere. If you welcome new experiences, new approaches to people and subjects, new insights into everyday life, then you cannot help but gather a treasure chest of wonderful ideas. Innovative teachers often find themselves changing, rearranging, recreating an offered idea until they have shaped something new and unique. Closed, rigid teachers, who reject everything that does not fit neatly into preordained compartments or formulas, never experience the interplay of ideas, so important a part of the creative process.

The ideas in this book are for you to play with! All of the suggestions have been tried and loved and shared in classrooms across the country. Add them to your knapsack. Let them be part of a fertile soil from which many seeds will grow.

As you read through the chapters, keep in mind some simple questions:

Do I like this idea?

Do I think it will work for me?

If not, how can I improve it, change it, rearrange it?

Your thoughtful answers to these questions will guide your choice of the activities best suited to your students.

Open-ended Ideas

Every activity included in the following chapters is open-ended. Each one could go on forever and never be boring or repetitious. Just because you have decided to stop at a certain point in an activity doesn't mean that the idea is finished. You do children a disservice if you lead them to think that they have completed an area of learning. I have heard nine-year-olds say "We finished the solar system," or "We already did poetry." What a shrinking of minds! Do not perpetuate that way of "learning" in your classroom. Always give your students the feeling that they are sipping from the overflowing cup of knowledge, never that they are draining it. Join the "anti-smug" campaign!

Always think MORE, never LESS. Ask yourself, "*What else* can we do?" The only limits on successful ideas are time and the reality of schedule structures.

Look to Your Students

In your constant search for ideas, don't forget your students. They will offer you unique ways to accomplish learning, often more effectively than any textbook. Some of the most memorable learning experiences I have ever had were suggested by the children. Norma Canner, a movement specialist, shared the wonder of such peak times. She said, "I came to teach and I stayed to learn."

Learn with Your Students

Be WITH your students in exploring as many creative experiences as possible. They need your presence as they write, draw, move, plan, improvise. Participate with them as often as possible; *you* too need to be nourished by exercises of imagination. A word of caution here: you are such a Very Important Person in the lives of your students that they are ready to copy whatever you do. Don't permit your works to be their *model*. Be the *last* person to share in the sharing, celebrating part of an activity.

The Most Important Questions

Throughout your teaching career there will be vital questions that need to be asked concerning the needs of your students and the most successful way for you to meet those needs. Cut through the often complicated jargon of the curriculum to find essential directions. Consider these questions:

What do I want my students to learn?

What teaching methods should I use to impart this knowledge to my students?

How will I know that my methods worked?

Remember, if you view the language arts curriculum as a life-centered, life-affirming study, your positive attitude will enable you to teach your students successfully.

One Last Note

The dividing of the components of the language arts curriculum into separate chapters is purely artificial. There is no resemblance to reality in this structure. In *real life*, these components are interconnected, interrelated, overlapped, and synthesized. As you read, you will naturally integrate the language arts areas into a healthy, whole language process. Pass that important news along to your students and help them make connections, see relationships.

4

Listening: A Forgotten Language Art?

"Pooh," said Piglet reproachfully, "haven't you been listening to what Rabbit was saying?" "I listened, but I had a small piece of fluff in my ear. Could you say it again, please, Rabbit?"

A. A. Milne[2]

Here lies Cliff, sprawled on the floor doing geometry problems, watching television, and wearing earphones that blare rock music into his ears. He looks at the television screen, reads the notes on the record album during a commercial, then settles back to his geometry problem. From another room, a voice broadcasts the news on the radio. The telephone is ringing. Cliff's mother tries to call him to dinner, but he can't hear her. Here lies Cliff, a modern child, tuning in and out of the world.

On the filled-to-capacity jet, the flight attendant stands at the head of the aisle explaining safety instructions that could mean life or death to the passengers. Look around the cabin. How many people are listening?

A family is going to counseling. The counselor's first challenge will be to find ways to encourage the family members simply to pay attention to each other—to listen to each other.

We are talking about a worldwide symptom existing not just in homes but in classrooms, offices, governments, and world organizations. *No one is listening*.

Listening as a Language Art

Let's take a closer look at listening. Human babies are excellent listeners. Most of our early learning is derived from listening, making sense out of the sounds around us, shaping those sounds into words and meanings. Because listening is such a vital part of how we learn language, our listening vocabulary is much larger than, much older than, our oral vocabulary. Babies understand more than they are able to say; their comprehension based on listening to the messages of others is greater and richer than their ability to respond verbally.

Given the importance of listening in language learning, it is shocking to think how often it is neglected. In fact, until very recently, listening was not even considered an essential component of the language arts curriculum. It was believed that listening was an automatic reflex, closely related to intelligence, and could not be taught as a skill in itself.

In 1928, Paul T. Rankin studied the distribution of people's everyday communication time and found that, of the 70 percent of their day spent in verbal communication, 45 percent was spent in listening.[3] In 1950, Miriam Wilt's study of the listening time of children in elementary school revealed that they were expected to spend over half of their school day listening. Most of the listening time was devoted to—the teacher.[4]

Another Wilt study, based on data received from hundreds of teachers in forty-two states and accompanied by on-site observations, showed that the teachers were not even aware of how much time their students spent listening. Wilt found that most of the teachers thought reading was the most important skill and what their students spent most of their class time doing. In reality, *the children were spending more time listening than in any other single school activity*. Wilt also discovered that rarely was there a real purpose for listening to what was being said. Stories or poems were not often read aloud; oral reading was seldom used to prove a point, give additional information, or provide enjoyment. In fact, most of the oral reading was merely a reiteration of material that had already been digested. The other oral language activities observed were largely verbal ping-pong with the teacher serving up questions to which children parroted answers derived from books. Listening was neither valued as a skill nor taught as a fundamental tool of communication.[5]

> Good boys and good girls always listen.
> To learn, we must listen.
> We must listen all the time.
> Good boys and girls never talk.
> But they always listen.
> We should listen and listen and listen!
> To *you*, teacher,
> and your words, your words, your words.
> Your words, your words, your words, your words!
>
> Albert Cullum[6]

The kinds of questions teachers ask evoke different levels of listening and responding. *Convergent* questions, which demand right/wrong, correct/incorrect answers, rarely stimulate higher-level thinking. *Divergent* questions, which encourage different approaches, insights, and explanations, inspire students to think through situations in a freer, more exploratory way, using prior knowledge and making new connections and discoveries in the process.

In classrooms where discussion is limited to convergent questioning, children often listen with tension (fear of being wrong), smugness at knowing the "right" answer, or apathy.

Imagine the kinds of listening and responding that would go on in the classroom if the teacher invited students to "think about Glenda the Good Witch and the ways she demonstrated her character. And, just for fun, if YOU had good magic like Glenda, what would you do with it?" Contrast that spirit of listening and participation with this common encounter:

The teacher asks, "What was the name of the Good Witch?"
John answers, "Glenda."
Short and to the point! Case closed.

Alice Keliher challenges,

Is it too cynical to say that children's not listening may well be good judgment on their part? Have we given them sounds worth being attentive to? Is there too great a tendency today to drill on the dry bones of technique and neglect the lure of poetry, folk tale, ballad and all the delights of imagination? To what in all the welter of sights and sounds should children give themselves? Is this not a matter of values?[7]

Listening Skills Can Be Taught

In 1952, the Commission on the English Curriculum of the National Council of Teachers of English published a report based on a five-year study. The commission's report called for listening to be considered a basic medium of learning and for listening habits to be taught, not left to chance. "From morning to night, the child is buffeted with the stormy winds of words. He needs help in a deluge. His school is about the only place where he can get help in selecting or rejecting, in understanding and using, the torrent poured over him."[8]

Today, listening is considered an essential component of the language arts curriculum. Listening skills *can* be taught. When people are trained to listen more carefully, they show improvement not only in listening skills but in other subject areas as well.[9]

The Findings   What have we discovered about children and listening in school?

1. Children listen more attentively in the morning hours when they are rested and well fed. They learn better in a comfortable, well-lit room which has no distracting clutter.

2. Children listen more attentively and respond with more intelligence if the teacher pauses a few extra seconds after each question and if the questions are open-ended and stimulating rather than yes–no, right–wrong ones that demand immediate monosyllabic answers.

3. Children learn listening skills through the give and take of discussions and through actively participating in a variety of experiences. Less time should be spent listening just to the teacher and more time should be spent talking and listening to each other.

4. Children listen more carefully to information and ideas if these are presented in a variety of ways and if they have relevancy and meaning to the children. Children are motivated to listen carefully if they see a purpose in listening and if their efforts to improve their listening skills are encouraged and praised.

5. Children's listening skills improve in an atmosphere that encourages them to express and evaluate ideas without fear of humiliation or criticism.

6. Children show improvement in listening skills when they participate in the formation of listening rules for the class.[10]

Listening: What's the Reason?

Sara Lundsteen defines listening as *the process by which spoken language is converted to meaning in the mind*.[11]

The need and desire for the mind to make meaning can be illustrated by an experience my husband had in college. He was taking a course in Experimental Psychology, and one of the experiments was to learn and then use a nonsense alphabet. A conscientious student, Howard tried to learn the nonsense letters, tried to do the assignments. But his mind balked. It refused to learn anything that made no sense!

We all learn differently. Perhaps you need visual clues to convert language into meaning. Or do you learn best through tactile-kinesthetic experiences? Are you a person who catches on immediately through auditory explanations? We need to provide opportunities *in all ways of learning* so that none of our students is left out of the process.

How Many Ways Do We Listen?

There is listening and there is *listening*. Our range of listening abilities covers a lot of ground between two widely separated extremes.

Passive Listening   hearing sounds but not interpreting them beyond bare recognition.

Intermittent Listening   following part of what is said but not grasping the whole message.

Unresponsive Listening   completely lacking facial expression or other signs of response.

Borderline Listening   missing the main point and focusing on a minor detail selected for personal reasons.

Emotional Listening   responding to selected words with fear, anger, or other emotions, failing to comprehend the whole message.

Careful Listening   comprehending the main idea, the organization, and the supporting data of what is heard.

Critical Listening   questioning the validity of what is said, rejecting any emotion-charged words, and maintaining a skeptical attitude toward broad generalizations.

Perceptive Listening   being aware of what is really being said, even if the words don't obviously express it.

Creative Listening   intellectually and emotionally appreciating what is heard. [12]

A teacher in one of my workshops shared with me a way of listening: she described loving teachers as listening with "the ear in the middle of their heart." (Write the word "heart." See the "ear" inside? Listen to your students with that special ear!)

Two Terrific Listeners

When Nessy and Jenny, two terrific sisters, were five-and-a-half and seven-and-a-half years old, respectively, their mental acuity, imagination, curiosity, and communicative abilities were outstanding. They were the best listeners I knew. They listened attentively to everything told to them and responded with interest and intelligence. They truly enjoyed listening. When told I was writing a textbook on the language arts, they responded enthusiastically with suggestions. "Tell teachers not to use boring books with no interesting stories and exciting sentences," they advised. I challenged them to suggest some exciting sentences. They thought for awhile and then Jenny exclaimed, "The British are coming!" Inspired by her sister, Nessy excitedly offered her contribution: "Land ho!"

We talked further about writing a book for teachers and each girl offered some advice. "Tell teachers to try to do very interesting things with their children, not just the same old things," said Jenny. And Nessy added, "Remind them not to scream or they'll strain their voices."

Their comments force me to face a bitter truth: I have often displayed bad listening habits, and I could have learned so much from these two children. My listening time in my student days was filled with daydreams, doodles, distractions, naps, plans for my future, focusing on an outside object like clouds, or focusing on an inside object like my growling stomach. I have checked out of conversations or lectures because I prejudged them as dull and didn't sift the wheat from the chaff, as good listeners should. I have made a judgment before I heard the person out, interrupting, rejecting, or ignoring the speaker's points and interjecting my own opinion before the speaker was finished. I have chosen only what's easy from what I heard, not bothering to stretch my mind to understand parts that were a little more complicated. I have forgotten that "good listening is dynamic, constructive—it's energy consuming. It's plain hard work!"[13]

Occasionally, I was lucky enough to have excellent, stimulating teachers to whom I gladly listened with all of my faculties. One such delightful teacher was Kenneth Koch, who in a lecture at Western Michigan University said something that all teachers in the world should write on the chalkboard of their minds and never erase: "Kids have an attention span equal to one's interestingness."

Examine Your Own Listening Habits

Before you walk into the classroom to teach listening skills, honestly evaluate your own skills as a listener. Do you listen attentively to others? More importantly, do you listen to kids?

> A teacher who really listens to children is sensitive to responses and recognizes their importance, finds much in them to indicate the depth of students' understanding and the pattern of their thought. Listening to children and interpreting their responses appropriately contribute to the teacher's ability to capitalize upon teachable moments for individualized instruction and provide support for struggling young minds.[14]

The importance of your own example as a listener cannot be emphasized enough. So often a variation of the following occurs:

"Miss Smith, I can think of a fourth cause for the Civil War."

"Only three are necessary for our quiz, Randy."

As you grow aware of the importance of good listening habits in your relationship with your students, you will begin to participate in meaningful speaking–listening activities. You will become a creator of ideas, an appreciative listener, a more effective learner, and a discriminatory critic. Through your efforts and example, you will help your students develop these qualities. Logan and Logan consider critical listening so important that without it they fear our very civilization may be lost. "The true, the false, the genuine and the charlatan, the orator and the spellbinder vie for our attention and we must learn to judge the worth as well as the words."[15]

The example you set as a courteous, attentive, responsive, clearly communicating listener is more important than any lesson plan on listening! When children are listened to by caring adults, they feel encouraged to express ideas, opinions, questions, and feelings. Their verbal language is greatly enhanced by teachers who are supportive listeners.

Keep all these facets of listening in mind as you consider this question: Since children in school spend a great deal of their time listening to the teacher, if you were a child, would you want to listen to *you* for several hours a day?

Students' Rules for Listening

Children are conscious of the need to establish rules to guide listening. Given the opportunity, they will surprise you with their valuable recommendations.

Sam, eight years old, was interviewed on his ideas for good listening rules. Here are his suggestions:

1. Sit down and listen.
2. Look at the person speaking.
3. Don't play around.
4. Don't make faces.
5. If you can't understand something, raise your hand and ask.
6. Listen harder for fire drills, for when someone explains something important, or if someone is telling you how to do something.
7. You can relax and listen to a story or a poem or a puppet show.

Barbie, nine, Marianne, ten, and Michelle, twelve, made up listening rules for a club:

1. The signal is to whistle two times. That means quiet.
2. Shut up.
3. Look at who's talking.
4. Do not interrupt.
5. Wait your turn to talk.
6. Raise your hand.
7. Whoever is talking should make it interesting. Don't drag, don't mumble, speak clearly.
8. Listen real extra carefully for important things like plans or instructions for trips and things.
9. Get all the facts before we decide on something.
10. Don't just sit there. Ask questions and give your opinions.

Barbie, Marianne, Michelle, and Sam included many basic requirements for good listening habits in their lists. Without using academic jargon, the children clearly described different categories of listening for different purposes.

1. Listen with awareness, appreciation, and enjoyment.
2. Listen for information, for directions, for comprehension of sequences, for discrimination between different words and sounds, for main ideas, and for summaries of ideas.
3. Listen critically and learn to evaluate and analyze what you hear so that intelligent decisions and conclusions can be reached.

Getting Attention

Before the first step is taken toward any teaching goal, a certain prerequisite must be met: whether you are about to give an assignment, introduce a lesson, or dismiss your class for lunch, you will have to get their attention. Few education courses truly prepare teachers for the disruptive, undisciplined confusion that sometimes lies in wait for novices. Creative teachers have a variety of ways to get their classes' attention. Here are a few examples of successful, widely used signals.

1. Blow a whistle, shake a tambourine, play a chord on a piano, or strum a guitar.
2. Flick the light off and on, ring a bell, or sing a special song.
3. Say "freeze," clap your hands, or use the football referee's "stop the clock" gesture.
4. Count down from ten, set a timer, or invent special hand or body signals.
5. Create a fantasy friend who can get the class's attention.

Include "Attention Getter" as one of the classroom jobs to which students are assigned. Some other attention-getting devices:

1. Put on an old hat called your "quiet, please" hat. Whenever you wear it, it means quiet. A variation is for a different child to be chosen each day to wear the hat to call the class to attention.
2. Whisper very quietly, so that the children will have to be alert to understand what you are saying.
3. Hold up a large cardboard ear and put your finger to your lips. Each child could make a pair of "listening ears" and take them out when you hold up the big ear. Or pantomime it!
4. Use three large cardboard signs that say "Stop," "Look," and "Listen." The signs are held up by three children whenever attention is needed.
5. Make a special flag. Raise it for attention.
6. Use sign language.

In classes rich with a diversity of interesting learning experiences, you need only begin the beloved activity to immediately get attention: hold up the book you are reading together, turn on the music the class enjoys, or start the project the group has decided on.

It is interesting and stimulating to have more than one way of getting attention. Experiment with your class. Together you will discover and invent methods that are your own.

Attention-Getting Metaphors for Motivation

Be aware of your own language in communicating with your students. We often unconsciously humiliate children in our attempt to get and keep their attention. Have you heard, or said, "We're not starting this lesson until Scott stops playing with his pencil like a little kindergarten baby! We're waiting for you, Scott—as usual!"

That kind of language comes from the Culture of NO, from a vote for Death instead of Life.

Consider creating metaphors for motivation. For example, imagine human beings as cars:

"Is your engine ON or OFF? Uh oh, turn it on!

Is your gas tank full or empty? Fill it up!

Wow, we need some air in our tires. They're flat!

Hey, kids, are you in Neutral? in Park? We can't go anywhere in Neutral or Park. Let's get in gear.

I hear static on your radios. Let's get those dials tuned in just right.

Your lights are off. Turn them ON. Turn on your BRIGHT lights. Now we're ready!"

Or imagine your kids are slumped in their chairs, definitely NOT paying attention. Tell them, "Kids, your backs are in the shape of the letter C. C'mon, let's get them in the shape of the letter I. What a difference! Now we're ready to begin."

Once the metaphors have been established, the kids need only such code words or signals as "Tune in" or "Brights ON!" or "Clear your signals" to remind them to be alert and attentive.

A last word on getting children to pay attention. Be sure that you have something worthwhile to share before you call your children to attention. Don't repeat yourself endlessly or they will tune you out. Be clear in your purpose. Once you have the attention of your class, you can begin to move toward your first major goal.

QUESTION: What do I want my students to learn?

ANSWER: I want my students to learn to listen with awareness, appreciation, and enjoyment.

Listening Activities   I

The Body

Through discussion and discovery, establish an ongoing interest in the wonders of the body, with an emphasis on listening abilities. Children love to talk about themselves and their own development. In an atmosphere of trust and acceptance, they will contribute feelings and personal experiences that are often valuable as lesson-launchers. For example, Dan told his classmates that when he was very young, he thought people could hear from all parts of their bodies.

He told secrets to knees, whispered into elbows and shoulders before he discovered that *ears* were important to hearing.

Awareness

Intersperse expressions of listening awareness whenever the opportunity arises. For example, a kindergarten teacher says to her class, "Imagine, boys and girls, to be able to hear that puppy bark in the middle of all that playground noise. Isn't it lucky our ears are so keen that we could hear that little lost whimper and help the pup?"

Or a fifth-grade teacher advises her students, "We'd better listen carefully to the weather report. We don't want to have our field day in the rain, do we?"

The Silence Game

Montessori teachers play a Silence Game, developed by Maria Montessori, to prepare children for listening. They ask the children to "make a silence," to make their bodies totally quiet and still. They relax the feet, the legs, the entire body. When everyone is completely peaceful and quiet, the teacher speaks softly, "We're going to listen; then we'll talk about what we heard." The group sits and listens. After a few moments, still speaking softly, the teacher asks each child in the group, "What did you hear?" and the children respond.

Spin-offs
   a. After the children have played the Silence Game a number of times, their responses may be taped and played back to them.
   b. Write a class poem from the list of things the children heard.
   c. Base a choral reading on their list.
   d. Translate their sounds into creative movement.
   e. Create drawings, murals, or sculptures based on the sounds.
   f. Add your own (A.Y.O.) spin-offs.

Sound Walks

Invite your class to share a walk with you. Keep a fast-moving pace. Return to the classroom and discuss the sounds heard on the walk. Write the sounds on the board as your students give them. (There probably won't be very many.) Before the class has a chance to become restless, announce that they are going on another walk. This usually meets with surprise and delight. Walk exactly the same route as before, only this time slow down, pause frequently, take your time to take things in. Return to the classroom and discuss the specific sounds heard on the walk. Write these sounds next to the list of sounds from the first walk. There should be a sharp contrast between the two groups of words. This contrast will provide a focus for discussion about how alert and aware we can be if we decide to really use our natural abilities, our remarkable powers.

A group of third graders took the two walks and compiled their lists.

First Walk (Fast)	Second Walk (Slow)
We heard:	We heard:
street noises	a car starting
traffic noises	an airplane zoom
birds	a loud car muffler
children talking	a dog barking
the teacher talking	our shoes shuffling
	some children humming
	trees rustling
	John whistling
	an ambulance siren
	cars beeping horns
	twigs snapping
	a puddle splash
	the teacher whispering
	ourselves breathing
	Andy burping
	birds chirping

"How many things do you think we miss seeing and hearing every day when we're in a hurry and don't pay attention?" is a question that usually provokes responsive answers. Children will draw conclusions from the experience as they share their feelings and words. Following naturally from your discussion, a variety of activities will suggest themselves.

Spin-offs
   a. Have your students draw a picture of the walk or one aspect of it.
   b. The class can write a story, newspaper report, or picture-story about the walk.
   c. Ask the kids to draw cartoons showing the contrast between the two walks.
   d. Use movement and pantomime to demonstrate the slogan "Take your time and take things in!"
   e. Use the words on the board as a resource and write letters to pen pals, family, friends, or another class describing the experience.
   f. Make up a puppet show about the walk.
   g. Write about the two walks in journals.
   h. Use the tape recorder to make up a radio interview of two people who went on a short walk and a long walk and are discussing their findings.
   i. Share the experience by making up a route at home and inviting a friend or a brother or sister to take the two walks.
   j. Add your own (A.Y.O.) spin-offs.

Listen Here

Wouldn't it be wonderful if every classroom had a small space, a special place, where a few children at a time could sit quietly listening and thinking? It could have a name of its own and have a throw rug or some floppy pillows to sit on, a pack of inexpensive postcards of beautiful paintings to look at, a music box with a very delicate chiming song to listen to, and some thoughtful books to read. Add a small plant, pussywillows, or dried cornstalks to smell and touch, a notebook to which a child's own thoughts could be added, and crayons and drawing paper to use if one wants to. It would be a special thinking, feeling, listening place where children could discover the peacefulness within themselves.

Bring In a Sound

R. Murray Schafer, a Canadian composer and teacher who is doing fascinating experimental work with listening education, describes silence as "a pocket of possibility. Anything can happen to break it."[16] Schafer asks students to bring an interesting sound to class. Some of the sounds students have shared are a balloon filled with air, then the air gradually let out; a metal clacker; a music box. One boy repeated the word "animal" over and over. He observed that the more he repeated it, the less it seemed to fit the thing it represented and the more it became a lulling sound with no meaning.

Spin-off   Ask the students to bring something from outdoors that makes a sound, something that they *find*. On a clear day, a break from indoor education is always refreshing and this assignment usually guarantees interesting results and effective exchanges of observations and ideas. Kids have brought in and demonstrated the sounds of

dry grass

small pebbles

acorns

pieces of old newspaper

clumps of dirt in discarded paper cups

leaves

twigs and sticks

"Bird-Wirds"

In this modern age, our ears receive a cacophony of sounds, most of which we ignore. But, just as a dog's sensitive ears catch a relatively inaudible whistle, so we can sometimes catch a certain voice or a special melody through the thundering sounds around us—if we press our *awareness* button and start *really* listening.

Children are fascinated by silence and sound and respond immediately to all discussions related to these phenomena. Every single day you probably hear the sounds of birds. How deep is your awareness of this daily experience?

One of my favorite assignments is to "listen to the birds and find words to describe their sounds." I have asked hundreds of classes of people of all ages to enjoy this experience. At the end of a week of listening, we share the findings. Here is a partial list of the "bird-wirds" gathered by second graders.

"Bird-Wirds"

cheer cheer chirp	drink your tea	whistle
kay kow kay kow	crook crook	arrogant
zzzzzzeeeeee	c'mere c'mere	dominate
good morning	not now not now	scold
all is well	eat eat eat	lullaby
tweeedle tweeedle	woe woe woe	joke
cheer up cheer	jivii jivii jivit	gossip
yik	uu wu uu	complain
ok ok ok	chee chicup chee chicup	twirp
chip chip chip	harmonica	blend
brrr brrr	squawk	drone
jee wit jee wit	squeak	argue
itchurk	nervous	peep
cheerio		gurgle

This experience is a wonderful people exercise to discover how tuned in you can be if you don't tune out.

Spin-offs

a. Tape the sounds of birds.

b. Tape the children's "bird-wirds."

c. Paint a mural of birds and intersperse the "bird-wirds" with the pictures so that when you look at the mural you will imagine that you hear it as well as see it.

d. Find poems about birds and see how many descriptive "bird-wirds" are used to convey their sounds.

e. Improvise creative movement using birds as inspiration. Add sounds.

f. Cut out pictures of birds and make individual collages using the cutouts and the "bird-wirds" for designs.

ₗg. Experiment with musical instruments and improvised sounds to find ways of conveying the sounds of birds.

h. Make bird puppets and present a sound-filled puppet show.

i. Write poems about birds and their songs using the "bird-wirds" as a resource.

j. Draw or paint individual pictures of birds. Add their words to the picture.

k. Add your own (A.Y.O.) spin-offs.

Noisy/Quiet: Listen and Gather Words

This listening–thinking–talking–writing–*doing* activity strengthens awareness of listening and develops appreciation for the creative possibilities related to an original listening experience. Remember, listening and talking precede writing as older components of the language arts!

Noisy   Desks are clear; board is erased; attention is on you, the teacher. Write across the top of one side of the board the word "noisy"; then turn to your students and ask them to think about noisy things that they hear. Give them a few seconds to think. It's up to you to decide to have the children raise hands, talk out, go-around-the-room-and-take-turns—whatever sharing procedure you like. Be sure everyone is encouraged to contribute. *Don't* get into a big discussion about any of the words, because it will slow down the gathering process and inhibit children from spontaneously contributing ideas.

You'll find that noisy words are very popular and that you have to write very quickly. In just a few minutes, the board will be filled. If, occasionally, you find a lull, fill the gap with a challenging question:

> What are noisy colors?
> Noisy holidays?
> Noisy words?
> Noisy times of the day? noisy places?
> What are noisy foods? activities?
> What are noisy instruments?
> What are noisy television shows?
> Who are noisy fairy-tale characters?

The number of words children of all ages gather in a few minutes' time is astonishing. Because children *know* more words than they can spell or read, they need opportunities like this to contribute some of their knapsack knowledge in a nonthreatening atmosphere.

Here is a sample of noisy words from a fourth grade.

We Listen to Noisy Sounds (Noisy Words)

scream	volcano	Cape Kennedy	red
shout	earthquake	bombs	firecrackers
thunder	crash	boo	boog-alooba
crunch	pow	soccer game	rock and roll
4th of July	vooom	lions roaring	stamp
trucks	missiles	elephants trumpeting	popcorn
airplanes	rockets	horses stampeding	circus
Halloween	construction	zam-zap	tornado warning
jumping	bang	alarm	recess
clapping hands	smash	siren	traffic jam
foghorn	stereo	ambulance	tap dancers
bongos	creak	factory whistle	

Spin-offs

a. Read all the words aloud together or in any spontaneous choral arrangement that lends itself to variety in tone and expression. At this point, the children will realize, perhaps for the first time, that the words not only *sound* noisy but *look* noisy. This intermingling of the senses is a wonderful mindstretcher and should be experienced as often as possible throughout the curriculum. Appreciation for both the written and spoken word will follow such important discoveries.

b. Challenge your students with questions.

Is it possible to write about "noisy" without using any noisy words?

How would we write a lively, noisy sentence about a noisy place?

Do the words in our sentences *look* and *sound* noisy?

c. Everyone (including the teacher) writes a poem (call it a word-sketch, arrangement, piece, or gathering if you don't want to call it a poem) with the title "Noisy." The words on the board can be used as a resource. Try to write words so noisy that you can really hear them. *Write for only a few minutes because the longer the time period, the more likely children are to cross out, correct, doubt, or worry about what they are writing.* Reassure your class that in this exercise imagination, not spelling, counts. Emphasize that enjoyment is important and that the papers won't be graded because this is not a test. This is an activity in which everyone succeeds! Try using a noisy musical selection as inspirational background music.

Often kids will write their "noisy" piece in the shape of a noisy object like a firecracker or cannon. This adds interest and life to the work. Always follow any writing exercise by sharing everyone's work. *Sharing is an integral part of listening appreciation and enjoyment.* Set an example as a responsive listener.

This is the time to encourage and support all creative efforts in a nonjudgmental manner so that your students truly learn that your classroom is a safe and positive place for them and that they don't have to be afraid of criticism or humiliation. Read your own piece last (sharing is a two-way street!). At this point, follow the advise of poet–teacher Kenneth Koch: "The most critical thing I'd say to the kids is, 'That's terrific!'"

Here are two examples of a third- and a fifth-grader's individual pieces about "noisy," written in about one minute.

Listen to Noisy Sounds

Popcorn pop and corn
Bongo bongo beep beep
Jets boog-alooba rock and roll
Bless my soul
I'm stereo.

> Ray
> Grade 5

Noisy Sounds I Hear

My lion roars very loud.
He's a carnival circus 4th of July lion.
I found him in a stampede.
He rides a fire truck and rings the bell.

> Betsy
> Grade 3

d. Rewrite, illustrate, and then display the "noisy" pieces on the bulletin board or in a booklet. (Old greeting card catalogues are great for these projects, and stationery stores are usually generous about giving them to teachers.)

e. Tape music and sounds to go with the different pieces; then use the pieces for oral reading. Combine them with creative dramatics and movement, and have your students present a show to younger classes or to parents.

f. Write a group poem about "noisy" using the words on the board as a resource. Ask the class to put noisy ideas together. Suggest that they listen to the sounds and rhythms of the words while you write them down.

g. Cut out, draw, paint, or print a collage of noisy words, pictures, colors, and designs. This project can be done individually or in groups.

h. Make a tape-recording that includes as many words from the gathering as possible. The children can say each word and follow it with its sound or say all the words followed by all the sounds. Experiment.

i. The children might choose just *one* word from the "noisy" board to concentrate on and express in writing, movement, music, or art. Or the group can decide how to express their chosen noisy word. Noisy words lend themselves marvelously to movement. Imagine how many ways we can express "roar" or "rocket" or "burst" with our bodies. A child can show the movement and have the rest of the class guess which word is being demonstrated.

j. Listen to *one* noisy word. Write about it for one minute.

k. Add your own (A.Y.O.) spin-offs.

Quiet   This may be introduced immediately following "noisy" sounds or a day or two later, depending on your schedule and needs. The important thing is to leave the noisy words up, either on the board or on a chart, so that they become familiar.

Write the word "quiet" across the top of the board and ask the group to sit very still, relax, be peaceful, and think about quiet things they like to listen to—quiet people, quiet places, animals, sounds, colors. Once again, write down all their ideas, which should fill the board. Always be ready to interject challenging questions if needed.

What is quiet food?

What is quiet music? quiet time?

What are quiet things you can do?

What are quiet clothes? colors? places?

Here are examples from a third-grade class gathering on "quiet."

We Listen to Quiet Sounds (Quiet Words)

early in the morning	tiptoe	wind chimes
tiny little animals	night	cats
ssshhhhh	old people	lullabies
sleeping	pink and grey	hum
snow	eggs before they hatch	library
whisper	turning pages	slow
when the rain stops	a leaf falling	flannel

Spin-offs

a. All the same possibilities for discussion, activities, and spin-offs that were used for "noisy" can be used for "quiet." However, a new experience is introduced because we now have two groups of words: noisy and quiet. How these words look to the eye, sound to the ear, feel in the mouth, and are imagined in the mind provide a startling and dramatic contrast.

With your students, contrast the two lists of words. Ask the students to write a line of noisy words or a noisy sentence and then, underneath, a line of quiet words or a quiet sentence. Then write another noisy line followed by another quiet line. Perhaps some children will want to begin with the quiet words and follow with the noisy ones.

After the writing exercise, read the papers aloud, sharing the noisy and quiet ideas. The children should have no problem identifying which lines are noisy and which are quiet. After this activity a fourth grader said, "The quiet words sound quiet and make me feel quiet when I hear them. The noisy words wake me up."

Remember, you are an important participant!

This technique of alternating contrasting elements is a marvelous way to introduce poetry that has an A/B/A/B rhyme scheme. The activity will also help students develop appreciation for well-chosen, vital words in whatever form they are presented: stories, ballads, poetry, or songs. Jesse Stuart said that he began to try to write poetry because of "the wind I heard in the dead trees and the loneliness of sounds at night."[17] After this experience you will find children listening carefully to the words they hear and becoming very critical if the words in stories are dull and lifeless. (Try word-gathering on fast/slow, bright/dull, hot/cold. Add your own list and activities.)

Here are samples of third graders' noisy/quiet papers, written, as always, in a very short period of time. Read them aloud. Can you tell which are the noisy lines and which are the quiet lines?

Noisy Quiet	Noisy Quiet
A clap of hands	A tuba playing
A worm going into an apple	A feather dropping
Feet stamping	Firecrackers popping
A bud blooming	A ant walking
Crash! A building getting built	Cars and trucks going by
The first flight of a butterfly	A butterfly flying
A mother scolding her son	A bomb explodes
A boy sucking a lollipop	Wind blows
A scream of a lady	
A cat having kittens	Roy
Linda	

b. Discover such noisy and quiet poems as Sandburg's "Fog" or "Jazz Fantasia." Read them aloud.

c. Listen for the noisy and quiet parts in music.

d. Divide the class into Noisy and Quiet groups and let them decide many ways to express noisy and quiet. For example, the Noisy group sings a noisy song; the Quiet group moves quietly; the Noisy group presents noisy pictures; the Quiet group hums a lullaby. The Noisy group improvises noisy music, while the Quiet group improvises quiet music. The Noisy group says noisy words in a variety of loud tones, and the Quiet group responds with quiet words in a variety of soft tones. If possible, have the groups change, so that everyone has the opportunity to experience both qualities.

e. Create puppet shows with Noisy/Quiet characters.

f. Tell stories with noisy and quiet parts.

g. Add your own (A.Y.O.) spin-offs.

Sounds

This could be included in "Noisy/Quiet," but it is important enough to warrant a section of its own. Words are very much a part of us. They are deeply embedded in our psyche and have a great effect on our feelings and behavior. Consequently, the more aware we are of our own personal vocabularies, the greater our insight, understanding, and appreciation of language, learning, and communication in general.

Sounds We Love   We all love the sound of some words. When we were babies, we gabbled, gurgled, babbled special sounds that amused us or made us feel good. Some of those sounds are words, and some are just that—sounds.

In Eleanor Cameron's wonderful book *A Room Made of Windows*, Julia, a young, budding writer, keeps lists in her journal of "the most beautiful words" and the "most detested words. . . . Under the beautiful words, which began with 'Mediterranean' and 'quiver' and 'undulating' and 'lapis lazuli' . . . she added 'mellifluous' which she copied from a piece of paper Mrs. Gray had given her at school. . . ."[18]

Here are some favorite-sounding words gathered by a second grade.

We Love the Sound of These Words

babbling brook	sunshower
Siamese	tiddly-winks
whippoorwill	Queen Anne's lace
salamander	butterfinger
collie	roller coaster
gingerbread	gossamer wings
boomerang	tic-tac-toe
yo-yo	bouncy ball

Here are samples of junior high students' favorite-sounding words:

We Love the Sound of These Words

dazzle	corncob	rhododendron
flick it	harmony	Rumpelstiltskin
Timbuktu	Amsterdam	Guatemala
Fuji	Shanghai	icicle
cool	nugget	sunshine
bountiful	wallaby	sandalwood
munch	mystical	
twilight	tintinnabulation	

Spin-offs

a. Make up words that sound good to you.

b. Discuss how the sounds of certain words affect us. Words have power. We listen to them, and they evoke different feelings in us. If we just hear the words "pizza" or "rainbow sherbet," we get a vivid picture in our minds of something delicious. We see it, we taste it. The sounds of the words alone can make us feel hungry.

c. Children enjoy gathering their favorite-sounding words. Even though many of the younger children do not yet know how to write or read, they love to say the words, hear the words, and have you write them down on the board or in their notebooks. Your students will learn how to write and read those favorite words more quickly than they will impersonal, irrelevant words taken from a standardized list.

I once discussed the sounds of favorite words with two first-grade classes. In a few minutes, the children had filled the blackboard with wonderful-sounding words. They were amazed at the number of words they knew. I told them I believed each child could think of 500 favorite-sounding words and if they asked their families and teachers to help them gather the words, we would have a celebration: a word party!

A month later I received a call from the teachers of those two classes. Their rooms were filled to capacity with favorite-sounding words. We had a wonderful party! Their walls were papered, from floor to ceiling, with their favorite words!

d. Make a favorite-sounding word mural with pictures and illustrations.

e. Draw favorite-word posters. Illustrate the words.

f. Write about any one of the favorite words.

g. Interpret favorite words in movement. (One of the most beautiful improvisations I have ever seen was second graders turned into a merry-go-round to express that favorite word.)

h. As stories, poems, and books are read, take time to notice how many favorite words are used.

i. Write poems, stories, and songs using wonderful-sounding words. Read aloud.

j. Add your own (A.Y.O.) spin-offs.

Sounds We Hate   Now go in the opposite direction and discuss the sounds of "Words We Don't Like to Hear." We are surrounded by a storm of words, some of which jab through and pierce us. And some we use to jab others. Listen to these words, write them on the board, discuss how they sound and how their sound and meaning affect us.

Here is a sample of a first grade's list.

We Hate the Sound of These Words

touch	waltz	cobra
gross	shut up	disease
fatigue	corpse	bomb
repulsive	tongue	smog
kiddo	gland	pollution
chick	mucous membrane	scrawny
obnoxious	Caucasian	fat

Spin-offs

a. Read aloud the words from both the love and hate lists. *Listen* carefully as each word is read. The children should read aloud with you and listen. *No written description can adequately prepare you for the experience of listening to this contrast of sounds.* Try reading one word from the favorite list followed by a word from the hate list. You and your students will be astonished at what you hear.

Here is a sample of the favorite/hate combination of a second-grade class. Say the words aloud and listen to them.

sunshine	daisies
hate	kill
rainbow sherbet	how nice to see you
stupid	shut up

Did your voice change tone, inflection, volume, expression as you read the different words?

b. Take turns reading the various words in different ways or have a "favorite" group and a "hate" group reading the words or groups of words alternately.

c. With your children, be aware of how writers select words to affect the reader in different ways. Even the youngest children will be very responsive to the words they read and hear and will even grow critical of wishy-washy, blah words. Because they have discovered that they themselves have the ability to use powerful words that can make people feel wonderful or terrible, they appreciate writers who use green, growing, sweet-smelling words to convey spring; cold, icy words to communicate winter; or noisy, colorful words to describe a carnival. They will have no patience with writers who use correct but ordinary, lifeless words. And isn't that ability to *listen with intelligence and awareness* what goal number one is all about?

d. Add your own (A.Y.O.) spin-offs.

Listen with Magical Ears

Don't just half-listen to music, poetry, stories. With your class, really concentrate and give yourselves completely to the listening experience. Put your whole self in! Ask your students to clear their minds of distracting thoughts. Ask them to pretend that they have Magical Ears that can listen to the deepest heart of sound. With these ears, they can hear the brightness and color of music, the melodies of words, the rhythm of poetry, and the true meaning of stories. If they concentrate, they can vividly picture the images that words and music evoke and can be filled with ideas and feelings from the listening experience.

CAREFUL

Never ask your students to listen to something for pure enjoyment and appreciation and then test them on it later. That is an example of the countless betrayals children experience when adults are not honest with them. Many of my generation of students learned to resent and dislike the most beautiful music because our music appreciation program taught us that we had better learn that music, those composers, spell-it-all-right, or we would flunk. So we memorized such lovely melodies as "Humoresque" with these original lyrics: "H-U-M-O-R-E-S-Q-U-E spells 'Humoresque,' written by D-V-O-R-A-K." If you know the piece, you will find our lyrics go perfectly with the melody.

Spin-offs

   a. Children of every age and background can learn to love to listen to great music and literature if it is presented to them in an exciting and interesting way. Pat Conroy's almost totally illiterate Yamacraw students learned and loved such classical works as Beethoven's Ninth Symphony, Verdi's *Aida*, and Rimsky-Korsakov's "The Flight of the Bumble Bee."

And the kids seemed genuinely to like the stuff. One morning Top Cat leapt off the bus, ran into the classroom, and informed me that "The Flight of the Bumble Bee" was played on the Andy Williams Show. Later in the year, Lincoln and Mary reported that they heard "The Dance of the Sugar Plum Fairy." . . .
   When I brought Leonard Bernstein's Children's Concert to the school, Leonard was a mild, if not overwhelming, success. His orchestra played several of the movements we had memorized and when they played those pieces, the kids would hoot and slap each other, then say, "That's old Shy-Koski."[19]

   b. Share music that you love with your students; discover new music. Always try to go from the familiar to the unfamiliar. Soon, the unfamiliar becomes the familiar and on you go to learn something new.
   As often as possible, correlate listening with other expressive forms. Ask the kids to draw, write, or move *as* they listen, *after* they listen. Discuss with the children how the music made them feel, what pictures, colors, and ideas came to their minds as they listened with their magical ears.

CAREFUL

If you encourage children to draw or write their feelings and impressions of music, do not criticize or reject their personal interpretations. *Night on Bald Mountain* is frightening to me and I draw a scary picture or write a scary story about the images conveyed to me by the music, but ten-year-old Bill finds *Bald Mountain* more exciting and adventuresome than frightening. His art and poems reflect <u>his</u> responses.

c. Listen to the music your students already know and love. Probably no group of people has a greater influence on today's children than do contemporary musicians, singers, and songwriters, who are affecting mores, fashions, and the language as well as music. Many of the songs your class already knows have excellent lyrics that can have great value in the classroom.

Ask the children to share their favorite songs. Set aside a few minutes at a time to listen to the various selections. If possible, have words on the board or on hand-outs for the children to follow as they listen. The poetic quality of many of the popular songs may surprise you. Composers from Bob Dylan to John Lennon, from Bruce Springsteen to Prince, have written excellent lyrics and melodies. You will be giving students an opportunity to learn from something important and relevant to them.

I once taught a class of junior high students, some of whom had transistor radios grafted to their ears and would, at any given pause, flick them on. One day, instead of asking everyone to turn their radios off, I suggested that they leave them on. The class was shocked. "Has this teacher flipped her wig?" said the looks they threw me. I asked them to take out paper and pencils.

"Let's *really* listen to five songs. Don't write the name of the song on your paper. Just write Song Number One, Song Number Two, and so forth. Let's listen closely to the songs as if we never heard them before. Listen to the words, the instruments, the rhythms, the mood. As quickly as we can, let's write down any feelings, opinions, ideas, images, or thoughts that come to mind."

The results were remarkable. The kids listened with concentration and intensity. Every single person wrote eagerly. Probably for the first time, a teacher gave credence to some of "their" sounds. Our sharing of their music was a wonderful reference point for future listening experience. *Because I listened to their music with attention and respect, they later were unusually attentive to poetry and music new to them*. Here is a sample from their responses to music.

Listening to Song Number Two

I see a lot of kids hopping around
dancing and the color it makes me
think of is a flashy green . . . blue . . .
yellow and the brightest colors. It
puts me in a mood to walk real fast
through a crowded town looking in the
windows but not really looking at anything.

Joanna

d. Listen to as many as possible of the superlative records available, from Prokofiev's *Peter and the Wolf* to Bill Cosby's comedy albums. Picture what is happening, imagine the story, and enjoy the shared experience. Any one of these listening-for-pure-pleasure moments can launch a celebration of activities if you and your class want to go in that direction.

e. Set aside time each day to read to your class from poetry, fiction, or biography. Be sure that you read something that *you* really like and believe your students will like as well. Don't choose a book that you have no feelings about. Ask your students to listen with their Magical Ears, so they can vividly picture, sense, and understand the reading. Talk about the book—celebrate it.

When we share stories, poems, and legends with children, the value of the experience is immeasurable. Children are wonderful listeners who want and need to hear the stories of the human family. Eudora Welty devotes the first third of her excellent book *One Writer's Beginnings* to Listening. She catches the children's hunger for the stories:

> Long before I wrote stories, I listened for stories. Listening *for* them is something more acute than listening *to* them. I suppose it's an early form of participation in what goes on. Listening children know stories are *there*. When their elders sit and begin, children are just waiting and hoping for one to come out, like a mouse from its hole.[20]

Reading in a monotone or a voice devoid of expression detracts from the experience for both the listeners and the reader. The human voice is an instrument that can be tuned to change tone, pitch, volume, inflection, quality of sounds (clear, husky, shrill, nasal). Practice reading aloud so that you will be able to use your voice in the most interesting ways possible. Of course, your students should enjoy this kind of practice, too.

CAREFUL

f. Listen to paintings; listen to houses; listen to trees. Encourage your class to use their Magical Ears to look at a painting or a photograph and imagine the sounds of it. Children of all ages have listened to seascapes, landscapes, cityscapes, and caught rhythms, colors, dialogues, music, and words. My favorite artists are Monet and Renoir, and I have always shared their paintings with all of my classes. We have listened as carefully to great canvases with our ears as we have looked with our eyes. Tune up your own Magical Ears and imagine the sounds, words, and songs in all the interesting places in the world.

g. One of my favorite experiences, which I have shared with children and adults of *all* ages, is to listen to music with your whole body and soul.

Relax, stretch out, lie down, close your eyes. Imagine that your body has thousands and thousands of tiny pinpricks on it, so small that you can't even see them. Listen to the music and imagine that it must go through all those tiny pinpricks before it can get inside of you. Once it gets through, it flows into all the parts of you and fills you. If you really listen with all your powers of concentration and imagine how the music is trying to get inside of you, after a while it will make you want to move. You might want to move just a hand or

your head. It doesn't matter. You will be filled with the music and *it* will decide how you want to move.

I have played everything from Greek folk music to Copland's *Billy the Kid*, from Native American chants to Rossini's *William Tell Overture*, and have found the response consistently enthusiastic. When I introduced the exercise to preschoolers, I was happily surprised at their excitement. They talked for weeks afterward about the "music coming in and filling us up."

It would seem that even preschoolers are aware of how fragmented our lives have become and are hungry for opportunities to truly give themselves to holistic experiences.

h. Add your own (A.Y.O.) spin-offs.

Share Something from the Five Senses

From the thousands of stimuli we receive each day and usually forget, everyone (including you) chooses one sight, sound, smell, taste, and touch to share with the class orally, in writing, through movement, art, music, or improvisation. This can be part of your sharing time. This daily exercise in gathering sense impressions really affects children's awareness of and increases their appreciation for the ordinary miracles of every day.

Spin-offs
   a. Have the children keep journals in which to jot down their five sense items each day.

I saw a jet plane
I smelled cut grass
I touched the tire on my bike
I tasted chocolate milk
I heard Bruce Springsteen's
new song.

                    Don
                    Grade 5

b. This exercise lends itself to one of the most immediately successful creative writing exercises that I know. Use the word series based on the senses: "I see," "I smell," "I taste," "I touch," "I hear"; add, if you want to, "I feel" or "I know." With your students, write a "sense" poem on the board. Here is a poem written by a fourth-grade class on a lovely spring day.

Tuesday in May

We see robins hopping in the grass.
We smell tulips.
We taste lemonade.
We touch the leaves on branches.
We hear birds chirping and the ice-cream truck ringing its bell.
We feel warm and happy.

c. Write individual sense poems. Use them as a source for oral, choral, or silent reading, creative dramatics, movement, and art projects.

d. Each day write five different sense impressions on five slips of paper and deposit them in shoeboxes marked Sights, Sounds, Smells, Tastes, and Touches. Use them as resource material for numerous follow-up activities.

Once a week, or whenever you want to, empty the slips of paper out of one of the shoeboxes and have the children sit around and look at, for example, all the *sounds* they listened to and gathered over the last week or two. They may choose any one of the sounds they want to illustrate or write about. Or the class can write a group poem composed of their favorite sounds from the shoebox or design a bulletin board of pictures and sounds under the heading "Last Week We Heard" or "Have you heard."

e. The children can cut out or draw pictures of their different sense images and deposit them in shoeboxes for future activities, such as a *sound picture*— a collage in which everything evokes a sound.

f. Take turns telling about or showing your different sights, sounds, smells, tastes, touches. Tape the sharing or write the words on the board as they are said. People are always amazed at the number of words they share in such a short time. After a while, being alert to what is around you will become a habit for you and for your students.

g. Add your own (A.Y.O.) spin-offs.

Correlate Listening with All Areas of the Curriculum

If you add the dimension of listening to whatever subject you are studying or discussing, learning will be enriched and imagination and appreciation will be developed. For example, if you are discussing *winter*, one of the subtopics of your focus could be "Let's stop for a few minutes and *listen* to winter. Imagine the sounds of winter. What winter sounds could we record on our magical tape recorder?" This is a time for listening, imagining, and quiet sharing.

Spin-offs
   a. Share photos or paintings as inspiration for listening.
   b. Take a winter walk and listen to winter sounds.
   c. Listen to familiar music like "Frosty, the Snowman" or "Rudolph, the Red-Nosed Reindeer" or unfamiliar "winter" mood music like *The Planets* by Holst.
   d. Listen to stories like "The Snow Queen" by Hans Christian Andersen or "The Snowy Day" by Ezra Jack Keats.
   e. Listen to poetry like "Stopping by the Woods on a Snowy Evening" by Robert Frost.
   f. Explore the feeling of winter by expressing words such as *melting, chunky, crunchy, quiet, deep, cold,* and *hard* through movement.
   g. The students' journals could include lists of winter words. Here is a page from Tommy's journal.

I Hear Winter Sounds

snow melting	snow balls hit cars
ice cracking	branches crackle
ice-skate blades cutting the ice	tires spinning
ski swoosh	snow tapping on the roof
clump clump in hard snow	wind blowing through the trees
snow balls whiz	

   h. If the dimension of listening is included in all curriculums and classroom areas, you will see a growth of fluency and comprehension in oral and written language, as well as a deepening awareness and appreciation of the miracle of everyday life, demonstrated by the children in your class. *Take time out to listen with them to the sounds of*

Events	*Places*	*Feelings*
circuses	jungles	sadness
state fairs	deserts	happiness
football games	rivers	anger
festivals	cities	jealousy
parades	farms	
historical events (like	playgrounds	*Weather*
the Westward Journey)	countries	hurricanes
	houses	thunderstorms
	indoors	blizzards
	outdoors	tornadoes

People	Holidays	Times
Native Americans	Thanksgiving	early morning
pioneers	Christmas	midnight
cowboys	Chanukah	dusk
miners	Cinco de Mayo	noon
fire fighters	Fourth of July	
construction workers	Halloween	
factory workers	Kwanza	
old people		
babies		

i. Expressing personal feelings in original and effective ways is a difficult challenge. So many of our old, traditional words have been devalued, overused, and misused. Often we find ourselves using trite phrases to shape our deepest feelings. Translating feelings into the senses is an effective way to grapple with these real but evasive existential items. If we made a movie about happiness, what sounds would we tape for the background of the movie? Or what do you hear when you think of anger?

j. Add your own (A.Y.O.) spin-offs.

How Do I Know These Methods Are Working?

We want to know, we *need* to know, if the experiences we offer our students succeed. If not, where did we lose the idea? the kids? Tuned-in teachers are constantly evaluating. It's a continuous process built into the *doing*. But we still need to take a few minutes to sit back, look at a whole experience, and learn something from it about our effectiveness.

Formal evaluation is always a difficult problem. I have taught in schools where more effort went into hammering out evaluation methods for a program than went toward the program itself. The program bombed, but the evaluation was terrific!

In keeping with a spirit of simplicity and directness, I suggest the following methods to aid you in honestly evaluating your activities in listening with awareness, appreciation, and enjoyment.

Use Your Eyes and Ears

Be aware of and alert to what is going on in your class at all times. Be WITH your students. Look at them. See them! *Listen* to them. Be sensitive to their expressions, moods, reactions, verbal and nonverbal messages. (If the whole class is yawning, stretching, and sitting dazed and detached during a listening time, you shouldn't need more complicated methods of investigation to conclude that the activity is falling short of success.) Be keen and honest. Keep a place in your plan book or journal for your observations of each child. Or write notes to yourself to answer some of the following questions.

Checklist for the Class

1. Did your students listen with interest and courtesy?
2. Did they participate with enjoyment and involvement in the listening and the activities accompanying the listening?
3. Did you see evidence of their positive responses in daily sharing of new words, sounds, and sense-awareness; interest in follow-up activities; desire to have more activities in which listening is the basic component; willingness to initiate their own projects?
4. Which areas did the children find least interesting?

Checklist for Yourself

1. Did I pace the experience according to my students' needs? Was it too slow? Too rushed? Did I lose them because I went too far with it? (Timing is very important.)
2. Did everyone in the class demonstrate interest and involvement?
3. Was I aware of the children who did *not* respond favorably?
4. What extra efforts did I make to involve those children and elicit their feelings and ideas? (Draw a circle that takes them in.)
5. Would I use this activity again the same way?
6. How would I change it to make it better?

Let us move on to our second category of listening goals.

QUESTION: What do I want my students to learn?

ANSWER: I want my students to learn to listen for information, directions, and main ideas, to comprehend sequences, and to discriminate between different words and sounds.

Listening Activities   II

How many times have you asked directions at a service station, listened to the person giving them to you, then promptly forgot them even before you drove out of the station?

How many times have you purchased something new and then, as the salesperson explained how to work it, blanked out and had to have all the instructions repeated?

If you want to witness extraordinary listening, watch a dance rehearsal during which the choreographer is directing dancers in complicated, intricate patterns. You will see how quickly the dancers comprehend the instructions. Observe how rarely they ask the choreographer to repeat. Notice how they immediately translate the directions into movement, demonstrating a virtuosity of minds and bodies.

If you want to witness extraordinary listening, observe a football team listening intently to the coach. As moves and combinations are explained, every eye and ear is focused on the speaker.

Your students are very interested in dancers and athletes, in easily recognized people who have trained themselves to concentrate, pay attention, comprehend—*listen!* Talk to your class about such examples of good listening. Explore other role models for good listening. Fire fighters learning their work? Doctors listening to an explanation of a new life-saving medication or procedure? Would you want a fire fighter who hadn't been a good listener to come to your rescue? Would you feel confident with a doctor who hadn't listened carefully to the lecture about the new procedure?

The school day is filled with directions and instructions. Whether the activity is a crafts project or a fire-drill procedure, it is important for children to listen to the words spoken, comprehend their meaning, and put them into action. Enjoyable ways to teach those listening skills are so numerous that we will have room for only a sampling—just enough for you to launch out on your own even as you read.

Directions

Always begin with simple directions. For many young children, a one- or two-step direction is more than enough to start with. "Bob, will you take this ruler and put it on the back table, please" is the type of functional direction that enables children to meet with immediate success.

You can turn this kind of direction-giving into a game in which children are asked to find something in the classroom that is a particular color or shape and bring it to the front of the room. After the items are gathered successfully, ask different children to put them back.

Colors, numbers, shapes, and letters are all good materials for these very simple direction-following games.

Movement Instructions

These suggestions can be related to any subject area or any aspect of the school day, can take from two minutes to ten minutes, can be sprinkled as often during the week as you wish, and are successful with *all* children of all academic abilities. They liven the scene and can be used when you need a change of pace. Here are examples of the many types of movement instructions possible. These are not necessarily related—try to imagine them in their various contexts.

Anyone wearing tennis shoes, clap your hands.

If you are wearing the color blue, tap your desk three times.

If you saw "Sesame Street" on television yesterday, touch your knees.

People whose first name begins with the letter "L" please stand up and blink your eyes.

Further exercise your students' bodies by giving them familiar exercise instructions, such as "stand up" or "touch your shoulders." Or try some distinctive variations, such as "put your thumb on your nose" or "tap your head."

Challenge the kids with unusual movement instructions that make them think. Label the sides of the room north, south, east, and west, and ask the children to face west and jump five times or to walk to the east. Other instructions that require perception and also entail a reward are "If you have something on your face that rhymes with 'toes,' point to it, and then you may get ready for recess."

Prepositions are excellent as movement instructions for listening comprehension. The children can clearly show "over," "under," "near," "far."

Attendance-taking Listening Exercises

Start the day with your ear to the ground! Begin with the importance of listening by enjoying some of these attendance-taking variations.

Saying Favorites   Tell the children to listen to a special question. Then, when you call their names for attendance, they are to answer it. For example, "When I call your name today, tell us your favorite food. 'Brett.' "

Brett answers, "Hot dogs."

Other favorites are TV programs, musical groups, numbers, colors, animals, holidays, places, books, clothes, words.

As often as possible, jot down the children's responses. Now you have material for reading, writing, graphing, moving, and painting.

Our Favorite Animals

Seth: snakes
Zee: zebras
Elaine: cats
Jim: elephants

A variation on this attendance-taking activity is to ask the class, after all have responded, to gather the ideas they heard as you write them—or have the children write them—on the board. This trains the children not only to listen but to remember.

The information is valuable because it can spin off into many areas: Math ("How many people chose 'cats'? Let's graph our responses. Let's consider it a survey and do percentages."); Art ("Here's a large sheet of paper taped to the wall. Before this day is over, please add your favorite animal to it."). Use the information as a source for writing, art, and movement activities.

Moving Parts   "We aren't just interested in whether a person with your name is present. We also want to know if all your moving parts are oiled up, strong, muscley, and ready to begin a new day!"

Take attendance of different parts of the body. Everyone must listen carefully as a specific part of the body is called. As soon as the children hear the mentioned part, they must move it, shake it, blink it, bend it. Here's an example:

Eyes. Blink 'em.

Nose. Wiggle it.

Shoulders. Shrug. Up, down. Forward. Back.

All the way from nose to toes.

Now we're really present. All the parts of ourselves and our whole selves!

Accompany the exercise with drum, tambourine, or clapping, or with music that has a steady beat.

A delightful continuation of this is to ask the kids to

Move everything.

Move nothing.

Move one part of you. Two parts. Three.

This is especially satisfying for children with physical handicaps. By your suggesting parts of their bodies that are functioning, that can move, they are encouraged to feel more ABLE than disabled.

Songs, Games, Chants

Children already have so much material in their knapsacks that helps them follow directions and learn sequences. Draw from this wealth of familiar ideas and go beyond it. Expand and add to it. Some favorites are

Simon Says

Farmer in the Dell

Hokey Pokey

Red Light, Green Light

Mother, May I? or Giant Steps

Follow the Leader

London Bridge

Here We Go Loop di Loo

Found a Peanut

Call and response songs

Simple folk dances

Clarissa, age five and a half, was sitting with a group of children. She looked up, spotted a wasp's nest, and immediately sang a variation of "Have You Ever Seen a Lassie?" Clarissa sang, "Have you ever heard a wasp's nest go bzzz bzzz bzzz . . . ?"

The rest of the kids were delighted and joined the game. The participation and listening levels were amazing. In a few minutes, led by Clarissa, the kids had composed a 21-stanza song which became an instant favorite. Some of the stanzas:

Have you ever heard a robin's nest go tweet tweet tweet . . . ?
Have you ever heard a mouse hole go squeak squeak squeak . . . ?
Have you ever heard a frog swamp go ribbet ribbet ribbet . . . ?
Have you ever heard a butterfly's cocoon go whooosh whooosh . . . ?
Have you ever heard a hamster cage go chewy chewy chewy chewy . . . ?

and finally

Have you ever heard a person's house go ha ha ha ha ha . . . ?

You can see the value of encouraging the children to improvise songs, games, and chants. It didn't surprise me that the very same children whom classroom teachers complained about by citing their inattentiveness memorized *every stanza* of Clarissa's song and sang it every day.

CAREFUL

Don't choose any dance, game, or song in which the technical directions are so rigid and complicated that the fun goes out of the experience. If a right foot is called for and a child lands on his left, do not humiliate the child or stop the dance to correct. *Never single out a child!*

An Oral Scavenger Hunt

Divide the class into small groups. Tell them you are going to give them the list of items verbally. They must be fantastic listeners. You will only tell the list once and they must remember as many items as possible. Give them no longer than ten minutes to gather the items. Encourage the groups to work together and pool their resources. Instead of giving prizes to the first team, celebrate the findings of all the teams as together you share the items.

Some indoor items kids like to find are

a piece of paper with three boys' signatures

a piece of paper with three girls' signatures

something colorful (give them specific color or the general direction)

something with a number

a circle-, square-, triangle-, or oval-shaped idea or object

Some outdoor items are

a sign of autumn, spring, winter, or summer

a twig in the shape of a letter or number

pebbles

a sample of earth

After all the items are checked and shared and you have talked about the value of listening carefully, of thinking, of working together, celebrate the successful hunt with free time, a special story, a record, game, song, or project.

Telephone Messages

Use two toy phones if you have them; otherwise pantomime telephoning. One child is the caller; another child is the answerer who must respond (improvise, pantomime, use dialogue or action) to the caller's message.

For older children, a shoebox full of messages suggested by the students adds to the fun. For younger children, the message may be whispered into the caller's ear by the teacher or another student. *All the messages must be directed toward some action as response*. This is especially effective with small groups. Here are some sample messages:

Would you please see if my kitten is on your front porch?

I just ran out of eggs and sugar. Can I borrow two eggs and a cup of sugar?

We didn't get our paper today. Could you check your paper and find out what movies are on television tonight?

I think I see smoke coming out of your kitchen window. You'd better go look and then call the fire department!

Catch a Train, Bus, Plane

Transportation is a popular unit of study. A visit to a bus terminal or airport is a valuable experience because it provides materials for all the subject areas— geography, math, science, language arts, and human relations. Students can witness firsthand the need for listening and following directions as well as the importance of comprehension and clear thinking as they observe people going in many directions to reach their destinations.

Use actual bus, airplane, or train schedules or make your own schedules using places you are studying in social studies; for younger children, use "tickets" of different colors and letters. Designate certain areas of the room as gates or tracks.

Hand out a ticket to each child. (If you want to correlate this with math, have everyone "buy" a ticket to one of a variety of destinations.) Have the children pretend that they are in a terminal waiting room, reading or dozing or talking quietly to a friend. They must be ready to listen carefully when the announcer calls off destinations and departure times and places. When they hear their city and track or gate called, they must move quickly to it, ready for whatever you have in store for them, which might be something like this: Tell the people at Gate 1 that "Due to mechanical difficulties, this plane won't leave on time. Those of you going to Los Angeles via Chicago, please go to Gate 3. Those of you going to Dallas via Chicago, please go to Gate 1."

Improvise a scene in which unattentive listeners miss their call and don't make their connections. People learn as much from observing mistakes (but no one is humiliated because the improvisation is agreed on by the class and acted out by volunteers) as from watching a procedure progress without a hitch.

Discuss the importance of listening and following directions.

Movement Sequences

Children of all ages enjoy themselves and gain self-confidence when they decide on sequences of movement and successfully carry them out. This kind of activity can be correlated with all subject areas or introduced as a fun challenge by itself. The sequence is *plan, listen, remember, move.*

Here is a sequence of movements for clowns that a preschool class worked out, listened to, and performed happily and successfully—all in a very short period of time. *They* decided on the movement. Jangly circus music was a perfect accompaniment.

Clowns
funny walk forward
funny walk backward
fall down
jump up
do a funny trick
walk on tiptoes
spin around
jump five times

You will be amazed at how alert your students are to verbal directions, instructions, or reminders. I like to pretend I'm an announcer as movement suggestions are made. An example:

"Ladies and Gentlemen, you will now see the circus parade of horses. Here they come! What a wonderful sight!"

The children, excellent listeners, immediately turn themselves into circus horses, prancing and trotting.

Imagine the exciting sequences of movement that children can invent, listen to, and follow:

animals

people (cowboys, football players, dancers)

things that change form (tadpoles to frogs, caterpillars to butterflies, seeds to flowers)

events (circus, zoo)

transportation (cars, planes, boats, rockets, trains)

When your students grow very quick at this kind of challenge, reverse the sequences: begin with the last step and work backwards to the first.

Listen and Respond

Countless stories, poems, and songs are filled with specific actions or scenes that lend themselves to illustration, movement, or creative writing. The children should listen carefully, then express what they heard and learned in a variety of ways, by responding, for example, to this: "Think of all of the animals that chased the Gingerbread Boy. How many can you draw?"

Call and Response Songs   Numerous cultures feature folksongs in which each line is repeated. Popular singers like Ella Jenkins have reintroduced such songs to children around the country. Listening is the key! Listen as the line is sung and then echo it.

Many camp songs from your own knapsack may be just perfect for this purpose. Combine improvisation with such call and response songs as

>   Oh, you can't get to heaven
>
>   The prettiest girl I ever saw was sipping cider through a straw
>
>   Kumbaya

for delightful singing–listening–moving activities.

Mental Math

This is another excellent "listen, think, remember, do" exercise for older children. Use no pencils or paper. Clear desks and minds. Slowly and clearly direct the class to follow your directions and arrive at the right answer. Don't make your directions too complicated or let the students worry about the exercise. *Begin with very simple numbers* so that everyone succeeds. Emphasize the fun and challenge, not who wins or loses.

>   Think of the number 5.
>
>   Add 1.
>
>   Multiply by 2.
>
>   Subtract 2.
>
>   Divide by 2.
>
>   What is your answer?

Pictures and Designs

A variety of materials may be used: construction paper; colored cutouts of different shapes, letters, numbers; cardboard cutouts of people, houses, dogs, sun, trees, flowers. The children should use a blank piece of paper as a base. Instruct them to do any number of things with their materials, such as put a tree in the lower right-hand corner of your picture; put a boy in the left-hand corner of your picture; put the sun in the upper left-hand corner of the picture; find a red circle and put it in the middle of your paper, and so on.

After the children have successfully followed the directions, praise their listening abilities; then give them some free time to arrange a picture any way they want. The original, creative pictures should be displayed or shared.

A delightful variation is to use geometric shapes: think of circles as wheels and long, thin strips as tracks, and place them so that a story emerges about a train going cross-country.

Mission Control to Spaceship

Using materials from your scrounge collection, have the children construct an interior portion of a spaceship with dials, buttons, and various technical apparatuses, or designate a space in the room bordered by chairs that will serve as a stage for improvisation. The Mission Control team sets up a similar stage at the opposite end of the room. The Mission Control team members give directions to the Spaceship team. The Spaceship team either pantomimes, improvises, or uses dialogue to follow the directions. Be sure all the kids have turns on both teams and discuss the importance of carefully following directions.

A Puppet Follows Directions

This is an enjoyable listening experience to share with younger children. Use the kind of inexpensive puppet with a button in its base that, when pressed, moves the figure. You will act as the interpreter between the puppet and the class. Introduce the puppet to the children. Explain that the puppet has difficulty following directions and needs help from the class because they have been so successful at following directions.

Have the class decide on a signal, such as clapping their hands very fast. Then explain to the puppet that when the children clap quickly, he should move quickly, and when they clap slowly, he should move slowly. Let the puppet indicate that he understands, but, when he actually tries to do the exercise, he is unable to follow the class's directions. Encourage the class to give him several chances to get it right (they'll be eager to do so). When he does follow the directions, your children will be delighted. Through teaching the puppet, they will understand the importance for themselves of paying attention and following directions.

Another variation of this is to have your puppet follow a stop–go game. When the music plays, everyone moves. When the music stops, everyone stops. The puppet can do the opposite for a while until he understands.

My little furry dog puppet, Snowball, was having trouble following the directions agreed upon by a group of kindergartners. We were really getting impatient with Snowball.

I said, "Kids, we just don't have time to spend on this activity. Snowball will have to practice and practice till he gets it right."

The kids looked dismayed. Boy, Mim sure is mean.

"Well," I thawed, "shall we give Snowball another chance?"

Five-year-old Josh's eyes widened and he pleaded,

"Let's give him a million chances!"

Puppets and kids need a million chances on the road to success! Give them those chances.

Simple Oral Directions

Many fun, easy-to-make projects can be used as the basis for listening and directions exercises. Search through your knapsack and try to remember camp, scout, and club activities you enjoyed which you can share with your class. Help children to *listen carefully*, follow directions, and make various objects.

paper hats	knots
paper airplanes	paper-bag puppets
kites	books
paper flowers	cat's cradle
mobiles	word-picture stories
papier-mâché puppets	potholders

Guess the Sound

Teachers have used tapes successfully in many listening skills activities. If possible, have a tape recorder for use in the classroom. Otherwise you can reproduce the sounds yourself. Tape a series of sounds that are associated with certain places or experiences. Ask the kids to listen to the sounds and try to identify them through discussion, pictures, words, or movement.

Household sounds: vacuum cleaner running, doorbell or telephone ringing, door slamming

Outdoor sounds: car starting, horn honking, fire engine siren wailing

Animal sounds: dog barking, cat meowing, cow mooing, horse neighing

School sounds: bell ringing, children playing, chalk scratching on blackboard

Parade sounds: band marching and playing, people cheering

Spin-offs

a. Six children, one at a time, tape their own voices saying phrases like "Good morning, everybody." The students then listen to the tape and try to identify the speakers in order through pictures, written words, or out loud.

b. Students can help teach their classmates how to pronounce words that begin with special sounds. Each child is given a specific sound, such as *sl*, and he or she tapes words beginning with that sound. The children repeat the words they hear their classmate saying on the tape and, at the same time, read them from a sheet of paper. Vary this exercise by having one word on tape and in the list of words that doesn't begin with *sl*. The children listen to the tape and then circle the incorrect word on the written sheet.

c. Tape musical instrument sounds. This should always *follow* discussion and class activity involving the various musical instruments. Tape the sounds of the instruments studied and have pictures of the instruments on a table. When the children hear the musical sounds, they should pick the pictures in the order they hear the sounds. Older children can put pictures and names of instruments together in the order they hear the sounds. Follow this exercise by asking the kids to draw, pantomime, dance to, write about, or play their favorite instrument.

d. There are many ways to create an alphabet book, but by using a tape recorder you can relate the exercise to listening. Two children work together as a team. Each makes up an original list of alphabet words, such as "A is for apple," "B is for banana," and records it. Then, with a list of alphabet letters in hand, each child listens to his or her partner's recording and writes the words next to the corresponding letters.

e. On ten separate cards, the students list the class' ten favorite things in a particular category, such as different kinds of food. Then they record their lists individually, pronouncing each item clearly. For variation, they can pretend to be a disc jockey or a consumer advocate, or use any other voice they choose. The class listens to each student's recording and arranges the cards in the order in which the words are announced.

f. Gathering sounds is an activity that should last the whole school year. Set aside a few cassettes for background sounds of many kinds, including original sounds the children tape themselves. Use them in many ways; correlate them with puppet shows, creative dramatics, choral reading, creative writing, and art.

Listen for Special Sounds and Words

To reinforce any auditory discrimination exercise, ask your students to listen for a specific word and give an agreed-on signal when they hear what they are listening for. These few suggestions will give you an idea of the variety of activities possible.

> When you hear a word that is an animal, clap your hands.
>
> When you hear a word that doesn't rhyme, tap your pencil.
>
> Make cutouts illustrating characters of a story. When that character is mentioned, stand up and show the cutout.
>
> Listen to different parts of a story. When that part is read, stand up and act it out.
>
> Make original sounds in response to different words in stories.
>
> Join in reciting the repeating line or poem in a story.

When children know ahead of time that they are listening for something specific—something they recognize, like the different musical themes in *Peter and the Wolf* or the clues to the fantastic mystery of *The Westing Game* by Ellen Raskin—they are incredibly alert and responsive.

Jokes and riddles are excellent materials for listening experiences. See how quickly children "get it" as they immediately pass on their newly discovered gem to others.

Sound Shakers

Use small orange juice cans, plastic medicine bottles, cardboard containers, bandage boxes, or tobacco tins. Make sure that you have an even number of the same kind of container. Cover each container with the same paper so that they are all alike. Fill pairs of containers with the same item, such as dry beans, pebbles, sand, cornflakes, rice, safety pins, paper clips, or thumbtacks. The children shake each container and try to find its mate—the other container that has the same sound. They need to listen carefully to match these different sound shakers.

Clues to a Mystery Object

Every once in a while, choose an object that will serve as a mystery object, preferably one that is interrelated with another subject area. Tell your students early in the morning that you will give them three clues, one at a time, about a mystery object. They must listen very carefully for the clues because you will intersperse them in a quiet way during the course of the morning's activities. After lunch, ask the children if they heard the three clues. Many of them will surprise you with their accuracy in remembering. Write the clues on the board as the children share them. Discuss the possible object the clues might describe. Ask the children to guess what they think the mystery object is from the clues. Write all the guesses on the board. Then bring out the "Mystery Box" that contains the object.

You could have an object that the kids, with their eyes closed, could touch or smell or, if you choose, just introduce it in a more simple way.

Here is an example of three clues given over a period of two hours and told only once to a second-grade class. Almost everyone in the class remembered the three clues even though the children were having trouble listening to other information.

The mystery object is yellow.

The mystery object is soft.

The mystery object is small.

The object turned out to be a little chick, which launched a study of seeds and eggs and how things grow.

CAREFUL

Unless easy, give-and-take discussion and comfortable exchanges of ideas and opinions are integral aspects of your daily classroom life, *none* of the following ideas will be effective. If children do not feel their contributions are of value, if they are not challenged to think, wonder, imagine, and express their own questions, answers, and ideas without tension, competition, or fear, then all techniques are useless.

Open-ended Questions

Earlier we talked about convergent and divergent questions. Be aware of the type of question you ask and the kind of response it evokes. Make your questions divergent—open-ended challenges that stimulate thought and imagination.

If you want to encourage discussion and a hearty exchange of ideas, don't ask

Who were Dorothy's three friends in *The Wizard of Oz?*
What quality did the Cowardly Lion want the Wizard to give him?
Who did Red Riding Hood meet on her way to her grandmother's house?

These questions are conversation stoppers rather than questions that open a topic to further discussion and exploration.

As often as possible, spark thoughtful listening and thinking with divergent questions, such as

What do you think would have happened if Red Riding Hood hadn't met the wolf?
What if the Wizard of Oz was a *real* Wizard?
Why do you think the Cowardly Lion wanted courage?
What if you were the Cowardly Lion? How would *you* feel?

Generalizations and Specifics

Children of all ages enjoy the challenge of discovering the main idea. After discussing "main idea" with your class, explain that you are going to tell them a few sentences (vary the number to suit the language sophistication of the children) to which they should listen very carefully. As soon as you are finished, they must pick one of the sentences as the main idea.

Here is an example of a successful first-grade exercise:

Tippy chews up my sock.
Tippy hides my sister's shoes under the bed.
Tippy is a mischievous puppy.
Tippy eats the cat's food.

The main idea is "Tippy is a mischievous puppy."

Always try to give relevant and interesting sentences. Here is an example of a fifth-grade selection:

California has great forests.
California is bordered on one side by the Pacific Ocean.
Disneyland is in California.
California is a fascinating state with a variety of interesting things to see.
California has many famous athletic teams.
California is the home of Hollywood.

The main idea is "California is a fascinating state with a variety of interesting things to see."

Children also enjoy preparing their own lists to share with the rest of the class. The exercise can be translated into an art project as well by creating posters with different spaces for the various components and with the main idea written across the top of the board or the poster.

When children have many experiences in listening for the main idea along with opportunities for discussion, they are better able to use these thinking skills in reading comprehension, in writing, and in all subject areas.

Telegrams

Students in intermediate grades are each given a small piece of paper and asked to listen to a story. As soon as the narration is completed and the story has been discussed, ask the children to pretend that they are reviewers who must send a telegram about a news story to their newspaper, magazine, or television show. In just one or two sentences, and in a short time period (no more than three or four minutes), they must summarize the story as completely as possible.

Go around the room reading and listening to the reviews and discuss with the class whether most of the reviews conveyed the main idea of the story.

Newscasters: Listen and Tell

Everyone takes a turn at being the newscaster. The teacher spends a few minutes with the newscaster sharing different events of the day, main ideas, and details. Immediately following your private discussion, the newscaster sits in front of the room and broadcasts the headlines of the stories you told. Here is a fourth-grade experience.

Teacher to newscaster: "That was some storm last night. Did you see how flooded High Street was? Our front tree almost blew down! Oh, by the way, did you see that East High won the state basketball championship? They have such a wonderful team. Don't forget, next Monday is a holiday. There will be no school. What are you going to do all day? Hope you plan to have some fun!"

Newscaster to class: "This is your class news report. A huge thunderstorm hit the city last night. East High won the state basketball championship! Monday is a holiday. No school! Those are the headlines of the day."

Listen to the News

Turn on the radio and have the children listen very carefully to a news broadcast for the major stories. When the broadcast is over, discuss the major stories that were reported. Have the class dictate the headlines and write them on the board. If you and your students are consistently interested in the world around you, you will never need to search for listening ideas.

How Do I Know These Methods Are Working?

Probably no area of the language arts curriculum is easier to evaluate than the category of listening. When children are listening for information, for directions, for main ideas, and they are asked *to do something* about what they hear, you can readily observe if they have listened effectively. Because they are asked to do something as a result of their listening experience, the success or failure of the listening lesson is immediately apparent. In your own journal, honestly answer questions like the following.

Checklist for the Class

1. Do my students listen carefully for specific instructions and directions and follow through without major problems?

2. Which students have difficulty following instructions and directions? How can I help them? Are there topics of interest that will especially hold their attention?

3. Do my students comprehend information without asking for numerous explanations and repetitions?

4. To what listening experiences do my students seem to give their greatest attention? their least attention?

5. Do my students ask clarifying questions when necessary to help in following instructions? Do I encourage such questions?

6. Do my students successfully fulfill the purpose of the directions? Which students seem to be having the most trouble in this area? How can I help them?

7. Do my students feel good about their ability to listen and act on their listening?

Checklist for Yourself

1. Do I repeat the same thing over and over until it loses its effectiveness?
2. Do I encourage the fast learners and yet not give equal encouragement to the slow learners? Many teachers unconsciously give enthusiastic praise to the quicker students and give directions-on-top-of-directions in an impatient, negative way to the slower students who are having trouble with the assignment.
3. Do I give directions in such a rigid, uptight way that the fun of the project is minimized?
4. Do I enjoy the experience and feel that my students not only accomplished the goal but gained in good listening as a result?
5. Do I praise my students for their good listening abilities?
6. How did we celebrate their accomplishment?

We conclude with the third category of listening goals.

QUESTION: What do I want my students to learn?

ANSWER: I want my students to learn to listen more critically, to analyze and evaluate what they hear so they will be able to make intelligent decisions.

Listening Activities   III

As you consider the following suggestions for helping children develop critical listening skills, think about your own listening skills. Many of us have unconscious (and sometimes conscious) biases toward people of different sexes, races, cultural or economic backgrounds. A neighbor admitted to me once, "I never believe anyone who has a Southern accent!" As we create learning experiences to help our students develop intelligent listening habits, so let us become more fair and open-minded ourselves.

Listening to Commercials

If American children know one aspect of modern life thoroughly, it is the world of commercials. Many millions of advertising dollars are aimed at children as consumers. Many of the words and phrases filling their knapsacks are coined from commercial advertisements. Listen to various commercials and discuss which products use words that are the most convincing and persuasive. Discuss whether the product actually lives up to its promises. Ask the students to work individually or in groups to make up a product, create a commercial for it using as many persuasive words as possible, and present the commercial to the class, live or on tape. The class listens to the commercial and decides whether to "buy" the product or reject it.

Speeches by Public Figures

With your students, listen to the radio to speeches by and interviews with famous people. Many speeches are recorded on records and tapes. Discuss the language and tone used. Were the speeches factual or editorial? What information was given? What questions were answered? What questions were left unanswered? What conclusions were presented? What did the speaker want the listener to believe? Did the information given justify the conclusions?

Public Service Commercials

During all elections, political campaigns, and special community projects there are one-minute commercials advocating a special event or a political candidate. Try to listen to as many of these as possible with your class and then discuss the information provided during the one minute. Share questions about the information presented. Discuss available resources for further information on the topic or candidate.

During one political campaign, a fifth-grade class was astonished to learn that a particularly appealing candidate, who spoke eloquently and convincingly, had a voting record which showed that he had actually voted against many of the issues he later advocated in his speeches.

Listen to a Hero or Heroine

Ask the kids to choose a figure from American history to support in a class election as "An American Hero or Heroine." The children should present relevant information, justify their claims, try to persuade the rest of the class to vote for their candidate, make posters, prepare speeches and one-minute commercials. Build up to a convention where the final voting takes place.

A variation of this activity is to have the children pretend *they* are the candidates and speak for themselves in the campaign. Their classmates listen, think, talk, and make their choices.

Historical Decisions

History is packed with excellent material for encouraging students to think critically. Open to any page in a history book and imagine the listening, thinking, arguing, and deciding that finally ended in some type of action or in inaction.

With your students, discuss the importance of critical listening in such historical decision-making events as the Boston Tea Party, the American Revolution, the slavery question, exploration of the West, and construction of the railroad across the country. Act out these events and ask the characters pertinent questions that evoke discussion, evaluation, and decision making.

Panel Discussions

Many curriculum areas lend themselves well to panel discussions, question and answer sessions, and decision-making opportunities. A consistent correlation between current events outside the classroom and interests in the classroom should be made. The two worlds should be joined as frequently as possible as they are really one world. It always shocks me to hear of classrooms where current events are never discussed.

Three class experiences in critical listening come to mind as excellent examples of what can be done to integrate current events into the curriculum.

A fifth grade read about the two major political parties trying to choose a city in which to hold their political conventions. The children imagined how the different cities were trying to persuade the political parties to choose them for their conventions. Students volunteered to do research on their favorite cities and present information to a panel (members of the class). The panel listened carefully, asked intelligent questions, and finally decided on two cities for the two political conventions.

Fourth graders read that the city zoo had been given a grant to build a new animal house and that the directors of the zoo were considering different proposals. The fourth graders decided that they would have their own hearing. Committees representing different animals spoke before a panel of the class. The class listened intently as the advocates of favorite animals tried to persuade the panel to use the grant for their animal. Great excitement and interest sparked the activity.

A sixth grade completed a very challenging unit on drugs with improvisations based on discussions and research. They improvised situations in which intelligent listening was of vital importance, such as two children trying to persuade a third child to try a new pill; an older brother or sister trying to get a younger sibling to experiment with acid; three high school pushers trying to convince sixth graders at a party to be cool and try some drugs. The class listened attentively, as did the recipients of the pressure. Questions were asked, ideas were exchanged, and the importance of critical listening was stressed.

Plans / Programs / Projects / Proposals / Procedures

In language-rich environments, where childrens' opinions and ideas are valued and respected, where their contributions to the operations of the class are welcomed, critical listening and thinking skills are continuously being developed.

Students are offered many opportunities to contribute to decision making regarding field trips, schedules, free-time activities, special programs, enrichment projects, and classroom rules and procedures. Working with partners, in small groups, or with the class as a whole, children enjoy numerous experiences in the give-and-take of everyday challenges. They need to listen carefully to options, to alternatives. They need to ask intelligent questions and listen respectfully to the comments of others. When students *know* that they have an important part to play in the success of their group, discipline problems are often minimized and high-level listening, speaking, and critical thinking skills emerge.

Take advantage of the many opportunities inherent in your daily plans to encourage your students' participation.

Listen and End It All

Children listen to a story in which the ending is left out. They suggest ways to end the story based on what they have heard of the story so far. They tell their endings, act them out, draw them, or write them.

Story Characters Come to Life

Tinker Bell says, "If you believe in fairies, clap your hands."

The bad boys try to dissuade Pinocchio from his destination.

The Wizard of Oz tells Dorothy and her friends that they must destroy the witch.

Children can improvise the persuading characters, while the rest of the class listens and decides if they would be influenced. How would the stories end if the characters weren't convincing? If the other characters had said "No!"?

Community Resources

A wonderful Arab proverb reads "Every neighbor is a teacher." Your community is rich in human resources that have a vital role to play in deepening and expanding the learning experiences of your students. Most communities contain a diversity of cultures. Our children need to meet people whose backgrounds may be different from their own.

Invite members of the community who are willing to share occupations, skills, experiences, travels, and hobbies with your class.

Prepare for the visit!

You would be shocked to know how many classroom visitors are greeted with polite indifference. Questions aren't asked. No response is given.

Compare the sad description given above to this memorable incident: I was visiting a class as an Author during Book Week. The minute I walked into that sixth-grade room I was greeted by twenty-seven hands lifted in the air waving large question-mark-shaped papers with questions written on them. Obviously, the children had not only talked about what they wanted to know from the visiting author, but had decided on individual questions and had gone one step further by clearly writing them on their question-mark papers. What a sign of LIFE!

And what excellent listeners! What excellent questions!

"Are all the people in your stories real or did you make them up?"

"Where did you get your ideas?"

"What made you start writing? What got you interested in it?"

The session was charged with active, involved, responsive, critical listening, talking, thinking.

Yes, good manners and courtesy are important in programs involving classroom visitors, but they are minimum requirements. Aren't we all hungry for the excitement of honest interjection? Curious and full of wonder, we want lively, responsive exchanges. We are eager to meet new people, to learn of their lives, to listen to their stories!

Help make that happen with your students.

How Do I Know These Methods Are Working?

After working together on thoughtful, intelligent listening activities and exercises, a fourth grader confessed to his teacher that, for the first time in his life, he had a good discussion with his older brother instead of a fight about something. "I asked him why he wanted to go to the Science Center without me and he told me some reasons. We talked about the reasons and I listened to him and asked him some more questions. After, he said, 'Why don't you come with me to the Center, Louie?' and I did. But that was the only time I ever just quietly asked him *why* he wanted to do something. It worked out real good."

Checklist for the Class

1. Are your students listening more carefully to everything they hear?
2. Are they asking clarifying questions and demonstrating critical thinking?
3. Are they making fewer absolute statements?
4. Are they backing up their beliefs and conclusions with specifics?
5. Are they listening and responding to each other in more intelligent ways?

Checklist for Yourself

1. Am I being too judgmental by injecting my personal opinions or biases into discussions and exchanges before the children express their own?
2. Am I trying to improve my role as a facilitator by asking thoughtful questions, steering children to think out their own opinions and reasons, helping them to discover their own thought processes?
3. Did I notice the children who did not demonstrate any growth in listening and thinking? What am I going to do about the children who never raise their hands to express an opinion, ask a question, or share an idea, or who don't seem interested in listening at all? How can I involve them?

4. How can I encourage all the children in my class to listen to and evaluate what they hear with greater thoughtfulness and intelligence so that they arrive at more sound conclusions?

Walt Whitman wrote, "I think I will do nothing now but listen." What do you hear?

ENDNOTES

[1] Walt Whitman, "Song of Myself," *Modern American Poetry/Modern British Poetry*, combined ed., ed. Louis Untermeyer (New York: Harcourt, 1950) 59.

[2] A. A. Milne, "Tigger Is Unbounced," *The World of Pooh* (New York: Dutton, 1957) 253.

[3] Paul T. Rankin, "The Importance of Listening Ability," *English Journal*, College Edition, 17 (1928): 623-30.

[4] Miriam Wilt, "A Study of Teacher Awareness of Listening as a Factor in Elementary Education," *Journal of Educational Research* 43 (April 1950): 626-36.

[5] Miriam Wilt, "The Teaching of Listening and Why," *Readings in the Language Arts*, ed. Verna Dieckman Anderson (New York: Macmillan, 1964) 50-56.

[6] Albert Cullum, *The Geranium on the Window Sill Just Died But Teacher You Went Right On* (New York: Harlin Quist, 1971) 8.

[7] Alice V. Keliher, "Childhood Education," *ACEJ Journal* (November 1965): 131. An editorial by a noted educator.

[8] David and Elizabeth Russell, "Listening," *Readings in the Language Arts* 45.

[9] Trivett, "The Effect of Training in Listening for Specific Purposes," *Journal of Educational Research* (March 1961): 276-77.

[10] Yvonne Gold, "Teaching Listening? Why Not?" *Elementary English* (March 1975): 421-22. An article of great interest.

[11] S. Lundsteen, *Listening—Its Impact on Reading and Other Language Arts* (Urbana: NCTE/ERIC, 1971).

[12] See P. S. Anderson and D. Lapp, *Language Skills in Elementary Education* (New York: Macmillan, 1979).

[13] Ralph G. Nichols, "What Can Be Done about Listening?" *Readings in the Language Arts* 57-68.

[14] Marlin L. Languis and Lorren L. Stull, "Listening to Children," *Childhood Education* (Nov. 1965): 167-68.

[15] William M. Logan and Virgil G. Logan, *A Dynamic Approach to the Language Arts* (Toronto: McGraw, 1967) 39, 55.

[16] R. Murray Schafer, "Ear Cleaning: Notes for an Experimental Music," *When Words Sing* (Scarborough, Ontario: Berandol Music, 1967).

[17] Jesse Stuart, *To Teach, To Love* (Baltimore: Penguin, 1973) 51.

[18] Eleanor Cameron, *A Room Made of Windows* (New York: Dell, 1971) 10.

[19] Pat Conroy, *The Water Is Wide* (New York: Dell, 1972) 67.

[20] Eudora Welty, *One Writer's Beginnings* (Cambridge: Harvard UP, 1984) 14.

5

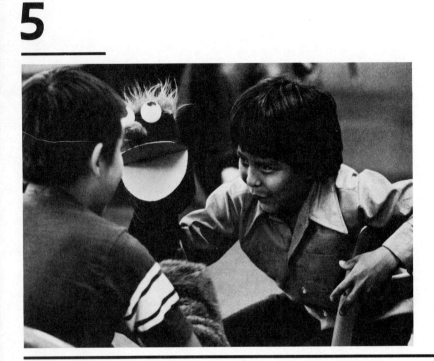

Talking in the Classroom—ssshhh!

The second flame in the universe is the flame of language.
People look for each other with words of fire
and a tongue of fire that stammers
is better than a head full of brains
that is silent.

FROM A CHASSIDIC TALE[1]

Talking with one another is loving one another.

AFRICAN PROVERB

Good News and Bad News

This is an introductory section of opposites. Votes for LIFE or votes for DEATH. Maryruth K. Nivens adopted the ancient symbols of "thumbs up" and "thumbs down" in an article contrasting schools that encourage and affirm to schools that merely "warehouse" children.[2] If none of these familiar ways of expressing joy or dismay works for you, try the old football rally "Yaaaaaay!" or "Boooooo!" as you read along.

Booo or Yaaay?

Jackie is five years old. All last week she was so excited about starting kindergarten that she would hardly eat or sleep. Today, her third day of school, a crestfallen Jackie steps off the bus. "Like a balloon with all the air out," her mother glumly describes her.

What happened to turn an eager, joyful child into a headbent, sorrowful, dejected little person?

"Mommy," Jackie relates her painful experience, "the teacher said that I talk too much. She punished me and made me lie down on the rug that everyone walks on. I don't want to do that." Tears fill her eyes. "Know what else she did, Mommy? She gave everyone a piece of paper and didn't give me one. When I get to be a teacher, I'm not going to give anyone one. Not even fruit cocktail!"

Yaaay or Booo?

Tom Griffin's fifth graders hurry to their classroom every day: they don't want to be late for their "morning meeting," a lively, warm session of going over the day's schedule; sharing personal, school, or world concerns; exchanging ideas. "We call it 'Loose Ends,'" Tom explains. The meeting is marked with courtesy, turn-taking, good listening, and trust.

Thumbs Down or Thumbs Up?

Nivens describes a school that she worked in and that her children attended. The children "were forbidden to talk in the lunchroom. This rule was neither fair nor sensible, and attempts to enforce it created more problems than the rule was supposed to solve."[3]

Good News or Bad News?

A class of sixth graders was buzzing excitedly in small groups, deciding which aspect of Sumerian culture to celebrate and share with the class.

"Time's up!" the teacher announced.

"Can't we have a few more minutes?" the kids pleaded. "We have so many more ideas we didn't finish talking about!"

"Go for it!" the teacher agreed, and they did.

A Vote for Death or a Vote for Life?

The sixth-grade teacher gave out a complicated project, two mimeographed, single-spaced sheets of paper, and a rather terse explanation.

The students were tense. After school, one courageous individual asked the teacher for clarification.

"I don't understand what you want," he ventured.

Sternly, his teacher responded, "If you have to ask, I have to downgrade it already!"

The class worked on the project in frightened silence, each child interpreting it alone. Finally, our more outspoken boy thought he figured it out, and began to work on it with a measure of enthusiasm.

When the projects were returned, his had a very low grade. His teacher said, "You missed the whole point!"

Thumbs Up or Thumbs Down?

Third grader Brett was having trouble "getting" his homework assignment. His mother hovered over him, worried and trying to be helpful at the same time.

Brett calmly reassured her, "Don't worry, Mom. We'll talk about it in school tomorrow and I'll understand it then. That's how we do it."

Good News or Bad News?

Five-year-old Carl attends a "progressive" kindergarten that guarantees parents that their children will read within the year. The rules are very strict. Carl had little to report the first week of school. Finally, he came home with the announcement,

"I met a friend today!"

Ecstatic, his mother asked, "What's his name?"

Carl answered, "I don't know. We're not allowed to talk."

Yaaay or Booo?

As you read this page, thousands and thousands of children are sitting in silent classrooms, praised and rewarded for quiet passivity. They are called "good" children because they make no waves, rock no boats, never disturb class routines with unnecessary questions or opinions. Such stifling of our children is probably one of the most deadly of all sins. Erik Erikson called it "the mutilation of a child's spirit."

A Vote for Death or a Vote for Life?

As you read this page, thousands and thousands of children are learning in language-centered, child-centered rooms stamped with numerous opportunities for a variety of interactions; engaging in one-to-one, small-group, whole-class discussions; enriching their language by *using it;* being actively involved in the plans, programs, and process of their school days. In such classes, you hear the kinds of music Geraldine Lee Susi described:

> I observed teachers and students working together in small groups. I heard laughter. I heard stories of childhood, of dreams, of embarrassing moments, and of imagination all shared and enjoyed. As feelings and past experiences were shared, there was a human element introduced which allowed for a common bonding."[4]

Can We Talk?

Language and thinking are so inextricably intertwined that it is almost impossible to deal with them as separate processes. The basis of all language arts components is thinking. Your language reflects your level of thinking. You need words for your thoughts. You have thoughts that are shaped into words. The two are totally interdependent; they nourish each other. Can you imagine yourself thinking without words? Remy Gourmont considered thinking as but another form of feeling and our thoughts as subvocal speech. From the first chapter of human history, one of the oldest and most universal ways human beings have expressed their thoughts and feelings has been through the spoken word.

> Since the spoken word is so important a component of the language arts curriculum and since facility with oral language is essential to the well-being and success of the individual in our society, how is it possible for children to be taught their language in silent, rigid classrooms? How can children be taught their language by having them keep still?[5]

Ruth Strickland represents the thinking of many of our major educators as she laments, "No development in American Education has been more detrimental to good language growth than the traditional pattern of screwed-down seats arranged in rows so that each child lived and worked in a little island of isolation as completely cut off from the fellowship of his groups as it was possible to make him."[6]

John Goodlad spent eight years studying thirty-eight schools. The result of his research, the book *A Place Called School* (McGraw, 1983), has been widely read and highly regarded. In an interview with *The Instructor* magazine, Goodlad discussed some of his findings:

> We found a flat, neutral ambience, an atmosphere that most students accepted as normal. Many students thought many of their teachers' actions, like asking questions, were not for the purpose of teaching but for the purpose of controlling the class. . . . Chances were 50–50 that when we walked into a classroom, we would find students listening passively or doing seatwork. We had to describe the atmosphere as emotionally flat. . . . We observed consistent and repetitive attention to basic facts and skills. Instruction rarely went beyond the imparting of facts. Back to basics is where we've always been. . . .[7]

But he also found

a high level of interaction between teachers and students in grades one through three. In general, children in the first three grades liked their classroom activities, too. Teachers didn't depend so much on textbooks and they used a wider range of teaching practices. Unfortunately, this variability fell off about fourth grade. . . .[8]

Yes, the physical design of classrooms is a very important factor in the development of children's language. A classroom with permanent, nonmovable furniture often presents an obstacle to the easy interchange of ideas and informal group work so essential to learning oral language. But equally lamentable are the screwed-down minds of those educators who believe in only half of Ecclesiastes' words—"a time for silence and a time for speech"—and who limit children's oral language experiences to talking to the backs of heads or standing, with voices tight and hearts hammering, before a large, impersonal group of faces while their "talks" are graded in a marking book. How can children gain competency in this most essential skill if their experiences in speaking are limited to formal reports and to responding to teachers' convergent questions with monosyllabic answers? How many hundreds of thousands of inarticulate, inhibited, insecure men and women have come out of our schools over the decades, handicapped in personal relationships, blocked in career opportunities, and facing life's challenges with extinguished powers of expression and communication?

Are We the Slow Learners?

Along with listening, oral language has a history of being ignored and passed over in teacher education as well as in school curriculum guides. For many years, it was widely believed that listening and speaking were by-products of instruction in reading and writing and did not need to be emphasized as essential skills in themselves. However, in 1952, the National Council of Teachers of English (NCTE) stated that the English language is an instrument of thought and communication, and, in addition to developing critical thinking abilities, "young people have a need to develop a sense of security in their own use of the language of the civilization in which they are being educated."[9]

The NCTE included in its statement the importance of children learning language "not merely as a medium of communication, but also for the expression of their own thoughts and feelings. Emotional stability frequently comes through creative self-expression. Young people need to learn how to release creatively their pent-up emotions and to express their innermost feelings and perceptions."[10]

In 1963, the Speech Association of America decried the lack of attention given to oral language and noted that in too many schools instruction in speech was represented only in extracurricular activities. In an official document called "The Field of Speech: Its Purpose and Scope in Education," the Speech Association defined educated people as those "capable of transmitting their meanings with accuracy, correctness, and clarity. . . . In the education of such people, knowledge and skill meld inextricably. . . . Human beings cannot avoid being essentially and significantly communicators . . . the arts of communication in speech and language are humanistic. . . ."[11]

Moving from the sixties to the eighties, we find a process of rediscovery. Articles, research, books, symposiums devoted to oral language flourished. Oral language was slowly becoming a major, vital component of the language arts.[12]

David Dillon, the editor of *Language Arts*, one of the journals published by the NCTE, devoted the February 1984 issue to "Talk." Why did he call the issue "Talk" instead of "Oral Language"? He saw Talk as more of a verb than Oral Language. Oral Language conveyed more formal images, such as oral reports, "Show and Tell," and listening exercises. Talk evoked dynamic images of small groups or pairs actively involved in shaping projects or solving problems, cutting across the curriculum, challenging, defining, supporting, questioning, wondering. Professor Dillon explained that Talk suggests more "informal, open-ended tasks for the primary purpose of learning and discovery for self. The emphasis is on meaning-making, transforming new information to make sense of it and bringing to the surface things known only implicitly."[13]

In his introduction to the Talk issue, Professor Dillon expressed his belief that Talk may well be the most powerful learning resource elementary children have at their disposal. He challenged:

> Why have we given it so little attention? Do we take it for granted? Do we consider it too ephemeral to investigate? Do we doubt its potential? Do we resist the alternative teaching model implied by its use?[14]

You have probably guessed the depth of my feelings about this topic. I am with the poet Pablo Neruda, who said, "For human beings, not to speak is to die."[15]

In less dramatic terms, Professor Anthony Adams, former chairman of the National Association for the Teaching of English and a lecturer at the University of Cambridge, England, was asked, "What happens if learners are limited or prohibited in the use of self-expressive talk?"

He answered, "There is a lot of evidence from sociolinguistics to support the view that for many children that is the end of learning. They switch off."[16]

What do you think? What are your beliefs, commitments, attitudes? Remember—as you believe, so you teach.

It's Your Turn

What were you taught about oral language, about talking, throughout your school years? Were you taught that "silence is golden"? That children should be "seen and not heard"? That you would get straight A's as long as you kept quiet? Or were you taught that your words were important, your ideas of value, and your questions and opinions worthy of respect and consideration? *Were you encouraged to speak your language?*

[handwritten margin notes: well-being, security, self-image; speak easily & fluently; express themselves; confident; greater success; spoken words most effective barometers of internal world]

No area of the language arts curriculum is more closely linked to your sense of well-being, security, emotional stability, and self-image than oral language. Many linguists now consider it "the" language and place it on a higher scale of value than the written word. Our time in history has even often been described as the "Era of the Spoken Word." Your family relationships, friendships, education and career opportunities depend greatly on the words you speak and the manner in which you communicate those words. How often have you based your impressions of other people on their spoken words? Individuals who speak easily and fluently, who express themselves with confidence in any social situation, have a greater chance for success in our society than do individuals whose words catch in their throats, whose palms sweat at the thought of speaking to anyone outside of their immediate families, whose minds blank when asked questions, and whose lack of self-worth is demonstrated by constricted, nervous stammers that distort their voices and convey negative vibrations to others. Your spoken words are probably the most accurate, effective barometers of the climate and weather of your internal world. In our society speaking and listening are considered so essential to successful communication and everyday living that some prominent educators rate those components as even more important than the ability to read. Children who score low in oral language skills generally tend to score low in achievement in reading and writing as well. Researchers have verified that children's awareness of themselves as individuals and worthy human beings emerges in direct relation to their ability to express themselves.[17]

When children are asked to share their feelings about successful teachers and teaching "methods," their responses are very homogeneous. Ask the children! You'll find that almost all of them highlight the fact that there are times for talking, for discussions, questions, and kidding around in every school day. Mary H. Mosley and Paul J. Smith asked hundreds of students for their opinions about successful learning experiences. They found five factors most often mentioned by the students (all of them liberally sprinkled with comments about oral language):

1. clear, complete explanations and concrete examples (encourages questions);
2. positive, relaxed learning environment (fun, jokes, freedom to talk);
3. individualized instruction (we are all different);
4. adequate academic language time (help students to learn);
5. motivation and interest (teacher is excited about the subject).[18]

The choice is yours. Will you choose as your role model Lisha and Tracy's second-grade teacher, who doesn't permit talking in school—"not even a whisper, not even one word, except at recess"?

"Oh," I asked, "was recess fun today?"

"We didn't get recess," Tracy confessed.

"We were punished," added Lisha.

"Why?"

"Some kids talked. Not even loud. Hardly at all. Now we don't get recess for two days."

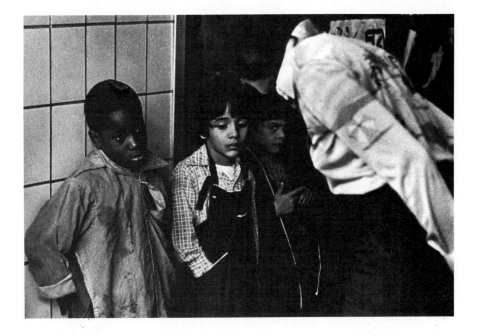

"Do you ever get to talk about stories or ideas?"

"NEVER! Our teacher doesn't go for that. She doesn't like to talk about things."

Or will you be inspired by Ronni Hochman, who believes that all education is special and shares her love of learning with her Special Ed middle-school kids?

> From the very beginning, from the day they walk into my room, the primary goal is to help them feel safe and free to speak and share without put-downs. Our rule is "Respect Each Other in Thought, Word, and Deed." We laugh every day but never *at* anyone, only *with*. We're constantly talking, kidding, joking, checking in on each other to see how we're feeling, how we're doing. You've got to ask the right questions so you get good, honest, real answers, not "uh." In my class, kids talk with each other, teach each other (peer tutoring), work with each other on projects, books, hobbies, lessons. Talking is paired with all instruction, in all subjects. It goes hand in hand with visual presentations. Listen—we have a great time!"

Thumbs up? Thumbs down? Good news? Bad news? A vote for Death or for Life?

Some Points to Remember

Good! You chose LIFE. Now, before we plunge into the pool of practical, 99 44/100 percent pure, successful ways to encourage TALK in your classroom, here are a few items that need extra highlighting.

You Are So Important!

Begin with yourself. Your part in encouraging free, natural, and easy communication in your room is pivotal, is vital. You are a collaborator, a participant, a sensitive listener, a mediator, a prompter, a helper, a questioner, an audience, a lecturer, a partner. You are more! You are a role model, demonstrating by your behavior positive, intelligent, aware habits of oral language, of talking.

Your response to the children's utterances affects the kind of learning that takes place in your room. Douglas Barnes studied these teacher–student interactions and found that nonjudgmental responses promote more learning. Teachers who welcome and accept students' ideas, clarify understandings, reflect or paraphrase concepts, and expand on the words of others encourage a free flow of communication.[19]

Do you take "the pause that refreshes"? Researchers have found that if you pause after asking a question, giving children a little more time to think about their responses, more language is encouraged and is of a higher quality. Teachers who pause again after the children's responses evoke further responses than those who have an immediate word of closure.

In language-rich, positive classes children have teachers who set up dialogues so that learning happens through interaction with others. Will you help that happen in your classroom?

Test Your Awareness Quotient

Your tone of voice, your pace, your facial expression, and your speech habits all contribute to the communication process. Do you speak so rapidly that it's hard to follow you? Slow down! Do you speak so slowly that you lose people in between words? Accelerate! Do you speak in a monotone? Is your pitch too high? Is your voice unconsciously scolding? Do you repeat the same word or phrase continually without even realizing it? One teacher continually uses "now then" in all of her conversations. Her class is so conscious of that repetition that they hardly listen to what she is saying.

What will your students hear when you speak? Are you aware of how you ask questions and what questions you ask? Are they usually closed questions with only right or wrong answers possible, such as "How much is 4 and 4? What's the capital of New York? What is the longest river in Africa?" Or are they open-ended, open-minded questions, such as "What do you think would have happened if Paul Revere had given the wrong message to the townspeople? How do you think President Lincoln felt when the South seceded from the Union?" Do your questions stimulate thought, wonder, imagination, explanation, conversation, expansion of ideas or do they usually end with a demand for the right answer: Albany is the capital of New York (2 points).

1. Do you consider free and natural speech as part of the human inheritance—as a gift that all humans are blessed with?
2. Do you feel comfortable and natural in situations where oral language is important?

3. Do you enjoy participating in conversations? In discussions?

4. Do you feel free to share your ideas, opinions, and questions with others?

5. Is your voice pleasant to listen to?

6. Are your sentences fluent? Is your language clear?

7. Do you think that oral language is an important component of the language arts curriculum and that all children must have many opportunities to learn and enjoy their language through experiences with the spoken word?

8. Are you interested in what children have to say?

9. Are you willing to become more aware of your own speech habits so that your communication with your students will not be hampered by unconscious obstacles? (I am still working on my Big Three habits: interrupting, interjecting, and anticipating!)

10. Do you see the connection between thinking and talking?

11. Do you enjoy talking with children?

Accept and Respect Your Students

Remember that children have been talking for almost all of their lives. They already have speech habits, grammatical structures, large vocabularies, and basic understandings of the language they have learned in their immediate environments. Many linguists believe that six-year-old children have grasped the fundamental structure of their language and speech patterns as well as they ever will, except for some minor changes that will be smoothed out through the educational process.

Your students may not speak the standard, more widely accepted English that would ease their way through the myriad social, school, and work situations ahead of them. Young children are so accustomed to their own speech sounds, expressions, mannerisms, and idiosyncracies that they don't even question them as correct or incorrect. Their language *is* their language. Linguists urge teachers to use the term "nonstandard" rather than the supercilious-sounding "substandard" for language that differs from the more generally accepted, informal, standard English. The most important steps you must take are to *accept the children and their language and make sincere attempts to understand their vocabularies, pronunciations, and idioms* which may be viewed as a language different from your own.[20] Consequently, your attempts to introduce your students to a more standardized English can be compared to introducing them to a foreign language!

CAREFUL

Language is very personal. If your language were criticized, wouldn't you feel humiliated and avoid the person who had found fault with you? Just as you would rather be corrected gently, quietly, and individually than in front of everyone in an authoritarian manner, so your students will be more responsive to correction or suggestions for language improvement if they are made in private.

Better still, don't TELL them—SHOW them by your example. Repeat or rephrase the child's words in more standardized English. For example,

Laura tells her teacher, "We don't go nowhere on Saturdays."

The teacher responds, "You don't go anywhere? Are Saturdays saved for something special?"

Betsy Dill, a teacher in an open classroom, said, "You must love the children sincerely and let them know it. They must know that you really trust them—without reservations—before they can trust themselves and feel confident that they can attempt new things. It is important that children know that even if they try something and don't do it well you still love them—and that how you feel about them doesn't hinge on what kind of work they do or what they accomplish. You love them because they are who they are."

Statistics tell the story. You will probably have a high percentage of children in your class who come from broken homes. Some of them may have a constellation of step families and relationships. Your language reflects your sensitivity to the situations of the children. We can no longer glibly announce, "Give this notice to your mother or father" or "I want your mother or father to sign this paper." The painful facts are that many of our children don't live with both parents and that the reminder of it is often very stressful. It's easy to learn to say "Please have one of the grown-ups at home sign this" or "We need permission from whomever is in charge at home for you to go on our field trip."

Our language reflects our caring and love for the children.

Some Words about Motivation

Let us assume that you have established a relaxed, informal atmosphere in which your children feel free to express themselves without fear of criticism or punishment. Let us further assume that one of your language goals is to help them develop an easy command of generally acceptable language because you know that poor speech habits, limited vocabularies, or drastic departures from commonly accepted usage can contribute to the insecurity and loss of confidence of anyone, no matter what their age.[21]

Suppose, then, that there are children in your class who obviously need a great deal of help with their language if it is to be raised to a more socially acceptable level. *Why should your students want to change their basic language*? Take the time to think about this question. Your answers are important to the philosophical framework within which you will be teaching each day. Why do you think Eliza Doolittle agreed to an experiment in linguistic metamorphosis? Do you think her dreams of being a "lady" and living a more cultured, luxurious life had anything to do with it? What was her motivation? Why should a child who says, "Me and him ain't gonna get no bus tickets!" or "Cwiff, did you hear the cwown?" want to improve those obviously in-need-of-improvement speech habits? Remember, you are not a speech therapist and will not be expected to deal with serious speech problems. But many speech problems can be corrected within a relationship of encouragement, positive reinforcement, reassurance, acceptance, and example.

Thomas R. McDaniel writes eloquently of the teacher's role in motivation. He uses terms like "inviting success" and "having high expectations." Interaction is the key. He asks you to remember that your interactions and transactions with students are central to successful lessons. Motivating teachers enjoy discussions, use humor, draw on personal experience, keep open minds, invite students to teach the teacher, keep a lively pace, and demonstrate genuine enthusiasm. The questions asked by such teachers give children every opportunity possible to show what they know, think, and value.

Professor McDaniel, who is the director of graduate education programs at Converse College, Spartanburg, South Carolina, offers this questionnaire.[22] How do YOU rate?

How Good a Motivator Are You?

Check your motivational practices by rating yourself on the questions below. Add your totals in each column. Score yourself as follows: 90–100, excellent; 80–90, good; 70–80, fair; below 70, poor.

	Usually (4 points)	Sometimes (2 points)	Never (0 points)
1. I believe my students are competent and trustworthy.			
2. I avoid labeling students.			
3. I avoid sarcasm, put-downs, and ridicule of students.			
4. I send explicit invitations to succeed.			
5. I listen to what my students really say.			
6. I let students know they are missed.			
7. I make good use of student experts in the class.			
8. I use heterogeneous groups to build interdependence.			
9. I teach leadership and communication skills.			
10. I avoid overemphasis on competition, rewards, and winning.			
11. I help groups evaluate their effectiveness in group *process*.			
12. I give equal time, attention, and support to low-ability students.			
13. I communicate high expectations to my students.			
14. I focus on future success rather than past failures.			
15. I look for what is positive in student work and behavior.			
16. I set and communicate clear goals for instruction.			
17. I use well-designed, thought-provoking questions to stimulate readiness.			
18. I use objects as "focusing events" to stimulate interest.			
19. I use brainstorming to stimulate interest before beginning a lesson.			
20. I use set induction activities that connect a present experience to a lesson concept.			
21. I ask low-risk, open-ended questions.			
22. I wait three to five seconds after asking a divergent question.			
23. I suspend judgment and redirect a question to get multiple responses.			

(continued)

24. I paraphrase and clarify responses instead of judging and praising.

25. I personalize learning.

Despite the fact that Mel Brooks, in his popular comedy album *The Two-Thousand-Year-Old Man*, describes fear as the oldest, most widely used form of transportation, you know that other, more positive emotions contribute to motivation. I truly believe that, with all of our marvelous teaching methods, techniques, devices, and materials, teachers miss the boat with many children because they fail to form the mutual relationships sparked with caring and affection that are essential to motivate children. Dip into your own knapsack and rediscover the times in your life when you were most motivated to learn, to grow, to improve. I am willing to bet that in many of those moments, there was a person in your life who believed in you, cared about you, and inspired you.

I saw this sentence tacked to a bulletin board in a teachers' lounge. It accurately and effectively describes the teacher–child relationship: "The best way to send an idea is to wrap it up in a person." You can be that person for your students!

As you begin the activities section of this chapter, remember and heed the words of the Little Prince:

"What a queer planet!" he thought. "It is altogether dry, and altogether pointed, and altogether harsh and forbidding. And the people have no imagination. They repeat whatever one says to them. On my planet I had a flower; she was always the first to speak. . . ."[23]

What kind of planet will you create with your students?

QUESTION: What do I want my students to learn?
ANSWER: I want my students to learn to express themselves easily, clearly, and effectively in all the many situations that involve oral language. I want my students to develop confidence and fluency as they enjoy many diverse experiences that encourage the free and easy flow of talk, of language interaction.

Language Activities

You Are a Major Language Experience

Ellen Clark senses that one of her fifth graders is troubled. She takes him aside and they talk together for a few minutes. The boy is plagued with family problems. At the end of the day he says, "You know, Ms. Clark, I never really had anyone talk to me like a person before."

Sister Iona, teaching first graders through the Workshop Way, says happily, "We're talking almost all day! Questioning, sharing, commenting, discovering. The teacher must constantly show interest, prod, poke, respond, initiate, and provide many examples of using language all the time!"[24]

Rodger Gerhardstein, who teaches older students, uses ideas that are valuable for teaching all ages. He keeps "attuned to what my students are into. What television do they watch? What books are they reading? What movies have they seen? What's happening with them? I let them know that I appreciate what they are about. If you aren't interested in what your students are doing, they aren't ever going to really talk to you!"

Roger Klein, an outstanding teacher, speaks of his students: "I take their ideas seriously. I don't pretend to be the expert. Try to be open-ended. You can't have a rigid agenda. Try to find out what the kids are interested in. You've got to try many ways to help them to open up. Sometimes I'm preposterous! But always informal, always flexible!"

Louise Bogart greets each child individually every morning with a warm handshake and a personal exchange: "These must be new red sneakers, Jon" or "How is your visit with your grandmother going, Sam?" She's tuned in! She knows what's happening with her students.

Anna was enthusiastic about her new teacher: "He's confident about the material. He uses good illustrations and explanations. He kept asking for comments and questions. He prodded! He wanted us to speak up. He looked directly at our eyes. We really paid attention! He moved and spoke with assurance."

I like to make promises to people. At the beginning of every day, I make four promises.

Promise One: *We're going to run out of time.*

Promise Two: *We're going to use ALL of our powers:* mind, body, memory, concentration, listening, vocabulary, comprehension, imagination—all!

Promise Three: *We're going to work hard.* We probably will need to take a break, get a drink, stretch and relax.

Promise Four: *We're going to have fun . . . or else!*

At the end of our time together, we go over the promises (which the kids always remember). It means so much to them that the promises are kept.

What promises can you make to your students each day as a preamble to the day?

Can you promise them that today they will do something mathematical?

Can you promise them that today they will see everything in colors? (Is this a color day?)

Can you promise them that today they will use memory or imagination?

Only make promises you KNOW you will keep!

Your Classroom

"There will be no lack of ideas for expression in rooms that are filled with things to look at and talk about."[25] Your room is a reflection of yourself and your students. It tells about your values, interests, and attitudes. Will it be a marvelous, magical place in which children live and learn or will it be just another room offering minimal opportunities? Will it be a room bursting with life and color, pictures and words, mobiles and hobbies, kids' poems and stories? A room of challenges, surprises, discovery, self-expression, movement, and life? Or will it be a room of packaged perfection, showing the evidence of rote learning and displaying only "A" papers? It's up to you to design a room to talk about, with room to talk!

Something Beautiful Space
Designate a portion of a wall or bulletin board for something beautiful. The children take turns contributing something they think is beautiful. They could introduce a picture, a design, a word, a poem, a flower—whatever they choose to share. Before their items are displayed, they share their "something beautiful" orally.

Something Funny Space
I can't sing enough praises for humor in the classroom. Human beings are unique in their ability to see funny situations, to make up and tell jokes, to perceive incongruities. Humor is a sign of comprehension, vocabulary, imagination, and intelligence. The playfulness of humor is a basic ingredient of creativity.

Reserve a space on the bulletin board, wall, or chalkboard for cartoons, riddles, jokes, and humorous articles and pictures. Here is the home of your more mirthful books. Share the humorous pieces orally before they are displayed. *Peanuts, Dennis the Menace, Nancy, Blondie, Garfield,* and *Funky Winkerbean* are examples of cartoons that appear daily in newspapers and tickle the funny bones of kids of all ages.

Some of the hilarious books I have seen highlighted in lively classrooms are *Pigs in Hiding* by Arlene Dubanevich (Four Winds, 1983), *Weekend in the Country* by Lee Lorenz (Prentice-Hall, 1985), *Breakfast for Sammy* by Cynthia Weissman (Four Winds, 1978), and *Kevin's Grandma* by Barbara Williams (Dutton, 1985). When such books are celebrated, the music of the room is laughter and talk.

I copied these riddles from a fourth-grade bulletin board:

What kind of underwear did the knights of old days wear?
  Fruit of aluminum
Why did Grandma put roller skates on her rocking chair?
  'Cause she wanted to rock and roll.

Make room for original jokes. Dan, a sixth grader, made this one up and presented it to the class with his friend Steve:

Dan: Look deep into my eyes. What do you see? (opens his eyes very wide)
Steve: I see a spoiled, selfish, rotten, mean kid.
Dan: Too deep.

The class loved the joke and enjoyed improvising it with different partners. Original cartoons based on it were displayed in the Something Funny Space.

Picture of the Day   From your ever-growing file of pictures collected from magazines, newspapers, advertisements, and old books and periodicals, choose a picture of an especially interesting face, place, event, or scene for the children to look at and talk, think, ask questions, tell stories, and write about.

The following are open-ended questions you might ask.

What do you see in this picture?

What's happening in this picture?

How does this picture make you feel?

If the person in this picture could talk, what do you think he or she would say?

Make believe you are in the picture. What do you see? Smell? Hear? How do you feel?

Encourage the children to bring in their own pictures to discuss.

Current Events Space   Set aside a space for newspaper items, clippings, and news photos. Encourage children to follow news events and read the daily newspaper in class and at home. The newspaper should be part of everyday learning. There are always items of interest to hold the attention of even the youngest children: sports events, television programs, feature stories on special events or famous people or things. Besides all the news of wars, accidents, and international misunderstandings, there are always news accounts of people performing great acts of courage and compassion—all of which lend themselves easily to lively exchanges of ideas and opinions in class discussions.

Plant Place   Whether or not plants are included in your lesson plans, they have a definite contribution to make toward stimulating oral language. Children care for plants, observe their growth, share excitement about a new leaf or a new bud.

I visited a class that had so many plants of different varieties it looked like a greenhouse. The children eagerly told me about each one. It was obvious from their enthusiastic conversations that oral language experiences bloomed in their classroom as well as the plants did.

Children in one kindergarten class plant every seed and pit they find. Often nothing grows, but once in a while they are lucky. A beautiful avocado plant sprouted for them from a pit they planted. There is constant conversation, observation, comparison, and the discovery of growing things in the class. What will grow in your classroom?

Pet Place   Students care for, study, watch, play with, and discuss their pets with classmates. Pets are a great resource for developing cooperation, responsibility, lovingness, and conversation. The kid's own pets and classroom pets provide material for all kinds of projects, such as the following:

Draw pictures of them.

Make up songs, stories, or poems about them.

Keep daily logs about them.

Write observations about them.

Improvise movement based on their movement.

Talk about them.

You may find children who don't talk to other children talking quietly to a gerbil or a rabbit. And, sometimes, the gerbil or rabbit will answer back! It depends on the magic in your room.

Collection Place   Children are the greatest collectors. They gather and save everything—from stamps to bottlecaps, seashells to garden pebbles, baseball cards to holiday cards.

Provide a space for students to share their collections. You may have such an enthusiastic response that the children will need to take turns and schedule a display date!

Of course, they will want to tell about their collection. How did they get started? What inspired them? You won't need to encourage questions and discussion. They're built into the enthusiasm of sharing something special, something meaningful like "Hey, can I bring in my collection of fossils? Arrowheads? Doll furniture?"

Science Experiments

I read an article recently that decried the lack of interest in and enthusiasm for science on the part of older students. Somehow, many children lose their curiosity and their excitement for observation and experimentation. (Can you guess why?)

Even if science experiments are not in your curriculum, children are interested in seeds, in how plants grow, in animals, rocks, the earth, rainbows, colors, our own amazing bodies. Simple experiments evoke questions, observations, comments, comparisons.

One of the highlights of teaching fifth grade one year was Andy's interest in geology and the way he shared this individualized subject with us. He even demonstrated how a volcano works with *almost* real eruptions. I won't tell you how. Maybe Andy is in YOUR class and will share that scientific concept with you! It was the main topic of conversation for days!

Book Nooks and Game Shelves

Every room needs a special place set aside for books and magazines brought in by you and your children, read and shared for enjoyment only. Carry a steady supply of old and current issues of *National Geographic, Life, Newsweek, Time, Sport, Sports Illustrated, Mad, Jack and Jill,* and other periodicals. They always provide inspiration for conversation, discussion, and projects.

Checkers, chess, backgammon, Go to the Head of the Class, Sorry, Trivial Pursuit, and other popular commercial and educational games are not only effective learning activities but also offer opportunities for children to talk quietly with each other, sharing in the give-and-take of the game process. You'll find that one of the most successful celebrations for finishing a hard day's work is to save some free time for games, reading, individual projects, or any classroom activity children choose. Children invent original games as challenging as any found in a store.

Projects in Progress

A real conversation piece in every dynamic classroom is one that must be completed by the children, one that challenges them to add their own contributions. Here are some examples:

A Blank Wall for All Seasons Tape up a large sheet of mural paper and leave it blank. Talk with the children and write suggestions on the board to go with the discussion. Here's an example of an introduction.

"Well, kids, we've been talking about spring. Now let's get some good ideas for spring images—sights, sounds, smells, textures, ideas." (Gather these together with the children.)

"Here's a blank wall just waiting for images of spring to be added to it. Whenever you get inspired, please draw, paint, write, or paste a spring idea to it. And how about signing your name to whatever you contribute?"

Then leave it. Talk will flourish. Ideas will be exchanged. The paper is large enough for contributions by all. In a few days, you will have one of the most memorable bulletin boards of the year. Try this activity with all the seasons, holidays, events, subject areas.

What more creative challenge than beginning with blank paper, empty space, silence? Everything is possible.

Go Fly a Kite and Other Addition Projects   Children respond with enthusiasm when they add on to something and see it enriched by their contribution.

I saw a bright and lively board of kites. The children designed and added their own kites to the sky background. On the kites and interspersed with them were poems, haikus, and words about kites.

Try this activity with animals, boats on the sea, flowers in a garden, houses, family trees, favorite books (design the covers), and foods.

Class Time Line   Begin by drawing a line around the borders of the room or across the top of the front wall, or by hanging an actual clothes line. Start the time line by cutting out the date of your birth, accompanied by baby photos or any other interesting birth material. Further along the line, add another item from your life—perhaps graduation from high school or college, marriage, or the beginning of your teaching career. Discuss the time line with your students, pointing out the milestones in your life and asking the children to contribute their birth dates, pictures, and souvenirs to the time line. In time, every child is represented on the line. They discuss and share each item as it is added to the line.

These projects are ongoing. Leave them up so children can help them grow, can see what ideas have not been included. The sound of these projects is the buzz of kids sharing ideas, exchanging suggestions, checking in with each other and their teachers. Nice sound!

Metamorphosis: A Language Adventure

Renoir Room   Nothing generates more enthusiastic talk than a major metamorphosis of your entire room. Albert Cullum, in his inspiring book *Push Back the Desks*, describes how his sixth grade turned their classroom into a Renoir room. They emptied their room of desks and chairs, cleared the walls and bulletin boards, and displayed fifty-four reproductions of Renoir paintings. They read, researched, discovered, talked, reported, lectured, and shared their findings and feelings with each other and with other classes. Cullum writes, "A whole new world of words opened up to them—*impressions, spontaneity, inspiration, technique, contemporary, classical, realism, modern, creative freedom* . . . . What a wonderful new wealth of words the students learned, used and understood."[26]

Hawaiian Room   I visited a sixth-grade class which had turned its room into Hawaii. The children greeted visitors with original flower leis, Hawaiian welcome chants, and glasses of papaya and pineapple juice. Original and commercial travel posters were hung from the ceiling. A mural of the skyline of Honolulu and the exotic silhouettes of volcanic mountains against pure blue sky and gleaming ocean covered the walls. Original models of sugar cane and pineapple plantations, Buddhist temples, Japanese pagodas, and Pearl Harbor were displayed. Origami renditions of tropical flowers like bird of paradise, plumeria, and poinsettia brightened the corners of the room. The children told legends and myths of the Hawaiian gods and people. They presented Hawaiian songs, accompanied by movement and real instruments. Every aspect of the project required planning, conversation, discussion, and cooperation.

Can you think of subjects or interesting topics that lend themselves to such an approach? It's something worth talking about!

Spider Mountain When children create a total environment, all the communicative and creative arts flourish! I spent a day with children enjoying a "Days of Creation" program. Each group had designed and constructed its own special space, its own unique environment. One group had turned their outdoor space into a huge spider web, with string criss-crossing from tree to branch to bush. They called their space "Spider Mountain" and had explored it thoroughly. They discovered a stream with rocks the shape of a brain and a heart; they found a handprint on one of the stones. They made up stories about treasure maps and buried treasure. They drew the treasure maps! Characters were created and placed in strategic locations in their web, including a nest of spiders belonging to Fayette.

We sat at a picnic table and I asked the kids about Spider Mountain. They *told* me everything! I tore off large sheets of paper from a slapped-together pad and suggested that we write about Spider Mountain.

Here's what the kids wrote from telling, from talking, from sharing adventures and imagination.

Spider Mountain

In Spider Mountain, in Spider Mountain,
there are three treasures buried;
there are three treasure maps.

In Spider Mountain, in Spider Mountain,
ten people looked for treasure.
Ten people did not come back.

In Spider Mountain, in Spider Mountain,
empty shoes walk without feet
and a hat looks for a head.

There's a rock near the bridge
in Spider Mountain.
There's a hardened heart and a lost brain.
There's a scream on the bridge
of Spider Mountain.
There's writing on the stones
and mist in the fog.

Handprints are fossils
in Spider Mountain.
Beware the welcome, turn away.
Fang greets you. The King eats you.

In Fayette's nest, babies wait to hatch,
wait to catch
you
in their huge web.

In Spider Mountain, in Spider Mountain
George and the Tick are a team.
When one gets caught, the other helps.
The Servant serves the King.

Won't you come visit us
on our Spider Mountain?
Drop in anytime to play.
You'll only hear "Hello" in Spider Mountain.
"Goodbye" is a word we never say!

Robin Howard, 10
Erin Klingbeil, 9
Karen Levy, 9
Kerrie Lewis, 10
Marlee Boerner, 10
Monica West, 10
Julie Wolfe, 11
Mandi Wolfel, 9
Christine Zahller, 9
Paula Strahl, 9[27]

Equally as powerful as the poem was the kids' awareness of the power of the process itself. They were surprised, delighted, and fascinated by the way their spoken words found patterns, images, and rhythms on paper. They laid a golden egg! (But if a goose never lays any eggs at all, what chance does it have to lay a golden one?)

They experimented with choral reading of the poem, trying different voices, different tones, different arrangements. They "wowed" the rest of the group when they shared their work.

Original art, music, drama, poetry, and dance don't emerge out of NOTHING, out of emptiness, out of a vacuum. As children create imagination-rich environments, even if only in one small corner of a room, even if in a shoe box, they find they have a lot to think about, talk about, and write about.

Give them those opportunities!

Celebrations in the Classroom

Annual holidays such as Thanksgiving, Valentine's Day, Christmas, Chanukah, Easter, Passover, Halloween, Chinese New Year, Kwanza, Cinco de Mayo, Japanese Boys and Girls' Days, United Nations Week, Black History Week, and

Brotherhood Week provide countless opportunities for oral language activities as well as enrichment activities in *all* curriculum areas. Students discuss and plan special programs and projects to celebrate the holidays, share ideas and feelings about the events, and express themselves in many effective ways. But there is no reason to limit your special events to just those expected times. Your room is your world, and in your world you and your students can celebrate many original happenings that stimulate all the language skills—especially oral language. Creative teachers around the country approach familiar holidays in diverse and imaginative ways. They also initiate special times that are reasons to celebrate and learn. Here are a few examples.

Special Person Day A child's name is picked from the names in the Special Person sack. A letter goes home to the family telling that Susie will be a Special Person on, say, the following Wednesday and any anecdote, story, or item that her family can share about Susie would be very welcome. The family is also invited to the classroom for Susie's day. Susie's name is mounted on the Special Person board. She receives a Special Person badge in the shape of one of her interests. If she likes horses, the badge could be in the outline of a horse. Susie brings things to share with the class, including photos, pets, and personal treasures.

The children talk about why Susie is special. They share anecdotes about her. Everything about Susie goes on the Special Person board. Susie chooses one favorite thing to do that day. It could be singing a certain song, playing a special game, or reading a favorite book. Afterward, another child's name is picked from the Special Person sack so that all children can have a turn. The teacher is the Special Person one day during the last week of the year.

Color Day We all love to talk about colors, so choose one color to celebrate with a special day. Let's say the children chose orange. On Orange Day, they think orange, speak orange, wear orange, draw orange, sing orange, move orange, read and write orange. They begin with concrete, realistic images of the color and move toward more abstract feelings. What is orange music? How does orange make us feel? How does orange make us move? What is the touch of orange? What are words that make you think of orange? Let's write an orange poem. Let's make up an orange dance. Let's write with orange pens and crayons. Let's make up orange math problems. Let's take an orange walk. Let's talk in orange voices. What other ways can you think of to celebrate a color?

Animal Day Children love to talk about animals. Plan to celebrate an animal with a special day. Check the Color Day for ideas to use to celebrate Animal Days.

Make Up Your Own Holiday Ella Jenkins' delightful chant "It's a Holiday" (*"Jambo" and Other Call and Response Songs and Chants*, Folkways Records, 1974) inspired movement and drama interpretations in answer to the challenge "What if YOU could make up a brand new holiday? What would it celebrate? What would it be called? What special things would happen on that day?" and so on.

Kids of all ages thought up new original holidays, such as

Smiles Day	Circles Day
Backwards Day	Singing Day
Stand Tall Day	Special Words Day
Play Day	Jumping Jacks Day
Peace Day	Tree Day

Through excited exchanges of ideas, they chose slogans, colors, activities, symbols, and foods to celebrate the new special occasions.

See *I'm in Charge of Celebrations* by Byrd Baylor (Scribner's, 1986).

Favorite Book Day   If you are reading a book with your class, celebrate it with a special day.

A fourth grade enjoyed Tom Sawyer Day. The children came to school dressed as characters in the story. They retold the story and discussed their favorite incidents and characters. They improvised scenes from the story. They made stick-puppets and presented a Tom Sawyer puppet show. A small group composed a ballad of Tom Sawyer, which they taught to the rest of the class. Tom Sawyer book jackets and posters were drawn and displayed. Tom Sawyer appeared as the guest on a "television interview program" and answered questions from the "audience." Injun Joe attempted to explain his actions.

Teachers like Maureen Reedy find that talking about favorite books can't be contained in just one day! She and her fourth graders talk constantly about the favorite book they are reading together. The characters in the book are practically members of their family. The children are so involved in the story that they live it—wondering what *they* would do if *they* were caught in the plot. There is a continuous celebration of ideas accompanying the reading of the book, whether it be *A Taste of Blackberries* by Doris B. Smith (Harper and Row, 1973; dealing with death) or *Do Bananas Chew Gum?* by Jamie Gilson (Lothrop, 1980; about a student with disabilities who is finally understood and accepted by his classmates) or *The House at Rose Street* by Mimi Brodsky (Archway, 1968; about racial prejudice).

Contrast the dynamic interaction of the fourth graders in Maureen Reedy's fourth grade with this scene in Nat's high school English class. First, the GOOD news: What a list of books Nat's class was assigned! *The Grapes of Wrath, To Kill a Mockingbird, All the King's Men*, and *The Pearl*, to name just a few. Now, the BAD news:

We never discussed any of the books. Whenever we started a new book, the teacher gave us a sheet of paper with the things she wanted us to know about it, like the theme, characters, and what to remember. Then we had less than two weeks to finish it before our essay test and short-answer test. If you didn't understand the book—tough. Like, *All the King's Men* had a lot to talk about. . . . Well, they all did, but we never talked about them. I guess the point was to see how many books we could read—like speed reading or something. I didn't get anything out of it. I'd rather spend a month on one book and really get into it.

Thumbs up or thumbs down?

Unbirthday Party   All the children celebrate their unbirthdays. Small, homemade gifts and cards are exchanged. A grab bag of surprises, riddles, jokes, and songs is available. They share unbirthday cupcakes while unbirthday games and songs are played and sung. The kids take turns telling what they want for their unbirthday. Imagination, humor, friendship, and cooperation foster a celebration of oral language.

Pen Pal Day   Discuss the idea of making pen pal friends with another class in another school, perhaps in another state or section of the country. Arrange with the teacher of the other class to embark on the adventure. The entire class can become involved, not just those individuals who like to write letters.

Before any letters are written, children draw pictures of themselves, bring in photos of themselves, or write descriptions of themselves to *accompany their own voices recorded on a cassette tape*. Each child has a turn on the tape to introduce himself or herself to the pen pal friends.

A package is sent to the other class containing the pictures, photos, and tape cassette. A while later your class should receive a similar package from their pen pals. The names of all the children in the other class are written on the board with their pictures mounted over their names. While the cassette is being played, the children listen to the tape, look at the pictures, and try to imagine their new friends' personalities. The children might draw names for pen pals. All year, tapes, letters, and pictures are exchanged. The project is a continuous topic of conversation and discussion. The lives of all the children are enriched by new friendships and experiences in language as communication.

Try this project with the residents of a nursing home.

Sharing in the Classroom

Probably no activity in the elementary classroom is interpreted in more diverse ways than Sharing Time, which ranges from a rigid, ten-minute period confined to one morning a week with prearranged sharers to "We share all the time! Whenever children have something to share, that's the time to share it!"

Sharing Time, unless it's totally destroyed by strict, limited interpretation, can be one of the most effective talk times of the day.

Share, Show, and Ask   The person who is sharing tells about his or her subject, shows something if there is something to show, and then is asked questions by the rest of the class.

Groups of Sharers   The kids are distributed around the room with their sharing items or stories. The class divides up into small groups, visiting with one of the sharers at a time. After a few minutes, the children move on to another sharer. It's like a marketplace or festival of sharing.

Sharing Partners   Each sharer has a partner. The partner introduces the sharer and subject to the class. Example, from a fourth grade:

"This is John Jackson. He is very interested in coins and last year he got one of the Olympic commemorative coins as a birthday present from his uncle. Now, here is John."

Mystery Sharing   The sharer presents the item to be shared as a mystery hidden in a pocket, bag, or container. The class tries to guess while the sharer provides hints.

"Today I'm going to share something that's very small and fragile."

"Is it alive?"

"No."

"What color is it?"

and so on.

All Sharing   Because there are so many children in a class who never share, some teachers have sharing days when all the children are asked to tell their favorite television program, their favorite song, their favorite book, food, word, time of year, day of the week, color, place. The children's responses are easy to translate into charts, written words, art projects, and songs. Here's an example of this group sharing improvised into "My Favorite Things" (from *The Sound of Music*). Enjoy this excerpt from a second-grade sharing time:

Carol likes pizza and Bobby likes ice cream.
Deshawn likes tacos and Kim likes hot dogs.
Evan likes steakburgers bathed in french fries,
These are a few of our favorite foods. . . .

Teacher as Sharer   Nothing is more meaningful and exciting to students than when you, the teacher, share something with them. Sharing means you care enough to want to give of yourself and your life to others.

Creative and loving teachers share seashells, pieces of petrified wood, black sand, picture postcards, stones, and other souvenirs of trips they have taken. Louise Johnson, a first-grade teacher who "always, always" brings in "something to share with the children from my vacations," one year found little pieces of wood. She put moss on them, made them into "woods creatures," then set them on the windowsill. "These are for you," she told the class. "Look at them for a while, find one that you especially like, listen to it, and when you can bring it to me and tell me what story it told you and what you were talking about, it's yours forever and ever to take home and keep!" After three days, every "woods creature" had found a new home!

Sharing through Oral Reports   Oral reports are so much a part of every classroom and, so often, a cause of anxiety in so many children that space is needed to share ideas on maximizing the enjoyment and creative challenge inherent in oral reports and minimizing the tensions accompanying them. Oral reports are made by individuals or small groups or committees and usually follow a time of research and information gathering about a specific topic. Clarity of purpose, organization, and comprehension are important elements of this type of communication. Don't forget that reports are really a *sharing* of knowledge and discovery. When children are excited about their topics and enjoy the research process, their motivation for sharing their material orally is greatly increased. As often as possible, children should be able to choose their own areas of concentration, even if their choices upset your plan for the study. Children should be given the freedom to present their material in imaginative and creative ways.

During oral reports, don't sit in judgment of the speaker with your marking book out; be part of the audience, guiding the presentation and enjoying the sharing. Your role as a responsive listener includes encouraging and supporting the speaker in every way possible. Your interest and appreciation are of paramount importance to a child's feeling of success and accomplishment. Students should be encouraged to use props, constructions, audiovisual materials, dramatic skits, puppets, charts, illustrations, *anything at all that adds life and interest to their presentations*. One teacher, anxious to make oral report time a true experience of sharing and exchange, reorganized her chairs in a semicircle. Children who had studied similar topics together sat near each other. The class had a round robin oral report time to conclude their unit on Native Americans. Each child had a turn sharing something interesting about Native Americans that the kids had discovered in their research. Everyone was involved. No one was singled out for criticism; everyone received an A.

When students are given opportunities to take responsibility for projects and procedures, they demonstrate great competence and intelligence. Here are rules a fourth-grade class made up for oral reports. They printed them on a chart and conscientiously tried to follow them.

1. Are you speaking in a natural voice?
2. Can your voice be heard?
3. Are you looking at us when you talk?
4. Did you organize your talk?
5. Do you know what you want to say?
6. Did you make your talk interesting?

Group Reports   An excellent example of group reporting is News Team. There are many variations of this program. For our sample, we'll take a close look at the News Team approach enjoyed by the fifth graders in Tom Griffin's class. He explains,

> We have a six-reporter team plus one commercial. We have an anchor person, national, international, room and local, sports, weather, and entertainment reporters. The kids get to try most of the assignments during the year as

different teams are responsible each week for a large weekly news report. All week the reporters gather information, helped by the other students during morning meetings or informally during the days. They organize their material, go over their notes, and prepare to present their news reports the way a television news team would do. Clear speaking, eye contact, well-presented material are what we look for. The person in charge of the commercial makes up a product with the advertising package to go with it. One of the best was a safety belt commercial presented at one of last year's News Team reports. One of the boys dressed as an old woman who survived an auto accident. She/he boasted to the "camera," "I was fine! Thanks to the belt!" That little slogan became our biggest subject for kidding around. At the end-of-the-year festivities, the kids got together and, in one voice, shouted, "Fifth grade was a pain, but I was fine—thanks to the belt!" We still laugh about it!

Now News Teams from Tom Griffin's room exchange with News Teams from the fifth grades of Molly Davis and Tom Dill.

"Apathetic" and "nonverbal" will never describe these lucky fifth graders!

A challenging variation on this idea is to create "time machine" News Teams. If you are studying early American history, have an early American News Team, giving you the events and happenings of THAT time. How about ancient Egyptian, prehistoric, or Native American Indian News Teams?

CAREFUL

Save your grades for short-answer quizzes and exams that check specific information. If you must mark children's oral reports, do so with all the "sweetness of soul you possess," for a harsh grade on an oral report, especially one presented in a more imaginative and creative way, is a sure method of squelching originality and freedom of expression. How would you feel if the project you worked so hard on was organized and presented in what you thought was a clever and enjoyable manner only to be awarded a C − or a 70?

Talk Walks

Walking and talking go together as naturally as breathing and living! Talk and walk in all seasons. As I write this, it is autumn. Look for signs of autumn. If something lying on the ground represents the season, bring it back to the classroom. Share the treasures of pine cones, brightly colored leaves, twigs, acorns. Talk about the sights. What can you do with these wonderful gifts?

Here's a third-grade list of suggestions about what to do with the acorns gathered on a walk:

Acorns

eat them	make up a game with them
give them to the squirrels	use them as balls
make buckeyes out of them	make them into necklaces
make faces and caps	make little boats from caps
make puppets	use caps as dolls' chairs

The walk goes from talk to song to art to reading to writing to dancing to puppets to crafts to science to whatever you and the class want to do. There's always more to do than there is time in which to do it.

Wonder Times

There are so many things to wonder about! What do you wonder about? Imagine wonder-full questions children might ask if you would give them the chance.

Wonder times are quiet times when no answers are necessary. Everyone has a turn to wonder out loud about something. The children may comment on or add to a question, but it is not required. Often, teachers discover topics of vital concern to the children, and then can guide further exploration and discovery. If you don't encourage children to wonder aloud together, you may never hear a child say, "I wonder if caterpillars know that they are going to turn into butterflies?" "I wonder why the pool wasn't open. The ocean never closes!" "What does my mommy do when I sleep?" "What do I look like inside?" "Who will be my mommy when I grow up?"

Dawn Heyman told her third graders, "The only bad questions are the ones we don't ask." In classes that hallow the spirits, minds, and imaginations

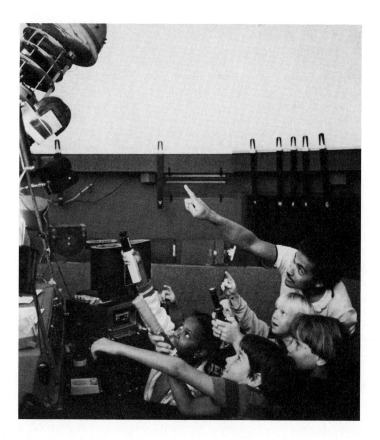

of children, questions are always on the agenda. Whatever words are spoken or written. The question board, the wonder board, fills with Big and Little questions. Questions are the kind of language arts exercise Jan Hammock's third graders enjoy the most. You never can tell what may develop from a single question. Third graders asked

Why is there color? (Carol W.)
How were letters formed? (Jennie L.)
Why do people love? (Becky)
How do people laugh? (Chris V.)

and Steve confounded the group with

What am I? Who am I? Why am I?

Once, a long-ago child whom we would now diagnose as Learning Disabled asked a lot of questions. One of the things he wondered about and asked about was "How come the sky looks blue?" That question helped lead that child, Albert Einstein, toward his amazing Theory of Relativity!

A Smorgasbord of Other Talking Times

Children are bursting with things to say! Some of them don't talk very much at home. In many classes, talking is not encouraged. Where do all their words go?

The Chinese call it "Talk Story." The Jews call it telling "Bubbe-Mayses" (Grandmother stories). Black Americans call it "rappin'"—telling how it is, telling what's happening. For thousands and thousands of years, we human beings have transmitted our culture not by the written word but by oral language. Vertically and horizontally, *the stories of the people* (their daily and historical experiences, anecdotes, chronicles, tales, legends) were handed down and handed across *by word of mouth*.

When the great holy man of the Oglala Sioux tribe, Black Elk, wanted his story known, he called for the historian John Neihardt and *told it to him*.[28] After an amazing journey across the world and back to his roots in Gambia, West Africa, Alex Haley found a story-telling "griot," an oral historian, to *tell him* the story of his people.[29] Most of the great cultures of the world have passed along their stories from person to person, from mouth to ear to mouth!

This rich and fascinating tradition is our childrens' heritage. We need to give them numerous opportunities to participate in this uniquely human process so they can continue passing along "the stories," the "happenings," by kibbitzing, rappin', spinning yarns, sharing talk-stories, "noodling around,"[30]— talking together.

Telling Tales in School

All people have stories to tell, and they enjoy telling them unless they have learned to be afraid of criticism or ridicule. Students should be encouraged to

tell stories, parts of stories, or just beginnings of stories. There are many wonderful variations of storytelling activities to explore. The stories of younger children can be written down by you or by older students. This is an excellent sharing project for two classes. Children love to tape record their stories, illustrate them, act them out, and improvise movement for them. Double the fun by giving children the chance to make up stories together. Round robin stories are passed around the group with each person adding a part to the story. Or stop your reading of a familiar story in the middle and ask the children to add original endings. Stories should always be shared.

Greg (age 4) Tells a Story

Once upon a time there was a bird's nest in a tree and there was a bird in it. The sister bird fell out. The brother bird flied out. The mother bird wiggled her nose and fell out and the father stayed in the nest and took care of them and then he took them to the bird hospital. They went back home and lived happily ever after.

Todd (age 4) Tells a Story

Once upon a time two boys named Todd and Gregory were on the Lost Sea and Robinson Crusoe came and saved them. Robinson rode out on his horse and put Todd and Greg on his pony. He took them back to the cave and they lived happily. Amen.

In many traditional cultures, storytelling is so important a part of the lives of the people that the storyteller has an almost sacred role. Often, the storyteller wears a special headdress, necklace, or costume as the story is told. Children are delighted with that idea and stories flow more easily when special clothing is worn, the storytelling object is held, or the storyteller sits in a special chair.

CAREFUL

Don't grade or mark children's stories unless everyone who tells a story gets an A, extra credit, a star, or a happy-face badge or sticker. The quickest way to kill creativity is to criticize it or correct it harshly. Let the creativity flow. Corrections and suggestions can always be made at a later point in the process. The children will want to write neatly, correct their spelling, and punctuate their sentences because they will want people to be able to read and understand their stories. How do you celebrate the stories?

Everybody Talk   When Louise Bogart senses that her students are bubbling with things to say, she stops everything, gathers them together, and gives them all a chance to say anything they want to, anything they want the class to hear. The children say what is on their minds. They do not have to connect ideas. This is not a discussion but an opportunity to talk, which most children enjoy and need.

Small Talk   In Ellen Clark's fifth-grade class the last half hour on Friday afternoons is reserved for small talk. All week, the kids write whatever is on their minds—problems, complaints, questions, ideas to share—and drop them into a brightly decorated handy box. They don't have to sign their names.

On Friday afternoons, they sit on a rug, open the box, and read one item at a time and discuss it. The session is like a collective "Dear Abby"! Here are two examples of items discussed.

"I don't know what to be when I grow up. I can't decide on whether to be a vet or a teacher. How do you decide? What about college? How much does it cost? How long does it take? Do you want to go to college?"

"What do you do if you have a teacher you don't like? I hate the language arts specialist. She won't help me when I have a question. She never asks, she just tells you and she never smiles."

Some of the responses to the second question were

> You're stuck, so make the best of it.
> Try to do something to make her smile.
> If she can't help you, find someone else who will.
> Write her a poem.
> Talk to her quietly.

Sense-full Talks   Pass around pieces of cut-up apples. Have the children taste them and talk about their reactions. Then have them taste familiar and unfamiliar foods and talk about them.

"Close your eyes. Here is something to taste. How does it taste to you? What do you think it is?"

Put together items of different textures, such as cotton balls, pieces of leather, tree bark, and confetti for the children to touch, think about, and talk about. Expand this idea to the other senses.

One to One   Children need to talk to each other on a one-to-one basis in order to enrich their own language learning. In many classes, they never have that opportunity. In creative, exciting classes they have many chances for one-to-one conversations, learning with and teaching each other, planning, just "rappin,'" sharing talk-stories.

Listening Chair and Speaking Chair   If two students have a disagreement or a problem to solve together and they are having trouble going about it, sit them down in two chairs and designate one chair as a Listening Chair and the other as a Speaking Chair. The person in the Speaking Chair has a turn to speak without being interrupted. The person in the Listening Chair must listen without interrupting. Then reverse the roles.

Friendship Day (Every day should be Friendship Day)   Give the children animals or shapes, numbers or words, to match with another person. When they find their matching person, they are given the chance to sit quietly together, talk to each other about anything they want, and plan something to do together that day, such as eating a snack together, drawing a picture together, playing a game together, doing a puzzle together. Later in the day, give them some free time to carry out the plan they made together. Do this frequently and give the children a chance to have quiet talks with different people on Friendship Day.

Partners or Buddies   Children are very good teachers and they like to learn from each other. They like to help each other. Research has proved that "peer teaching" is very successful, not just for academic improvement but for human relations as well. As often as possible, encourage students to work together, help each other, tutor each other, read together, check their assignments together, and talk about ideas and plans with each other. If you really want to develop your class into what Chick Moorman calls "The Our Classroom,"[31] a class of cohesion and trust, of respect and sharing, then you will find hundreds of ways for your students to be buddies and partners together.

Talking in Small Groups   Children need time to be together in small groups. They can play games, work on projects, plan skits, or read plays. They can solve problems and compare their solutions to those of other groups. Even if the kids just talk together, it's important.

Discussions   Too often, class discussions are really teacher-centered monologues with occasional one-word answers from the students who raise their hands. Discussion really means *to speak together about,* and all children should feel safe enough to participate in the discussions and free enough to share their ideas and questions. Discussions are most successful in small groups of five or six children. The purpose and topic of the discussion should be made clear to the participants. Discussions can center on everything:

problems to solve

books and stories

units of study

current events

holidays and special occasions

concepts and feelings

classroom plans, projects, and procedures

When children work out the few simple rules for discussion, emphasizing courtesy and clarity, such as "Write ideas on the board" and "Listen to all ideas with respect," they tend to be more responsible participants.

Encourage everyone to participate. You may have to go around the room and ask for everyone's opinion just to involve the entire class. Many children won't offer their opinions but will respond when asked.

You will have to provide direction frequently to keep the focus of the discussion clear. You can do that harshly or with great sensitivity and awareness.

During the course of a discussion, it is valuable to *summarize* or encourage the students to summarize major points in order to recap the information agreed on up to that time. This way the discussion can continue with greater clarity and purposefulness. Another subtle thing creative teachers do is *restate* children's questions and comments or ask them to restate their ideas.

Tom says, "The Mexicans weren't treated no good."

A creative teacher might say, "Tom, you didn't think the Mexicans received fair treatment? In what ways?"

You are not stopping the discussion to correct grammar or usage, but are adding your own sample of more standard language without humiliating the speaker. You are also encouraging the children to think through their ideas and to try to express them more clearly.

Children should not dread discussion times as frightening or threatening but rather should enjoy them as stimulating exchanges of ideas and opinions that enrich their understanding and knowledge and strengthen their self-image and self-confidence. Some conclusions should be reached if possible.

Engage in brainstorming often. Ask all the children to really feel free to share whatever ideas they have on the topic. *Never permit a put-down of any idea!* Brainstorming is very effective in gathering and shaping ideas for projects and programs in an atmosphere of trust and respect. Students should discuss every aspect of their school day. They should be active participants in decision making, contributing their ideas at all levels of class life. Only by using oral language in all aspects of the day, in all ways, do children learn their language. A sixth-grade teacher told this story:

> Our class is going to a cemetery next week. We're going to read tombstones and do grave-rubbings. And do you know what? The whole idea came from the children, not from me. We have been studying the history of our country and talking about the early settlers and some of the houses and streets that are still in existence. The class got very excited because they knew of a little cemetery in back of an old church where hardly anyone goes. Well, we're going, and I guess you could say this is the first field trip planned by students for the teacher!

Happy Talk   "Happy Talk" is one of the most delightful songs in the musical *South Pacific*. From *The Wiz*, the rock version of *The Wizard of Oz*, comes the song "Don't Nobody Bring Me No Bad News." Put these ideas together to focus on Talk Times that feature only good news! Sometimes it's important to help people get in touch with the things that are right and good in their world! Here are a few second-grade contributions to Happy Talk Time as ideas were passed around in a circle.

> "Ice cream is delicious. I love Bubble Gum flavor." (Kevin, 8)
> "Once I saw a rainbow." (Susie, 8)
> "My dog is cute." (Tawana, 8)
> "Remember when the clown came to school?" (Jill, 8)

Happy Talk is contagious. Spread it!

Puppet Talk   Children love to talk to, with, and for puppets. If puppets are regular members of your classroom, they are ready and waiting for children to give them life. So often, the shy, insecure child will respond beautifully to interaction with puppets. Encourage the continuous use of puppets in teaching lessons, improvising stories, retelling familiar stories, singing, and in free play.

Talking to Ourselves   Young children, especially, show a virtuosity in language development when they are engrossed in play. Heads bent over toys, dolls, props, they are totally involved in their play situation, their play drama. They give voices to different characters in their story, show amazing skills at narrative and dialogue, and demonstrate comprehension, vocabulary, and appreciation for the way language enriches life situations. Your scrounge box, toy box, or play area will beckon to the children. They'll improvise telephones, houses, cars, spaceships. Just give them the time to explore and create. Eavesdrop and enjoy![32]

Plays and Skits   Although many excellent materials for play production are available to teachers, I think the BEST plays are those the children create themselves, out of situations and resources that compel them. When children are encouraged to talk about everything going on, when they see that their

spoken words are also written words, they realize how easy it is to "make a play." More on play-making in the next chapter.

Magic Circles for Problem Solving

Dr. William Glasser, author of *Schools without Failure,* is credited with coining the term "magic circle" to describe a place for problem solving and for sharing important feelings. Sometimes teachers designate a special place in the room for these more serious discussions. I have seen children gather on a special "magic circle" rug or carpet to have this meeting. Whether you follow Glasser's terminology or remember the sacredness of circles as shapes, you'll find that a circle of children and teachers talking together, respecting and caring for each other, is an effective way to encourage thoughtful, positive oral language experiences. A third-grade teacher shared this example:

> There were complaints from the children about being disturbed by others while they were working. I said, "Let's take time and give attention to this problem, and see if we can't find a way to solve it." We cleared a space and sat on the floor in a circle. We discussed all aspects of the problem and listened to all the complaints and ideas for remedying the situation. Here are some of the solutions agreed on by the class.

> 1. When people are reading, do not disturb them.
> 2. When people are working on a project, don't talk to them unless they want you to.

3. When people are busy working around you, speak in a very low voice.

Sitting together in our Magic Circle and discussing ways to solve problems has really made a difference in the climate of our room.

Sandwiches and Other Oral Directions

In our fast-paced, complicated, technical world, people need to be able to give directions clearly and accurately. A fun way to introduce the subject of giving directions is to ask your students to think about the different steps involved in making a peanut butter and jelly sandwich.

After they have given the topic their attention, ask children to volunteer (or you call on them) to be direction-givers and listener–doers. Perhaps you'll want to have four or five pairs of students demonstrate.

Give the listener–doers two slices of bread, a knife, a jar of peanut butter, a jar of jelly, and a napkin. One child at a time has a turn to give a listener–doer directions for making a peanut butter and jelly sandwich. The listener–doer responds to each step in the process even if it is out of sequence, even if it hinders the making of the sandwich. The results of the activity are often perfectly constructed peanut butter and jelly sandwiches or hilarious messes. In one fourth-grade class, the direction-giver forgot to tell the listener–doer to open the jar of jelly. The sandwich stopped at the peanut buttering of one slice of bread!

After all the demonstrations are complete, the class discusses the importance of clarity and accuracy in the giving of directions. Ask your students to guide a group in following directions for games, crafts projects, or some everyday activities. One fourth-grade group so thoroughly enjoyed the experience that the teacher never had to assign direction-giving to each child, because everyone in the class wanted to participate!

Some of their directions were for

> making potholders
>
> making cats' cradle designs with string
>
> playing tic-tac-toe
>
> tying shoelaces
>
> making a paper airplane
>
> learning a new game
>
> doing the "moon walk"
>
> learning map directions
>
> learning a new cheer

Singing in the Classroom

There's a universal proverb: "If you can talk, you can sing." People sing their lives. Singing frees the spirit, is important in personal expression, exercises vocal cords, and is an ancient and honorable way human beings learn their language! Involved in song, children often forget their insecurities and fears. In fact, many songs help children gain confidence. You will be surprised at the number of "nontalkers" who benefit from many singing experiences. Whether children learn their alphabet letters through the ABC's song or their geography from songs like "M I S S I S S I P P I" or their numbers from "This Old Man" or about historical characters from songs like "Davy Crockett" or about dramatic events like the sinking of the *Titanic* from songs like "It Was Sad When the Old Ship Went Down," songs and singing are a vital part of language learning, language development.

Very young children know the lyrics to popular songs. My preschoolers lisped the words to songs by Lionel Richie, Michael Jackson, and Tina Turner! In addition to the excellent albums produced by such classroom favorites as Hap Palmer, Ella Jenkins, Patty Zeitlin, and Raffi, you have a world of folk music, classical music, music from around the world to choose from, to share with your students.

A poignant incident comes to mind to illustrate the importance of songs in the lives of children. My mother came to this country from Rumania shortly after World War I at the age of 16. Recently, she and my father were taking a walk around Rockefeller Center in New York City. The Center was bright with the colors of the flags of all the nations. My mother had an instant idea: "I wanted to find the Rumanian flag. But," she explained, "I forgot the colors. I looked at all the flags and couldn't find it. Then, I remembered the little song we learned in school that told the colors of the flag. I sang it to myself, remembered the colors, and found the flag!"

You do not need to sound like Frank Sinatra or Ella Fitzgerald to encourage singing in your room. Your enjoyment of singing, the value you give it, your willingness to correlate it with all areas of the curriculum, will provide inspiration enough for successful experiences.

A friend was substituting in a kindergarten class when the children asked her to sing them a song. She blushed, saying that she had an awful voice, but the children insisted that she sing. She swallowed her self-consciousness and sang "Row, Row, Row Your Boat." When she finished, she apologized for her voice. "That's OK," a kindergarten boy comforted her. "You did your best!"

Do your best! If your best needs help, invite parents, community resources, other teachers, other students to sing with your class. Your own students, with your encouragement, will provide leadership and material. Don't forget to discover the many songs your students already know, love, and can't wait to sing! Write your own lyrics to popular melodies!

As often as possible, correlate movement patterns with singing. Clap hands, tap fingers, stamp feet, create finger and hand plays to accompany songs. The next chapter shares numerous movement ideas.

Serendipity in the Classroom

Often the unplanned, unanticipated surprise moment turns out to be the most meaningful time of the day. Veteran teachers verify that spontaneous happenings often provide material for their most successful learning experiences. If you are an open, flexible person responsive to the children and their interests, responsive to the environment around you, you will discover many opportunities for exciting oral language adventures.

Rainstorm   In the middle of the day, the sky darkened with gathering clouds and it began to rain. The children kept looking up from their reading books to the windows. The teacher looked too, and discovered the change of weather. Thunder rolled and a crack of lightning flashed through the sky. The rain fell in torrents.

"Let's close our books for a while and watch the rain," the teacher suggested to the delight of the already distracted children. They stood at the window and watched the storm. They listened to the sound of the rain. They talked about the rain and how it made them feel. They wrote about rain and drew pictures of rainstorms. The teacher reported this as one of her most enjoyable teaching days.

Doodle-Bugs   I was about to begin a unit about the farm with a group of kindergartners when Bobby interrupted by showing his bruised finger and complaining about the pain. The other children crowded around to see the important finger. Finger was replacing farm as the topic of the day! Bobby was wearing a shirt that had "I Am A Doodle-Bug" written on it. I touched his shirt and read it aloud. "I never saw a Doodle-Bug, did you?" I asked the class. They nodded their heads. Certainly.

"What does a Doodle-Bug look like?" I asked. They dropped to the floor in various Doodle-Bug positions.

"How do Doodle-Bugs move?"

"Very fast."

"Very slow."

"Kinda bumpy."

"They crawl."

Ideas bounced around the room. "Show me," I said. The kids rolled, slithered, crawled, slid. They finally decided that they wanted their Doodle-Bugs to move backwards, which they enjoyed demonstrating.

"Do Doodle-Bugs make sounds?" I asked, applauding their movements.

"Of course they do!"

Again—ideas exchanged, sounds explored. They finally agreed that Doodle-Bugs make a peppy, squeaky sound, which they all made with great concentration.

The children and I discovered tricks Doodle-Bugs do, games Doodle-Bugs play, and how Doodle-Bugs sleep. Finally, when all the Doodle-Bugs were asleep, I began a story about Doodle-Bugs on the farm. The Doodle-Bugs discovered all the aspects of the farm that I wanted to share with the children. Through sharing ideas, movement, improvisation, songs, games, pictures, and stories, we covered the farm from field to barn and enjoyed every minute.

Will you make room for Doodle-Bugs in your curriculum?[33]

The Last Word

Some students will be reluctant to talk in the classroom. Don't force them, single them out, or humiliate them. Always encourage them to become involved, to express themselves, and let them know that you care about their opinions and ideas and will respect them. One teacher said, "I put my kids in such fun situations that they almost have to participate—they can't resist!" The best teachers I know always wait a few seconds longer for answers and responses. Take that extra time to give children the chance to speak. If you have a few reluctant talkers in your class, occasionally take them aside in a small group and have a quiet talk with them. Sometimes, the competition in a large, verbal group is too much for inhibited children, and they need experiences that assure and encourage them.

Experienced teachers will testify that, often, children who do not participate, who hardly speak, will go home and report in detail what "we did today." To illustrate, one of Candace Mazur's favorite subjects to enjoy with kids is *trolls*. She has about a hundred experiences to celebrate trolls. The children are excited with her as they move, make sounds, improvise stories, create dances, design masks, and sing troll songs in their free-spirited exploration. On one of their troll journeys, Candace noticed that one boy was completely holding back. He stood on the side, didn't move, didn't say a word. Arms folded, he seemed hardly interested in the activities. Candace chalked it up to "You win some; you lose some." That night, the parents were invited to an Open House. A very enthusiastic couple greeted Candace with this news:

"I don't know what you did today, but our son came home and turned his whole room into a troll cave!"

Their son was the boy who never participated!

Remember to keep drawing circles that take kids IN!

Creativity in the classroom means fun. Fun means that total silence will not reign at all times. The sounds in your classroom will be those of children talking, laughing, exchanging ideas, and learning together. The most beautiful classes to visit are the ones in which everyone is involved in exciting projects. There is always movement, sound, and life; the classroom reflects the dynamism of life. Talking is not a crime! The only check is volume. Reread the list in Chapter 4 for ideas on getting attention. Once you and your students agree on the signals, volume control is easy.

How Do I Know These Methods Are Working?

Because your relationship with your students is honest and authentic, you have made them aware of how important it is for them to develop competency, ease, and fluency in oral language in order to improve communication. Your students are an important part of the process of evaluating how successful your efforts have been. Their ideas, suggestions, responses, observations, and conclusions about oral language activities are an essential aspect of their individual and group development. After all your oral language activities, leave a few minutes for evaluation with your students. I listened with joy to a group of first graders talk about a discussion they had about birthday presents.

The teacher asked, "Well, I think we all had a chance to share today. Did we leave anyone out?" No. Everyone had contributed something to the birthday presents discussion. The children were glowing.

"Sandy wasn't mean to me today. He let me talk!" a tiny, blue-eyed girl said. Sandy puffed proudly.

"I think a good thing about today's discussion was that no one was mean. Everyone talked and everyone listened," the teacher praised.

"But Rena talked too low. I could hardly hear her!" aggressive Andy criticized. Rena flushed.

The teacher to the rescue: "Maybe we should all try to talk loudly and clearly so everyone can hear us, because we're all interested in what everyone has to say." The teacher wrote these important ideas on the board.

Be Sensitive to the Feelings of Children

If children understand the goals of learning, they will take pride in their growing abilities in communication and self-expression; they will be pleased with their developing competence and confidence in articulating ideas, opinions, feelings, and questions. A constant emphasis on the positive rather than the negative, on suggestions rather than criticisms, on encouraging rather than discouraging, should be the pattern of evaluation with your students.

An effective challenge to your students following most oral language activities is "How can we improve our discussion?" or "Can you think of ways that would improve the way we give oral reports?"

"John, you had so many interesting things to say, but when you looked down at the floor, I missed hearing them. Let's *all* try to aim our words at the people we're speaking to!"

It's fun to experiment and students can easily see the value of your suggestions when they try them out for themselves.

Tension, anxiety, and loss of self-confidence are to be avoided at all costs. Harsh criticism, humiliation, and rejection absolutely guarantee one thing: the squelching and smothering of a child's freedom of expression. Remember that "Teaching is one of the few professions that permits love."[34]

CAREFUL

Evaluating Oral Language

There are three areas to focus on in your evaluation: your class as a whole; each individual student; your own role. Write checklists for each of these areas, keeping your language simple but pertinent.

Checklist for the Class

1. Did the group seem interested in the activity? in all of it? in parts?
2. Did the activity inspire wide participation or did just a few children become involved?
3. Was basic courtesy practiced during the activity or were there frequent interruptions, distractions, or outbursts?
4. Would I repeat this activity in the same way? How would I change it to improve it?

Checklist for the Individual Child

1. Does the child participate in classroom activities in general?
2. Does the child participate only in some activities and sit out others?
3. Does the child work and play silently?
4. Does the child talk easily to other individuals? Whom?
5. Does the child talk easily to the group?
6. Does the child contribute ideas when participating in small group discussions?
7. Does the child express his or her ideas with ease? with difficulty? with confidence? with hesitation?
8. What kinds of things does the child talk about most freely?
9. In what kinds of situations does the child talk most comfortably?
10. Is the child responsive when asked questions during discussions? during small group meetings?
11. Are there any areas in the child's oral language behavior that need extra attention? What?
12. When does the child seem most at ease and happiest?

Checklist for Yourself

1. Approximately how much time did I spend today asking questions of my class, explaining, giving instructions, scolding, discussing, conversing, sharing? What kinds of questions did I ask?
2. Did I invite the students to plan or decide together about an activity or program?
3. Did the children have the chance to express their ideas freely?
4. Did I go out of my way to encourage or praise a more reluctant, shy child today?
5. Did I make time today to speak quietly for a few minutes to each student on an individual basis?
6. In what ways did I help the children to improve their oral language skills today in a nonthreatening, supportive way?

7. How did I stimulate discussion today?

8. Did I share anything of myself today?

9. What did I find out today from the children about themselves that I didn't know before?

10. Did I leave enough time after each of my questions for the children to take a breath, think about the question, and then answer it?

11. Was I courteous and respectful? Was I an appreciative and responsive listener?

12. In what ways can I improve my role in encouraging oral language?

13. What was the most enjoyable part of today? When was I most at ease and comfortable?

14. Did I enjoy talking to my students today?

15. Do I think they enjoyed talking to me?

"Teach them the right way to use the voice. Teach them to read with their ears as well as their eyes. We must teach them the sacredness of human communication."[35]

ENDNOTES

[1] Adapted by Dr. Marc Lee Raphael, Department of Jewish Studies, Ohio State University.

[2] Maryruth K. Nivens, "Is Yours a Thumbs-Up or a Thumbs-Down School?" *Phi Delta Kappan* Feb. 1985: 427–29.

[3] Nivens.

[4] Geraldine Lee Susi, "The Teacher/Writer: Model, Learner, Human Being," *Language Arts* 61.7 (1984): 712–16.

[5] J. Murray Lee and Doris May Lee, *The Child and His Curriculum*, 3rd ed. (New York: Appleton, 1960) 301.

[6] Ruth Strickland, *The Language Arts in Elementary School* (Boston: Heath, 1957) 132.

[7] Marge Scherer, interview with John Goodlad, *The Instructor* Jan. 1984: 56–58.

[8] Scherer.

[9] National Council of Teachers of English (1952), in Lee and Lee, *The Child and His Curriculum*. For further information of the statement, write to National Council of Teachers of English, 1111 Kenyon Road, Urbana, IL 81801.

[10] NCTE.

[11] Speech Association of America, "The Field of Speech: Its Purpose and Its Scope in Education," SAA Symposium, New York, 1963.

[12] Some excellent books on oral language:

C. Ausberger, M. J. Martin, and J. Crieghton, *Learning to Talk Is Child's Play: Helping Pre-Schoolers Develop Language* (Tucson: Communication Skill Builders, 1982).

B. Bos, *Before the Basics: Creating Conversations with Children* (Roseville: Turn the Page, 1983).

K. E. Nelson, ed., *Children's Language* (Hillsdale: Earlbaum, 1983) vol. 4.

P. H. Berne and L. M. Savary, *Building Self-Esteem in Children* (New York: Crossroad/Continuum, 1985).

L. S. Vygotsky, *Thought and Language* (Cambridge: MIT P, 1962).

Kenneth Goodman, *Language and Literacy: The Selected Writings of Kenneth Goodman* (Boston: Routledge, 1982) vol. 2.

G. Pinnell, *Discovering Language with Children* (Urbana: NCTE, 1975).

Joan Tough, *Focus on Meaning: Talking to Some Purpose with Young Children* (London: Allen, 1973).

[13] David Dillon, Introduction, *Language Arts* 61.2 (1984).

[14] Dillon.

[15] Pablo Neruda, *Language Arts* Feb. 1984: 124.

[16] "Talk and Learning in the Classroom: An Interview with Anthony Adams," *Language Arts* 61.2 (1984): 119–24.

[17] An excellent summary of research in oral language has been written by William H. Rupley, *Elementary English* Apr. 1974: 519–24.

[18] Mary H. Mosley and Paul J. Smith, "What Works in Learning? Students Provide the Answers," *Phi Delta Kappan* Dec. 1982: 273.

[19] See the works of Douglas Barnes: *From Communication to Curriculum* (Hammondsworth: Penguin, 1976), and *Communication and Learning in Small Groups* (London: Routledge, 1976).

[20] See the work of Roger Shuy, Walter Wolfram, and William Riley, "Linguistic Correlates of Social Stratification in Detroit Speech," Cooperative Research Project 6-1347, Part LV (East Lansing: Michigan State U, 1967) 2–5; Robert Rosenthal and Lenore Jacobson, "Self-Fulfilling Prophecies in the Classroom: Teacher's Expectations as Unintended Determinants of Pupil's Intellectual Competence," American Psychological Association Meeting, Washington, D.C., Sept. 1967, reprinted in *Scientific American* 218.4 (Apr. 1968): 20–25.

[21] Strickland 144.

[22] Thomas R. McDaniel, "A Primer on Motivation: Principles Old and New," *Phi Delta Kappan* Sept. 1984: 46–49.

[23] Antoine de Saint Exupéry, *The Little Prince* (New York: Harcourt, 1971) 76.

[24] For information of *Workshop Way*, write to Grace Pilon, Xavier University, P. O. Box 47, 7325 Palmetto Street, New Orleans, LA 70125.

[25] Lee and Lee 301–305.

[26] Albert Cullum, *Push Back the Desks* (New York: Citation, 1967) 52.

[27] This experience happened at a "Days of Creation" arts program for Camp Ken-Jockety, Galloway, Ohio (Seal of Ohio Girl Scouts), Summer 1985. The poem was published in the children's magazine *The Kids' Connection* Fall 1985.

[28] John G. Neihardt, *Black Elk Speaks* (New York: Pocket/Simon, 1972).

[29] Alex Haley, *Roots* (Garden City: Doubleday, 1976).

[30] Phillip Lopate, *Being with Children* (New York: Bantam, 1976).

[31] Chick Moorman and Dee Dishon, *Our Classroom: We Can Learn Together* (Englewood Cliffs: Prentice-Hall, 1983).

[32] See Laura E. Berk's "Why Children Talk to Themselves," *Young Children* July 1985: 46.

[33] Mimi Brodsky Chenfeld, "Doodlebugs and Other Basics," *Phi Delta Kappan* Mar. 1978: 479–480.

[34] Theodore Roethke, *Straw for the Fire* (Garden City: Doubleday, 1974).

[35] Roethke 163.

6

Movement and Drama: Old Ways of Learning

There is no race without a history of dancing and unless physically restrained, all children dance.

OLGA MAYNARD[1]

Children play. Wherever we find children, we find play. They pretend. They try on life. Play is as natural to children as eating and sleeping. It is a fundamental force in growing.

GERALDINE BRAIN SIKS[2]

Melissa is two and a half years old. Watch as she bounces from room to room involved in the important business of playing. She hop-skips toward you, flops on the floor, and pops up again to mix and serve you a delicious invisible meal. She pumps gas into her tricycle and drives it around the living room collecting invisible, but heavy, trash cans. She loves trash collection day! Now she's a letter carrier with an important message for you. Open it before she turns into a doctor curing a sick teddy bear.

Meanwhile, look at Greg, who is five. Today he is a firefighter, whizzing past on the firetruck to save a burning building. Yesterday he was a sheriff keeping crime off the streets. Now he's practicing his "twirling" so he can lead the parade. Tune in tomorrow to find out who he will be. You can be sure that he won't be just sitting still. He will be skipping, jumping, zig-zagging along in the universal dance of childhood. Every day children demonstrate that "the most interesting distance to a point is not a straight line!"[3]

Take a walk around your neighborhood and watch the children. What are they doing? On my walk this afternoon, I noticed these scenes: one group of kids was practicing cartwheels on a lawn heaped high with autumn leaves; a group of six- and seven-year-old girls was performing high school cheers that they had learned by observation; one little band of "break-dancers" was so involved in their choreography that they didn't even wave as I passed them; and the four kids sitting on a nearby porch, heads together in deep concentration, told me that their game was "too complicated to explain it to you, Mim!"

What do you notice?

By watching Greg, Melissa, and all the children move and play, you will discover what interests them, what is important to them, and how they feel about themselves, other people, things, events, and relationships in their environment. For them, each day is a new adventure, a new triumph, a new link with what was learned and enjoyed the day before.

Leave your neighborhood and travel the world! Wherever you go, no matter the country or customs, children will play, children will move. This is the language, *the work*, the way of learning of childhood.

Do You Remember?

When you were a child you sang, danced, and playacted. Through your games, you rehearsed various lifestyles and characterizations, practicing and preparing for adult life. While you played, the game *was* your reality. If you were normally shy and quiet, you might have become bold and aggressive in imitation of the character you were playing. You made up songs, invented dances, and composed intricate, dramatic plots. You rarely played in silence, probably accompanying your activities with a variety of words and sounds. You may have disguised your voice to express a change of character. You used various props to add authenticity to your games. A towel tied around your neck made a magic cape; an old bathrobe became a dress for a princess; pebbles were money, macaroni, or treasure. You didn't live in a vacuum. Your movement and games evolved from

an idea, a story, a television program, an event, a person, a place, an object—
something that caught your imagination.

Try to remember how deeply and for how long you stayed fascinated by a
favorite story, idea, or game. *Young children have remarkable attention spans
for the subjects that compel them*. They don't become bored with the same story
played for days and sometimes weeks. Repetition is part of the rhythm of childhood.

Not only did you learn to express yourself through movement and drama,
but you *learned your language!* And you learned a lot about the world around
you as you tried to make sense of it, tried to understand its complications. Your
play became another way of knowing, another way of comprehending feelings,
conflicts, relationships, concepts.

Ruth Sawyer believes that children are the freest, most universal creators.

> Left unhampered, they begin very young to put into everyday life a series of
> masterpieces of creative thinking and doing. . . . They work with direction.
> They strike at the core of what they would express. They have nothing to
> discard because they have accumulated nothing unnecessary. It is as if they
> were always saying, "This I like. This I will make-sing-play-be."[4]

When Do Children Learn to Be Afraid?

Most babies are not born afraid or inhibited. They delight in exploring the
world around them, discovering their own powers, experimenting with sounds
and shapes. The tragedy in our society is how soon our children lose their
freedom to play, how quickly their enjoyment in expressing themselves through
movement and "acting-out" is frozen. They too soon learn to repress their
spontaneity and inventiveness; to inhibit their original ideas, observations, and
feelings; to settle into stereotyped patterns in a world of Right and Wrong and
very little in between.

Since I began teaching in 1956, I have noticed a pattern. Of course what
I give you here is a generalized description, but I know that many of you who
have worked with children of all ages will recognize its validity. I call it the
"chronology of creativity." It goes something like this:

Preschoolers and kindergartners   bouncy walks, eager and open faces,
ready for new experiences

First and second graders   traces of bounce, more shy and hesitant,
more "wait and see"

Third and fourth graders   shoulders a little slumpy, arms folded, giggly,
whisper to each other, attitudes more skeptical

Fifth and sixth graders   I call these kids the "wall people." Often it seems
as if some powerful glue has fastened them to a wall where they wait, wary of
a new experience, needing to be lured into it. Their expressions are self-

conscious, often suspicious, and they hug their arms tightly to their bodies. "Show me! Convince me!"—they seem to be challenging.

Seventh grade and above I call these the "Pompeii" kids. Their bodies, minds, and spirits are caught in the lava from the volcano, trapped inside the hardened lava for thousands of years until a dedicated, determined, persistent teacher helps them break out.

(I share these images with the children if they seem to need them. If the images fit. I share them as a way of expressing my commitment to protect and encourage their freedom of expression, as a way of asking them to join in the effort.)

Please note that in the eighties, with the push on younger children to enter programs that emphasize skills and academic achievement, the kindergartners no longer fit this chronology. Many have already lost their eagerness and openness for new experiences as a result of such high-anxiety education.

Virginia Tanner, nationally known for her work in movement education, reports that

> the child at the age of four seems to possess tremendous creative energy, but by the age of nine seems to have had it so dimmed that it is no longer a source of rich fulfillment. Could it be that through unimaginative teaching methods and lack of vision, hours of unguided television, stereotyped toys, we are stifling the very thing that will bring all children their greatest moments of happiness?[5]

Gladys Andrews, another pioneer in movement education, sadly observes children who no longer move and play joyfully and spontaneously.

> It seems appalling that much of children's vibrant, natural zest may be lost or submerged as they grow older. From the second grade upward, children are apt to appear hesitant, self-conscious, inhibited, bored and uninspired. When this is true, something tragic has happened to their way of learning and to their urge to explore new realms and tell about them.[6]

Is this sad chronicle of diminishing creative powers inevitable? Do young children have to lose their joyousness and lightness of spirit and become closed, uptight, self-conscious adolescents? Can the older children be helped to revive and rejuvenate their creative energies so they are able to rediscover the exhilaration of self-expression, of experimentation, of playfulness?

Just as Americans are jogging and cycling and working out to keep their bodies in shape, so programs are needed to keep minds and imaginations in shape. Bodies have to be warmed up so they can fully express human emotions, themes, and ideas. Imaginations have to be enriched so information is not the sole goal and single-level understanding is not the product.

"What flower was the War of Roses named after?"

"The rose."

"Good. You made Honor Roll."

Jenny walked up to her third-grade teacher and asked, "Is this language arts?"

"Yes, Jenny."

"Well, we had the language. When do we get the arts?"

Basics to the Rescue

There is a great deal of talk today about movement and drama and their place in the curriculum. Some people consider these areas "way-out ideas." Others call them "frills." I presented a program in a city that had just voted down its school levy. One of the teachers told me, "Creativity is out of the program. The arts are out!"

The arts have never been out of the human program. They are the oldest ways we have communicated and expressed ourselves. They are the REAL "basics." Movement, drama, visual arts, and music are as ancient as the first shrug, strut, grimace, grin, pendant, or pigment; as old as the first foot tapped to express nervousness, victory, or anger; as historic as the first clap of hands to show pleasure or celebration; the first mask to frighten away enemies or to send off a hunting party.

We know that our cave ancestors marked their lives with drama, with movement, with the arts. They left ritual objects, musical instruments, palettes and brushes, wall paintings that showed bodies in movement patterns, bodies dancing.

Olga Maynard reminds us that "for the greater part of time and the greatest number of people, there have been no divisions between music, dance, and drama, between poetry and song. . . . Music as magic is the oldest form, stemming from the prehistoric time when dance was religion, science, art and entertainment for mankind."[7]

> We are a rhythmic race. Our hearts beat, our blood courses, we breathe, and walk and run, in rhythms. We are creatures of a turning planet. . . . We walk and run, the simplest forms of locomotion, from the instinct by which we dance.
>
> We speak; therefore we sing. Above all other forms of life we are able to make articulate and meaningful sounds as self-expression and communication.
>
> It is because we are so shaped and motivated as human beings that we dance, sing, make music and poetry. And because of them, are made to feel and to think.[8]

Just as these human arts have blended through history, so they continue to connect all subject areas in classrooms that invite them to enrich learning experiences.

This chapter could very well have been scattered throughout the book, combining with every other chapter, for the arts combine with all the components of the language arts curriculum as well as all subjects. But many, many teachers are still reluctant to invite movement and drama into their classrooms.

Many teachers do not feel confident including these arts in their program. With or without failed school levys, they "cut them out." So here we give them their own chapter to highlight their importance, to help you see how easily and naturally they fit into your school day, and, more important, how hungry you and your students are for their bright presence.

Even though movement and drama are totally integrating kinds of activities, for clarity and as a demonstration of accessibility they will be discussed separately. (Keep them linked in your mind as you read! Keep making connections!) We'll begin with movement.

Expression through Movement

Simply defined, movement experiences (or movement education) center on the use of the body in expression and communication. The movement activities are a way of learning, a way of thinking, a way of knowing. Movement is vitally linked to language and is a language of its own. In many cultures, the language of the body is sacred and conveys legends and stories, religious beliefs and customs. In many cultures, special rituals combining dance, drama, music, poetry, and visual arts cure the sick, make crops grow, cause rain to fall, and bless babies so they will grow strong and healthy.

Often, children who have difficulty *explaining* an idea or a concept—for example, "up"—easily demonstrate their comprehension of "up" through movement. We have a language of movement that illustrates our perceptions and understandings. Prepositions, verbs, adverbs, relationships (spatial and interpersonal) are expressed naturally through movement. Superlatives jump off a dry page in a text to charm children with the challenge of interpreting one of the Seven Dwarfs—"Sleepy," "Sleepier," "Sleepiest"—with each level another body shape! *Language at the core! Another valid way of knowing!*

In programs around the country for people who suffer from emotional and mental disorders, dance and movement have been rediscovered as important therapeutic components (something our ancestors knew very well!). The exciting news is that movement education has also moved back into the lives of our *unlabeled* students!

Movement in the classroom is simply returning this oldest of the arts to its rightful place—as PART OF EVERYTHING—*not separate from but part of* all other areas of the curriculum.

Movement activities have very few requirements: a willing teacher; a group of children; a little time; a little space; an idea; a climate of trust; enthusiasm, encouragement, respect, safety, enjoyment, and success.

Perhaps at this very minute, you feel like putting down this book, shifting your position, standing up, stretching, bending, shaking out your muscles. Why don't you do just that?

Now, don't you feel more relaxed? Less tense? Less restless? Better able to concentrate?

Movement is a sign of life! When something stops moving for a long time we say it's dead. We don't teach children to move. They already know how to move. Tragically, when they come to school they often are taught NOT to move.

With all our knowledge about and memory of moving, we still instruct children to "sit still" for long periods of time and often punish them for moving. One third grader told me that the only time his class was permitted to move around was during recess, and today they were punished and didn't get recess because so many children were wiggling in their seats during class.

The human body is an incredible machine, capable of expressing many levels of emotions and ideas as well as performing Olympian physical feats. For some children, moving their bodies may be the only effective way of communicating and evoking a response when all other methods have failed. Scientists tell us that many children learn more easily through imaginative, creative movement and physical activity than through the conventional, abstract methods of written and verbal messages.[9] Most children love to move and will eagerly share their ideas about moving, often more easily than their ideas on other topics. Through movement, they develop confidence and fluency in communicative skills as well as positive self-images. James Moffett believes that "nonverbal communication provides the best pathway to speech."[10]

Kate Witkin writes eloquently of the values and practicality of movement education in her book *To Move, To Learn* (Schocken, 1978). She sees movement activities as ways to totally involve children in the learning process, in the joy of learning. She reminds us that the ancient Greeks celebrated the harmony between the body and the mind and made of this harmony an aesthetic. All aspects of the curriculum are enhanced by success-oriented movement and arts-related experiences.

Fresh from classrooms, Marlene Robbins, a dancer and dance educator working in many programs and schools with people from preschoolers to senior citizens, talks freely and with great dedication about movement and learning:

> Movement is the most exciting aspect of learning. It makes information personal. Take the story of Peter and the Wolf. If the kids hear the story and the music, they love it. But, if they get to move to it, get to be Peter, the duck, the bird, the wolf—then they *really* experience the story. They know how the characters feel. . . . Movement enriches all subject areas. It makes learning fun. If we're working with number concepts, we go beyond reading the number, writing and recognizing it. We clap it, step it, jump it, discover its rhythm in time. . . . Movement activities allow you to be nonjudgmental, noncompetitive. We're not talking Bad or Good or Right or Wrong. In a safety net of success, movement gives you a chance to explore ideas from all sides. . . . When people move in a safe, relaxed way, they go beyond inhibitions and self-consciousness to freer, higher levels. At a recent teachers' meeting, I started with an easy warm-up sitting right in our chairs, simple exercises that evolved into people taking turns leading. That led to a little improvised story. Faces changed. People went from serious and nervous to laughter and playfulness. One of the teachers described the experience as "movement to feelings of love, to feelings of joy."
>
> This is possible in any classroom. I see so many children spending hours sitting still. Movement gives them the opportunity to go from a passive way of learning to a more active, involved level. You can see the kids go from being slumped indifferently to concentrated, alert, curious, excited bodies. It helps people to get excited about thinking. So many times we learn in compartments and our thinking is confined to little boxes. Movement helps expand thinking and learning into the circle of ideas. . . . We never *really* know how individuals learn things, so the more avenues we offer, the greater the possibility that more and more people are reached in meaningful ways. . . . Isn't that the goal of education?[11]

At this writing, Marlene is involved in a process of bringing together people from all generations to share words, music, memories, and movement in creating a multidimensional community experience.

In this chapter you will see how easily movement activities can be correlated with every aspect of the language arts as well as with the general curriculum. You don't have to be a dancer yourself to encourage your students to move. You just need to enjoy moving and believe in its importance in the curriculum. If presented without tension and rigidity, movement is the one experience that will guarantee all children success.

The activities are divided into two sections: Movement and Drama. However, you will find that movement and drama overlap and intertwine naturally. In the classroom, teachers blend them, link them, or let one evolve from the other. As you read, synthesize. Relate the ideas to other subject areas and see how naturally they flow together.

Enough said. Get moving!

QUESTION: What do I want my students to develop?
ANSWER: I want my students to develop self-confidence, awareness, imagination, self-expression as they learn about themselves, their language, and their world through diverse, enriching movement experiences.

Movement Activities

Exercise Break

Take advantage of the current emphasis on physical fitness to devote a few minutes a day to warm-up exercises. Exercises can be done right at the desks, tables, or chairs. Your students will be glad that you care enough about their physical–mental harmony and well-being to include an exercise break in the daily schedule. Both you and your students will *feel* better and *learn* better.

Exercise with imagination. Include Exercise Leader as one of the daily classroom "jobs" or responsibilities. Encourage the children to work out their own exercise sequences. There are hundreds of ways to enjoy exercise times. Here are just a few samplings:

Favorite exercises to favorite music

Sequences written on the board. Here is a favorite sequence from a fourth grade: (1) Stretches. (2) Bends. (3) Torso twists. (4) Jumps. (5) D.Y.O.T. (Do Your Own Thing—this is part of most of my warm-ups!)

Body Part exercises: head, arms, hands, shoulders, legs, A.Y.O.

Animal exercises: cat stretches, puppy wiggles, frog hops, A.Y.O.

Holiday exercises
Halloween: skeleton shake-out, robot's rigid movements, witch-crooked and
        pointy, A.Y.O.

Seasonal exercises
Winter: throwing (snowballs), shoveling, skiing movement, A.Y.O.
Summer: swimming strokes, rowing movement, lawn-mowing pushes, A.Y.O.

Parts of Speech exercises
Nouns: clowns, jugglers, farmers
Verbs: jump, hop, march, tiptoe
Adjectives: big, little, strong, weak
Adverbs: gracefully, clumsily, lightly, heavily
A.Y.O.

Nursery Rhyme exercises
Ups and Downs: Hickory Dickory Dock
Jumping Over: Jack Be Nimble, Hey Diddle Diddle
Falling Down (kids love to fall down): Humpty Dumpty, Jack and Jill
A.Y.O.

Alphabet exercises: Change bodies into, say, the letter *T*. If you were the letter *T*, what exercises could you do? Experiment and discover! Turn on music and have a *T* party. Try *I*, *X*, *Y*.

Four Directions exercises: Whatever we do, we do it to the north, the south, the east, or the west. We can do the same exercise four times or change our exercises for each direction (for example, facing north, do jumping jacks; facing south, touch your toes).

Follow the Leader: Every person leads an exercise (don't force reluctant leaders). Move quickly around the room. After everyone has a turn, go to D.Y.O.T. Then change—do another Thing![12]

Show Me

A magic phrase that almost instantly adds the dimension of movement to any learning experience is "Show me!" Here are a few examples:

You are reading and talking about trees. You have trees on your minds. "Show me the shape of a tree. Let's see your branches."

You are studying space and talking about antigravity. "Show me how an astronaut moves in space. Are you wearing special boots? How do you walk?"

You are learning about antonyms. "Show me the opposite of 'down.'"

"Show me" works perfectly with another suggestion, one that is more *real* than theoretical. "What if someone didn't speak or understand English? We would need to communicate to that person in another way. Show me how we would communicate these ideas":

Welcome to our classroom!
Please be quiet.
Listen!
Let's have a drink of water.
Now we are going to write.
A.Y.O.

Songs

Children of all ages love songs that involve movement. Younger children never tire of "The Eensy Weensy Spider," for example. If you have had camp experience, you know that even cool middle-grade kids will sing and move to numerous intricate camp songs! Go beyond the familiar, preset movement songs and with your students create original movement to accompany *any* song. Children easily add movement to such songs as "I've Been Working on the Railroad" and "This Old Man." A group of sixth graders choreographed a very powerful movement accompaniment to "Follow the Drinking Gourd," a song that helped slaves communicate the road to freedom.

A good way to loosen muscles and inhibitions is to encourage the children to "conduct" the music. Ask them to "play instruments" (imaginary) to the music and watch strumming, clapping, drumming movement patterns emerge.

Imaginative teachers like Jay Brand are always open to experimentation and discovery. I watched Jay work with a group of third and fourth graders as they started conducting to his offering of music. Some of the albums Jay shared with his students were

Boogi Woogi Parties
Olatunji (African drums)
Ravel's *Bolero* and *Spanish Symphony*
Benny Goodman's *Swing into Spring*
Rimski-Korsakov's *Scheherezade*

As the kids conducted to this diverse selection of music, Jay encouraged them to imagine actions or events the music suggested. The conducting freed the kids to go on with improvisations *to* the music that included little scenes of ordinary gestures like brushing, sweeping, painting, eating, and jumping.

Fingerplays   These are very popular in the early grades. Once again, don't rely solely on those fingerplays found in books and magazines. Often, the best ideas come from you and your students making up your own fingerplays to enrich poems, chants, and songs.

Games   Those that involve movement, such as "Ring Around the Rosy" or "Farmer in the Dell," are part of every child's experience and familiar to us all. Movement games like "Hokey Pokey" are easily expanded with such stanzas as "You put your elbows in . . ." or "You put your shoulders in . . ." or other less celebrated body parts.

Improvisations   Original movement games are easy to learn and so much fun for you and your students. "This Is What I Can Do" is a singsong chant with a leader in the middle. The child in the middle does something, such as dancing, hopping, clapping, making a funny face. All the children follow, and then another child takes a turn in the center.

The chant goes like this:

> This is what I can do.
> Everybody do it too.
> This is what I can do.
> Now I pass it on to you.

A nice variation of the game is to say the children's names: "This is what Sara can do. . . ."

Everyone moves and participates. Everyone wins. Make up your own chants and games.

Stories, Ballads, and Poems

Children love to move to stories and poems as they are read or after they are read. Movement activities evolve naturally into reading, writing, and art sessions.

After improvising movement about birds, the first graders became so inter-

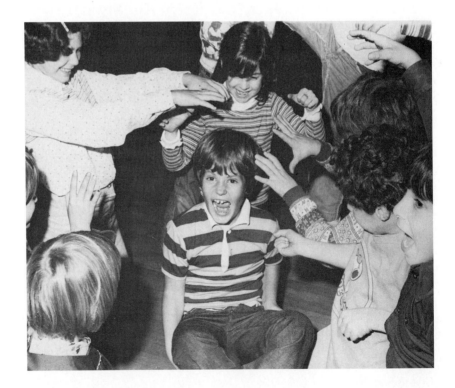

ested in them that, for a long time after, they were reading and writing about birds.

Many stories already suggest movement. There's lots of running in "The Gingerbread Man." We've changed the chant to "Run, run as fast as you can. You can't catch me. Nobody can!"

In our version of "The Three Little Pigs," the children are the flimsy houses of straw and sticks that easily *fall down* when the wolf huffs and puffs. Boy, do they show their muscles and resist the wolf's hot air when they are the house made of bricks!

Watch older children change from inhibited to eager when asked to "work out" some stories, poems, and songs to present to *younger classes*. They are proud to be a touring group of strolling minstrels and troubadours.

Don't feel you must adapt an entire book or story for movement interpretation. Often just a few scenes or themes evoke an enthusiastic response. Celebrate those parts. For example, children especially love the scene in Robert McCloskey's *Make Way for Ducklings* (Penguin, 1976) in which Michael, the friendly police officer, stops traffic in a busy intersection to allow Mrs. Mallard and her ducklings to cross to safety. We turn the children into groups of traffic vehicles (they choose their vehicles, of course!). The teacher is Michael, who stops the traffic and waves along another group of children, turned into mallards, who quack and waddle across the "intersection." This is the kind of delightful activity that causes "Can we do that again?" requests and you will have to repeat it over and over until every group of children gets to be the ducks!

Some favorite stories that I have shared with children in movement interpretations are *Where the Wild Things Are*, by Maurice Sendak (Harper and Row, 1963); *The Emperor's Nightingale*, by Hans Christian Andersen (Schocken, 1981); *Play with Me*, by Marie Hall Ets (Viking, 1955); *The Snowy Day*, by Ezra Jack Keats (Viking, 1962); and *In My Mother's House*, by Ann Nolan Clark (Viking Seafarer, 1972).

You don't have to pick parts. The children enjoy moving as a group, interpreting their own monster shapes and movements, for example, in *Where the Wild Things Are*. Shake out the monster shapes and become a kid named Max sailing and rowing across the sea. In *The Snowy Day*, we all lie on the floor and make snow angels or walk around the room stepping in snow, making footprint designs, making tracks.

Many poems *already* suggest movement. Read and listen to the poems and do what they say. For example, Shel Silverstein's "Dancin' Pants" gives you verbs such as *bounce, whirl, twirl, jiggle*, and *prance*. "Orchestra" tells us to play our first instruments, our own bodies. The silly poem "Two Witches" by Alexander Resnikoff plays with words and imaginations as it tells the story of the itchy witch. "Wiggly Giggles" by Stacy Jo Crossen and Natalie Anne Covell is a terrific poem to move to as an often-needed tension break. Try it following a test. What about *before* the test? Experiment! David McCord's "Every Time

I Climb a Tree" encourages climbing, growing movement. And what do we see as we climb the tree? *Show it.**

Children's original stories, poems, and songs can always be used to inspire movement. Here is an example written by kindergartners and first graders. Supply the choreography from your own imagination.

Hop, hop,
Kangaroo.
Stop, stop,
Kangaroo.
What are you going to do,
Kangaroo?
Boo hoo,
Kangaroo.

Hop, hop while drinking pop.
Jump, jump while getting mumps.
Skate, skate with a plate.
Hike, hike, ride a bike.

Crawl like a caterpillar.
Swim like a fish.
Sneak like an alligator.
Make a wish.

Choreograph Your Own Videos The decade of the eighties introduced videos to American pop culture—movement and drama to go along with songs. Most children KNOW the words to most popular songs of the day; they are already rich with those language resources. Encourage them to create movement to accompany their favorite songs and to share their "works" with the class. Be sure the *words* to the songs are included (write them on the board, or have the kids make copies of the words and run them off, or copy them on a large sheet of chart paper). You'll be delightfully surprised to discover that, often, children who have not had many successes in academic areas are outstanding "movers." Give them these opportunities to succeed. Give them every opportunity to succeed!

In 1985, the song "We Are the World," composed to symbolize the need for famine relief for hunger-stricken Ethiopia, was adapted by children of all ages and celebrated with powerful movement accompaniment. One of my favorite ways to evoke movement responses was to ask every child to "be a leader" and set a movement pattern expressing the theme of caring, loving, helping, comforting, and/or sharing. Each person led a particular movement. The group followed. Simple and meaningful.

*Shel Silverstein's "Dancin' Pants" and "Orchestra" are published in *Where the Sidewalk Ends*, by Shel Silverstein (Harper and Row, 1974). "Two Witches," by Alexander Resnikoff, "Wiggly Giggles," by Stacy Jo Crossen and Natalie Anne Covell, and "Every Time I Climb a Tree," by David McCord, are published in *The Random House Book of Poetry for Children* (Random House, 1983).

Words

Words are wonderful movement stimulators. You can move to the sound of words, create patterns to the rhythm of words, and explore ways to interpret the meaning of words through the body. Although we can only touch on a few of the ways words can be used to motivate creative movement, imagine the endless possibilities. Think of all the words you know that command movement. Some words make you move from place to place, such as *race, march, prance, gallop, run, crawl, stalk, hobble, stagger.* Other words, such as *collapse, twist, shake, whirl, sag, droop, pounce,* make you move in particular ways. We all respond to words like *snowman, clown, car wash, tunnel, revolving door, rocket ship, puddle, rubber band,* and *orchestra* with body shapes and movements that express their unique interpretation of the words.

Students can work as a group or individually and improvise movement for one word or many. Help children discover that words go beyond spelling, reading, and writing. Sometimes they have a life of their own!

After your students have practiced their spelling words all week, used them in sentences, copied them over and over, put the spelling words that lend themselves to movement interpretation in a box or bag. Divide the class into small groups and have each group pick one word. Give the groups only a few minutes to work out one or two ways to "show" the meaning of their word. ("What if someone didn't speak English? How could we show them what we mean?") The purpose is *not* to present the word as a riddle, with obstacles to its meaning, but to convey the word *as clearly as possible* through movement.

You can easily imagine how children will immediately think of ways to show such words as *transportation, friendly, practice, cooperation.*

Let Me Make You a Preposition You Can't Refuse Many teachers complain that their students don't "get" prepositions. These words are excellent moving activities. Have fun with them. Play with variations and SHOW their meanings.

"Show me Jack-Be-Nimble jumping *over* the candlestick. Did Jack jump *under* it? Let's see Jack jump *under* it. *around* it? *behind* it? *near* it? *far* from it?"

Native American prayers and chants are rich with prepositions because those words help connect people to all the forces of the universe. The Navajo morning song repeats this chant:

> May it be beautiful above you
> May it be beautiful below you
> May it be beautiful before you
> May it be beautiful behind you
> May it be beautiful all around you
> May you walk in beauty.

When I share this chant with my students, we affirm each direction—above, below, before, behind, all around—by reaching toward it with our arms and hands. When we come to the final direction, "*in* beauty," we spread our arms wide to take in the morning, the day, the world.

Music

Listening to music is an important, enriching human experience. Many schools do not have music specialists, but classroom teachers who care can correlate music with all aspects of the curriculum so their students are not deprived of this valuable experience. As often as possible, expand listening into movement. You don't have to choreograph a ballet for your class. Human beings naturally respond to music through movement. You will see that children move differently to Spanish flamenco music than they do to Old English country music. In an atmosphere of trust and freedom, children will not be afraid to reach out to new experiences. Since they *can't be wrong* about how they interpret the rhythms and melodies, they will be themselves and respond to something beautiful, fiery, pulsating, or melancholy.

A sixth-grade class was studying space. They were very involved—reading books, writing reports, forming committees, working on projects, and collecting pictures. One of the children brought in the record album for the film *2001: A Space Odyssey*. When it was played, it created such eerie, outer-space feelings that the group wanted to move. They improvised very effective movement that conveyed the emptiness, the weightlessness, and the mystery of space life.

Your part in the experience is to encourage, motivate, and support. The movement will come from the children and you. Listen and move. Let the music move you. Be eclectic. Correlate music and movement with other curriculum areas.

Basic Rhythms

Walking, skipping, hopping, galloping, running, marching, jumping, clapping, leaping, and turning to the accompaniment of recorded music or song, drum beats, tambourines, or rhythm sticks are favorite activities of all children. They enjoy making patterns and games out of natural, basic ways of moving.

Spin-offs a. We need to stretch our imaginations and encourage exploration. Ask everyone to walk. Then ask if that is the only way they can walk. All the walks will change. High, low, loud, soft, graceful, angry—the possibilities are limitless. In my experience, the record number of different walks tried was won by a group of fourth graders who created thirty-two walks. Try changing ways of jumping, hopping, running, skipping. You will be amazed at how inventive you and your students can be.

This is an excellent way to free mind and body to discover the many patterns humans are capable of choosing.

b. Combine two basic movements, such as running and stamping. This kind of spin-off works well with the whole group, smaller groups, partners, or individuals. Experiment with several variations: run, run, run, stamp; or run, run, run, run, stamp, stamp. Combine with numbers: four runs and two stamps. Combine with rhythms: four fast runs and two slow stamps. Combine with direction: four fast runs forward and two fast stamps zigzag.

Pictures Move Us

You should already be collecting photographs, prints of paintings, illustrations from magazines for use in countless creative endeavors. Use those visual images as stimuli for movement responses. For example, look at a picture of posies in a pattern. Ask your students, "Can you take those shapes? Show me." Suggest that the children bring the designs to life.

Or ask, "If you were in this picture (say, a beach scene) what would you be doing? Imagine you *are* in this picture. Where are you? How do you feel? How do you move? Show us."

Or say, "If you see a person hiding in this painting, take her shape. Turn yourself into the hiding person."

We have "moved" through art exhibits, museums, and art galleries, turning observation and comprehension into movement. Follow with creative writing and your own art activities. Add music!

Best Tricks

Every person has a specialty! Yours may be standing on one foot. Mine may be doing a backward somersault. Whatever our best trick, we are proud of it and love to do it. Talk about favorite tricks with your students. Ask them to practice their favorite tricks without paying attention to anyone else. Remind them that every person is different, unique, and has special ways of moving. The word *competition* must be removed totally from these experiences. After a few minutes of practice, turn on the music and ask the students to perform their favorite tricks to it. If time permits, have each child show a trick and have the others try to imitate it. This gives all the children a chance to lead and a chance to follow.

Spin-offs   a. Next to each person's name write the trick demonstrated. The result is a lively class movement "poem," which can be read, recited as a choral piece with rhythms and music accompanying it, illustrated, or dramatized.

Here is part of a third grade's "poem" following a "best tricks" session.

Aren't We Great?

James stood on his toes and jumped in the air.
Amy lifted one arm and one leg and didn't lose her balance.
Peter did two cartwheels.
Jean did the splits.
Andrew rolled across the floor.
Mrs. Chenfeld clicked her heels.
Marcie skipped very high.
William spun around on his stomach.
Mario stood on his head.

b. Movement challenges—such as How wide can you stretch? How far up can you reach? How high can you jump?—are all enjoyable, accessible ways to develop body awareness, appreciation, and comprehension. Children who may not pass a spelling test or who read with anxiety often find immediate success in such activities.

Animals

One sure way to get children to move, think, talk, and share is to introduce the subject of animals. Animals rank high in popularity. Imagine kids' response to this challenge: Can you think of a movement that comes from an animal?

I hope that you are ready to *see* the response in movement and to *hear* it as well—because exciting ideas will tumble out so quickly and enthusiastically that you will have to catch them and sort them out.

"Cats pounce!"
"Horses gallop!"
"Snakes crawl!"
"Horses neigh and stretch their necks!"
"Dogs roll over!"

Write the ideas on the board and have the children move to each one of them. Constantly remind them that of all the ways to hop or gallop or crawl, they are only doing a few.

Spin-offs   Ask the class to concentrate on exploring the various movements of one animal. They can imitate the movements suggested by each of the children in the class.

a. "Which animal shall we choose?"
"Snake!"
"What kinds of ways do snakes move?"
"Crawl." "Curl up." "Stretch."
"Let's do each of these."

This activity quite often becomes the beginning of an original story, which the class can later complete, and then write and illustrate.

b. Focus on one of the common animal movements like jumping. Discuss the many kinds of animals that jump. Do they all jump the same way? Imagine how much fun you and your class will have demonstrating different animal jumps, combining them, making new patterns from them. It's easy to go one step further and discover jumpy sounds and music. You might even find yourselves composing jumping poems and stories and drawing pictures that make your whole room jump.

It's possible to spend weeks and months studying just one of the basic movements. We should encourage awe and appreciation for the wonder and complexity of life—never foster a simplistic "know-it-all" attitude!

In what other ways can you extend animal movement? Do you see how easily it correlates with the other language arts components as well as art, music, science, and social studies? Remember, animals play a prominent part in many cultures.

The Chinese calendar is divided into a zodiac of twelve animals. Is this the Year of the Mouse or the Year of the Snake? In thousands of ceremonies around the world, animal masks are worn by dancers as they perform dances devoted to different animals. Poems and songs about animals are chanted. You will discover how naturally a social studies unit can be enriched by exploring movement ideas.

How Many Ways to Cross the Floor?

Another immediately successful and enjoyable activity for children of all ages is to ask the class to think of twenty-five different ways to cross the floor. After the initial shaking of heads and groaning, ideas will come easily. Write them as quickly as you can on the board as the class does them.

Here is a list of twenty-five ways to cross the floor that third graders said and did in about ten minutes.

walk	roll	whirl	stagger
march	tiptoe	crawl	dance
skip	walk backwards	sneak	leap
run	stamp	fly	kick
hop	tap dance	swim	dribble (basketball)
slide	jump	jump backwards	robotlike
skate			

Forgive me for pointing out again the obvious correlation between this exercise and many other curriculum areas, including a new way of looking at language as expressed by an exhausted third grader who said, "Boy! These words sure get you sweated up!" These verbs really ARE *action* words!

Telling Time Is a Moving Experience

Telling time is difficult for many children, especially with the popularity of digital watches! But *all* children enjoy using their arms to imitate the hands of the clock. One first grader who was having difficulty learning to tell time experienced his first success when he expressed the shape of 2:45 with his arms and then recognized that time on the class clock a little later. He jumped out of his seat, flung out his arms, and shouted, "It's a quarter to three! I know *that* time!"

Spin-offs   Groups of children can create a clock with hands that move. The tick-tock rhythm of time is an excellent accompaniment.

Turn Yourself Into . . . and Other Movement Challenges

Children of all ages respond immediately to and demonstrate great imaginative powers for movement-inspiring questions such as

If you were the rain, how would you fall?

If you were a ball, how would you bounce?

If you were a rainbow, how would you glow?

What if you were a snowshape? How would you melt?

What if you were a jack-in-the-box? How would you move?

Vary such exercises with equally enjoyable movement suggestions. Remember, we are talking language: vocabulary, comprehension, following directions . . .

Turn yourself into a whisper. How would you move?

Turn yourself into a shout. How would you move?

Turn yourself into a sneeze, a hiccough.

Turn yourself into the Tin Man, Dorothy, the Scarecrow.

Turn yourself into Thumbelina. How would you move?

A.Y.O.

Seasons and Weather

Give daily weather reports through movement. Children dance storms, thunder, lightning, snow, drizzle, wind, cold fronts and warm fronts (one group is the heavier, stronger cold front; the other is the lighter, softer warm front). One of the most memorable weather movement experiences I ever had occurred when I was working with a group of fifth graders shortly after a terrible tornado. We decided to dance a tornado. The children took the shapes of houses and buildings and created a village with their bodies. The group dancing the tornado whirled frantically through the "village," scooping up buildings and houses, leaving some walls standing while others fell. After the dance, the children poured out their feelings, memories, and fears of the tornado. Teachers said that the children had been reluctant to discuss the event and that the movement session really "opened them up and freed them to talk about it."

Always correlate movement with writing, art, music activities.

Circles and Other Basic Shapes

Basic shapes can be explored, discussed, and understood more clearly through movement. Here is an example of a fourth-grade session on circles.

With their teacher, the children drew circles in the air with their hands, traced circles on the floor with their feet, and formed circles with their fingers. They discovered parts of themselves and their clothing that had circular shapes: eyeglasses, cheeks, belly buttons, earrings, a polka-dotted shirt, buttons. They looked around the room and discovered more circles: clocks, doorknobs, a wastepaper basket rim. They thought of other things that have circle shapes: pizza pies, wheels, bubbles, hula hoops, happy-face buttons. They thought of events and activities that have circles in them: basketball, ferris wheel, birthday cake, bowling.

The most joyous circle movement I have seen children create was a huge merry-go-round with horses going up and down, children holding on to poles, and the entire carousel going round and round while the music played.

Conclude your circle session with a discussion. How do circles make you feel? What colors do you see when you think of circles? What places remind you of circles? What sounds make you think of circles?

Move on to squares. Shape your learning experiences! One first grader discovered, "There are no corners in a circle!" Write, sing, paint, and move!

Machines and Group Movement

Kids love to make machines with many moving parts, accompanied by sounds and producing something. A group of ten to twelve fifth graders created a fabulous machine that turned logs into toothpicks. All this with bodies! Al Genovese found this group movement activity to be one of the most successful and enjoyable he had ever experienced with his students.

A simple way to introduce the idea of machines is to ask one child to start a mechanical movement and keep repeating it, with an accompanying sound. Another child adds another mechanical movement and sound and so on, until all the children have contributed their special patterns and sounds. The result is usually terrific.

When children discover that they can work together and build wonderful machines with their bodies, they extend this talent to other experiences. Divide the class into groups of ten or twelve children. Challenge them to talk together and choose *one shape* to create using all their bodies as part of it. The shape can be abstract or can depict something real. It can move or be still. Children of all sizes and ages have made the most imaginative shapes in very short periods of time. Give them a few opportunities to make different shapes. Remember, they must talk together, think, share ideas, and cooperate *before* their bodies move. Here are the most outstanding shapes I remember from elementary schools throughout the country:

> a snake
>
> a house with rooms and doors that opened and closed
>
> a wall
>
> a barbed wire fence
>
> an automobile
>
> a typewriter

Jay Brand challenged his first through fourth grade summer school students to create machines with their bodies. He was amazed! "They were brilliant," he exclaimed as he described the children forming popcorn poppers, toasters, pinball machines, can openers, and record players with their collective bodies.

Magic Floors

> What if this floor wasn't wood? What if it turned into ice? How would you move?
>
> What if this floor changed into sloshy mud? How would you move?

Each new condition created for your floor will result in new ways of moving. Students of all ages enjoy making up "what if's" and responding to them. Some of the wilder "magic floors" kids have suggested and moved on are

> a floor turned into quicksand
>
> a floor that we thought was rocks but was really sleeping alligators—and the alligators woke up!
>
> a floor that was a dark and narrow path to a mysterious place
>
> a floor that made us lose our balance
>
> a floor that bounced us
>
> a floor that turned into an ocean

Your floor can be a magic carpet. Add music to the experience and visit other countries and cultures. A fourth-grade teacher, wondering how to introduce a unit on Eskimos, used the "magic floor" idea and changed the floor into ice. She then asked her students to imagine that they were wearing heavy, fur-lined clothes and boots. How did the ice and heavy clothes make them move? They responded to the suggestions, improvised movement, shared ideas, and launched "the best unit on Eskimos I ever taught."

Changes

Life is full of changes; nothing ever stays exactly the same. Children are fascinated by objects or animals that change shape. They like to share their thoughts and observations and grow in awareness and responsiveness. Their ideas inspire movement.

Here is a selection of ideas to be used with children of all grades. In each situation, the idea was translated into original movement. You will note that, in some cases, the idea of change was applied to a larger theme. Open-endedness is the rule for these experiences. There is no room for rigid, preset answers to contrived questions.

tadpoles to frogs

caterpillars to butterflies

acorns to oak trees

seeds to flowers

ice to water to steam

babies to old people

transportation: from feet to spaceships

seasons: winter to spring to summer to autumn to winter

ancient times to modern times (for example, from cooking over a fire to cooking in a microwave)

A group of fourth graders interpreted the idea of chicks, from growing *inside* eggs through hatching to becoming fluffy, active birds. During the process, one of the girls lost an earring. After the activity, we looked for it. One of the boys asked, "Kyra, where were you lying when you were hatching?"

I couldn't help but think of the many movement ideas we have waiting to be hatched!

Change Body Shapes   A favorite movement activity is to hold one body shape, then change to another body shape and hold it. Keep changing and holding—or call it moving and "freezing." Use any strong rhythms, any music with a heavy, steady beat. Encourage the children to experiment with interesting body designs. Watch them move from familiar to more original and creative as you go along.

Moving Statues

One of the best ways to get people moving is to suggest that they be a statue of someone or take the shape of something. Teachers report that they have been very successful in launching movement activities through this approach. In each case, the statue moves, then freezes again. The original shape sets the pattern and feeling of the movement to follow. Here is an example from a sixth-grade movement session correlated to a lesson in social studies.

Be a statue of a pioneer. Feel the shape. Feel your muscles holding the shape. How long can you stay that way?

Move your statue. Move as a pioneer. How does this person want to move? Can you move your statue for one minute? (Fiddle music, hand-claps, tambourine taps, or silence can accompany the activity.)

Go back to your original shape. Hold it!

Spin-offs   a. Extend the exercise into creative writing by writing for a few minutes from the point of view of each statue-person. Write about how you feel as a pioneer, dancer, explorer, and so on.

b. Correlate the statue exercise with art; take the shape of a piece of sculpture or a figure or object in a painting and add original sounds and music.

Movement Enriches All Learning

Seeds   Kindergartners examined seeds and discussed how plant life begins from them. They remembered that when they began they were very small, even smaller than the smallest seed. The teacher suggested, "Let's make ourselves as small as possible. Curl up and tuck under." The children and their teacher felt the beginnings of growth in their bodies as they slowly unfolded, uncurled, stretched, reached, rose up, and took shape. They compared their present powers and skills to their beginnings. "Look what we can do now!" They proudly demonstrated various movement patterns. "It all started with seeds!" a breathless five-year-old summarized.

Solar Systems   Fifth graders studied the solar system. They read, discussed, and reported on stars, planets, asteroids, and other celestial objects. Words like *revolution, rotation,* and *orbit* became a part of their everyday vocabulary. One day, during a discussion, a girl admitted that even though she could give the definitions of such terms, she didn't *really* understand them. The admission evolved into a movement experience featuring a moving, orbiting solar system.

One child was the sun. Planet-children placed themselves in relation to the sun. Moons, asteroids, and comets found their places. The children rotated in place and, because the solar system is continually moving, the entire group of heavenly beings also orbited the sun. One of the fifth graders wrote in his journal, "Today was the best day of my life. Our class made ourselves into a planetarium."

Geography   Jungles, deserts, swamplands, islands, mountains, volcanoes are studied by children across the grades. Enrich the study with movement extensions. Bodies shape jungles. Animals and people move differently on hot sand deserts than on swamplands. Volcanoes erupt. Show us! A group of children demonstrates volcanic eruption. How does lava move?

Holidays and Special Events   Packed with their own native images, customs, costumes, special vocabulary, themes, and music, holidays and special

events lend themselves naturally to enriched learning opportunities for children of all ages. Many teachers, while including art, writing, reading, and drama activities in the celebration of a holiday, rarely think of movement as a vital component of the festivities. Yet it's so easy and accessible!

Children love parades. Almost every holiday can be celebrated with a parade of the characters, ideas, and animals inherent in the occasion.

A Halloween parade will surely be different from a Thanksgiving Day parade! A group of fourth–fifth graders celebrated Presidents' Day by marching as tall, straight, proud Abraham Lincolns and then by making a parade of boats to carry George Washington across the Delaware River. The children rowed, then stood and commanded the troops as President Washington had.

Abraham Lincoln walked miles to school. How many do you think he walked? Six? Let's walk around the room six times, one time for each mile. Did Abe walk in all kinds of weather? All seasons? Maybe each mile had different weather conditions. So we walk in six different ways because we love books and learning as much as Abe did! The "Battle Hymn of the Republic" or "God Bless America" or another American history song plays as the children walk.

An assembly of elementary school children talked about Martin Luther King, Jr., and how he helped people to move from feeling hopeless and downtrodden to feeling free, strong, and proud. They sat scrunched in their seats, contracted into their smallest shapes. While a group of children read Dr. King's "I Have a Dream" speech, the entire auditorium of students and teachers slowly, slowly evolved from closed, tight, huddled figures to open, taller, stronger, lighter, freer bodies. By the end of the reading, every body in the auditorium was lifted, stretched up and out, expanded and strengthened. We felt freedom in our bones! The simplest of activities. The most moving of moments.

An example of a special event that lends itself well to a wide variety of movement activities is the circus. Over the years, I have shared celebrations of circus ideas with virtually thousands of children. These are just a few suggestions out of all that is possible. Interpret them, change them, rearrange them to fit your own needs. But most of all—enjoy!

Always gather information first. The children will give words to express their feelings about and knowledge of the circus. Ask for sense words—sights, smells, tastes, textures, sounds. Circus characters, animals, and emotions will pour out. Write the words on the board as quickly as possible. Words like *clowns, acrobats, jugglers, lion tamers, tightrope walkers, circus band, horses, elephants, exciting, colorful* will crowd the list.

Encourage the children to practice moving to different circus words, one at a time. Have everybody turn into a circus clown. Clown nose. Hat. Funny clothes. Tricks. Clown walk. Then shake out the clowns and go to the next circus character.

Once a group (including you) has practiced moving to many characters and you have encouraged the children to differentiate between each one, to show each animal's unique qualities through movement (I like to challenge them by kidding, "If you're a lion, don't look like an elephant!" and so on), then the fun *really* begins.

"Now that we've had a lot of practice with all the circus people and animals, let's have a circus parade!"

When the music begins, each person moves as one of the circus characters. When the music stops, they freeze. While they are frozen, they decide on the next circus character. When the music starts again, the children should move like their second character, and so on. Use any marching, carnival, or parade music.

The children have a chance to explore many different ways of moving as they share ideas. So often we put them in rigid situations. "You're on the clown committee!" we say, and cast such a permanent spell that a child must stay a clown forever. Activities like the one described above give them choices and freedom to change and try new patterns.

During the circus activity, I tell the kids, "If there's an idea that we didn't practice and you want to do it, go ahead." One time I noticed a boy just walking in an ordinary way, looking at the lively, bouncy circus panorama around him.

"Who are you?" I asked as we paraded together.

"I'm the owner!" he informed me.

To expand the concept of the circus parade, designate three areas of your room or gym for three "rings" and divide your class into three groups. Let each group decide what's happening in its own ring. Once an entire elementary school created a circus. Each class had an area of the gym and had decided on its contribution to the festivities. We gave each class a number, put on lively, circus-y music, and the fun began as each class—elephants, monkeys, lions, jugglers, tumblers—presented its "act," in the assigned order, in its own section of our multi-ring circus.

> You will notice that, after a totally involving movement experience, students' writing, art, and oral language projects become more original, vital, and imaginative. Pictures, stories, posters, newspapers, poems, diaries, bumper stickers will catch the excitement, the dynamic vocabulary, the children have discovered through movement.

These movement suggestions are just a few of the countless ideas possible. The other chapters in this book highlight movement activities as well, presenting them as intertwined, integral parts of the language and learning processes, as valid ways of knowing and understanding.

I hope that you will now think MOVEMENT in relation to all curriculum areas. Remember, education is a moving experience!

Many teachers are concerned about discipline and control during movement activities. Here again, respect, cooperation, and consideration are primary values. Without trust and mutuality, none of these suggestions will succeed. Paying attention, listening, following directions, and "getting it"—grasping the idea—are qualities to be emphasized. Two stories I tell children are so effective as motivators for those desired attitudes that I must pass them on to you.

> One boy had a life-long dream of being on the high school football team. He spent his younger years working out, lifting weights, exercising. But he never practiced paying attention. When he finally tried out for the team, he was the strongest and the toughest but—*he didn't make it!* He couldn't follow any of the coach's instructions because he had never learned to pay attention.

> A young girl wants to become a dancer. She practices, stretches, keeps in shape. But she never practices paying attention. When auditions are held for a part in a dance production, *she doesn't make it.* Her body is in great condition but, sadly, she has never exercised her mind: those powers are out of shape!

Both stories are true, and they really hit the kids!

Keep rules simple:

When we move around the room, we all move in the *same direction* (safety).

Work out a signal for closure. "Freeze!" or "Red Light!" are excellent verbal signals. "Shake it out," with a jingle of a tambourine, is also very effective. Keep it simple.

Movement activities are so much fun that your students will work hard to see that they happen again and again.

Keep competition out of the activity.

The key words are *cooperation, consideration,* and *paying attention.*

Begin with movement activities that take up only short periods of time. Enjoy those moments and build on successful instances to more complex challenges.

Remember, "children move because movement gives them a tremendous lift, a sense of freedom, exhilaration akin to flying high above the waters, above the clouds, above the earth and into the sky. . . ."[13]

Keep things moving!

Drama in the Classroom

For too many years, drama, along with movement, was considered an unnecessary frill, advocated by a few avant-garde teachers on rainy days *if* the students had finished all their *real* schoolwork. Fortunately, in the last two decades educators have taken a new look at drama and discovered (or rediscovered) it to be a vital, fertile field with practical applications of great value to classroom life and to the lives of children.

As we have noted, the natural work of all children is play, is pretending, is trying on life through imagination. This activity, basic to human existence, is now appreciated as an essential component of the language arts, an integral part of learning, touching every subject, every curriculum strand.

A bold statement reaffirming play as a basic right of children was circulated by the U.S. National Committee for Early Childhood Education, the Association for Childhood Education International, and the National Association for the Education of Young Children. It is an important document for you to know about.

A Child's Right to Play

Why play?

Children's play is often depreciated by adults who think of it as a mere time filler rather than an essential component of healthy development. Were these adults to follow the lead of an increasing number of researchers and teachers, examining closely what children do when they play, they might understand why play is so essential to the child's well-being and competence.

Play is a very special activity with distinctive features that set it apart from other behaviors.

When children play their interest is self-directed. They are intrinsically motivated to solve problems that stem from either the physical or the social world and are important to them.

When children play they are not as concerned with particular goals or ends as they are with the variety of ways a goal may be achieved. In play they experiment with possibilities and become more flexible in thinking and problem solving.

When children play their behavior is not literal. Much of what they do stands for something else. They represent their experiences symbolically. Their ability to conceive objects and situations as if they were something else is thought by researchers to contribute to later skill in hypothetical reasoning and the understanding of abstract symbols and logical transformations.

When children play they free themselves from external rules, from the restrictions imposed by adult regulations, and from the realities imposed by time and space. Paradoxically, however, children generate rules for their play situations and establish roles and plots. Close study of such play reveals that children's negotiations with one another are complex. They make longer utterances and use more varied vocabulary than in other situations.

When children play with objects they discover what they can do with them. Increasing their own repertoire of behaviors in this way contrasts with the exploration of objects in which they establish what properties the objects have. Both play and exploration, involving on the one hand the familiar, and on the other the novel, are essential to children's understanding of the world and of their own powers.

Finally, *when children play* they are actively engaged. Their attention is not easily distracted. Children who are unable to so involve themselves in play signal that something has gone seriously amiss in their development.

Adults who give serious consideration to these distinctive features of children's play will recognize that play is as essential to the child's all-around development as adequate food and rest. They will understand why those who wrote the United Nations' *Declarations of the Rights of the Child* set the right to play parallel to such rights as special protection, adequate nutrition, housing, health care, and education.

Children realize their right to play when the adults around them appreciate and respect their playfulness and provide ample time and space for them to play. Materials and equipment are also important, although they need not be elaborate. The crucial role that parents and teachers have in responding to and supporting children's play ideas, while not overwhelming them, becomes increasingly evident.

Play, the child's way of coming to terms with personal experience in and knowledge of the physical and social world, is never sufficient in itself. Adults must also provide ever-expanding opportunities for children to learn from their own actions and observations, as well as from being told, the nature of the people and of the things that surround them. But it is in play that children come to terms with those realities, comprehend them more, and more effectively create new possibilities for dealing with them.[14]

Probably the most influential person in the field of drama education is Dorothy Heathcote. Her work, beginning in her native country of Great Britain, is recognized around the world. I urge you to read her book *Dorothy Heathcote: Collected Writings on Education and Drama*.[15]

Heathcote is passionate in her focus on drama as a powerful learning tool. She respects and values the knowledge and experiences of the students. She wants, through the drama, to help children build on past experiences and to help them gain a deeper knowledge of themselves, of what it is to be human, as well as an understanding of the society they live in and its past, present, and future.[16]

She does not see the role of teacher as passive, as that of an onlooker or observer. The teacher intervenes, directs, participates, enables, challenges. The teacher takes a role in the drama, becomes part of it, helps shape it. She asks teachers to free themselves from the burden of being instructors—"people who must know everything"—and invites them to become "sharers in learning experiences with their children, enablers, and seekers after excellence."[17]

Drama is a way of making the ordinary extraordinary; of deepening understandings; of sharpening feelings, perceptions, and imaginations as teachers and children go beyond the purely informational level of exchange so common in so many classrooms.

History Test

1. The Mayflower carried Pilgrims from England to America. It landed at Cape Cod on November 21, 1620.

Answer these questions about the sentence you just read:

What was the name of the ship?

What were the people on the ship called?

On what date did the ship arrive in America?

Underline the correct answer:

The Mayflower landed at Key West / Cape Cod / San Diego.

Now we know it. Don't we?

Try substituting nonsense in the text.

1. The Gigglygump carried penguins from Mars to Morocco. It landed at Disneyland on May 40, 1902.

Now let's have a test. We know it, don't we?

So much of the learning that takes place in schools is of this level. Drama in the classroom gives children the opportunity to feel the ship, live the Pilgrims' lives, know the journey (65 days on rough seas), discover the complex emotions felt upon landing, share the courage and the fears. Drama gives children the chance to find the dynamic energy of the curriculum as it unfolds its possibilities for real meaning, for real comprehension.

When children are involved in drama experiences they are good listeners, articulate talkers, "movers and shakers," eager planners, decision-making participants in the give-and-take of ideas in a climate of cooperation and respect. They use all their powers. Their BRIGHTS are ON! They enjoy *learning*, becoming fluent in personal expression and in communication, more reflective, curious, and understanding of themselves and others.

CAREFUL

If there are some children who have already grown layers of inhibition and are hesitant to join *any* open-ended, creative activity, *don't force them to participate.* Always include them in the planning and discussion. Give them peripheral, safe ways of entering the activity, such as "Jed, you're sitting far away enough so that you have a good view of this scene. Does it seem scary enough to you?" Keep making circles that "take them in."

QUESTION: What do I want my students to learn?

ANSWER: I want my students to develop self-confidence, awareness, imagination, and self-expression as they enjoy learning about themselves, their language, and their world. They can do this through diverse experiences in informal dramatic activities, which stress cooperation, spontaneity, originality, participation, interaction, and decision making.

Drama Activities

Props for Playing

Children love props. Games of make-believe become even more believable with a realistic touch: a hat, a cane, an umbrella, a dish. Organize a "scrounge campaign." Have your students write to their families asking for "old stuff" to use in the classroom. Such requests often result in a cache of supplies that children can use in many different creative activities, from sculpture to creative writing to drama.

When props are combined with time to play and experiences to draw from, the value of the activity is immeasurable. Students can be encouraged to try different roles rather than limit themselves to rigid stereotypes. Children need the freedom to play many different parts in their important games of make-believe. They must feel free to use the props as they choose without fear of ridicule. Girls pretend to be doctors, firefighters, and astronauts. Boys pretend to care for babies, type letters, and wash clothes.

A kindergarten's trip to a post office launched a week of playing post office. Using props such as large cartons, hats, old envelopes, and paper bags, the children built a post office in their room.

A first grade's trip to a bakery stimulated a flurry of mixing, baking, and selling baked goods, helped considerably by the old pots, pans, and cartons contributed by parents and friends.

Inspired by a unit on archeology, a group of fifth graders created their own archeological dig site which they filled with scrounged and originally constructed "artifacts." They had many adventures on their journeys to discover the buried history.

Warm-Ups

Just as you need to warm up before you play a musical instrument or participate in a sport, so you and your students need to loosen the body part by part (stretch, bend, shake out tension) and relax the mind to get ready for dramatic expression. Here are samples of teachers' favorite warm-ups for all grade levels.

Make Faces   The human face is a kaleidoscope of changing expressions. Children love to make faces. Here is their chance to make sad, funny, crazy, ugly, beautiful, surprised, sleepy, angry, or mysterious faces.

Shake Out and Shape Up   In other cultures, human hands are used to convey intricate meanings. American culture limits the range of expression communicated by hands. Shake out your hands and experiment with various ideas, such as fists, "hello" hands, "goodbye" hands, working hands, destructive hands, gentle hands, clumsy hands, helping hands. Consider how easily the other parts of the body lend themselves to this kind of experimentation and exercise.

How Many Sounds Can You Make?   Exercise the vocal cords with a warm-up. Each person in turn makes a different sound. You may want to go around twice, or you may want to tape the sounds.

How Many Ways Can We Say . . . ?   You know that one person can say "Glad to meet you" in an icy voice and intimidate you while another person can say the same words and warm your heart for the day. Discuss the many ways of communicating a single word or phrase. Voices can convey excitement, nervousness, anger, sarcasm, mischief, love. Each quality brings a different dimension of meaning to the spoken word. Choose a word or phrase and ask each person to repeat it in a different way. Some favorite words and phrases of classroom teachers are *this is for you, thanks a lot, come again, hello, goodbye, oh, help help, you're really nice*.

This round-robin warm-up really helps children to understand the importance of pitch, tone, stress, rhythm, gesture, facial expression, and posture in communication.

Pantomime

Pantomime is one of the oldest, most widely used and enjoyed forms of nonverbal communication. It involves physical movement—gestures, facial expres-

sion, and full action—without words to convey situations, characters, relationships, feelings, and objects.

Always start with simple ideas. Encourage children to work their pantomime from the inside out. Begin with their own thoughts and feelings about the subject and let them find expression in the body, so that anyone who looks at them will be able to see what is being communicated. People enjoy working in groups or as individuals. No one approach is right for everyone, so experiment with many ways.

Despite the fact that pantomime is a nonverbal art, you'll find that the kids often want to add words to their pantomime exercises, thus demonstrating how naturally pantomime serves as a springboard to oral language. Never prohibit a child from adding speech or sound to a pantomime activity. Encouragement is your most important contribution to the process, because creativity is always threatened by discouragement.

The pantomime exercises below range from simple to complex.

Comb your hair. (Is it long, short, curly, knotted?)

Eat an ice cream cone. (Is it smooth or chunky?)

Get dressed. (What are you wearing?)

Practice a musical instrument.

Perform some kind of work.

Make a telephone call from a coin-operated phone.

Surprise! What did you get for your birthday? Open the box and show us.

Be a magician and do a trick.

Be an inanimate object.

Be an animal and do something.

Be a character from a story.

Be a police officer directing traffic.

Be a pioneer family loading a covered wagon.

Show us one of the Seven Dwarfs. Show us all seven!

Be the crews of Columbus' ships. Show your reaction to sighting land.

Show us one of your hobbies.

Words are excellent stimuli for pantomime exercises. Keep good words for pantomime exercises written on index cards or small pieces of construction paper in a "grab-bag." The children can take turns grabbing a card and using the word on it as the idea for their pantomime exercise. Imagine choosing words such as *gardener, skater, criminal, clumsy, stuck up, shy, dentist* and conveying their meaning through body expression.

Not only is vocabulary enriched, but appreciation for language and human expression is strengthened as children learn new ways of interpreting what they know.

Improvisation

Improvisations are informal dramas that evolve from ideas or situations agreed on by the players. There is no set dialogue or plot, no lines to memorize. The participants create their own dialogue, movement, action, and plot as they interact with one another and interpret the situation from their point of view. You don't need to send away for a resource kit of ideas for improvisations. *Material for improvisation is everywhere.* Familiar, everyday events and happenings, as well as those based on special studies and lessons, are equally valuable in providing experiences for creative dramatics. So many teachers know that their most inhibited, reluctant, silent children often speak more easily in situations in which they express characters other than their own. "This isn't me, Johnny, speaking. This is Daniel Boone!" they seem to say. They are also telling us that they desperately need all these opportunities to practice language in a safe and enjoyable way. With enough encouragement and experience, Johnny may soon feel confident enough to express Johnny.

Your informal drama sessions can be complete in themselves or can develop into full-scale correlations with other subject areas.

Here is a sample of different experiences that can easily be translated into improvisations.

Everyday Situations

Becky finds a kitten.

Laura loses her housekey.

Michael "gets" a new baby brother.

A new student is joining our class tomorrow.

These ordinary happenings provide excellent material for short, informal improvisations. Children find themselves in situations that cause them to think, act, respond, communicate. Whatever they do has value. There is no correct or incorrect answer. Discussion often precedes and follows the improvisation and further understandings are gleaned from observing and participating in the activity.

The New Student   A class of fourth graders was told that a new student would soon join them. They discussed how it feels to be a "new kid" going into a strange, unfamiliar situation. They talked about the range of responses—from hostile to helpful—that a group might have to a new person. The discussion quickly turned into a drama when the teacher suggested that they explore some of the ideas and feelings involved in such a situation. She encouraged the children to articulate any attitude, even try on a point of view that wasn't natural, just to add that dimension to the "story." Here is an excerpt from the session:

Teacher: We have a new student coming. Now, let's see if there's room for an extra desk.
Danielle: She can sit next to me. (moves her desk)
Joe: How do you know it's a girl? Maybe it's a boy.
Jason: What's the new kid's name?
Teacher: LaDonna James.
Gretchen: That's a weird name. Don't put her near me. I'm crowded enough.
Melinda: That's mean.
Gretchen: Who cares?
Danielle: There's room for LaDonna here.
Tanya: I'm glad we're getting another girl.
David: There are too many girls in this class.
Teacher: I think we have just the right number of boys and girls in this class with LaDonna. Any suggestions to help make LaDonna welcome?
Greg: Just be our regular selves.
Jason: We'd scare her out of here being our regular selves. (laughter)
Gretchen: I don't go out of my way for anybody.
Tanya: You could be a new kid someday, Gretchen. (other kids agree)
Joe: We could kind of greet her with a special handshake—like this. (demonstrates)

The drama went on for a few more minutes. In the discussion that followed, a few children commented on how harsh Gretchen's words sounded. Gretchen agreed and admitted, "After I started being the 'bad kid,' I felt uncomfortable and wanted to switch over."

When the new student did arrive, the class welcomed her with unusual sensitivity and warmth. The teacher credits the drama session with helping the kids make positive decisions in the actual situation.

Stories, Songs, and Poems   After children share a story, song, legend, or poem that they especially like, enrich the experience by encouraging further interpretation through improvisations.

Here is an example of how a third-grade teacher started her class off on improvisation. "I wonder how Little Red Riding Hood felt as she walked through the forest. I wonder what she was thinking about. How would you feel if you were Little Red Riding Hood on your way to Grandma's house with a basket of goodies? Did she skip along? Did she hum to herself? What do you think? Let's imagine ourselves as Little Red Riding Hood going to Grandma's."

The whole group put baskets on their arms and took off for the forest (middle of the room). After a few minutes of walking, the children began to improvise dialogue.

"I wonder if Grandma made my favorite cupcakes."

"I hope I don't meet anyone dangerous in this forest."

The teacher gave further impetus to the improvisation by asking, "What if the wolf were friendly?"

"What if Grandma hit the wolf?"

"What if Grandma weren't home?"

Ballads, legends, and tall tales are excellent improvisation starters. When children read and listen to traditional literature in song and story, they are delighted to interpret, continue, or change the material in original ways. Give them many opportunities.

Name-dropping; Hats and Shoes; Grab-bag Suggestions

Name-dropping   Place the names of characters past and present, real or mythological, into a bag. Ask the kids to pick names and create spontaneous, informal scenes in which their characters meet and exchange dialogue and action. Improvisations should not last longer than a few minutes. The important goal in all these activities is to give children many opportunities to experience a great variety of language skills.

Hats and Shoes   These clothing items are excellent for inspiring imaginative improvisations. Scrounge a variety of hats and shoes. Who do you become with a witch's hat on your head? A baseball cap? A feather headdress? A flowered bonnet? Step into these shoes. An old saying tells us "Don't judge a person until you've walked a mile in his shoes." Give the children a chance to walk in someone else's shoes. Imagine the person. Who is this person? Name? Occupation? Action? Feelings?

Correlate the improvisations with creative writing, art, music.

Mix and match. Have small groups of children in hats interact with children in shoes. Be in for a surprise at the fluency of language and ideas!

Grab-bag Suggestions   Have the children write down ideas for three people to act out. Each idea, serious or humorous, must contain an interesting dramatic situation. Place the ideas in a grab-bag. Here is an example of a sixth-grade improvisation.

Three mountain climbers are attempting to conquer Mt. Everest, but they encounter a bad snowstorm. Do they manage to reach the peak? The three climbers are very different people. What happens to their relationship in this situation?

Curriculum Improvisation   Pat and Brian Edmiston studied with Dorothy Heathcote at the University of Newcastle in Great Britain. How do they adapt Heathcote's rich and multifaceted approach to drama to the realities and exigencies of American classrooms? In this excerpt from an interview, Pat and Brian articulate the importance of drama as a learning medium as well as an end in itself:

> Drama is always about people and always in a social situation. We are talking about attitudes, viewpoints, choices, problems and solutions to problems. Through drama, we can make these interactions very relevant. We give children the power to make decisions, to create living art. We don't need to do whole stories. Sometimes we take one episode and close in on it. Listen to the way kids respond to a book you are reading or a discussion about a particular theme. When they react to a situation with "I wouldn't do that! I'd be scared!" that's a cue to you that a dramatic episode is waiting to be explored. Help the kids go from "If I were, I would . . ." to "I am, I will and I do."[18]

They talked about their experiences with fourth and fifth graders who were reading Virginia Hamilton's *The House of Dies Drear* (Macmillan, 1968), a story about a modern boy and his family who move to a house in Ohio that was once an important part of the Underground Railroad; the house is filled with characters who have mysterious memories.

On brown butcher paper, Brian and Pat made a very large map of an area near Dayton, Ohio. On the map they drew three roads, a river, areas indicating trees, and a railroad line. They asked the kids to draw in their own homes.

"Where do you live?" They challenged them with such questions as "Do you live near the river? Do you have a boat? Do you have two horses?" Many of the kids drew houses similar to the house of Dies Drear.

Now the students were closer to the story. What about a sanctuary? Isn't it a risk to hide a runaway slave? Some of the abolitionists were jailed. Were the slaves afraid? Where can we hide them? Do you have a hiding place in your house? Show it to us. Can we use your horses? What signals can we use to indicate the markings and the plans? How long can someone stay in that hiding place? It's so small.

Because the children chose to live the story, they wrote letters and journal entries about the night the slaves arrived, about the jailed abolitionists, about how each group felt. They created a museum and their letters became the artifacts. They took field trips to houses in the area that were part of the Underground Railroad.

They felt the fear and hope of the slaves. They took the risks of those who helped them. They discovered that imagination is a time machine. It permits us, through drama, through the arts, to directly experience the lives of characters and events far from us in time but close to us in our humanity, in our capacity to feel.

What episodes in your curriculum material are waiting to be explored through drama?

Puppets in the Classroom

Puppets have been around for centuries. They enriched the lives of the ancient Greeks and preserved some of the traditions of the Roman theater after the collapse of the Empire. Punchinello entertained Italy in the fourteenth and fifteenth centuries, then moved to France and England in the seventeenth century. In England, he was called Punch, and he performed with a puppet named Judy. Punch and Judy shows are still popular in England today. Hans Christian Andersen, Lewis Carroll, Goethe, and Voltaire were fascinated by puppets and even wrote original plays for their own puppet theaters.

Teachers all over America are welcoming puppets into the classroom and making them a vital part of everyday learning. Puppets can be used to explain or describe something, give directions, say funny things, tell stories, ask questions, and create dramatic situations to which children respond. Puppets provide children with many opportunities to expand their language skills as well as challenge their imaginations. Students who are reluctant to talk to anyone often feel more confident talking through the characters of puppets. Children enjoy performing puppet shows for each other. They then have a chance to ask questions about and experiment with the puppets after the show.

There are excellent resource books on puppets and puppet making, but the best puppets are often the original ones children create from scrounged materials.[19]

Puppets can be made from

paper bags	broomsticks
fingers	shadows
fists	peanut shells
sticks	pipe cleaners
gloves	socks
hands	papier mâché
marionettes	

Puppets can become regular members of your classroom, improvising book reports, explaining something, telling a story, adding yet another dimension to a lesson. Teachers like Ellen Clark and Libby Blaho know that "a lot of kids who normally won't speak in front of people feel safe and relaxed when they get behind the puppet stage." In their classrooms there's never a time that some group of students isn't developing a new puppet plot to share with their classmates.

Paper Bag Dramatics

Using several paper bags, put three objects, or three pictures, or three words into each. Or try putting one object, one picture, and one word in each!

Object Ideas

leaf	string
paper clip	shoelace
envelope	mitten
comb	penny
pen	eraser
rubber band	

Picture or Photo Ideas

people	designs
places	colors
things	

Word Ideas

telephone	teacher
scissors	baby
horse	Indian
igloo	rattlesnake
firefighter	airplane
frying pan	

Divide the class into small groups, and let each group choose a paper bag. They have only a few minutes to look at its contents and make up a skit using the objects, pictures, or words in any way they want. Encourage the children to use body movement, speech, sounds, pantomime, and props.

A marvelous variation of this idea is to give each group, without their knowledge, a bag containing *the exact same contents*. When the skits are presented, the imagination and endless creative talents of human beings will be demonstrated more clearly than through any lecture or textbook.

Potpourri of Creative Dramatics Activities

Classroom teachers like Kay Callander, who integrates the arts with all subject areas, have knapsacks full of imaginative combinations of ideas. Here are a few of Kay's:

a. Show a film with a good story line to the class but turn off the sound. Children discuss what they think the story line might be by watching the characters' facial expressions and body movements and the location and setting of the action. Then run the film again with the sound.

b. Dramatize stories by changing the roles of the characters. Switch the protagonist and the antagonist. What happens?

c. Listen to a piece of music and then make up a story using the music as background.

d. Read stories in which the dialogue is repeated. Children can use the refrain from, say, "The Giving Tree" or "The Gingerbread Man" as they improvise a story.

Be aware of the resources in your own community. Dancers, mimes, and dramatists are excellent classroom visitors and program presenters. Our children need all the opportunities possible to enjoy live performances.

How Do I Know These Methods Are Working?

Are your students growing more confident, relaxed, courageous, and aware? These qualities will be reflected in everything they do, in the ways they move and speak, in their attitudes and behavior, in their oral and written work.

Because there are, as yet, no tests to adequately measure such qualities, you will have to be sensitive and responsive, alert to the changes in your students, cognizant of and caring about situations and relationships in your room. When children are encouraged to learn in an atmosphere of trust and safety, they communicate important information to you about their sense of well-being and accomplishment.

As in all evaluations, the children's opinions and feelings are most important. They have valuable knowledge to contribute. Take time to discuss various drama and movement experiences with your students. Their feedback, both verbal and nonverbal, will help you to shape an even more effective program.

Checklist for the Class

1. Did they enjoy the activity?
2. What were some of the things they learned?
3. Did they cooperate? respect the ideas of others?
4. What was the best part of the experience?
5. If they didn't enjoy the experience, why not?
6. If the value wasn't clear, why not?
7. How can the activity be improved?
8. Did everyone participate? If some didn't, why not?
9. Did one or a few children dominate the activity?
10. Were the nonparticipators interested observers or indifferent rejectors?

Checklist for the Individual Child

1. Did he/she participate? How?
2. Is there a pattern to his/her participation or rejection?
3. Did I make time to meet privately with this student if he/she seems to be rejecting the activity?
4. Which of the student's interests can be included as material for *creative activities* (magic words!)?

Checklist for Yourself

1. How well did I organize the activity?
2. Did I encourage everyone to participate?
3. Did I go out of my way to reassure reluctant students?
4. How can I involve those who are reluctant to participate?
5. Did I demonstrate that everyone's ideas were of great value?
6. Did I participate or sit back and watch the action?
7. Did I dominate the activity or was I too passive?

8. Did I enjoy the activity?

9. What did I learn from the experience?

10. How can I improve my role in such activities?

There is no end to the material in this or any chapter. The chapter stops because there is a limit on specific time and space. But as it stops, be inspired by the *go* words of Ruth Strickland.

In order to preserve the imagination, uniqueness and originality of children, there must be opportunity to enjoy the fanciful material as well as factual and realistic material and the opportunity to make up stories, original dramatic plays, games and art creations. Expression is essential to mental health and wholesome intellectual development.[20]

ENDNOTES

[1] Olga Maynard, *Children and Dance and Music* (New York: Scribner's 1968) 5.

[2] Geraldine Brain Siks, *Creative Dramatics: An Art for Children* (New York: Harper, 1958) 85.

[3] Emma D. Sheehy, *Children Discover Music and Dance* (New York: Holt, 1963) 158.

[4] Ruth Sawyer, *The Way of the Storyteller* (New York: Viking, 1947) 116. Sawyer's original remarks refer to "the child"; I have changed them from singular to plural.

[5] Virginia Tanner, Commencement Address, Wilson College, Chambersburg, PA, 2 June, 1963.

[6] Gladys Andrews, *Creative Rhythmic Movement for Children* (Englewood Cliffs: Prentice, 1955) 22.

[7] Maynard 4.

[8] Maynard 3–4.

[9] Robert E. Samples, "Are You Teaching Only One Side of the Brain?" *Learning Magazine* (Feb. 1975): 25–28.

[10] James Moffett, *A Student-Centered Language Arts Curriculum* (Boston: Houghton, 1968) 41.

[11] Marlene Robins, interview with the author.

[12] Movement activities and suggestions are highlighted in such books as Anne Lief Barlin, *Teaching Your Wings to Fly* (Santa Monica: Goodyear, 1979); Mary Joyce, *First Steps in Teaching Creative Dance to Children,* 2nd ed. (Gloversville: Mayfield, 1980); Joyce Boorman, *Creative Dance in the First Three Grades* (New York: McKay, 1969); ———. *Creative Dance in Grades Four to Six* (Don Mills, Ontario: Longman, 1971); Mimi Brodsky Chenfeld, *Creative Activities for Young Children* (San Diego: Harcourt, 1983).

[13] William M. Logan and Virgil G. Logan, *A Dynamic Approach to the Language Arts* (Toronto: McGraw, 1967) 92–93.

[14] Millie Almy, "A Child's Right to Play," in "Reaffirmations: Speaking Out for Children," *Young Children* (May 1984): 80.

[15] Dorothy Heathcote, *Dorothy Heathcote: Collected Writings on Education and Drama,* ed. Liz Johnson and Cecily O'Neill (London: Hutchinson, 1984).

[16] Heathcote 12.

[17] Heathcote 13.

[18] Pat and Brian Edmiston, interview with the author.

[19] For an excellent article on puppets, see Myra Weiger, "Puppetry," *Elementary English* (Jan. 1974): 55–65.

[20] Ruth Strickland, *Language Arts in the Elementary School* (Boston: Heath, 1958) 151.

Some other books that encourage the development of a creative approach to language and learning with an emphasis on the importance of play are

John Warren Stewig, *Informal Drama in the Elementary Language Arts Program* (New York: Teachers College Press, Columbia University, 1983); Andrew Fluegelman, *The New Games Book* (New York: Doubleday, 1976); Maria Montessori, *The Secret of Childhood* (New York: Random House, 1972); Rollo May, *The Courage to Create* (New York: Norton, 1975); Abraham Maslow, *Toward a Psychology of Being* (New York: Van Nostrand, 1968); Robert J. Martin, *Teaching Through Encouragement* (Englewood Cliffs: Prentice-Hall, 1980).

7

Literature:
Carry It On!

I said at the start that I am a lover of children's books. And so I am,
and so I'll always be. . . . For at their best, their language, their art,
their seriousness of intent measure up to *any* standards of excellence.
. . . And the beauties and truths and delight that they can offer to our
children can meet the deepest needs of the heart and the mind.

JUDITH VIORST[1]

If you were asked to list the important needs of human beings, you would probably begin with the rudimentary needs for survival and move on to the spiritual, social, and humanistic requirements that we all share. Robert Havighurst studied the American people and concluded that they had certain basic "tasks" to accomplish. Read his list of developmental tasks and see how many correspond to your list of important human needs.

Developing a satisfactory self-concept

Learning to get along with peers

Developing skills in reading, communicating, and using numbers

Developing scientific and social concepts necessary for effective everyday living

Developing values, attitudes, and conscience

Developing self-direction[2]

I would add the necessity of developing imagination, creative abilities, and aesthetic appreciation.

Why, in the beginning of a chapter on literature, am I asking you to think about important human needs?

The answer is simple.

People Need Literature

I believe that literature comes closer to meeting all of our basic human needs than any other component of the curriculum! Through literature we learn about ourselves, other people, other places, and other times. We dip into the wisdom of accumulated human knowledge; we gain insights into human situations and social and historical events. Through literature we discover what is possible in human experience and imagination, and our own lives grow in richness and depth.

May Hill Arbuthnot writes about how books can enrich life, enhance our sense of life's significance, and provide a source of comfort, wisdom, and pleasure. She feels that children need literature to widen their horizons, deepen their understanding, and give them broader social insights. They need books that minister to their merriment or deepen their appreciation of beauty. They need heroism, fantasy, and good down-to-earth realism. And they need books that, in the course of a good story, help them to develop clear standards of right and wrong.[3]

Leland B. Jacobs, a beloved figure in American education, speaks and writes eloquently about his feelings for literature. At a recent reading conference, "Jake" Jacobs told his audience of teachers, "Literature is an illumination of life and living. . . . Literature gives readers the opportunities to walk in the shoes of someone else, to be somewhere else. Literature helps kids *know*, helps make things come together."

An excellent example of the ways in which literature fills needs is the diary of Anne Frank. The house where Anne stayed in Amsterdam still stands and is open to the public. There you can see the hidden stairway, the bare, tiny rooms, Anne's bulletin board with pictures of her favorite movie stars, and the pencil marks on the wall where Anne's father measured the children and kept track of their growth. On another floor of the house, you can see something very valuable to you as a teacher. This floor is devoted to the diary itself and the many responses to it from people around the world. In one of the showcases are letters and charts from teachers who have read the diary with their students. One teacher diagrammed the numerous educational experiences her class shared through their reading of Anne's diary. Here is her chart.

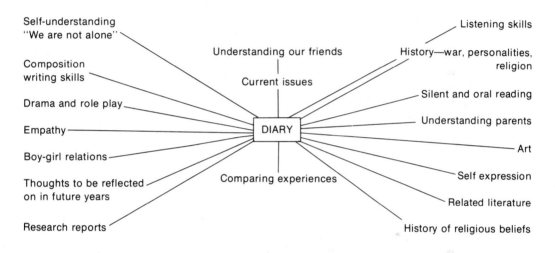

How many important human needs as well as language learning skills were explored by that class as they shared a literature experience? The possibilities for in-depth involvement and multilevel activities in any given literary work are limitless! A book can become more than print on bound pages between two covers. It can become part of our existence, leaving a permanent mark on our psyche. Think about the books that have meant the most to you and imagine, for a moment, on how many levels and in how many areas they have affected your life.

Harold Brodkey, in a powerful essay called "Reading, the Most Dangerous Game" writes in strong words about the influence of literature on our lives:

> Reading always leads to metamorphosis, sometimes irreversible, sometimes temporary, sometimes large-scale, sometimes less than that. A good book leads to alterations in one's sensibility and often becomes a premise in one's beliefs. One associates truth with texts, with impressive texts anyway. . . .
>
> After all, if you don't know what's in good books, how can your life not be utterly miserable all in all? Won't it fall apart with fearsome frequency? The best of what this species knows is in books. Without their help, how can you manage?[4]

What Do You Believe?

Now is the perfect time to get in touch with your own feelings about, and experiences with, literature. How you teach such a vast and important area of the language arts will depend on your own attitudes, beliefs, and commitments.

Long before the first words were written or read, stories were passed from one generation to the next. No matter what catastrophes occurred, the literature of the human family was carried on, recited around fires, sung by wandering minstrels, interpreted by dancers, actors, and artists, and eventually scratched on wood, clay, stone, and paper.

Vivid examples of this phenomenon are the Arthurian legends, told and retold for hundreds of years, enriching the *oral* tradition from the fifth century A.D. until the fifteenth century when Sir Thomas Malory collected the stories in his book *Le Morte d'Arthur* (printed in 1485).

First told *before* the Middle Ages, these stories continued to inspire writers and composers for centuries. In the mid-twentieth century, Alan Jay Lerner and Frederick Loewe wrote a musical based on T. H. White's play *Camelot* that can still be enjoyed on the live stage and on film. To me, the most poignant scene in the play is the last. Here, Camelot is in ruins; the Round Table is no more. Arthur sits alone in the lull before battle. His beautiful Guinevere is guilty of treason and has been sentenced to death. His best friend and loyal knight, Lancelot, has betrayed him. Into the midst of this gloom, a young boy enters. He wants to join King Arthur and the Knights of the Round Table. King Arthur knights the child and bids him to return to England and *tell* the story. As long as the story is told, Camelot, Arthur, Guinevere, Lancelot—all the characters and adventures—will live.

Just as Arthur asks his new young knight to *tell* the stories, so we teachers are knighted for the same purpose. Literature, the birthright of all children, is a precious gift that we must pass on.

Reverence for Literature

Children are curious, full of wonder; their eyesight is not yet completely blurred with stereotyped images. They still hear new sounds and unusual patterns of words, playing with rhymes and rhythms as naturally as they touch and move. Their imaginations are rich with drama, story, poetry, and myth. They want to know about everything—"not only about the past of their own country and people, but of all times and all peoples, about the history of ideas . . . about birth, life, sickness and death, about the beginning and meaning of life."[5]

Thoreau said, "Every child begins the world again." Children help us look at the world as if everything were new, everything possible. Unless the mind and spirit are enriched, unless the imagination is used and challenged, unless the creative powers are appreciated and strengthened, they are lost, sometimes never again to be found. Helping children to develop a real and lasting love for literature is a way of ensuring the preservation of those special qualities that define the best in human life.

The word that wants to write itself on these pages is the word *sacred*. I am not alone in my reverence for literature. Those whose lives are committed to literature in the classroom speak in one voice—a voice of urgency, of belief, of communion with all that is of most value in human history. They do not see literature as a "free-time reward" for those few students who finish their "real work" early and have time to read some book for a few minutes until the next lesson begins. They do not see literature as material for skills and drills, as fill-in time between more substantial subjects, or as reasons for book reports. They view literature in its most cosmic, humanistic, awesome proportions. It is no less than "the imaginative shaping of life and thought into the forms and structures of language. . . . The province of literature is the human condition; life with all its feelings, thoughts and insights. . . ."[6]

John C. Manning, president of the International Reading Association (1985–86), spoke to the second general session of the IRA's annual convention. He challenged and inspired the audience with his speech titled "What's Needed Now in Reading Instruction: The Teacher as Scholar and Romanticist." Some excerpts:

> Those of us who serve the schools as teachers of reading need to immerse ourselves in the world of books, stories, poetry, and drama. We need to know the literature appropriate and appealing to the children . . . who come to our schools to learn to read. . . . We need to seek within literature those lines that speak to eternal truths, those stories that have taught through the ages, that poetry which has opened our intellects and consciences to an understanding of goodness, truth, and beauty. We must ourselves be at all times well read, so that we may use the literature and history of our birthright as teachers to inform, to entertain, and to inspire. . . .
>
> Through the teaching and use of language we need to enlighten our students to recognize and appreciate the inherent dignity of all human labor through words of gratitude and thanks, to relieve physical and emotional pain through words of understanding and compassion, to seek justice and equality through words of good moral sense and common decency. And for all of us to seek through language and reading a universe of peace in our families, neighborhoods, cities, states, and nations in the only world we can together share.
>
> The greatest gift we can give to the children and students who come to our schools is the unbridled romantic love affair with language and books in historical context and literary form. It is that gift which shall remain long after the sweet gentle memories of school have dimmed and faded forever more.[7]

Speaking of Good Books

Take time to think about literature in your own life. Talk to your family, friends, and classmates about their experiences and memories. Literature makes a stimulating topic of conversation. Share memories. What are the earliest stories you remember? What lullabies, ballads, or songs were chanted to you? What fairy tales, nursery rhymes, legends, or myths were told to you in your childhood?

What people and places from your favorite stories stand out vividly in your memory? Can you remember ideas, feelings, and revelations first introduced to you through poems and stories? How did your favorite books inspire you, move you, and stimulate your imagination?

Rumplestiltskin is part of my life. I am always waiting for him to spin my chaff into gold! The crocodile who swallowed an alarm clock in *Peter Pan* is another of my constant companions. He is forever lurking nearby ticking away our time. How many times have you seen *The Emperor's New Clothes* in living color in the headlines of your daily newspaper or TV newscast? What stories and characters are following YOU around?

Are you Jack? Cinderella? Sleeping Beauty? one of King Arthur's Knights of the Round Table?

Find a Book to Love

Throughout these pages, you have been urged to rekindle those memories of early experiences that were meaningful to you. If you do not remember the books that you loved when you were a child and how you loved them, will you be able to "pass on the good news" to your students? If you think of literature only as a required subject and not as an important part of your life, what kind of attitude will your students catch from you?

Suppose you try to remember but find little in your experiences to inspire you. Does that mean that you can check out of this chapter untouched? Does that mean that you will not be able to teach literature in the joyful, meaningful way that it must be taught? What do you think? Here is my advice.

Find a book to love. Read it. Perhaps as you are reading it, time will stop for a while. Maybe chores will wait, the telephone will go unanswered, dinner will be late. You will begin building experiences into your present structure that strengthen "the wonder of the printed page—the beauty of language and illustration"[8] so that you can truly share new feelings with your students that are as valid and important as rekindled memories.

Remember that you, the teacher, have a world of books at your fingertips waiting to be discovered.

Your importance as a role model, as a living example of someone who *loves* books and *loves* to read cannot be emphasized enough. Children learn more from what you *do* than from what you *say*. If you truly want to pass on the stories, pass on the wonder, then you must start with yourself and begin your own love affair with literature.

Roger Gerhardstein always read his own book during silent reading time in his high school English classes. He was reading Leon Uris' *Exodus* and must have exuded such concentration and intensity as he read that his students asked him the name of his book. Later that day, Roger stopped into the library. The librarian told him that his students had rushed in and taken out every Uris book on the shelves.

Include the value of personal example and inspiration in your conferences with parents. So often, parents complain that their children don't read in leisure time, but, if asked, they admit that reading for pleasure is not one of their own priority activities. Invite the childrens' families to join in the reading commitment. Remind them that "the best way to send an idea is to wrap it up in a person."

A Book for Every Child

Annie, a very verbal two-year-old, visited an early childhood program. While her mother talked with the director, Annie spotted the bookshelves. Reaching toward them, she pleaded, "Please, may I have too many books?"

Her mother picked out books and laughingly explained Annie's original terminology: "Too many means *a lot!*"

How lucky we are to live at a time when there are "too many" excellent children's books! Today there truly is a book for every child. The range of children's literature is a feast for all to enjoy. Explore the world of children's literature and discover adventure, mystery, history, drama, humor, and beauty— the richness of the human heritage caught in the written word.

Through literature, children may discover in books new friends from backgrounds and cultures different from their own. Vital human issues, often difficult to talk about—like social justice, equality, fairness, cooperation—may be clarified and comprehended for the first time through involvement with stories in which characters make decisions in believable life situations. Children who never left their streets or towns may discover the greater world and its beauty and wonders in the pages of books. And, if we keep looking and offering, reading and sharing, we may help children find THE books that speak personally to them—like mirrors, like reflections of themselves caught in words. They are not alone! (See "Some Further Resources" at the end of the chapter.)

Picture Books   Don't let the label fool you. Picture books are not limited to young children. This merging of art and word beckons to children of all ages, including adults. Writers and artists have pooled their talents to create works of beauty, wit, and wisdom. Their works can be found on the picture book shelves of children's libraries. They cover a wide range of ideas and topics, corresponding to all phases and stages of children's lives. In all cases, the story is enhanced by the pictures. The fusing of the two arts creates a rich, lively, literature experience that nourishes imagination and deepens the meaning of the text. Often, the pictures themselves are quality works of art. Browse through the picture book section of your nearest library. Check the list of outstanding winners and runners-up of the Randolph J. Caldecott Medal. Each year since 1938, the most distinguished American picture book has been honored with this medal, named for the nineteenth-century English illustrator who pioneered the field of illustration for children. Share your discoveries with your students. There is a picture book waiting right now to become your favorite.

Traditional Literature   Myths, fairy tales, and fables—those works of wonder, mystery, or adventure provide a constant source of enrichment. When we discover the recurring universal themes in folk literature, we develop understandings and insights that strengthen us as members of the human family. Various cultures can be studied through their legends. All peoples have wondered about the mysteries of the universe, from the puzzle of creation to the incredible, yet everyday, phenomenon of life. Despite our complex, technical society, we still don't know the answers to the most basic questions about the origin of life. Telling myths and fables is the imaginative way people throughout history have expressed their wonder, asked questions, and offered explanations.

In his stimulating book *The Uses of Enchantment: The Meaning and Importance of Fairy Tales,* Bruno Bettelheim asks readers to consider the vital role these unique works of art play in the lives of children. Fairy tales not only hold children's attention, entertain them, and arouse their curiosity but also enrich their lives, stimulating imagination, helping to develop intellect and clarify emotions. Fairy tales are attuned to children's anxieties and aspirations, fully recognizing their difficulties while suggesting solutions to the problems. Bettelheim believes that more can be learned about the inner problems of human beings in any society and about the right solutions to their predicaments from fairy tales than from any other type of story.[9]

Anne Thaxter Eaton reminds us that

> through legends and folk tales, all of us . . . recognize our heritage from the
> past, the courage and heroism, the love of soil, the spirit of adventure, the
> devotion to a cause, the steadfastness and loyalty which make people today
> willing to fight and endure in order that the spirit of man may continue to
> exist in nobility and freedom. . . . Imagination grows by what it feeds on.
> Without sustenance, it shrivels.[10]

Poetry   Theodore Roethke believed a "poem is a holy thing." He considered poetry "one more triumph over chaos!"[11] How do *you* feel about poetry?
Do you like it, love it, fear it? Or are you perhaps just indifferent to it?

Poetry is probably the most mistaught area of literature. How many of us
learned poetry by rote, quizzes, exams, and authoritative questions and answers?
Because many of us were taught poetry as if each poem was a math problem
with the solution arrived at by a set formula, we probably missed the most
important aspect of it. Poetry might be the most elusive type of literature. It is
difficult to catch with a definition. It evokes highly personal responses. Some
definitions of poetry are almost as exciting to read as poems themselves! Myra
Cohen Livingston writes eloquently about poetry:

> It is, after all, a personal thing; its meaning to each human being is private.
> It invades the innermost thoughts; it clings to and bolsters the inner life. It
> is not something to be rationalized or explained; it is not an abstract principle;
> it is not part of an all-about book which arms with facts; it is not a piece of
> logic with which to startle others or to alter the course of scientific knowledge.
> It is not something to be classified. It cannot be proved.[12]

Leonard Clark warns,

> If poetry is omitted from the lives of very young children or if it is allowed to
> play only a minor part in their experience, there is a serious danger that
> powerful, though undeveloped, feelings will remain only partially satisfied
> and ideas, though not fully formed, will be confined to too narrow a range.
> This is a bold statement to make and it is important to make it at the present
> time, when so many other agencies are at work in the world—whether will-
> fully or not—to undermine the foundations of wholesome childhood—to seduce
> it from its normal pattern of growth and to keep it ignorant of its cultural
> heritage.[13]

I urge you to read poetry. Find the poems and poets who speak to you.
Discover words that express your deepest thoughts and feelings, that describe
how you see, and that ask the questions that are on your lips.

Edith F. Hunter wrote, "It is the nature of human nature to want to share
with those we love the things we really enjoy."[14] In keeping with that philosophy,
and to demonstrate the power of poetry in the classroom, I want to tell you this
story.

For three years I taught tough, "underachieving," borderline drop-out high
school students in Upward Bound, a federally funded program aimed at moti-

vating capable but turned-off teenagers to recommit themselves to education as a real value in their lives. One summer I taught four classes of creative writing a day. On this particular day, I gathered some of my most beloved poems and brought them in to share with *all* my students. Among my treasures were poems by Walt Whitman, Carl Sandburg, Lawrence Ferlinghetti, Edna St. Vincent Millay, Nikki Giovanni, and Anne Sexton.

I decided to share the poems in basically the same way with all the classes, with only a few differences. With all the classes, I talked about how I wanted to share some of my favorite poems because I wanted my friends to be part of something I loved. With all four classes, I read the poems and wrote the names of the poem and poet on the board. The first class was just asked to listen. The second class was asked to listen and jot down their thoughts or feelings as the poems were read. The third class was asked to listen and, *if they felt like it*, when the poem was finished, write their own poem about the poem they had just heard. The fourth class was asked to listen and, *if they felt like it*, continue the poem. *No assignments were given in any class*.

At the end of the day, I stopped into the library. The librarian was very angry at me. "You really should organize your program better," she scolded.

"Huh?" I remarked intelligently.

"Isn't it ridiculous to give *four classes poetry assignments on the same day?*" She flung out her arms. "Those kids piled in after lunch and cleaned out the poetry shelves. Now, the next time you should plan things better!"

Poetry, like traditional literature, can be part of everything you do. Don't box it into one unit of study ("Oh," said the third grader, "we already finished poetry.") or separate it from your life or the lives of your students. There are poems about *everything*. Many poets, like A. A. Milne, Mary O'Neill, David McCord, John Ciardi, Shel Silverstein, and Eve Merriam, write especially for children. Many of *your* favorite poets can be shared with children.

CAREFUL

A poem is not a math test or a spelling quiz with right or wrong answers. Don't judge, criticize, or grade a child's interpretation of a poem. The best way to destroy a child's interest in poetry is to put it in the realm of a workbook drill and present it in the same way as a multiplication principle.

Realistic Fiction   When I started teaching in the mid-1950s, the country was ablaze with civil rights issues. Reports of segregation, racial prejudice, hostility dominated the headlines. Imagine teaching fifth graders American history during that time. The kids wanted to know, "What's happening? What are Sit-Ins? Why are people throwing stones at little children in New Orleans?" We looked for books dealing with prejudice but found NONE. In disbelief, I visited the children's librarian at the New York State Library in Albany and was told, "The are *no* books for kids about prejudice or any other controversial issue. Controversial issues for children's books are taboo!"

That was the year the picture book about black and white bunny rabbits was removed from library shelves!

I was very distressed. I wrote a book called *The House at 12 Rose Street*. It was about a black family moving into a white neighborhood, based on a true incident in Leavittown, Pennsylvania. For almost *ten* years, the book was rejected by every major publisher. Always the same response: the story is good BUT we aren't publishing anything controversial. In 1966 the book was published in hardcover by Abelard-Shuman. In 1968 it became an Archway paperback. In 1980 it was adapted for an after-school television special.

I share this chronology to emphasize the changes in choices for children from the fifties to the eighties. Today, you and your students can find realistic novels running the gamut of current issues—from divorce to desertion, from drug abuse to sexual abuse, from terminal illnesses to mental disorders.

Books of realistic fiction help children develop insight into complex social and emotional situations. These are tough times and so many of our kids are wading through very difficult waters. Fortunately, there are many books out there waiting to help them on the voyage.

Ericka, suffering from difficult interrelationships in fifth grade, reads Louise Fitzhugh's *Harriet the Spy* (Harper & Row, 1964) and finds a kindred spirit.

Lonnie, sixth-grade cool kid, faces the arrival of a new baby at home with anxiety. Norma Klein's *Confessions of an Only Child* (Dell, 1975) is his treasure!

Bernice Cullinan thinks of realistic stories as both mirrors and windows of life:

> The many experiences they allow us can be had safely; we can sail around the world without fear of shipwreck or suffer blindness without loss of sight, while still probing the emotions of the moment. We can also rehearse experiences we might someday have; we can fall in love, undergo a job interview, experience the birth of a child. These practice sessions with story help prepare us for reality, creating expectations and models that influence our reactions to real events.[15]

Modern Fantasy and Humor   Today, it's easy for a child to make factual, informational books the center of his or her reading. The great number of such books reflects our technological society. But we all have a need for mysterious or humorous material that challenges our imaginations, amuses and entertains, or gives us food for fantasy. Many psychologists worry that we cut off a child's experiences with fantasy and make-believe too early, thus shrinking the imagination. Animals that talk, time machines, spiders that spin wondrous webs, earth children who search a strange planet, and bears who talk in hums as they play with their friends in the "100 Aker Wood" are the stuff that feeds healthy young minds.

Young children are drawn to stories that relate to their own immediate world. The familiar is comforting. Once there is recognition, playfulness is possible. Remember, children are individuals. There will be some children who *never* want a frog to talk or a witch to melt! Be aware of the children's interests and responses.

Children need to laugh, need to be intrigued. Most children need to enter another realm of human existence, where the fantasy world the writer conveys is as real and believable as the one in which the children actually live.

Biography and Historical Fiction   We human beings are curious. We want to know everything about other people's lives. We can often learn from the lives of others, no matter who they are. We learn from other people's courage and faith. We learn from the mistakes and choices they made in their lives. Every age of history has stories written about it. Individuals from every walk of life have their stories on the pages of books. Their stories become a part of our own knapsack of experiences.

Informational Books   In keeping with the idea that there is a book for every child, remember that not all children will be drawn to fiction, folk tale, or fantasy. There are books about every topic under the sun waiting for those curious fact-finders. Brightly illustrated, well written and well organized, Joanna Cole's *A Frog's Body* (Morrow, 1980) or David Weitzman's *My Backyard History Book* (Little, Brown, 1975) are examples of the kinds of fact-filled, informational books available to our young readers.

If you are still in need of definitions of children's literature, the following two statements should clear up any problems.

Charlotte Huck observed that "a child's book is a book a child is reading and an adult book is a book occupying the attention of an adult."[16]

And May Hill Arbuthnot commented that "a book is a good book for children only when they enjoy it; a book is a poor book for children, even when adults rate it as a classic, if children are unable to read it or are bored by its content."[17]

At the end of this chapter is a list of resources that can aid you in discovering excellent books. Make the effort to use whatever is helpful in this important search, which has as its goal the nourishing and enriching of children's lives through literature. Lois Lenski has words of inspiration on the vital importance of helping children discover literature:

> We never for a moment believe that children really like the cheap, the tawdry and the commonplace. If that is what they feed on, it is because they have been given nothing better. We know that, once they are given the opportunity, they will always respond—as instinctively as flowers turn toward the sunshine, they will respond to the good, the true and the beautiful.[18]

Will Literature Live in Your Room?

Remember that you, the teacher, are largely responsible for your time and space and what happens within those boundaries. Will yours be a roomful of books? Even if you are lucky enough to teach in a school with a fine library, you still need to fill your room with books. Gather books from the community and local libraries (who are unusually generous to teachers). Don't shortchange your students. Be sure that the books in your room reflect the wide spectrum of children's literature. Surround them with folklore, poetry, realistic fiction, biography, historical fiction, humor, and fantasy. Know your students' interests and find books that meet their needs. No one in your class should ever be able to grumble, "There's nothing to read!"

Sometimes we can become so involved in the activities that enhance and expand the book that we forget about the book itself! A good book is a rich and fulfilling experience in itself. There is no substitute for the direct and satisfying encounter with a good story, poem, or play.

Will You Read to Your Students?

Anna Grace is a young singer now in her mid-twenties. She remembers sixth grade more vividly than any other elementary school year because of one fact: "That was the year our teacher read to us every single day. It was the highlight of the day. We all looked forward to listening after lunch. She read in a great way, changing her voice with each character, getting different moods and tones to fit the story."

No matter our ages, we love having *a good reader* read to us. Read with expression and enthusiasm. Experiment with sounds and voices. Your voice and your body are instruments.

Whether you read a chapter of a book at a time until you finish it, a short story, or a group of poems, read to your students every day!

Whenever possible, tape your reading. Children often love to listen to a story over and over again. Take Charles Laughton's advice: "Choose a book you're comfortable with. Read nothing because you think you should. A book read from a sense of duty is almost certain to be a crashing bore. The pleasure of reading aloud comes principally from sharing something you like with someone you like."[19]

Encourage Your Students to Read on Their Own

Most of this book is filled with OLD NEWS. It may *seem* new and novel only because we've forgotten about it. Encouraging children to read silently and individually each day is a very old way of enjoying reading, but we've grown so technical and technique-oriented that we've forgotten how important that set-aside time is to developing appreciation for books. Now, most schools have begun to adopt it as part of their required reading program. They even have a name for it, Sustained Silent Reading, and even use initials—SSR! But we know how natural and enjoyable a "program" it is!

Set aside some time each school day for your students to read books of their choice, comfortably and quietly. Start with ten or fifteen minutes a day, leaving time to share the books. This is not the time to drill, test, criticize, or correct. If John chooses a book on a fifth-grade level, and he reads on a second-grade level, let him be. Freedom of choice means just that. We need the freedom to learn to make choices, good and bad.

Dewey Chambers reminds us "the real reason for the teaching of reading in our schools is to produce readers of books, not children who just know how to read. The gift of reading and the opportunity to use that gift is a sacred trust of all teachers."[20]

Everyone should be encouraged to read and discover the reward in the joy of reading. If you want to teach children to hate books, test them on their favorite books, quiz them on the books they choose to read on their own, use the contents of their favorite stories as material for drills. A popular writer of children's books told a group of teachers, "I have read questions about my own stories in children's workbooks that even I could not answer!"

Charlotte Huck reminds us that "it is possible to teach a child to read and to hate reading. . . . At the same time it is just as easy to teach children to read and develop a love of reading. I believe that schools can be joyful places where the quality of living is equal to the quality of learning."[21]

You can't measure love, but isn't that what you hope will happen between your students and their books?

Invite Storytellers into Your Classroom

In communities across the country, people who are good storytellers are waiting to be invited to share their tales with children. Check your community's resources, such as local librarians, grandparents and other relatives, senior citizens, fellow teachers, and students.

If a good storyteller is unable to come to your class, take the class to the storyteller. Or if this isn't feasible, use the excellent recordings of great storytellers. There are fine tapes and recordings of children's literature. On a visit to a third-grade class, I discovered these records in the "Listening Corner":

The Bears' Christmas and Other Stories, read by Stan and Jan Berenstein (Caedmon Records)

A. A. Milne's *The House at Pooh Corner*, told and sung by Carol Channing (Caedmon Records)

Hans Christian Andersen in Central Park, stories told by Diane Wolkstein (Weston Woods Records)

The Folk Tellers (Tales to Grow On), Barbara Freeman and Connie Regan (Weston Woods Records)

Recordings cannot take the place of live storytellers, but they are effective resources in a listening area of your room. Often you will see children listening with earphones to the stories during "free time."

Don't forget an excellent resource for storytelling—you and your students. Encourage the telling of stories—whether original stories or familiar ones—by individuals, groups, round-robin style, or by the class as a whole through choral voices. Music, art, creative writing, and movement are natural extensions of stories.

Special Reading Places

Do you remember how you loved special places when you were a child? Children still have those places. They love to build structures and play, hide, talk, read, and write in them. If you were to travel across the country, you would see children in creative classrooms reading in, on, or under

lofts	barrels	umbrellas	mats
pup tents	rugs	benches	pillows
bathtubs	rocking chairs	bean bag chairs	tables
crates	boats	tree houses	corners
carpets			

With your students, plan special reading places where children can "escape" to enjoy a book undisturbed and undistracted. For inspiration, read this description from Betty Smith's *A Tree Grows in Brooklyn*.

Home at last and now it was the time she had been looking forward to all week: fire-escape sitting time. She put the small rug on the fire-escape and got the pillow from her bed and propped it against the bars. She chipped off a small piece of ice and put it in a glass of water. The pink and white peppermint wafers bought that morning were arranged in a little bowl. . . . She arranged glass, bowl, and book on the window sill and climbed out on the fire-escape . . . breathed the warm air, watched the dancing leaf shadows, ate the candy and took sips of the cooled water in between reading the book.[22]

Book Reports

CAREFUL

In too many classes, reading and enjoying a book isn't as important as the book report. Many children love and understand books but fail book reports! Assigning regular book reports, grading them for spelling and punctuation, or criticizing the opinions and feelings they contain are not ways to "pass on the good news" of literature.

There are so many easy ways for children to keep records of the books they read. They can fill out index cards with title, author, publisher, and a few descriptive lines and recommendations about the book. The children can keep their own files or contribute to a class book file that is then available to everyone as a resource. Or they can keep book lists in a special section of their notebooks. Some classrooms have book trees growing in them with construction paper leaf shapes on which children write the title and author of each of their books with a few pertinent comments. Remember, this is *not* a contest.

Another variation is a pocket chart, mounted on the wall, with a pocket for each child. The students fill out special book slips for each book read and drop them into their pockets. Or set aside a special space or board for book-response cards on which the children write brief summaries and opinions of books. The cards are often brightly illustrated.

Professor John E. Davis likes to experiment with different ways of reporting on books. Here are examples of some of his favorite approaches:

He provides index cards in three colors—green, yellow, and red. He tells students, "If the book is one of the best ones you have ever read, write the report on a green card. If you feel the story was just so-so, write on a yellow card. If the story was one that made you wonder why you bothered to read it at all—if, in fact, you were able to complete it—write the report on a red card."

He provides a supply of transparency material—clear plastic, bleached X-ray film, or even kitchen plastic wrap—and transparency markers. If a student wants to (optional, of course), he or she makes a transparency and uses it on the overhead projector while telling about a book just read. John suggested this to a fifth-grade teacher who adopted the idea. One boy in the class who never read *any* books wanted to make a transparency. His desire to make a transparency was so strong that when he discovered he would have to read a book to make one, he read a book!

Will you offer many options?

Many imaginative activities can evolve from, introduce, and enrich books. Within each book lie countless seeds of possibilities to heighten the experience of the book itself (never to replace it!).

Think of *sharing*. Isn't that what we really do when our feelings about books spill over to our neighbors and are expressed in other activities? Think of *responding*. Give your students plenty of ways to respond, plenty of choices.

I like to ask kids to share a book *any way they want to:* tell it, write it, draw it, show a scene from it, sculpt it, dance it, turn it into a puppet show, design a symbol for it—the ideas are endless. And always include the ordinary form of book report as an alternative (the index card or book report sheet with standard questions). Sometimes people don't feel creative, and we need to respect that response.

Bernice Cullinan reminds us that

> Children should be allowed to explore their own responses as well as to share the responses of others, and to discuss all responses in the light of the text itself. A teacher who wants to hear only one kind of response to a story will soon have children who read "for the teacher" rather than for themselves; for they learn to give us what we value; if we applaud the narrowly focused, one right answer, that is what we shall be given. A teacher who encourages each child to work out a personal response, to share that response with others, and to return to the text for verification will soon have students who read for pleasure, immersing themselves in the stories and becoming critically aware.[23]

Because we are human beings, we want to continue something we love, to celebrate it, to share it. The next section of this chapter is full of wonderful ways to do just that. Only remember that what you are celebrating is something meaningful and enjoyable in itself.

QUESTION: What do I want my students to learn?
ANSWER: I want my students to fully experience and enjoy literature as an important part of their lives.

I want my students to grow in awareness, knowledge, insight, appreciation, creativity, and language development through a literature program that connects and enriches all strands of their curriculum.

I want my students to begin a love affair with books that will last a lifetime.

Getting the Kids Hooked on Books

You, too, have a smorgasbord of choices of how to catch your students' attention, how to catch them in your magical net as you begin reading a new book to them or encourage them to read on their own. There's always the direct approach: "Here's a book. Read it." Or "Today we begin reading a new book. Its title is————." But you can be more imaginative and have more fun in this launching process.

Many teachers start with *objects* from the story or book. Reach into your "Story Bag" or "Story Pocket" or "Story Knapsack" and pull out a special object. It's a stone. What does a stone have to do with our story for today? We wonder together, looking at it, examining it. Aha! *Stone soup!* What other objects are waiting to begin stories?

John E. Davis likes to tease the kids. Sometimes he reads just a small portion of a story and adds a question or suggestion that will "sell" the book to students. He had fun with *The Pinballs* by Betsy Byars (Harper & Row, 1977). He read the first two paragraphs of the book:

"One summer two boys and a girl went to a foster home to live together. One of the boys was Harvey. He had two broken legs. He got them when he was run over by his father's new Grand Am."[24]

John stops the reading. Dramatic pause. Then he tempts them further with "I wonder what else could happen in that story?"

You can imagine the response!

With Thomas Rockwell's *How to Eat Fried Worms* (Dell, 1975), John takes more of a "hard sell" approach. He reads the first three pages of Chapter One, "The Bet." Next he skips to the last chapter, "Epilogue." He then says, "If you are at all interested in how Bill went from making the bet with Alan to the point that he thinks he might be the first person in history to be hooked on worms, you'll enjoy reading this story."

And you can be sure that they do!

One of Ronni Hochman's favorite ways to get her students excited about books is to gather a large variety of paperbacks and "introduce" them to the kids, holding them up, reading from the back covers, summarizing a little and encouraging a lot. She was in the midst of one of these sessions when she held up the book *Chocolate Fever* by Robert K. Smith (Dell, 1978).

"This book is about a boy who can't get enough chocolate. He *loves* it! He has a passion for it!" She felt a sudden inspiration and continued playfully, "We all have cravings, don't we. I do. You do. Let's talk about some of *our* passions. I have one. I love it so much. It makes me feel good. I can never get enough of it. I'll tell you mine, if you'll tell me yours!"

The kids took turns telling their "cravings," with *pizza* and *ice cream* heading the list of popular responses. When Ronni's turn came, she asked, "Can anyone guess mine?"

Stephen's hand shot up. *"Us?"*

In Ronni's class, her students learn not only about love of learning but also about feeling loved!

Tom Griffin likes to write his own songs. He brings his guitar to class and plays it. He writes songs about books he is going to read to his fifth graders. Here is the song he wrote to introduce *Tuck Everlasting* by Natalie Babbitt (Farrar Straus & Giroux, 1975), a "heavy," magical story about the possibilities of eternal life and the realities of death.

Would You Like to Live Forever?

This is the story of a family named Tuck
Who came upon some very unusual
  luck.
They were heading from the East to the
  frontier country
Through a forest that never seemed to
  end
When suddenly they saw it—it was
  right around the bend—
It was a woodland spring of water
From which they all would take one
  drink

And the things that began to happen—
   you never would think
What's it like to live forever? Just ask
   one of those Tucks.
He might just tell you it ain't such good
   luck
And he would know because he's a
   Tuck.

This also is the story of a young and
   lonesome girl
Her only friend a toad, oh, what a
   lonesome world.
Well, one day she decided to take a
   walk outside in the wood.
It was there that she stumbled upon
The Tuck's secret of the wood.
Would she like to live forever? That's
   the choice that she had
But the question in her mind—would
   she be happy or sad?

Living forever sounds so good—at
   first—
But after 500 years would you be living
   a curse?
Your family and all your friends—they
   died long ago.
What else could you do? Where else
   could you go?
Would you like to live forever? I put
   this to you.
If you had a choice, what would YOU
   do?

It's something that I'd like to ask all of
   you.
Would you like to live as long as the
   sky's been blue?
It's something that you'd really have to
   think about.
Don't leave any room for doubt.
Forever and a day you'd always be
   here.
Living a life without any fear.
But, what about the magic and the fire
   in your eye?
Can it keep you burning when you
   know you'll never die?
Would you like to live forever? I put
   this to you.
If you had a choice, what would YOU
   do?

Enjoy the challenge of starting the kids off with excitement, anticipation, curiosity. Remember, the most ordinary thing can become extraordinary in the hands of a creative teacher. Explore! Experiment! Enjoy!

Activities That Celebrate Books

Talk

Professor Herb Sandberg is a proponent of the natural, enjoyable exchange of feelings and ideas that can be communicated about books and book characters. With children of all ages, he conducts discussions so lively, so dynamic and inspiring, that you might think they are talking about people they know intimately. When people love books, the action, characters, theme, and conflict become part of their lives. Partners, small groups, whole classes can discuss such topics as

What is the book about?

Who are the characters?

Which parts were most interesting to you?

Which characters were your favorites? Why?

How did you feel as you read the book?

What did you think about?

What would you do if you were in that situation?

What did you learn from it?

How does this book compare with others on a similar theme?

Would you recommend this book?

Sing

Songs and stories have been related to each other through history. There is a song about everything in the world: animals, holidays, places, people, events, feelings. Many of our popular folk tales probably began as ballads sung by minstrels wandering from village to village. Conversely, many songs, both modern and traditional, are based on literature. "John Henry" and "Robin Hood" are based on folk tales. "Richard Cory," "The White Rabbit," "Guinevere," and "The House at Pooh Corner" are all modern songs based on poetry and fiction.

One fourth-grade teacher claims that her best year of teaching was 1976, our nation's bicentennial year. She was excited about learning the history of our country through its songs and stories and her students caught the spark. Songs and stories overlapped. The children discovered that, through songs, they could trace the groups of immigrants coming to America. Songs told them about the building of railroads, the life of the whalers, the barges on the Erie Canal. Songs about people, places, and events carried over to stories on those same topics. The children devoured them all.

Don't wait for our nation's tricentennial year to help children discover that songs can help them trace the lives and experiences of earlier Americans. Think of the many songs you know or have heard that can enrich a book about farmers, slaves, cowboys, sailors, miners, or Native Americans. Every people, every country, every region has its songs. If you are studying a culture, read the stories and poetry of the people of that culture and sing their songs.

Write your own songs! Kids are great composers!

Listen to Music

Marvelous music for operas, ballets, musicals, and symphonies has been based on literature. Once a story is read and loved, how exciting it is for children to experience it on a different level.

Have the children listen to the music and then draw and write their feelings as they use their imagination to combine their knowledge of the original story with a musical expression of it. Start the activity with questions: How does a writer evoke suspense? fear? joy? anger? How does a composer evoke those same feelings?

Here is the start of a list of musical compositions based on literature:

Ravel   *Mother Goose Suite*

Stravinsky   *The Firebird; Song of the Nightingale*

Rimsky-Korsakov   *Scheherezade; Le Coq d'Or*

Tchaikovsky   *Sleeping Beauty; Romeo and Juliet, Nutcracker Suite*

Grieg   *Peer Gynt Suites*

Kodály   *Háry János Suite*

Copland   *Billy the Kid*

Create Sound Effects

Use rhythm instruments, body sounds, and voice variations to compose background music for a favorite story or poem as the words are spoken by a group or an individual. Tape this oral reading and background sound. For example, poems about Native Americans are enhanced by rhythmic percussive sounds; Halloween stories lend themselves to a wide assortment of eerie, mysterious sounds. Combine this activity with improvisation and movement.

Dance the Book

Many poems and stories are excellent stimuli for dance improvisation. All through history, dancers have interpreted legends and myths through body language. In many cultures each movement and posture of the body represents a specific word or idea and audiences "read" the dance as they would a book.

With children of all ages, I have explored ways to dance stories, poems, characters, and plots from favorite works of literature. Here are a few samplings from a file bursting with favorites:

Dance all the characters from A. A. Milne's "100 Aker Wood." Challenge with specifics: "When you work on movement for Rabbit, try to look just like Rabbit! Close in on his special rhythms and movement designs."

Fairy tales like "The Emperor's Nightingale" provide excellent material for creative movement. Work as a group but with individual choreography: "Show us *your* Emperor. How does he stand? How does he walk? Shape his statue. Move it." Then "Shake out the Emperor and move on to the Nightingale . . . and on to the tricky fellows . . . and now show us your Mechanical Nightingale . . ."

Sixth graders celebrated *A Wrinkle in Time* in dance. They chose the scene in which the little band of earth children arrive at a strange planet where everyone moves and acts in exactly the same way. The class divided into groups of earth children, bouncing, skipping, moving spontaneously around the room through the rows of robot-like people moving in rigid unison. The contrast was striking and perfectly caught the drama Madeleine L'Engle describes so powerfully in her story.

When you offer children *choices* in how they may respond to a book, you'll find that some kids choose to share their book in dance. One sixth grader choreographed a beautiful unfolding, expanding dance as her "report" on *Jonathan Livingston Seagull!*

Follow the movement experiences with creative writing and art activities. Kids need multidimensional experiences to enrich their comprehension and appreciation. Keep making connections!

See Chapter 6, "Movement and Drama," for more suggestions.

Illustrate the Book or Story or Poem

Even in schools without regular art programs, most kids will express their feelings and reactions to literary works they love through art. They enjoy illustrating a memorable scene from a story or line from a poem. They love the challenge of drawing or painting portraits of their favorite characters or landscapes of their favorite settings.

Even a group of cool, inhibited junior high kids responded enthusiastically to the challenge of illustrating their favorite nursery rhymes! The "hook" was that they were to share their illustrations with younger children who had somehow missed the fun of nursery rhymes!

Stories Good Enough to Eat

In many stories, a specific food is important for a character. The Queen of Hearts has her *tarts*, Homer Price loves his *doughnuts*, Winnie the Pooh is never without his *honey*, Peter Cottontail risks everything for those delicious *garden vegetables*, and *gingerbread* children are delicious to munch while reading the Gingerbread Man.

Children love to cook as much as they love to eat the results. See the end of this chapter for suggestions on stories good enough to eat.

Dramatize, Improvise

Characters speak and move. Stories are action-packed. Things happen. Emotions change. The plot thickens.

Children work individually, with partners, in small groups, or as a class to interpret and express parts of stories, favorite scenes, especially compelling exchanges of dialogue, or individual characters.

Experiment with pantomime, puppets, choral reading, masks, props (any combination of drama components) to give a book even greater impact.

A very simple, delightful way to dramatize a story is with *chairs*. The children design a large paper shopping bag for each character in a story. They slip each bag over the back of a chair; each chair defines a specific character. When the children sit in the chairs, they *become* the characters and dramatize the story.

For example, imagine how delightfully the story of Goldilocks and the Three Bears is presented as children take turns sitting in the Baby Bear chair, the Mother, Father, and Goldilocks chairs. I visited a kindergarten where the story was retold by groups of four children until everyone had a turn.

Try this idea with the Seven Dwarfs: have each chair be a dwarf's chair, and have each child who sits in a particular chair turn into that dwarf! Go down the line of dwarfs, and have each respond in character to questions from the rest of the group. Leave a little extra time so that everyone has a turn!

Combine this idea with Musical Chairs!

Ideas beget ideas.

A.Y.O.

Map a Book

Many books, such as *The House at Pooh Corner* and *The Hobbitt* already have maps accompanying them. Children will enjoy designing a map to go with the action of a book. Give them the chance to draw or construct a relief map to accompany a story they like.

Paper Dolls from Book Characters

Many children love to cut figures out of cardboard and then design clothes and costumes and improvise dialogue and situations for them. Use characters in a story as the subject of the paper dolls project.

Make a Class Mural

After you and your students share an especially exciting book, you all may decide to celebrate the book with a mural in its honor. Tape a large piece of paper to a wall or board and discuss your plans. There are no set rules for creating murals.

Some murals are free-flowing. Each child contributes a design or illustration expressing any part of the story he or she chooses. Others are devoted to illustrations depicting highlighted scenes from the story. Murals can also be divided into sections and follow the story in chronological order, from beginning to end.

Children may work individually or in small groups. The important thing to remember is that everyone's contribution should be encouraged so that everyone will enjoy the creation.

Dioramas

Sometimes called "shoebox" stories, dioramas are three-dimensional models depicting a scene. Sometimes the shoebox is left open to reveal the scene immediately. Sometimes it's closed with a hole cut in the side to offer a more mysterious secret view. The background is painted and figures and objects from the book are arranged in dramatic action. Children love using a scene from a favorite book as the subject for a diorama they share with their classmates. Often, the part of the book that stimulated the diorama is written out and taped to the outside of the box.

My husband vividly remembers his shoebox scene of the flying monkeys and the witch from *The Wizard of Oz*. He used pipe cleaners covered with papier-mâché for the monkeys and witch. He used green terry cloth for grass and cotton puffs for clouds. After almost fifty years, he still remembers the complexion of the witch and the frightening expressions on the monkeys' faces.

Keep a full scrounge box ready for such projects.

Discover Mythology

After reading legends and folklore with your students, look for references to mythological and legendary people and places on maps and in our daily lives. How many cities in the United States are named Athens? Who are the planets and stars named after? Who are the oceans named for? What about the names of rockets and ships? This is an activity that will last throughout the year.

Write Your Own Myth

After reading myths and fables, the children will want to create their own. Discuss the common themes and structures shared by so much of folklore, such as the Hero, usually an average person, who overcomes great obstacles to achieve a specific goal. In folklore, good and evil are always clearly defined. Magical objects and symbols are used, and numbers take on special significance. Certain words or phrases develop magical qualities through repetition. There are many ways to stimulate children to write their own myths and fables. Here are just a few suggestions.

Spin-offs
   a. After they have read a legend, ask the class to *continue* the adventures of a favorite Hero or Heroine or make up a new Hero or Heroine and write a new adventure or magical story. Add illustrations.
   b. Have the children draw a map of a mythological place and then write a story using their map as the landscape. One group of fourth graders made up a map and wrote individual stories based on its terrain.
   c. Your students might write their own explanation for the beginnings of the earth, animals, trees, fish, mountains, rivers, flowers, stars, volcanoes, storms, night, and day. Correlate with art, drama, music.
   d. Have the children collect objects that would make good symbols to use in a myth, such as a golden slipper, a key, a magic wand, a scarf, or a special pair of eyeglasses (without lenses). The children can choose an item and write a myth using the object as a major ingredient of their stories. Improvise them. Dance them.

Write a Newspaper

The children can work individually, in groups, or as a whole class. They choose a book to use as the subject of a newspaper article or as the basis for an entire newspaper. Editorials, news stories, crosswords, cartoons, feature stories, public service announcements, and other components of newspapers are written about the action and characters of their book. Each group of children can base their writing on a different book.
   Can you guess what book Judy Adlerstein's class is sharing when they call their newspaper the *Wonderland Times*?

Listen to Poems and Write Your Own

Poetry inspires poetry! When we listen to and read the heightened language of poetry, its music fills our imagination. There are so many wonderful ways to listen to the poetry of others. Here are but a few suggestions:
   Read a poem aloud. Encourage your students to write their own poems in the rhythm of the one shared.
   After reading a poem to the class, suggest that they try writing one using a similar rhyme scheme
      or that they *continue* the poem
      or how about a poem expressing a similar theme or topic?

or what about a *contrasting* poem? If the original poem is rhymed, try writing a poem in blank verse or the reverse?

The Stuff of Poetry   Seasons, animals, colors, time, places, events, changes, feelings are the life themes of all of us. Children enjoy experimenting with ways to write a variety of poetry celebrating language and ideas: try poems full of *colorful* words; peaceful, quiet poems; scary poems with frightening images; silly poems with silly words.

Books like Kenneth Koch and Kate Farrell's *Sleeping on the Wing* (Vintage, 1982) provide excellent materials for old and new ways of encouraging poems based on poems.

A.Y.O.

Make a Poetree

As you probably guessed, a poetree is a tree of poems. The children write their favorite poems on colored construction paper cut in a design that expresses the poem. A poem about balloons is printed on balloon-shaped paper. A poem about a cat is printed on paper cut in the shape of a cat. The poems are read to the class and taped to the poetree.

Biographies Speak for Themselves

After the children have read biographies, ask them to think of an original way for the subject of their biography to share the story of his or her life with the rest of the class. Here are some ways in which sixth graders shared biographies they had read.

Tecumseh   Cara made Tecumseh's head out of felt and left a hole for the mouth. She wrote his story on a roll of adding machine tape, which she put inside the head with just the tip showing. The other students could pull down the tongue and read his story.

Helen Keller   Fran moved carefully, haltingly, to the front of the room, walking as if she were blind. As Helen Keller, she talked to the class about her life of struggle and faith. Her voice carried the strained, unmodulated tones of someone who has finally learned to speak but cannot hear the sounds she makes.

Gather Favorite Quotations

As they read, students can write their favorite quotations in a special notebook. Then they copy those words into a class scrapbook and illustrate their contributions. As often as possible, have the children share these favorite words orally or illustrate them, using them as text for posters, pictures, discussions, creative writing, music, movement, and dramatics.

Here is a sampling from a few pages of fourth graders' favorite words from books.

Bob likes "Life is always a rich and steady time when you are waiting for something to happen or to hatch."[25]

Miranda likes "Once, when the sky was very near the earth, a woman hoeing in her garden took off her necklace and hung it in the sky. The stars are her silver necklace." [26]

Make a Montage

There are so many ways to organize this activity, which brings together the segments or parts of a whole in imaginative patterns. Here is just one example: A sixth grade class read a collection of Greek myths. They discussed them, wrote ideas and names on the board, and then divided the class into small groups. Each group chose one hero, heroine, or god to celebrate. Some of the ways they expressed their ideas: puppetry, pantomime, music, felt-board narration, shadow drama, and comic strips. When the parts came together in a montage, the festivities were memorable!

Nursery rhymes and fairy tales are also excellent subjects for a montage. A variation is to close in on *one* story or poem and highlight different scenes and themes from it.

Four Case Histories of Literature Celebrations

This is not a book of recipes but a sharing of experiences and suggestions with the hope that they will inspire you to mix your own magical festival of ideas. With that approach in mind, enjoy the following examples of how literature blends with serendipity, openness, enthusiasm, the arts, the language arts, and time to yield multilevel "peak" experiences that children will remember all their lives.

Solve a Mystery

Maureen Reedy's fourth graders are totally immersed in the complicated relationships of characters and events featured in Ellen Raskin's *The Westing Game* (Avon, 1980), an intriguing mystery with the challenge of finding an explanation for a murder that occurs before the book begins. A few of the activities Maureen and her students have shared:

The sixteen characters in the book are charted individually, their descriptions and actions recorded on strips hanging from ceiling to floor.

The fourth graders group into teams of four paralleling the teams of four players described in the story. Each child "becomes" one of the characters in the story.

As the book is read (fifteen minutes a day for the reading, fifteen minutes for discussion), clues are passed out to each team. As the days pass and the plot thickens, the teams meet and try to make sense out of their clues.

The children create a Westing Museum. They write all the important objects of the story on the board and assign an object to a person, complete with a very carefully written explanation. Such objects as a copy of *The Wall Street Journal*, a chocolate candy bar wrapper, and a diamond engagement ring begin appearing in the museum with excellent explanations of their significance.

As clues are given in the book, they are gathered in a central display area. The children have just figured out that many of the clues contain words that seem to come from "America the Beautiful." They have just copied all the words to the song to study it for hidden meanings.

The book is not over. This is the fourth week for *The Westing Game* and the class is still completely involved in the story despite the fact that almost all the children have bought or borrowed the book to read on their own with the sacred promise not to talk about any events that have not yet been read in class.

Excitement is mounting! Tune in tomorrow . . .

The Shakespeare Lady

Adina's invitation was printed on a felt scroll contained in a shoebox.

"You are invited to our Shakespeare play on Monday, November 4, at 1:00 P.M. I hope you can come. Please R.S.V.P. by November 1."

What a unique invitation. I later discovered that every invitation sent by Adina and her classmates was an original!

On November 4, we sat in the audience admiring the colorful banners displaying artistically written and designed quotations from Shakespeare. The children chose the quotes and, of course, created the banners.

> The play's the thing.
>
> All that glitters is not gold.
>
> 'Tis the mind that makes the body rich.
>
> Though I be but little, I am fierce.

Suddenly—lights and Elizabethan music. The procession began. We never saw Adina and her usually mischievous, mumbling, slump-shouldered middle-school comrades. Instead, we sat spellbound watching and listening to the proud figures of Queen Elizabeth, Lord Leicester, Calpurnia, Kate, and other compelling Shakespearean characters. Backs were straight. Gestures poetic. Eyes clear and unafraid. Every word pronounced perfectly and comprehended by the speaker. Plumes, capes, swords, crowns. The witches from *Macbeth*, Calpurnia's dream from *Julius Caesar*, "This England" from *Richard II*, "We Happy Few" from *Henry V*, "All the World's a Stage" from *As You Like It* were some of the scenes the players offered. What a transformation!

One parent whispered to me in a hush between speeches, "Shakespeare moved into our house!"

How fortunate that Adina's school had invited Dusky Reider, the Shakespeare Lady, to bring the Bard to the children. With the cooperation of Artists in the Schools, Dusky Reider moves in books, costumes, voices. Teachers, parents, and kids are summoned to the cause. Dusky brings her passion for Shakespeare, her belief that the children will learn to love and understand his works and perform them for others, and a deeper faith that their lives will be enriched by the encounter.

I invite them to learn about the plays of Shakespeare. No put-downs. A safe environment. We *try* voices—the witches' voices, the king's voice. I use my original Kentucky accent; then I speak in much clearer pronunciations. I tell them stories about the times of Shakespeare, about Queen Elizabeth. Everyone in the class has a part. I tell them that I know we're going to give a beautiful play working together as a family. They keep journals. We talk about everything we do. They always come through. Don't you think they did a wonderful job?

Who in your community is waiting to be invited into your classroom? And, if that person's calendar is full, there's always YOU!

The Lizard Lovers Club

Attention Lizard Lovers

The Lizard Lovers is a club that gets together on Thursdays every week. We get to eat lunch together and have fun. We have tests on Pinkwater books every week. We read books by D. M. P. (Daniel Manus Pinkwater) and anybody else.

Our differences from pods: Lizards are responsible, appreciate literature, read, are a little bit crazy, and are creative. Pods are ignorant of the lizard way of life (reading!). The pods need to have their minds and eyes opened.

We have had many new lizards join this year. We hope to get a lot more.

Books we have read: *Lizard Music, The Magic Moscow, Wizard Crystal,* and many more.

We are learning new songs and making new friends with people in other rooms.

We are not a fan club. We just like Pinkwater's books.

P.S. Lizards don't wear shoes.

Tee shirts. Logos. Weird language. Lizard bracelets. Newspapers. Plays. Stories. Letters to Pinkwater. Language fairs. Picture book contests. Pinkwater tests. Puppets. Correspondence to publishers, to *The New York Times Book Review,* to Wally (a figment of Pinkwater's imagination who became an excellent pen pal); an original radio play; telephone interviews; book charts; library shows . . . What's going on here? What is this all about, anyway?

The Lizard Lovers Club is an extraordinary example of serendipity, flexibility, synthesis, and fun. One summer, Paul and Jan Hammock, then teaching in a middle school, decided to have a little reading group that would meet every other week and share books. They invited a small group of sixth and seventh

graders to join. They walked to a nearby children's bookstore, paired up, and each pair picked a book. The chosen books had to be ones that no one had read and that all approved. They drew dates to determine the order in which the pairs would present their books. Each member bought copies of the six books and read each one before it was presented. *Lizard Music* by Daniel Manus Pinkwater (Dodd, 1976) was one of the books.

Paul remembers that the session about that book was by no means unanimously positive. He recalls a lively afternoon with strong feelings on all sides. Paul and Steve especially liked the book.

When school started that September, Paul, as a little joke, cut up an index card, wrote on it in black and green ink *"Lizard Lover:* Honorary Member," and presented it to Steve because they were the two who had really endorsed the book. Steve playfully showed his card to the others. Well, they had read the book, too, so why weren't they included in the honorary membership? Paul just cut up a few more index cards! The news spread! More and more kids came in claiming that they had read *Lizard Music* and wanted a card and wanted to be in the club. In three weeks, over forty kids in the school had read the book and joined.

Paul couldn't stop the tide. He called a meeting of the Lizard Lovers and the rest is history. By the end of the year, over two hundred children of all ages, parents and interested community members had "joined." A steady and lively correspondence with Pinkwater evolved, culminating in an unforgettable visit from the beloved author to his admirers, who had by now read *all* of his almost thirty books, including the galley pages of *The Snarkout Boys and the Avocado of Death* (Lothrop, 1982). The news of the Lizard Lovers Club traveled to both coasts and people were writing to the kids for membership from points east and west. For weeks the bookstores and libraries of the city were depleted of Pinkwater books! When a reviewer for *The New York Times Book Review* gave Pinkwater a negative review, the Lizard Lovers took pens in hand and the letters flew. That year kids read, wrote, talked, drew, dramatized, played, sang, sculpted, *celebrated* as they never had before.

This is only a sampling of the events and activities that occurred that year. Paul Hammock has an easy explanation for such amazing developments: "Things happen by accident and people shouldn't be afraid to make the accidents work. Roll with them!"

And he quotes from Pinkwater: "Sanity is contagious! Beware!"

Your Room Is a Web

Ellen O'Neill's kindergartners listened to *Charlotte's Web* and loved it. They wanted to turn their room into the corner of the barn where Charlotte spun her web. Ellen brought thin string to class and together they decided how to weave the web, where to attach the string, what points of the room were to be connected. They wove their room into a web! They moved as carefully as Charlotte through the strands of string. They improvised the different animals and people in the story. They cut out letters to spell Charlotte's magical words and attached them to the strings of the web. Just as the kindergartners were caught in Charlotte's spell, so your students will be caught forever in the magic of literature if you teach with enthusiasm, imagination, courage, and love.

Resources at Your Fingertips

What books to choose? What books do kids like? What are they interested in? The answers are a few minutes away. Use your community resources.

Visit Your Local Children's Librarians

A brief visit with our nearby children's librarians, Rosemary Anderson and Janis Wilson, yielded a wealth of information and ideas. Here are some of the things I found out: *Always* in demand are

Beverly Cleary's books
Betsy Byars' books
Judy Blume's books

The Little House on the Prairie books

C. S. Lewis' *Chronicles of Narnia*

Tolkien's books

S. E. Hinton's books

"Kids always ask for books about Pippi Longstocking (Lindgren), Encyclopedia Brown (Sobel), and the All-of-a-Kind Family (Taylor), and for Shel Silverstein's poetry books.

"Right now," the librarians observed, "many of the middle-school kids are interested in contemporary fiction, but not necessarily 'problem' fiction. They like stories with humor, such as *Nothing's Fair in Fifth Grade* (DeClements, Viking, 1981) and *Dear Lovey Hart, I Am Desperate* (Conford, Scholastic, 1977).

"If a teacher is reading a particular book to the class, we get so many requests from the kids in the class and their friends. For example, the last few weeks we can't keep *Where the Red Fern Grows* (Rawls, Bantam, 1974) or *The Doll House Murders* (Wright, Holiday, 1983).

"Younger children are asking for books by illustrators because it seems teachers are spending a lot of time studying the different illustrators' works and styles. There's a big run on books by Eric Carle, Brian Wildsmith, Ezra Jack Keats, Leo Lionni, and Tomie de Paola. The younger kids still always ask for books by Dr. Seuss, the *Curious George* books (Rey), the *Frances* books (Hoban), and Don Freeman's books, especially *Dandelion* and *Corduroy*.

"So many times, kids come in and say, 'I want a good book to read.' Then we find what they especially like, what other books they've enjoyed; then you go from there. Sometimes they tell you, 'We like sad books or fantasy.' Sometimes we can get them started on a new direction. We try to stay current with all the new fiction so we can honestly recommend it. You can't recommend something you don't like yourself."

Ask the Kids

Kids love to talk about books.

The Kids' Connection Magazine asked its readers (ages 5–13) to send in the names of their favorite books.[27] The response was tremendous. The list grew. Here are some of the titles submitted. (All of the books mentioned by Rosemary and Janis were included. These are *others* on the list.)

Tom Sawyer	*The Velveteen Rabbit*
Watership Down	*The Hundred Dresses*
Where the Wild Things Are	*Babar*
Down the Dark Hall	*The Pushcart War*
White Fang	*A Different Twist*
Charlotte's Web	*The Never-Ending Story*
The Witch of Blackbird Pond	*Winnie the Pooh*
Thunder, the Mighty Stallion of the Hills	*The Littles*
	The Pigman

The Runaway's Diary	*The Black Stallion Mystery*
The Haunted Bridge	*Star Wars*
Little Miss Tiny	*Choose Your Own Adventure*
Cinderella	*Bearbook*

At the end of this chapter are suggestions for excellent resources that will enrich your understanding and knowledge of children's literature.

How Do I Know These Methods Are Working?

We have, as yet, no *accurate* measure to gauge enjoyment, enthusiasm, interest, and appreciation. No methods have yet been devised that test a person's development of a lifelong love for literature. As these are among the basic goals of teaching literature, you will have to rely on evaluation techniques such as these checklists.

Checklist for the Class

1. What are my students reading?
2. Is there a pattern to their choices?
3. What does it tell me about their interests and concerns?
4. How do they feel about their books?
5. Are they learning from their books?
6. Are they using their creative energies to express their feelings about a book in different ways?
7. Are they incorporating vocabulary, ideas, and concepts from their books into their daily lives?

Checklist for Yourself

1. Do I listen to my students' comments, opinions, and ideas about what they are reading?
2. Do I talk with them about their books, comparing themes, discussing story lines, characters, mood, action, and words?
3. Do I offer my students many opportunities to share their books in a variety of ways and am I part of these experiences?
4. What am *I* reading?

What Books Mean to Students

When children love their books, they make them part of their everyday conversation and play. If you have children who don't enjoy reading, who are not reading anything that is meaningful to them, or are not participating in any related activities with enthusiasm or interest, consider them as deprived as any undernourished child. Help them search for that special book, that particular poem, that elusive story waiting to be found. Help them to find it and encourage them to love it.

Some Further Resources

Anthologies

Three examples of excellent anthologies of children's literature that not only offer hundreds of reviews, summaries, and recommendations of books across the field but also integrate literature with all strands of the curriculum are

Bernice Cullinan, *Literature and the Child* (New York: Harcourt, 1981).

Charlotte Huck, *Children's Literature in the Elementary School*, 3rd ed. (New York: Holt, 1979).

Zena Sutherland and May Hill Arbuthnot, *Children and Books*, 4th ed. (Glenview: Scott, Foresman, 1976).

Periodicals

All of the popular teachers' magazines include sections on children's literature. In addition, many journals feature information on new books for children. Examples are

The Horn Book Magazine

The Reading Teacher (International Reading Association)

Library Journal

The Bulletin of the Center for Children's Books (University of Chicago)

New York Times Book Review

Language Arts (National Council of Teachers of English)

Awards

The Randolph J. Caldecott Medal is given each year for the most distinguished picture book for children published in this country and selected by a committee of the Association for Library Services for Children of the American Library Association.

The John Newbery Medal is given each year to the book considered to be the most distinguished contribution to children's literature as selected by a committee of the Association for Library Services for Children of the American Library Association.

The winners and runners-up of both of these prestigious lists will start you off with an outstanding collection of the best in children's literature.

Human Relations

The books listed below will help you select children's books that improve human relations and encourage understanding of others who may be different from ourselves.

Guidelines for Selecting Bias-Free Textbooks and Storybooks (New York: Council on Interracial Books for Children, 1980).

Barbara Baskin and Karen H. Harris, *Notes from a Different Drummer: A Guide to Juvenile Fiction Portraying the Handicapped* (Ann Arbor: Bowker, 1977).

G. Simkins, G. Holt, and C. Simkins, *A Cross-Culture Reading Program* (Boston: Houghton, 1977).

John Gillespie and Christine B. Gilbert, eds., *Best Books for Children from Pre-School through Middle Grades* (Ann Arbor: Bowker, 1981).

Joan Fassler and Marjorie Janis, "Books, Children and Peace," *Young Children* 38.6 (Sept. 1983): 21–30.

J. Carr, "The Literature of Fact," *The Kobrin Newsletter* (Chicago: American Library Association) offers suggestions for informational books.

Judy Freeman, *Books Kids Will Sit Still For: A Guide Using Children's Literature for Librarians, Teachers, and Parents* (Hagerstown: Alleyside, 1984).

Carolyn Flemming and Donna Schatt, eds., *Choices: A Core Collection for Young Reluctant Readers* (Evanston: Burke, 1984).

Sharon S. Dreyer, *The Bookfinder: A Guide to Children's Literature about the Needs and Problems of Youth, Ages 2–15* (Minneapolis: Circle Press/ American Guidance Service, 1981).

"Good New Books about Native Americans," *Classroom Reading Teacher*, March 1984: 671–72.

Jane Manthoren, *Children's Classics: A List for Parents*. Write to The Horn Book, Park Square, Building 3, St. James Avenue, Boston, MA 02116.

Organizations

The organizations listed below offer information on all aspects of children's literature, especially on books that help children understand themselves and others. See also the listings at the end of Chapter 1.

International Reading Association
800 Barksdale Rd.
P.O. Box 8139
Newark, DE 19714-8139

National Council of Teachers of English
1111 Kenyon Rd.
Urbana, IL 61801

National Association for the Education of Young Children
1834 Connecticut Ave. N.W.
Washington, DC 20009

Association for Childhood Education International
11141 Georgia Ave. Suite 200
Wheaton, MD 20902

Anti-Defamation League of B'nai B'rith
823 United Nations Plaza
New York, NY 10017

National Association for the Advancement of Colored People
186 Remsen Street
Brooklyn, NY 11201

Integrated Education Association
School of Education
Northwestern University
2003 Sheridan Road
Evanston, IL 60201

New York Library Association
Children and Young Adults Services Section
15 Park Row, Suite 434
New York, NY 10038

American Library Association
50 East Huron Street
Chicago, IL 60611

Resources to Deal with Attempts at Censorship

Unfortunately, through the years attempts have been made by various community groups to censor books for children. Pressure is put on teachers, librarians, and school administrators. Tension and trauma often dominate the scene. When schools are prepared with a process and system for dealing with attempts at censorship, the confusion can be minimized. I urge you to think about the issue, read about it, and form a philosophy as sturdy and strong as a house made of bricks.

Such organizations as *The International Reading Association, National Council of Teachers of English*, and *The Council of the American Library Association* have come out with policies that are practical, articulate, and enlightened.

People for the American Way, 1424 Sixteenth St. N.W., Suite 601, Washington, D.C. 20036 is an excellent resource for sample procedures used by schools throughout the country to combat censorship.

Books Good Enough to Eat

Gretchen Anderson, *The Louisa May Alcott Cookbook: Twenty-eight Recipes Mentioned in Little Women* (Boston: Little, Brown, 1985).
Carol MacGregor, *The Fairy Tale Cookbook* (New York: Macmillan, 1982).
———, *The Storybook Cookbook* (Englewood Cliffs, NJ: Prentice-Hall).
Virginia Ellison, ed., *The Pooh Party Book* (New York: Dell, 1975).
———, *The Pooh Cookbook* (New York: Dell, 1975).
Katherine Hart, ed., *Pease Porridge Hot* (Austin: Encino, 1967).

ENDNOTES

[1] Judith Viorst, "The Books Children Love Most," *The Writer* (April 1976): 22.

[2] Robert Havighurst, *Developmental Tasks and Education* (New York: McKay, 1955).

[3] May Hill Arbuthnot, *Children and Books*, 3rd ed. (Chicago: Scott, Foresman, 1964) 2, 17.

[4] Harold Brodkey, "Reading: The Most Dangerous Game," *New York Times Book Review*, 24 Nov. 1985: 1, 44–45.

[5] Edith F. Hunter, "The Peace of Great Books," *Horn Book Reflections*, ed. Elinor Whitney Field (Boston: Horn Book, 1969) 298.

[6] Charlotte Huck, *Children's Literature in the Elementary School*, 3rd ed. (New York: Holt, 1979) 4.

[7] John Manning, speech, General Session, International Reading Association Convention, New Orleans, 9 May 1985. Reprinted in *The Reading Teacher* 39.2 (Nov. 1985).

[8] Dewey W. Chambers, *Children's Literature in the Curriculum* (Chicago: Rand McNally, 1971) 8–9.

[9] Bruno Bettelheim, *The Uses of Enchantment: The Meaning and Importance of Fairy Tales* (Vintage, 1977) 5.

[10] Anne Thaxter Eaton, "Children and the Literature of the Imagination," *Something Shared: Children and Books*, ed. Phyllis Fenner (New York: John Day, 1959) 82.

[11] Theodore Roethke, *Straw for the Fire* (Garden City: Doubleday, 1974) 260, 172.

[12] Myra Cohen Livingston, "Not the Rose," *Horn Book Reflections* 174–80.

[13] Leonard Clark, "Poetry for the Youngest," *Horn Book Reflections* 156–58.

[14] Hunter, "The Peace of Great Books" 294.

[15] Bernice Cullinan, *Literature and the Child* (New York: Harcourt, 1981) 289.

[16] Huck, *Children's Literature in the Elementary School* 3.

[17] Arbuthnot, *Children and Books* 2.

[18] Lois Lenski, *Adventures in Understanding* (Tallahassee: Friends of the Florida State U Library, 1968) 14.

[19] Charles Laughton, "Read It Out Loud," *Something Shared: Children and Books* 29–33.

[20] Chambers, *Children's Literature in the Curriculum* 13.

[21] Huck, *Children's Literature in the Elementary School* ix.

[22] Betty Smith, *A Tree Grows in Brooklyn* (New York: Harper, 1943) 20, 21.

[23] Bernice Cullinan, *Literature and the Child* 21.

[24] Betsy Byars, *The Pinballs* (New York: Harper, 1977).

[25] E. B. White, *Charlotte's Web* (New York: Harper, 1952).

[26] Natalia M. Belting, ed., *The Sun Is a Golden Earring* (New York: Holt, 1962).

[27] The list of children's favorite books is taken from the magazine *The Kids' Connection* 4.1 (Fall 1985). See also the annual October issue of *The Reading Teacher* for "Children's Choices," a joint project of the International Reading Association and The Children's Book Council.

8

Reading: "The Funnest Thing!"

"It's a Missage," he said to himself, "that's what it is. And that letter is a 'P,' and so is that, and so is that, and 'P' means 'Pooh,' so it's a very important Missage to me, and I can't read it. I must find Christopher Robin or Owl or Piglet, one of those Clever Readers who can read things, and they will tell me what this Missage means."

A. A. MILNE[1]

Pooh's little friend Piglet is equally confounded by the idea of reading. In "Rabbit's Busy Day," Piglet comes across grumpy Eeyore who is looking at three sticks on the ground that form the letter *A*. Piglet, of course, doesn't recognize the *A*. Eeyore lectures:

> Do you know what an *A* means, Little Piglet? . . . It means Learning, it means Education, it means all the things that you and Pooh haven't got. That's what *A* means . . . to the educated, not meaning Poohs and Piglets, it's a great and glorious *A*. Not just something that anybody can come and breathe on!²

The story of how Pooh will learn his *P* or how Piglet will recognize the letter *A* is one of the most controversial, thoroughly researched, and debated of all the components of the language arts curriculum. Let's face it: *Reading* means Learning. It means Education. It could be the pivotal factor in one's success or failure in life!

Before we plunge into a discussion of some of the recent developments on the reading scene, let's talk to one of our most vital resources—our kids. What do they have to tell us about their reading experiences?

Jon   Now in sixth grade, Jon knew his alphabet, spelled his name, and had begun to combine letters and form simple words when he was two years old. He loved to "read," completing sentences in stories and turning pages at the correct places in the texts. How did he learn to read? "From magnetic letters on the refrigerator door!"

Arthur   Sixteen and quick-witted, Arthur is an excellent mechanic who constructs new machines as well as he repairs ailing ones. He is in ninth grade, reading on a first-grade level. He knows how to drive but can't pass the written test. Talk to him about almost anything, but don't mention reading.

Elizabeth   When Elizabeth was in first grade she read on a sixth-grade level. Her favorite book was *Charlie and the Chocolate Factory*, which she read with dramatic expression, comprehension, and enjoyment. How does she remember learning to read?

"My father taught me. First, I read the newspapers with him. Second, we read the funnies. Third, we read Dr. Seuss books. And fourth, we read highway signs. Fifth, well, I guess I knew how to read."

Charles and Lee   Two years apart, close friends as well as brothers, Charles and Lee enjoy similar cultural, social, and family activities. They are both agile, intelligent boys who love athletics and the outdoors and are busy with many hobbies. There is one major difference between them. *Charles is a reader and Lee is not*. Both boys were avidly read to. Both enjoyed being read to. Charles, since babyhood, has been fascinated by books, magazines, newspapers. He read early and grew to be a devoted reader. Lee never chose a book if a toy was around. He reads satisfactorily, passes all of his standardized tests, and has no

difficulty deciphering unfamiliar words that might block his enjoyment of reading, but he would consider himself a nonreader without a moment's hesitation or regret.

Nessy and Jenny   These perky sisters have been reading since early childhood. When Nessy was in first grade and reading *Little House on the Prairie*, I asked her how she learned to read.

"I think I knew how to read when I was born."

"No, Nessy, you couldn't," I said. "No one knows how to read at birth. Everyone has to learn how to read. Can you remember how you learned?"

A minute of meditation resulted in this explanation: "Jenny taught me. Jenny sang the alphabet song and pointed to the letters. I had to say them as she sang the song. Then I learned easy words like *the* and *at* and *hat*. Those words led me to the big ones like *Wisconsin* and *America*, and *beautiful*."

When I asked Jenny how *she* learned to read, she responded immediately: " 'Sesame Street' and 'The Electric Company!' "

Miguel   When Miguel first came to this country from Guatemala, he spoke no English. Now, in sixth grade, he talks, writes, and reads in his new second language. How did he learn?

"Mostly from TV. Mostly from big signs like McDonald's, like Wendy's, like supermarket stuff, Cokes, and magazines like *Time* and," he grins, "rock and roll albums—Bruce Springsteen!"*

Understanding the Reading Process

Any textbook can easily be filled with countless case histories reflecting the wide diversity of reading abilities and interests of children. Based on your own knowledge of the reading habits and experiences of your friends, classmates, and relatives, you could probably write case histories that would provide further insights into the complexity of the reading process.

Examine your own reading history. Try to remember how you first learned to read, when you first learned to read, how you felt about learning how to read. Somewhere in your farthest memory (or perhaps your closest) is the knowledge of your struggles and triumphs as you listened, sounded out, absorbed, thought about, recognized, and finally deciphered the complicated code of written symbols that opened the world of reading to you. Making meaning out of visual symbols translated from auditory symbols and expressed through written symbols is *not* the simplest of human activities. If you could recall your emotion at the time, it might have equalled or even excelled the exhilaration experienced by Champollion when he deciphered the Rosetta Stone and thus unlocked the secrets of an ancient language.

Despite the fact that thousands of extensive studies have been conducted over the years, experts still cannot completely explain why Lee, who is able to read satisfactorily, is a nonreader or why Arthur, who can understand the fine details of intricate machines, cannot decipher the written symbols of his own language. Educators are still agonizing over the purposes and definitions of reading. Is reading a means or an end? Is word recognition the goal of reading, or is knowledge of the sounds of new words, ability to pronounce words, accuracy in oral reading, enthusiasm for reading, or comprehension of words the goal? What is beginning reading? Does beginning reading mean responding to material with understanding and comprehension? Does it simply mean naming and sounding letters? What influence does lighting have on reading abilities? What about class size? How can we effectively measure students' *interest* in reading? Do children need to learn the letters of the alphabet to learn to read? Every study raises as many questions as it tries to answer.[3]

Scholars articulate diverse and provocative philosophies. The offerings are dizzying. You can spend literally the rest of your life reading research reports and observations *about* reading. Do you agree with Kenneth S. Goodman, who looks at reading as a psycholinguistic guessing game? Goodman sees reading as a "selective process. It involves partial use of available minimal language cues selected from perpetual input on the basis of the reader's expectation. As this

---

*Young children share their experiences in learning to read and their ideas about letters and words in Mimi Brodsky Chenfeld's *Creative Activities for Young Children* (Harcourt, 1983). See pages 252–54.

In her travels and studies, Chall found that children generally seemed to react to an atmosphere created by the teacher and the program *together*. There was excitement, enthusiasm, and interest in some classes whatever reading program was in use. Conversely, in other classes children responded to each other and to activities with listlessness, boredom, and restlessness no matter what reading program was used. *Generally, it was what the teacher did with the method, the materials, and the children rather than the method itself that seemed to make the difference.*

Back to You

Your school system may have adapted any one of the many excellent reading programs available. You may be teaching in a tightly structured curriculum, orthodox in its following of one specific method. Perhaps you are fortunate enough to teach in a school where you are encouraged to use the best resources, combining decoding skills with meaning-emphasis experiences in a holistic, child-centered climate. Whatever your teaching scene, YOU bring yourself to the method, to the children. With your own interests, strengths, knowledge, life resources, personality, perception, instinct, imagination, you blend system-approved reading methods with *everything you know* as you try to reach each and every child. Be strengthened by this reminder from Paulo Freire: "Teaching kids to read and write should be an artistic event."

He laments the fact that many teachers "transform these experiences into a technical event, into something without emotions, without invention, without creativity." He sees many teachers working "bureaucratically when they should work artistically. Teaching kids how to read words in the world is something which cannot be really put inside of a program."[12]

James F. Baumann summarized some of the factors affecting success in reading achievement. He wrote, "In other words, *teachers* teach, not textbooks, workbooks, games, kits or media."[13]

There's no getting away from it! YOU *are crucial to the process.*

Early Intervention: Helping the Poohs and Piglets

Marie Clay, a New Zealand educator, is widely known for her observations of young children beginning to read. Why do some children read easily and others with great difficulty? She discovered that the children who learned to read easily had developed an understanding of "concepts about print": they knew that books had fronts, backs, pages; that print in the books is what is read; that print is made up of letters that form words and sentences and are read from left to right with the page on the left read first, followed by the page on the right; that the sentences are read from top to bottom and that there is an order to the words in the sentence and if you change the order you change the meaning. These children also had a sense of story.[14]

Clay's work with young children who were having problems learning to read beckoned Charlotte Huck and Gay Su Pinnell from Ohio State University.

They visited Clay in New Zealand and were deeply impressed with her success in helping young children overcome reading problems. They noted the remarkable results of her ten years of developing and testing certain strategies and decided to bring Clay's approach back to the United States and try it with American children. They began the program, which they called Reading Recovery, as a pilot program in the Columbus, Ohio, public schools. Their results were so impressive that in 1985 the State of Ohio General Assembly allocated funds to the Ohio Department of Education to train teachers around the state to implement the program. Gay Su Pinnell and Charlotte Huck are supervising the training and research.

Gay Su Pinnell is enthusiastic in her dedication to the approach. Here are some of her thoughts about the Reading Recovery program:

> Reading Recovery provides a second chance for young children at the risk of failure during their first year of reading instruction. With this early intervention effort, we hope to reduce reading failure. This is not a *method*. The focus is on helping children become independent readers by developing self-generating systems. *We want to enable poor readers to behave like good readers all the time!* In an intensive *one to one* relationship, teachers are trained to carefully observe and diagnose childrens' reading behavior and teach them effective strategies. The key to the program is the trained teacher who *observes* the child in detail, knows the reading process and procedures. The teachers' responsibility is to select books so that the children always read at 90% accuracy or above. Many opportunities are provided for children to read and reread easy material, simple material, to other children, parents, friends. The children write every day, constantly seeing the relationship between the reading and writing. Teachers never do for the children what they can do themselves but structure lessons so they can use everything they know and the tasks are made easy. We have found enormous progress in only a few weeks. Children who could be failing readers behave like good readers! This approach untangles the confusion while it's still easy. It shows that children failing in reading can learn to read![15]

R. Craig Roney adds an important thought to this focus on helping children with reading problems. He writes, "The knowledge that reading is both enjoyable and immediately useful" is a most important background experience. Children are consummate pragmatists. "If they neither sense immediate benefit from reading nor learn to enjoy the activity, they will regard it unfavorably and fail to develop the habit."[16]

Gay Su Pinnell counsels, "Teachers have to pay conscious attention to ways of helping."

We want to help children develop the lifelong habit of reading with enjoyment and understanding, don't we?

We can't stay away from YOU. Carl Rosen believes that you, the classroom teacher, are the dominant element in the issue of teaching reading. Your ability to recognize, nourish, and channel the interests and needs of your students and to create conditions that arouse thought, activity, and imagination is critical.[17]

Keep Making Connections, Seeing Interrelationships

Many outstanding scholars in the field of elementary education have found a high correlation between children's general language abilities and their success in reading: Reading is not separate from the rest of the language arts. These scholars believe reading is intrinsically linked to oral language, listening, and comprehension. From the first baby coos, through the babbling stage, to the first recognizable word, to the breakthrough into sentences, a child is preparing for reading.

When you see toddlers "read" a book by looking at the pictures and "tell" the story in their own words, you are observing many of the components of reading even though the child is not deciphering the actual words. The child is getting the idea of the story, being cued by the pictures, understanding the meaning of the story, enjoying the experience, reconstructing the story in original words.[18] Do you agree with educator Iris Tiedt that reading is one of several language skills, all of which reinforce each other, and that no language skill can be taught in isolation? William Rupley and others also view reading as an integral part of the language experience. They found that a child's ability to learn how to read is highly related to his or her present skills with the spoken language.[19]

Think of reading as a learning phenomenon that emerges from early language experiences and is related to all aspects of language activities. Remember that reading involves perceiving, achieving meaning, and reacting in a variety of ways.[20] This attitude toward reading will result in a classroom environment that will provide stimulating and dynamic language experiences for your students, an environment rich in appreciation for the many ways in which reading is an integral part of our daily lives, not an isolated or disconnected one. Your students will see that the chart noting their observations on the class's pet gerbils is *a reading experience*, as are the suggestions jotted on the chalkboard about where to go on a field trip, as are the rules of behavior voted on by the class, as are the story problems in the math assignment and the map exercises in the geography text. *Your* students will never hear what a group of fourth graders heard their teacher say after a fire drill:

"Well, we missed reading today because of the fire drill, so let's go on with social studies."

In your class, children will know that reading is part of everything they do, a vital component of all subject areas, a major aspect of all their experiences.

Your Many Choices

Throughout this book, we have been using words like freedom and flexibility in discussing creativity. In this chapter on reading, those words take on special meaning. The range of teaching methods and materials is vast and spreads out before the American teacher like an education smorgasbord. You will have resources at your fingertips and methodologies in your knapsack that were unknown when I began teaching over thirty years ago. It will be your responsibility to choose the approaches that most effectively meet the needs of individual students. Not all materials will prove successful with all children. You will probably create combinations of methods and resources. When faced with students who, for whatever reason—social, psychological, or physical—do not respond to the conventional teaching methods, teachers must rely on their own creative energies to devise ways to reach those students.

We have been discussing Code versus Meaning methods for teaching reading. I ask you to consider these as basic, inseparable components of the reading process. To only emphasize the mechanics of decoding is to shortchange the child. To neglect decoding skills and stress only meaning is to ignore the children who are struggling through a confusion of visual images and sounds. Children need all the basic understanding and skills possible in order to succeed at reading. They need to be able to use clues to recognize and identify words; they need to develop a large sight vocabulary; they must be able to learn words by the context in which they are presented, the pictures that illustrate them, their configuration, phonics, and other decoding aids. But just recognizing and identifying words isn't enough. Without an equal stress on meaning—comprehension, interpretation, and evaluation—reading becomes a mechanical exercise in the translation of written symbols.

Your commitment should not be to a particular material or method, but to the children, your *particular* students, whose needs must determine your approach. Students like Jenny, Nessy, Elizabeth, Charles, and Lee, who have learned the basic mechanics of reading, don't need endless workbook exercises and phonics drills. Arthur, Miguel, and others like them, caught in the tangles of deciphering a complicated code, will need your help to pinpoint their specific areas of difficulty and to find ways to solve those problems.

By all means, utilize the available standardized diagnostic tests that have been developed to assist you in determining your students' special needs. Such tests can provide you with valuable information about the kids' competency in reading skills, such as word identification, word meanings, comprehension, and vocabulary. Keep in mind, however, that no matter how comprehensive a standardized test may be, it is still that—a standardized test. It can be a valuable tool when interpreted wisely. It can yield information on various areas of the reading process to help you evaluate the needs of your students. But it cannot substitute for your firsthand observations. It cannot replace your own conclusions based on close classroom relationships with children. Remember that all your students, from Arthur to Elizabeth, will learn to read with more success, will learn to love reading, if theirs is a classroom with books of many types, on many subjects and reading levels. When books are read, shared, discussed, and interpreted in a climate of trust and mutuality, people find that reading becomes an important part of their lives, enriching and sustaining them.

We Learn from Each Other

Jeanette Shotter teaches first grade. She is a free spirit who constantly challenges her students and shares adventures with them. Her approach to reading is eclectic and her manner is dynamic. While her students are ecstatic about the way she teaches them, their parents are sometimes skeptical or confused. She meets with the parents to share her philosophy and the events in her classroom.

"How many reading groups do you have?" a parent challenges. "Twenty-nine," Jeanette answers. "That's when everyone is reading individually." She goes on to explain that sometimes they have two reading groups, when the class is divided into two sections, each working on a different part of a choral reading piece. Sometimes they have five reading groups, when a committee is looking up information on gerbils, one boy is off by himself reading his space books, the bulletin board committee is cutting out new words for a display, and so on. The parents quickly get the message, especially when they see the kinds of books and magazines their children are able to read.

Peg Schnittke, a reading consultant, lured a group of disinterested, apathetic fifth graders into a small room covered with maps of hidden treasure and pictures of pirates. She spun a web of adventure in which pirate ships on the high seas searched for lost treasure. With enough paperback copies of Robert Louis Stevenson's *Treasure Island* for everyone, the exciting experience unfolded, turning the once disinterested fifth graders into avid readers who branched out to other adventure stories, biographies of Stevenson, and their own original, dramatic interpretation of the book presented with great pride and excitement. The group improved in the standardized reading tests given annually by the school system.

Louise Bogart, like many Montessori teachers, creates an environment rich in materials and stimulating learning areas where her very young students can develop independence and self-confidence. She believes "children are responsible. They're in touch with the materials. They choose the materials they enjoy and learn best with. I start each child off with one or two sounds and letters. We say words that start with those sounds. They work at their own pace and often create their own materials [such as letter shapes or booklets]. Our children are reading at four and five years old. Once kids crack the code, there are no holds barred. They want to read everything!" Under a system with no official reading groups, no set of basal readers, no allegiance to any one reading method, Montessori children have done well in all standardized reading tests. "The danger of getting hooked into any one method is—What if it doesn't work with one child? You've got to invent a whole new method and materials."

Dawn Heyman's third graders come from low socioeconomic backgrounds, many from broken homes, often speaking nonstandard English. Her school system has adapted a reading program that is strictly structured. But even within the limits, Dawn explains,

> We take time. We talk about the stories. Even some stories that children don't show interest in, we find something in it to talk about. We relate it to our own experiences as people so reading is a pleasant time. . . . We use the words. Sometimes we'll play games with the words. Take *ie* making the long *e* sound, like "field," "yield," "shield," "fiend." We stop the story, look up the words. All the time we're finding meanings as we learn the technical facts about the word. Later, as a joke, we'll write letters that begin, "Dear Friendly Fiend." We have some laughs. We have fun with the reading.

Faye Moskowitz's lucky seventh graders will read, discuss, listen to, and come to appreciate a rich offering of literary works. Before school is over for the year, her seventh graders will read Steinbeck, Poe, Wilder, O. Henry, Twain, and Dickens. Faye, inspired by her own childhood experience of a teacher who opened the doors of reading to her, recalls that "like a magician, she could pull verbal rabbits out of a seemingly empty line of prose or poetry. She was our tour guide, our decoder, our tastemaker."[21] Now Faye passes the tradition on to her own students.

Creative teachers keep basic purposes clearly in mind as they "look for new ideas, change worn-out tactics, and never, ever fall into patterns that lead to student ennui." You may have students like Charles, Lee, Jon, Elizabeth, Arthur, Jenny, and Nessy in your class. You may have one official, approved reading program in your school along with the accompanying materials to implement it. Perhaps in your hands it will become an effective and successful learning experience for most of your students. Perhaps, too, you will notice that some children do not learn as easily through it as others. Some children learn through the intellect, immediately grasping ideas as they are presented. Others learn through the body—physically experiencing the idea. No matter what official method you may be using, you will still have to supplement and expand it, creating new ways to reach all of your students. Remember that the method is a means, not an end. The purpose of the method is to *teach children how to read* so that they can learn from and enjoy all the knowledge and beauty of human achievement that is shared through the written word.

Do you know that, when asked what they are doing and learning in reading, many children in our country give no response. Some have told me that they don't have reading. They never associated their workbooks, skill tests, phonics drills, and cassette exercises with reading. They never knew the purpose of those lessons. To those children, identifying and recognizing letters and words and pronouncing correct sounds to correspond with alphabet shapes had nothing to do with reading.

Caught up in everyday demands, it is easy for the classroom teacher to forget to pull together the various technical reading skills so that they become purposeful. When children see the purpose for their work, their motivation is multiplied. A fifth grader grumbled to his teacher, "I don't see why we have to waste all this time on these crazy *gh*-ending words." The teacher answered, "If you're in the middle of a terrific adventure story and you're right at the most exciting part and along comes one of these words ending in *gh*, you don't have to stop and wonder what it is and have trouble pronouncing it in your mind. You'll know it so you can read right on without interruption."

I remember three-year-old Larry's favorite question, posed endlessly in his toddler's lisp: "What's the weezon?" I hope you remember the "weezon" for it all!

Volunteers in the Classroom: Open the Doors

One of the most exciting developments in recent years is the growing involvement of community members in educational experiences for children. In more and more classrooms, parents, family members, and volunteers from the general community have committed themselves to taking responsibility in classroom activities and schedules.

An example of the many ways volunteers play an important and valuable role in the classroom comes from Jean F. Robinson's first grade. One of the first orders of business at the beginning of the school year is a note sent home asking for volunteers. Jean puts every volunteer to work! She uses all their skills and interests. One mother loves to cook so her time with the children is cooking time. Of course, cooking means the kids read recipes, go over ingredients, make sure they have the proper utensils and items for a successful culinary adventure. What do they use? An electric hot plate or frying pan. Keep it simple.

Jean's volunteers read with, are read to, play games with, write with, write for, listen to a small group of children or to one child at a time. They are involved in all of the activities and are permanent members of the class group. Jean has volunteers whose children long ago passed through her class. The children went on. The parents stayed! It makes a difference.

Ella Rappaport wasn't satisfied with simple retirement in a warm climate. She heard that the local school needed volunteers so she rounded up a few of her neighbors and they signed up. They have definite time periods, permanent assignments. Ella's is a third-grade class.

"Sometimes I work with one child. Sometimes a few children. We might go over math problems or the story they didn't finish in the reading assignment. It's very gratifying. I know it means a lot to the children for me to be there. It means a lot to me, too."

We need all the friends we can get! Reach out! People are waiting to be invited.

Families Play a Very Important Role

Whether two parents, one parent, step parents, grandparents, or guardians, the families of the children, their most immediate "world," are vitally important in the encouragement of and success in reading. When I work with family groups at conferences and meetings, I challenge them:

"What are you reading? When do you read? Do you read *with, near, around, before, after* your children? Do you read *to* them? *Listen to them* read? Do you *share* stories? *Enjoy* the reading time together? Is it a time you look forward to? Is it an important part of your lives?"

Take every opportunity to remind family members (in a nice way) to inspire, encourage, and share reading experiences with their children. They, along with teachers, are the central role models in their children's lives.

Knock on All the Doors

Before you delve into some of the many ideas that will help you enrich and enliven reading experiences in your classroom, I want to share an incident with you.

I was invited to spend a day with the reading teachers of a city, exploring "creative and innovative" ways to teach reading. The workshop was to be held in a large, historic church that filled an entire city block. I parked my car and, carrying my records, puppets, tambourine, and notebook, walked to the first door. It was locked. I knocked and no one answered. Puzzled, I walked to the next door in the old building. Again, it was locked and there was no answer to my knock. The parking lot was full of cars. I knew there were people inside the rambling building. I continued walking around the church, knocking on every door, finding each one locked, hearing no sounds from within. After a while, I began to feel like a character in a Kafka novel. I had almost made a complete circle back to my starting place when I came to the last door and knocked.

When it opened, the smell of coffee filled my nostrils and the sound of teachers laughing and talking rang in my ears.

Some children are like that building with many closed, locked doors. No matter how many times you knock or how many doors you try to open, it seems as if you won't get in. But persistence, faith—whatever form of spunk you want to call it—will keep you knocking. If you believe there's life inside a child, you won't give up; you'll find the approach that will touch the child and open the doors.

QUESTION: What do I want my students to learn?
ANSWER: I want them to learn to love reading and to comprehend everything they read.

You Are a Reading Experience

You, as teacher, are a continuing influence on your students. How do you see your role? How can you be a positive influence on the reading attitudes of your students? Share with your students your own interests, particularly those that involve reading. Consider reading an inseparable part of all the curriculum areas. Don't limit your materials to the standard basal text and workbook or think of reading as a separate subject limited to a specific schedule. Your materials should be as diverse and eclectic as life itself.

A basic, constant vocabulary in your room features the *names* of you and your students. Our own names are our *first* words, the ones closest to us, the ones that give us immediate reassurance and are the trunks from which our ever-growing, branching bloom of words reaches skyward.

Know your students and their interests. Remember that almost every human activity is defined by words and has within it every component of the language arts curriculum. Word skills and word relationships are part of everything we do. If your room is a room of words, your students cannot help but grow in reading awareness and competency. Remember, children know many thousands of words. They know many more words than they can read or write. They understand them and can use them in conversation. The more often you give shape to the words they already know and the more you surround them with familiar and new words that have meaning for them, the larger their vocabulary will become and the more they will feel a sense of achievement and pride in their success.

Remember, another constant and basic source of relevant and lively reading material is the written work of your students. Display, mimeograph, ditto their poems, stories, riddles, cartoons, songs, suggestions, questions, on a daily, ongoing basis. Don't hoard their words! Don't make your sharing of their works a reward for the highest achieving members of the class.

A sixth-grade teacher once told me, "Friday is the day we put up the best papers of the week." The rest of the week the walls were covered with commercial posters and charts. Do you think that that practice is carrying out the old commandment "Rejoice in all of your works"?

If your room is filled with the original materials of your students, it will be a dynamic and meaningful environment that can't help but stimulate growth in all learning areas, especially reading. You are giving your students a strong and important message: Their words are valuable. Their works are valid learning materials. Watch motivation and self-esteem grow! Since all the language arts are interrelated and interdependent, every activity suggested under the general categories of Listening, Oral Language, Creative Movement and Dramatics, and Literature can also be a reading activity.

ABC Activities

Letter of the Day

This is especially effective with younger children. Celebrate each letter of the alphabet by assigning it a special day. Have the children search the room to find the special letter, which you have tacked on to bulletin boards, desks, walls, or closets. When the children discover the letter, they then look around the room for objects that start with that letter. Suppose the letter is E. Gather and talk about objects that begin with E. Write E words on the blackboard. Draw or design pictures, posters, collages, or mobiles featuring the letter E.

Combine letters and colors for a Red Letter Day! How about a Blue or a Purple Letter Day? Combine it with numbers! Today we celebrate six words that begin with the letter P. Let's write them in pink or purple!

After a day of colors, letters, and words, first-grader Jeremy beamed, "Reading is amazing!"

Letters in Pockets

Louise Johnson, a first-grade teacher, uses an apron with many pockets for numerous activities. She introduces new letters by referring to one pocket as "Polly Pepper's Pocket" and pulling items from the pocket that begin with the letter P. "Busy Bossy Beth's" pocket introduces B words.

Alphabet People

This is an experience that will be greatly anticipated by children in the early grades. Dress up to represent a letter by drawing the letter on an old shirt, pinning the letter shape to your sleeves, pants, or skirt, wearing a paper hat with the letter taped to it or hanging from it, or carrying different items with you that begin with the letter. One teacher dressed up as the Tin Man for the letter T. His hat was in the shape of a T. He stood with arms outstretched in the shape of a T. He taped pictures of taxis, toys, telephones, and tennis racquets to his clothing. He announced himself with a shake of a tambourine and a recital of words that began with T. Then he did a tap dance. The class added their own T words, wrote them down, and illustrated them.

Celebrate the entire alphabet by having the kids pick letters to illustrate and animate.

Special Sections for Different Letters

Set aside spaces on the walls, bulletin boards, or chalkboards for letters. Make room for as many large and colorful letters as possible. Leave enough room under each letter so that the children can tape up words, pictures, and objects beginning with that particular letter.

A space set aside for *C* might have words like *cat, candle, cow, can, cough,* and *cap* along with all the children's names that begin with *C* and pictures and original drawings depicting *C* objects.

Leave the alphabet spaces up for a few days, preferably a week, so children can add to, use for creative writing, look at, read, and enjoy.

Alphabet Children and Other Moving Moments

Children preschool through junior high school will enjoy this activity. Ask your class, "Can you make a letter of the alphabet with your fingers?" Everyone can do it. Letters grow out of fingers and are immediately recognizable. The class continues the experiment and makes several other letters. After a few minutes, challenge your students to use arms, legs, and then whole bodies to make the shape of a letter. Many letters lend themselves easily to body interpretation. Children may request a partner to help them make a single letter. This leads to partners forming a two-letter word with their bodies. They spell *it, up, is, to, be, if, so, no,* and so on.

Older classes will want to go on to longer words. I have seen fourth, fifth, and sixth graders stretched across a gymnasium floor with their bodies clearly spelling *peace, love, brotherhood, exit, friend, happy.* Without being instructed, other children turn their bodies into question marks, exclamation points, and dots over the letter *i*.[22]

Expand the activity by dividing the class into groups of three or four and asking them to spell the *same* word, say, *cat,* but giving each group its own adjective to shape its body-letters of *cat* in a special way. The group "spelling" *proud* cat will have a different quality than the group "spelling" *scared* cat! This is an excellent way not only to celebrate letters and words but to demonstrate the purpose of adjectives. Spin off into art, creative writing, and improvisations.

Alphabet Dream Books

During a "rest" period, ask the kids to stretch out on the floor in the shape of a letter of the alphabet. Try different letters. Suggest that everyone try resting to, say, the letter *T*. Here come the two greatest words to inspire imagination: *What if?*

"Boys and girls, *what if* at night you had trouble falling asleep? Instead of tossing around, *what if* you tried shaping the different letters of the alphabet with your body. Wouldn't it be fun if you fell asleep in the shape of one of those letters and all of your dreams were of things that began with that letter? Here you are resting in the shape of a *T*. What might you dream about?"

Turn the activity into alphabet books. The children love to illustrate their alphabet dreams, showing themselves asleep in the letter shapes.

Darcell's dream book showed her asleep in the curled up shape of the letter *C*. What do you think she dreamed about? *Cats, cotton candy, clouds*, and *cars*. Her pictures illustrating her "dream" were, as she describes them, "dy-no-mite!"

Movement Questions

Questions involving movement lend themselves to recognizing alphabet letters. Try such enjoyable challenges as

Do you have a *T* in your name? Then clap your hands.

Does your name have a double letter in it? Then tap your fingers on your desk.

Look around the room. Do you see a word beginning with the letter *L*? Then blink your eyes.

Consonant Blend Kids

A fourth-grade teacher shared this as one of her most successful and enjoyable reading activities. The children are assigned, or pick, a consonant blend that they will introduce in an original manner to the rest of the class on a certain day.

The most memorable anecdote involves a boy who was to introduce the blend *SN*. When his day arrived, he was not in class for the early morning rituals of attendance and announcements. The teacher thought he was absent. Suddenly, there was a knock on the door. When the door was opened, there was the *SN* boy, wriggling on the floor with a homemade snake costume and mask. He hissed—"Sssnnnnn"—and said as he entered, "I'm a sneaky, snivelly, snotty, snorty, snarly snake. Snnnnnnnnn. Snnnnn."

The words the class added to his snake list were snarl, sniffle, snorkel, and sneeze. The children told round-robin stories about the snake using as many *SN* words as possible. They wrote about the snake, drew hilarious *SN* pictures, and improvised dramatic skits.

Ten More Ways to Celebrate Letters

1. Bake cookies in letter shapes. Eat them!
2. Find the hidden letters: children draw pictures or designs in which they hide the shapes of letters.
3. Metamorphosis: change the letters into designs or animals. Draw, paint, or construct the magically changed letters with scrounge materials.
4. Shape pipe cleaners, fabric scraps, felt, cotton puffs, and seeds into letters.
5. Write letters in sand, snow, mud, fingerpaint, clay, glitter.

6. Find letter shapes in twigs, stones, bark, stems, and leaves. Arlene Alda's imaginative book *ABC* (Celestial Arts, 1981) will inspire you and your students.

7. Gather these materials of the earth (see #6) and shape them into letters. They make very original exhibits.

8. Compose cheers or songs celebrating the letters of the alphabet. "Let's hear it for the letter *O*! Let's hear it for the letter *K*! What do ya say? O.K.! Yaaaay!"

9. Alphabet activities: with your students, gather ideas for a different activity for every letter of the alphabet. Here are a few of the suggestions from a second-grade alphabet activities chart:
   A: *Act out* an *animal, ask* a question, *arrange* the farm
   B: *Build* a sculpture, *blow* up a *balloon*
   C: *Cut* an interesting paper shape, *color* a weather report
   D: *Draw* a *design, dress* a *doll*

10. A.Y.O.[23]

Yours: A Room Full of Words

The constant presence of written words in your room will provide a daily vocabulary that can be enriched and expanded by adding interest/learning centers, special places, and new activities.

Today children are used to a dynamic, sometimes chaotic, environment pulsating with diverse sense impressions. Don't be afraid to decorate your room with dialogue ballooning out of a cartoon character's mouth or a stream of sky-writing on a blue bulletin board. The more unusual the better.

Students' Names

Always display the names of your students. If they can read nothing else, children are usually able to read their own names. It is reassuring to them to see that familiar, secure word in front of them. They can have immediate success because they can read their own names. And, after a while, they should be able to read the names of their classmates. Many skills exercises can be based on the names of your students. (See Chapter 10 on skills.)

Carol Seefeldt suggests using childrens' names as reading resources: write them on "cubbies, on paintings and artwork and other personal objects. Use lists of children's names . . . so similarities and differences between names can be observed. You might list all the children who have a birthday during each month, those who will go to the library on Tuesday, or those voting to name the guinea pig Christina and those voting to name it Andrea."[24]

Weather Words

There is weather every day. It provides opportunities to learn more sight words and to increase word comprehension. Assign a different child each day to give the weather report. The appropriate card is chosen from the Weather pocket on the board and shown to the class as the child talks about it. Movement can easily be correlated with weather by translating the word into actions. On some days, take the time to express the weather of the day through a picture, shoebox scene, or improvisation. Every single experience has unlimited scope.

Helper Words

All classrooms have helpers and all helpers have titles, such as Messenger, Money Collector, Eraser Captain, or Exercise Leader. Combined with children's names, these words are always interesting and always important to the program of the day. After a while, change the order of the Helper List so the children won't learn the words by rote. Humorous illustrations for each helpful job add a note of liveliness. Don't forget to add News Reporters and so on. Expand your concept of Helpers!

Curriculum Words

The names of school subjects, textbooks, units of study, and assignment words are excellent daily reading materials to be printed on the board, handed out on ditto sheets, or written on construction paper in bright magic marker colors.

Special Category Words

Seasons, holidays, and events stimulate a gathering of excellent vocabulary. Imagine the excitement of creating a bulletin board of spring words and pictures, Thanksgiving words and pictures, or field-trip-to-dairy words and pictures.

Spin-offs How easily the vocabulary of children is expanded along with their enjoyment of words that have special meaning in their lives! Bulletin boards of special words gathered around a theme are excellent resources for exciting spin-offs into other language activities.

> Use the words on the zoo board to write poems and stories about animals.
>
> Ask your students to choose five of their favorite words from the board and write about them.
>
> Have the children select words from the board to express in movement or improvisation.[25]

Posters

Ours is an age of posters. Our kids love posters, and classrooms might be covered with lively original and commercial posters.

I visited a sixth-grade class that was truly poster-happy. In just a few minutes, I jotted down the following philosophies printed on different posters.

> Imagination is more important than knowledge. (A. Einstein)
>
> The greatest unexplored area lies under your hat.

The joy of the heart colors the face.

We achieve according to what we believe.

The teacher and students shared some of the ways the posters were used in the class. Ask your students to do some of these:

Write about how they feel about the different ideas.

Discuss what the words mean to them.

Choose their favorite poster and tell why.

Break into small groups and present the meaning of the poster in different ways, by singing, making up a skit, writing a poem, and so on.

Tee Shirts, Buttons, and Bumper Stickers

Children love tee shirts, buttons, and bumper stickers as much as they love baseball cards, jewelry, and decorated lunch boxes.

Have a Wear-a-Word Day and invite everyone in the class to wear something with a word on it. Read and write all the words on the board, use them for creative writing, improvisation, choral reading, and art projects. Correlate them with social studies, political events, geography, and history. Humorous words on tee shirts or buttons will open the door to group discussion on the place of humor in communication.

Design original messages for tee shirts, buttons, and bumper stickers. Gather and display interesting examples of commercial items.

Spin-off   For a boost to self-image, encourage the children to turn themselves into the subject of a poster, button, tee shirt, or bumper sticker. Here is the text for a second grader's colorful poster about himself:

BILLY WALTERS
A BRAVE BOY
WHO LIKES CATERPILLARS

His poster was three-dimensional. The caterpillars were made out of painted cotton glued onto the paper. His eyes were two brown buttons and his hair was made of wool. He did get help spelling *caterpillars*, but after the posters hung around for a few days caterpillar was a word everyone in the class could read!

Letter and Word Mobiles

People of all ages enjoy making mobiles. Use hangers, string, and cardboard shapes; a larger shape expresses the theme of the mobile while the smaller shapes support the theme. Words written on the cut-outs are an important part of the mobile. Word and letter mobile ideas are everywhere. Here are a few I have seen hanging in various classrooms.

Snow Mobile (Preschool)   The word *snow* was printed on the card at the end of the central string and colored in by the children. On the supporting strings hung shapes of snowmen, snowballs, boots, and sleds.

Me Mobile (First Grade)   The children's names were the central theme of the mobile. On the supporting strings hung pictures of bicycles, pets, houses, cars, and toys, which expressed the various interests and family relationships of the children. Words like *My House, My Dog, My Bike, My Car,* and *My Wagon* were printed on the various cardboard-backed pictures.

Circus Mobile (Third Grade)   The children chose circus people and activities. Words like *clowns, lions, acrobats, giants,* and *dogs* were printed and drawn on the various circus shapes.

Book Mobile (Fifth Grade)   Instead of assigning a standard book report, the teacher suggested that the children create mobiles based on their books. The title of the book written on an original design was the centerpiece and surrounding it were different characters and scenes shaped, cut out, or sculpted.

Poetry Mobile (Sixth Grade)   Original and favorite poems were printed clearly and illustrated on index cards cut in silhouettes that expressed the theme of the poem. A poem about trees was written on tree-shaped cards. A poem about a house was written on house-shaped cards.

Names and Labels

Name-giving is one of the most important parts of every creation story. We give names to everything about us and within us. In keeping with this age-old activity, label *everything* in your room. Chairs, tables, chalkboards, bulletin boards, closets, desks, and other furniture gain in importance when a card bearing their name is taped to them. Children enjoy the naming and labeling process and definitely acquire an ever-growing sight vocabulary.

Ask your class to help you make up proper names for each labeled item. Many reading skills can be incorporated with this playful naming exercise. Here are examples:

Charles Chair	Able Table	Windy Window
Tom Table	Pesky Desky	Bright Light
Donna Desk	Bored Board	Desk at Rest
Frank Floor	Tall Wall	Art Cart

Print questions on a specific piece of furniture or a part of the room. Your students will enjoy responding to such questions as Why is Pesky Desky messy? or What are Tall Wall's three wishes?

Writing on the Walls

The importance of using the original writing of your students as reading material cannot be emphasized enough. Sadly, many teachers still display only "A" papers. If you offer opportunities for original written responses to a great variety of experiences, your students will provide your room with a deluge of wonderful reading matter. And motivation for clear handwriting and correct spelling and punctuation will be high because your students will want their classmates to be able to read their work.

Add your own questions, comments, and suggestions to the writing on the wall.

Scavenger Hunts

Scavenger hunts are always popular and can be simple or difficult, depending on the grade level. Write the list of items to be found on the board or duplicate it and give each child or team a copy. Include as many sight words (from room displays) on your list as possible. If you are working with specific kinds of words (like colors or numbers) in your lessons, use them. Make the items accessible yet challenging to the imagination. Here are some examples.

From a second-grade hunt
Find something blue
Find something small
Find something round
Find something with your name on it

From a fifth-grade hunt
A print of your hand
Something that helps you to write

A funny face

The names of five presidents of the United States (spelled correctly)

Instead of just piling up the found items, clearly label a different section of the room for each one, so that the children not only read the words initially but, after they find what it is they are looking for, must read the words again to put their object in the right place. When everyone is finished, celebrate the hunt by sharing the different items and interpretations of the list.

Free-Choice List

Teachers of all grades find a free-choice list a popular and important part of the school week. Print a list of interesting activities and display it in a special place. Students read the list, decide which activities they like, and complete as many activities from the list as possible, when they have time available. If a child reads the list and doesn't like any of the suggestions, he or she may write an original list of ideas and show it to you for your approval. Often students' suggestions are excellent and should be shared with the rest of the class and incorporated in future lists. Devote wall space to the various responses to the list. The following is an example of a fourth-grade free-choice list.

1. Write a story about an animal lost in space and read it to three people.
2. Make a felt picture-story for first graders to use.
3. Make a shoebox scene from your favorite book.
4. Make up a crossword puzzle or any kind of word puzzle. (These can be duplicated and handed to the rest of the class as a project.)
5. Draw a self-portrait. Write ten words that describe you.
6. Do you have any inventions in your mind? Describe one of your inventions and draw a diagram of it.

Mystery Game

On a special place on the chalkboard, write *Mystery of the Week;* underneath that write the first clue. Each day add a new clue. By the end of the week, the students will have five clues to read. You have not *said* anything. On Friday the children should write their answers to the mystery on a piece of paper. They can draw pictures to accompany their answers. Read all the answers out loud and discuss the mystery. Share ideas about how the clues helped or didn't help with the challenge. Then take out a special envelope marked Solution or Answer and write its contents on the board. Those who guessed correctly will be pleased, but minimize the competition among students by encouraging total participation. Praise the whole group for their intelligence and imagination.

Here is a list of clues used in a second-grade class.

Monday: I am an animal.
Tuesday: I think about funny things.

Wednesday: When people get mad, I kiss them.
Thursday: I sleep on top of my doghouse.
Friday: I pretend that I am a World War One Flying Ace.
Who am I?

Word Pictures

The children can draw pictures using words instead of visual images as the content. They may, for instance, draw the outline of the objects, then fill them with their defining words. The drawing below is an example of this.

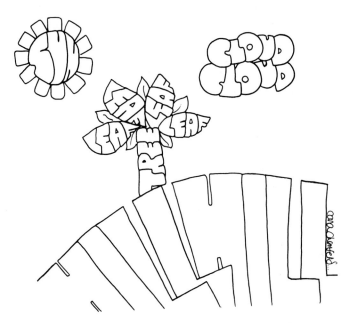

Class Journal

Just as a ship's crew keeps a daily log of its journey, so your crew of students can keep a daily record of your adventure-in-learning together. The journal is written by the class, printed on the chalkboard, and then copied by a helper into a book. The book may be illustrated by the class's original drawings or highlighted by samples of work pasted onto the page. The time set aside to write the log is valuable because it provides an opportunity to summarize the experiences of the day as well as a chance to discuss what was the most memorable part of the day. Have one of the children read the log aloud at the close of each day. Greeting card catalogues make excellent class logs that can be enriched with illustrations and additional class comments.

Notes and Message Boards

Teachers often scold students for writing notes. Perhaps they are missing a good educational opportunity. After all, someone must *read* the note in order to complete the exchange and someone must *write* clearly in order for the message to be understood. With this in mind, why not give your students an opportunity to write messages to classmates and have them answered? "Helpers" could deliver them (they will need to read the names on the outside of the notes in order to do so). Children will experience firsthand the need for correct spelling and usage and clear handwriting in order to have their messages understood.

You are probably familiar with message boards that advertise rides, cars for sale, or puppies for sale. If you have the space, set aside a Message Board so that the children can write messages to their classmates. This kind of board may prove to be the most popular reading material in the classroom.

I'm getting up a ballgame after school. Who wants to play?
                                                                Jed

Did anyone find my new pencil box? Please look for it.
Thank you.
                                                                Marcia

My dog had pups. If you want to see them, come over Saturday afternoon.
                                                                Robin

Telling Fortunes/Writing Fortunes

Children love to tell fortunes. Give each child a pack of index cards or cardboard squares with a letter of the alphabet printed on each card. For every card, a fortune must be written and illustrated (optional) to coincide with the letter. For example,

A	C	L
You will become an	You will become a	You will become a
Actor	Clown	Lawyer

D	S	V
You are very	You are very	You will find
Determined	Stubborn	Victory

Greg Siegler's kindergartners and first graders baked fortune cookies and wrote fortunes to stuff inside the cookies. Each child wrote three fortunes, one for him- or herself, one for a classmate, and one for a family member. They were feeling very frisky that day. Here are a few examples of those fortunes:

You will meet a unicorn.

You will turn into a banana split.

You're going to sing with Michael Jackson.

Magic Vocabularies

In the center of all the words we know, we have our very favorite words clustered around and connected to the things we love. Build close relationships with the people you live and work with and you will soon discover those special words that turn them from OFF to ON, from dull to bright. Here are two dramatic examples:

Donald is an alphabet child but all the letters add up to Slow and Failure. He hates school and everything related to school. He hasn't had one good day in school in his thirteen years. But I know something about Donald that his teacher doesn't. He knows the names of every professional football team in the country! He knows them backwards and forwards, right side up and upside down. He knows the cities, the reasons for the teams' names, the team colors, statistics, and players. Donald can't read from his basal text or successfully complete his workbook assignments, but he can mix and match, alphabetize, fill in the blanks, make puzzles and riddles on every football team from the Dallas Cowboys to the New York Giants! *Why doesn't Donald's teacher know about his "magic vocabulary"?* Through those glorious teams that Donald loves, he could find the way to reading success. "Teachers have to pay conscious attention to ways of helping."

Doug is a sharp, bright, "smart" fifth grader who daydreams a lot, often checks out of the stories in his reading book, is usually unchallenged by the limited vocabulary materials. I know something about Doug that his teacher doesn't. Doug is a "Dungeons and Dragons" kid. He's a master at the mind-boggling game. I visited Doug when he had to stay back from a family outing because of a sprained ankle. He talked excitedly about the intricacies of "Dungeons and Dragons." He rattled off words and terms that dazzled me. I asked him to scribble down some of the words connected to his beloved game. Here are a few of over forty words he wrote in less than five minutes.

characters	shield
modules	leather
experience points	armor
crossbow	levitation
quarrels	charisma
druid	invisibility
cleric	monsters
dwarf	magic item
wizard	magic user

In five minutes, how many ways can you think of to use Doug's magic vocabulary words to turn him ON? to catch him in your magical net? What words are in *your* magic vocabulary?

Surveys

What are the Top Ten Favorite TV programs in your class? Top Ten Favorite authors? ice cream flavors? singers? places to visit?

Always interesting reading materials are the opinions of the kids as they respond frequently to questions posted on large sheets of chart paper. Be sure there's room for every student to write an answer or opinion. The conclusions of the various opinion charts become another excellent reading resource!

Music and Song

All songs have words and all words can be read. Therefore, I urge you to consider music and singing as an important part of your school day. Music and singing are basic expressions of the human spirit.

Few people today have as powerful an influence over youngsters as do popular singers. When the words from songs your students know are used as reading material, the language experience is deepened. When students consider the words of songs valid reading material, they are alert, interested, and appreciative. Ask your students to write out the words to their favorite songs, then read the words and listen to recordings. Use the songs for choral reading or to sing along. Use the songs as ideas for art activities or to launch movement activities. Relate the ideas in songs to other curriculum areas, such as history or geography.

Newspapers

The newspaper is a daily source of ideas for exciting reading experiences. Many newspapers give training courses to teachers on how to use the newspaper in the classroom. If available, these sessions can be valuable, but if you open your mind to the numerous possibilities of using the newspaper with your students, you probably won't even need a course. Here are some questions based on the daily newspaper that can be used as reading exercises in the classroom.

What's your horoscope? What's your "sign"?

What's the weather? What's the weather across the country?

What's on television tonight?

What sports teams played yesterday? Who won? Who lost?

What movies are playing in town?

What advice did columnists give today?

What events are reported about our town? city? state? country? world?

Were any pets reported lost or found?

Did you see any bargains in the advertisements?

How many mayors', senators', governors' names can you find?

The possibilities to develop interests and knowledge and to expand the students' vocabularies are limitless. Any one of these questions can be developed into related activities, such as horoscopes to astrology to legends, or weather reports into a unit on meteorology.

Movement Is a Reading Experience

At a recent reading conference, I was about to begin my workshop, "Movement Is a Reading Experience," when a skeptical teacher grumbled, "How can movement be a reading experience?" Laughingly, I immediately shared some familiar written messages that involve movement instructions:

Walk	Elevator Down
Don't Walk	Bridge: Slippery When Wet
Resume Speed	Do Not Pass
Slow Traffic in Left Lane	Exit
Caution: Bump	Enter
Elevator Up	

I think by the end of the workshop she was convinced that there are countless ways to relate movement and reading.

We have space here for only a few examples of reading/movement activities. Read through the rest of the book for more ideas. As with all the suggestions in these chapters, sift them around in your mind and combine them with your own. "Reject nothing! Rearrange all!"[26]

Daily Exercise of Bodies and Words

Everyone needs an exercise break. Sitting still for too long a time encourages physical and mental fatigue. Taking only two or three minutes, you can share an enjoyable experience with your students, introduce a successful, effective language arts lesson, and get some exercise.[27]

Throughout the book we have shared ideas for such exercise variations as Exercise Leaders, Follow the Leader, Alphabet Exercises, Holiday and Seasonal Exercises, Body Parts Warm-Ups, and Animal Exercises. Here are a few more to add to your ever-growing list of ideas.

Read-and-Move Cards

Print movement words on index cards. Words such as *hop, skip, walk, march, slide, fall, tiptoe, clap, leap, stamp,* and *bend* will provide instant motivation. There are many ways to use these cards. The following ideas should help you to get started.

Each person picks a card, reads the word written on it (with some help from you, if necessary), and then turns the word into the movement described. After the child shows the movement, the other children have to guess the word.

Each child picks a card, reads the word, and leads an exercise based on the word.

Keep the cards available for spontaneous activities or display them on a chart or bulletin board. You will be amazed at how fast your students' vocabularies will grow.

Movement Grab Bag

On cardboard strips, print movement instructions for your students to follow individually or as a group. They can be simple or complicated. Fill a shoebox or manila envelope with the strips and keep them available as a constant source of *reading* and *moving* material. Continuously add to your collection, including your students' suggestions. A few samples:

Move across the floor as if you were being drawn by a magnet.

Walk across the room in slow motion.

Move across the floor as if you were the greatest giant in the world.

Make five different designs with your hands.

Ice-skate across the floor. Do tricky steps.

Stretch from down to up in slow motion.

Keep bouncing for one minute.

Body Parts Chart

With your students, gather names of body parts and print them clearly on a large chart. What a reading resource!

Place name cards of your students next to the names of the different body parts. Don't turn this into a drill session or anxiety exercise! Scoot around the room to quickly check (whisper) if each child knows the body part associated with his or her name. Then have each child lead an exercise featuring that particular part of the body.

Or try this same activity encouraging the exercise leaders to put their name cards next to the body part *they* choose to celebrate.

Have the class choose, say, five of the body parts to exercise. Spin off into a body poem.

This poem celebrates the five body parts a fourth grade exercised one day. The word *my* was added to the five parts written on the board in a list. Here's what the kids wrote:

> My toes are wiggly, bent, dirty, and tiptoe.
> My elbows are sharp, pointy, bony, and tickle people in the ribs.
> My ears hear whispering, laughing, and shouting.
> My fingers clap, play the piano, shake "no," and wave hello.
> My head is hard, round, movable, and full of ideas.

After the class recited this aloud, they quickly divided into five smaller groups, assigning each group one line of the "poem" to practice saying together with improvised body movements accompanying the words. (Don't give them more than one or two minutes to practice. I believe that the longer you give people to prepare material, the more inhibited, self-conscious, and negative they can become.) Afterwards, the whole class recited it together, led in movement by the various groups.

The poem was rewritten on a large piece of construction paper. Children illustrated it and it became a bulletin board display to be read and enjoyed.

Add these body-parts class poems to the class log! Encourage the kids to write their own individual pieces. Here's one from Cara:

> My toes are jelly beans.
> My elbows need room.
> My ears are pierced.
> My fingers are wearing rings.
>
> My head is smart.
>
> Cara
Grade 7

Footprints Are Words

This is a wonderful springtime activity to share with younger children. Spread a roll of white paper on the floor; at one end of the paper, fill a basin with tempera paint and water; at the other end, place a basin of clear water and towels. One at a time, the children take off their shoes and socks, step into the basin of paint, and walk, skip, hop, or slide—whatever they decide—on the paper. After they wash their feet and dry them, they tell you what they want written above or below their footprints. I have seen kindergarten rooms bordered by the footprint paper with lively words like

Frankie hops-hops-hops.

Judy skips-skippety-doo.

Debbie jumps like a kangaroo.

The class can use the mural as the basis for a movement poem, a choral reading, or related art activities.

"Words Sure Get You in Shape!"

So many words can be interpreted in movement. Start a gathering of vocabulary words and print them clearly on index cards or construction paper. After your children are *sitting* for too long, give them the chance to *show you* the words as you hold up the cards.

With a fourth grade, we had time to "show" about seven cards before library time. Some of the words the children read and showed me were *lift, crawl, tremble, sway, tree*.

When we stopped, one of the kids cracked, "Boy, words sure get you in shape!"

Add Words to Everything

One December day I was preparing for an inservice workshop at an elementary school. As I walked through the hall, I stopped short to admire one of the most colorful and lively winter murals I had ever seen. The children had painted, pasted, cut out, drawn sleds, snow shapes, snowballs, ice-skaters, animals—all on a long sheet of butcher paper. As I enjoyed it, a tiny thought kept buzzing through my mind. Something was missing. Finally, it hit me. ADD WORDS! I suggested that to the second-grade teacher who immediately agreed. At the end of the school year, a package was delivered to my house: the wonderful poster, rich with words—signs, dialogue bubbles, names on sleds, names on articles of clothing, labels, words on trees, snow words.

Add words to everything! I conducted a workshop for teachers that was held in the music room of a high school. Bordering the room were portraits of the great composers. A grim-looking group! Their piercing eyes glared down at us! At the lunch break, it hit me. ADD WORDS! We tore construction paper and notebook paper and, with a few magic markers, wrote words for our composers to be saying or thinking. We taped our words to the walls over the portraits. They made the day! We went from grim to grin!

Journey around your room. Look at all your spaces and special places, pictures, boards, closet doors, shelves, and panes. Add words!

A room is to read!

A Reading Walk Outside

A few minutes' walk away from your room and school will yield many valuable experiences that can be adapted to reading. As the children walk, they should record every word they recognize. Many of these will be traffic and safety words or words from automobile license plates and bumper stickers. When you get back to the classroom write down all the things seen on the walk and use them for reading material, as resource words for creative writing projects, skill exercises, art, music, and movement spin-offs. A second-grade class made a huge bulletin board telling about their walk. They had recognized and collected almost sixty words on their "reading walk." Words and illustrations dazzled all passersby. Of course, the favorite words they saw were Baskin-Robbins ice cream flavors!

A Reading Walk Inside

Take your students on a walk around the school. Have them bring a pencil and paper and write down any words they see during the walk. This can also be done on a visit to another classroom. When the walk is completed, have the children share with each other all the words they noted.

Translate the experience into creative dramatics, pantomime, creative writing, movement, and other readings.

Field Trip Words

Every field trip is a word-gathering experience and a reading trip. Trips to museums, factories, and firehouses will produce a vocabulary suited to each.

The poet Theodore Roethke said, "There is no end to what should be known about words."[28] The ideas and activities here are only a beginning.

A Few Last Words

Jon, Arthur, Elizabeth, Charles, Lee, Nessy, Jenny, Miguel, Pooh, and Piglet are waiting for YOU. Like all humans, they each have different needs, different

interests, different personalities. One reading program will not do for Elizabeth, reading five levels above her own, or for Arthur, a reading failure with a cluster of emotional problems connected to the word "read." No matter how excellent the method, it will not "work" evenly for Miguel, struggling to learn English as a second language, or necessarily turn Lee from OFF to ON. He's mastered the code but he couldn't care less. He recognizes words but he just doesn't like them!

Dedicated, imaginative teachers use everything possible to find ways of reaching each student. They do not—*cannot*—depend on cards or buttons, bubble gum comics or score sheets, basal readers or workbooks. For Donald, they'll chart the glorious teams of the professional football leagues. For Douglas, they'll sneak in "Dungeons and Dragons" vocabulary in worksheets and class stories. They are tuned in to the lives of their students. They know their magic vocabularies. They continually help children make connections across the curriculum; across the language arts strands; between school, home, and community; between reality and imagination. The environment they create with and for their students is exciting and dynamic, challenges involvement, evokes response. It is an active place rich with multifaceted experiences and learning opportunities. They want to help students crack the code so they can go on . . . and on. Maybe someday their students will feel about reading and books as Francie Nolan did in *A Tree Grows in Brooklyn:*

> The library was a little shabby place. Francie thought it was beautiful. The feeling she had about it was as good as the feeling about church. . . . Francie thought that all the books in the world were in that library and she had a plan about reading all the books in the world. She was reading a book a day in alphabetical order and not skipping the dry ones. . . .[29]

Patricia Morton describes her lifelong love affair with books and reading:

> I live books while reading them. I have gone back in time and forward in dreams. I have redone history and explored the mystery of a human cell. I have stood on the other side of this world, first in books and then in reality. Yes, books have been the keys to magic kingdoms, and have made those kingdoms my own.[30]

Your students are waiting to walk through those doors to magic kingdoms. Go with them.

How Do I Know These Methods Are Working?

You know what you hope to achieve with your students. If you wrote down your goals, they would probably read something like this.

1. I want my students to increase their vocabulary.
2. I want them to recognize words, understand their meaning, and be able to group them into ideas.

3. I want my students to read for many purposes.

4. I want them to enjoy reading, to read with competency, and to consider reading an important part of their lives.

No area of the curriculum is as thoroughly supplied with standardized methods of evaluation as reading. No doubt your school puts a high value on whatever testing system it has adopted and by using these tests you will have some idea of your students' reading abilities. But you cannot rely on standardized tests alone. In fact, your evaluation based on your own observations should be going on all the time.

Original Worksheets

As often as possible, use worksheets and exercises that *you* prepare based on words from class experiences. Every single skill can be taught more effectively by using materials that are relevant to your students rather than an impersonal list of words in a workbook. Since all people do not learn at the same rate or in the same way, you will always have to go beyond the workbooks, no matter what their quality. Remember the magic vocabularies!

Keep a file of each child's worksheets, exercise papers, and word skill samples; share the files individually so each child can see each step of his or her development. If you have an open relationship with your students, they will feel safe discussing their progress, problems, fears, and needs with you. You can gain valuable insight from knowing how your students assess their own learning.

Observe Your Students

Be aware of your students as they read both orally and silently. Be alert to how they respond to learning-center activities, read-and-do projects, and group reading sessions. Keep notes on incidents that you need to remember. Include positive, as well as negative, observations, such as a child's ability to use reading in relation to other activities. Create your own checklist to keep in mind as you observe and evaluate your students day by day.

Checklist for the Children

1. Is _____ able to recognize and identify new words?

2. Does _____ show competency in all the word recognition skills, such as pictures, context, configuration, and structural analysis? Where is help needed?

3. Does _____ show interest in reading? In what kinds?

4. Does _____ comprehend what is read, whether it is reading worksheets, class projects, learning center activities, directions, or games? In what areas is there difficulty?

5. Does _____ seek information through reading activities in all forms, such as silent reading, oral reading, listening to stories read aloud, doing projects and activities based on reading, or discussing reading materials?

6. What interest does _____ have that could provide valuable reading resources? What is _____ magic vocabulary?

7. In what area does _____ need further help, encouragement, and reinforcement?

8. What learning strategies are needed?

Checklist for Yourself

1. In what ways did I encourage reading today?

2. What experiences did I offer in reading today *in which each child could succeed?*

3. When and how did I take time to encourage and praise my students?

4. What can I share from my own experiences and interests that will provide a resource for reading development? from my children's interests?

5. What did I learn about my students and their interests that will help encourage their reading?

6. Did I miss any opportunities to link reading to shared classroom experiences? to relevant themes and relationships?

7. Did I notice which children were having difficulties today? In what areas?

8. How can I provide the most effective help? materials? skills exercises?

9. What did I do today that I would do differently tomorrow?

10. What will I do tomorrow that will expand vocabularies and spark further interest in reading?

I would like to share a feeling with you. Deep down, I believe that what every teacher really hopes for is to help students develop a lifelong love of reading. If we could look into the future, we would be happy to see that reading had become an enjoyable and important part of their lives. Of course we can't look into the future, but we can evaluate the present.

Nessy told me, "Reading is the *funnest* thing!"

A fourth-grade teacher found a student alone in the room, reading in a corner.

"Bobby, you're here all alone. Are you all right?" she asked in a concerned voice.

Bobby looked up, smiling. "I'm never lonely when I'm reading a book," he reassured her.

And that's what this chapter is all about.

Some Suggested Readings

Many books and articles provide up-to-date information as well as stimulating viewpoints across the reading spectrum. The following are examples of important resources.

Richard C. Anderson, Elfrieda H. Hiebert, Judith A. Scott, and Ian A. G. Wilkinson, *Becoming a Nation of Readers: The Report of the Commission on Reading* (National Institute of Education, 1985). Center for the Study of Reading, P.O. Box 2774, Station A, Champaign, Illinois 61820.

Frank Smith, *Reading without Nonsense* (New York: Teachers College Press, 1985).

Jonathon Kozol, *Illiterate America* (New York: Anchor/Doubleday, 1985).

Arthur N. Applebee, *A Child's Concept of Story* (Chicago: U of Chicago P, 1978).

Marilyn Cochran-Smith, *The Making of a Reader* (Norwood: Ablex, 1984).

Herbert Kohl, *Reading, How To* (New York: Dutton, 1973).

Glenda Bissex, *Gnys at Wrk: A Child Learns to Write and Read* (Cambridge: Harvard UP, 1980).

Kenneth S. Goodman and Yetta M. Goodman, *A Whole-Language Comprehension-Centered Reading Program* (Tucson: Arizona Center for Research and Development, 1981).

Frank Smith, *Understanding Reading*, 3rd ed. (New York: Holt, 1982).

Theodore L. Harris and Eric Cooper, eds., *Reading, Thinking and Concept Development: Strategies for the Classroom* (New York: College Board, 1985).

Dorothy Fink Ungerleider, *Reading, Writing and Rage: The Terrible Price Paid by Victims of School Failure* (Rolling Hills Estates: Jalmar, 1985).

Jerome C. Harste, Virginia A. Woodward, and Carolyn L. Burke, *Language Stories and Literacy Lessons* (Portsmouth: Heinemann Educational, 1984).

The many excellent journals and educational magazines available consistently publish important articles on reading. Some of them are

Phi Delta Kappan	*Journal of Reading*
The Reading Teacher	*Language Arts*
Educational Leadership	*Young Children*
Reading Research Quarterly	*Journal of Educational Research*
Review of Educational Research	*American Journal of Education*

ENDNOTES

[1] A. A. Milne, "In Which Piglet Is Entirely Surrounded by Water," *The World of Pooh* (New York: Dutton, 1957) 127.

[2] A. A. Milne, "Rabbit's Busy Day," *The World of Pooh* 231.

[3] I encourage you to keep informed of the latest reports and research in the field of reading. The journals published by the International Reading Association and the National Council of Teachers of English are excellent resources, as are professional periodicals such as *Phi Delta Kappan, Review of Educational Research, Journal of Teacher Education,* and *Reading Research Quarterly.*

[4] Kenneth S. Goodman, "Reading: A Psycholinguistic Guessing Game," *Theoretical Models and Processes of Reading,* ed. Harry Singer and Robert Ruddell (Newark: IRA, 1970).

[5] "Reading the World and Reading the Word: An Interview with Paulo Freire," *Language Arts* 62.1 (Jan. 1985): 15–21.

[6] Jeanne S. Chall, *Learning to Read: The Great Debate* (New York: McGraw, 1967).

[7] Chall 9.

[8] Jeanne S. Chall, *Learning to Read: The Great Debate,* rev. ed. (New York: McGraw, 1983).

[9] Chall, *Learning to Read,* rev. ed. 308.

[10] Chall, *Learning to Read,* rev. ed. 309.

[11] Chall, *Learning to Read,* rev. ed. 284.

[12] "Reading the World and Reading the Word" 19.

[13] James F. Baumann, *Journal of Reading* (Nov. 1984).

[14] Marie Clay's work is of great significance to classroom teachers. Her book *The Early Detection of Reading Difficulties: A Diagnostic Survey* (Auckland: Heinemann, 1972) is highly recommended.

[15] Gay Su Pinnell, interview with the author. For further information on the Reading Recovery Program, write to Gay Su Pinnell, Reading Recovery Project, Ohio State University, Ramseyer 200, 29 West Woodruff, Columbus, Ohio 43210 or Hilda Edwards, Coordinator, Reading Recovery Project, Ohio State Education Department, 65 South Font Street, Columbus, Ohio 43215. Ask for *Ohio Reading Recovery Project Technical Report* 1985, 1986. See also Gay Su Pinnell "Helping

Teachers Help Children at Risk: Insights from the Reading Recovery Program," *Peabody Journal of Education* 62.3 (Spring 1985): 70–85.

[16] R. Craig Roney, "Background Experience Is the Foundation of Success in Learning to Read," *The Reading Teacher* (Nov. 1984): 196–99.

[17] Carl L. Rosen, "Reading and the Disadvantages: Some Psycholinguistic Applications for the Classroom Teacher," *Views on Elementary Instruction*, ed. Thomas Barnett and Dale Johnson (Newark: IRA, 1973) 13.

[18] Nila Bantan Smith, "Early Language Development: Foundation of Reading," *Elementary English* (Mar. 1975): 399–402.

[19] William Rupley, "Language Development and Beginning Reading Instruction," *Elementary English* (Mar. 1975): 403–408.

[20] Miles A. Tinker and Constance McCullough, *Teaching Elementary Reading*, 3rd ed. (New York: Meredith, 1968).

[21] Faye Moskowitz, "Why I Read to My Class, *New York Times* 3 Aug. 1986, sec. 12: 62.

[22] Mimi Brodsky Chenfeld, "Alphabet Antics and Concept Clowning," *The Instructor* (Jan. 1975): 60.

[23] See the chapter "We Learn Our Letters and Words," in Mimi Brodsky Chenfeld, *Creative Activities for Young Children* (San Diego: Harcourt, 1983) for many more suggestions.

[24] Carol Seefeldt, "What's in a Name? Lots to Learn," *Young Children* 39.5 (July 1984): 24–30.

[25] Very interesting ideas for vocabulary development are presented in Robert J. Marzano, "A Cluster Approach to Vocabulary Instruction: A New Direction from the Research Literature," *Reading Teacher* (Nov. 1984): 168–73.

[26] Theodore Roethke, *Straw for the Fire* (Garden City: Doubleday, 1974) 183.

[27] Mimi Brodsky Chenfeld, "Moving Moments for Wiggly Kids," *Phi Delta Kappan* (Nov. 1976).

[28] Roethke, *Straw for the Fire* 188.

[29] Betty Smith, *A Tree Grows in Brooklyn* (New York: Harper, 1947) 18–21.

[30] Patricia Morton, "Doors into the World," *The Reading Teacher* (Dec. 1984): 260–61.

9

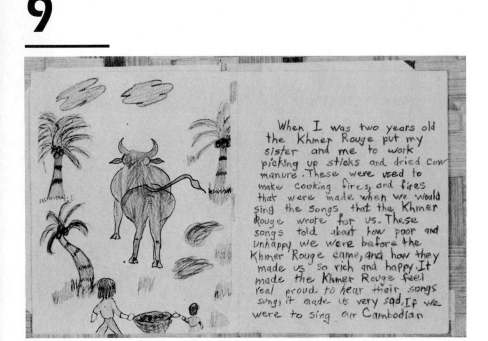

When I was two years old the Khmer Rouge put my sister and me to work picking up sticks and dried cow manure. These were used to make cooking fires, and fires that were made when we would sing the songs that the Khmer Rouge wrote for us. These songs told about how poor and unhappy we were before the Khmer Rouge came, and how they made us so rich and happy. It made the Khmer Rouge feel real proud to hear their songs sung; it made us very sad. If we were to sing our Cambodian

Write?
Of Course Write!

Far too long and far too much, we have thought of reading and writing as technical language matters when the fact is that composing and comprehending are deep operations of mind and spirit.

JAMES MOFFETT[1]

Children Are Eager to Write

Recently, while on a filled-to-capacity jet, I had a few hours to closely observe the behavior of an adorable ten-month-old baby who sat on his mother's lap pounding, tapping, tickling the tray in front of him. Most of his concentrated activities centered around books he was "reading." He turned pages, pointed to pictures, made sounds as if he was reading, kept at this for a long time. His other equally involving interest was in "writing." His mother gave him a pencil and paper. He busily "wrote" on the front, the back, all across the sheets of paper. From my view across the aisle, I would almost think he was writing *real* words! He held the pencil firmly in his little hand. He knew what to do with it. He delighted in the doing. *Children are eager to write!*

I was very lucky. My friend and neighbor Gregory, now the assistant drum major of his high school band and an accomplished rock and roll percussionist, allowed me to be part of his *whole life* of growing. I watched him grow from a toddler to a sheriff, a cowboy, a rock and roll singer, a guitar player, a letter carrier, and, just before he began kindergarten, a writer! Since babyhood he had scribbled on paper and solemnly *read* me his words. When I jogged, he stopped me on the street and "wrote out" speeding tickets. He "wrote" stories and read them out loud to me. When he was almost five, he knew his letters, numbers, and a few key words. One day, an event occurred that has remained clearly etched in my mind. The summer before kindergarten, he knocked on my door and asked how my writing was coming along. I asked him if he would like to write something for me.

HOHOHO GREGORY
I LOVE YOU TODD
PAPPA TO KIM TO
I LOVE YOU GREG

He worked hard on his paper, not letting me see it until he was finished. Then, clearing his throat and looking very important, he read: "Ho! Ho! Ho! Gregory. I love you Todd. I love you Papa. Kim too."

He was very proud of his note and wanted me to read it too. *I couldn't contain my excitement at seeing the first letters Greg ever wrote form words I could read!*

As I read and reread his writing, he listened with a mix of attentiveness and emotion that is difficult to describe. He breathed so deeply, almost holding his breath, as I read his words. A magical moment! Excitedly, he asked, "Didn't you love the 'Ho! Ho! Ho' part? I thought you would especially like that part!" Then he said goodbye and waved his paper in his hand like a flag of victory.

Children are eager to write!

Most children in our country share Gregory's enthusiasm for writing. They scribble on papers, books, furniture, walls. They make writing part of their play, signing their names in make-believe cursive with the flourish and illegibility of physicians writing prescriptions. They *want* to learn how to write, and they practice long before they ever go to school. Most children will be eager to sit down to write letters and words. And when their words are read and understood by others, they will be jubilant.

Look at the photo of Kevin's hand, below. In spite of the fact that Kevin is not holding the pencil correctly, his purposefulness is evident. Like Gregory, Kevin's determination is fierce, his motivation is high, and his pride in his ability to write is obvious. That moment in our own lives, when we discovered the

miracle of written communication, is waiting somewhere in our memories to be rediscovered and appreciated. Can you find it in your knapsack?

Smiles Are Like Upside-down Rainbows

When Lisi was four and a half, she looked at the world and all its wonders as if it had only recently been created for her. Her mother wrote down some of Lisi's observations.

A Poem about the Snow

The snow on the trees is like animals,
Polar bears and white elephants.
The snow on the ground is like cotton and white fur.
The snow comes down like little raindrops, one by one.
I don't know what it sounds like coming down,
I can't hear a bit.
The snow is very quiet coming down,
like a little bunny hopping.
The sky is like light blue snow.
The mountains are like big piles of leaves.
The clouds are like shadows of the mountains.
The sun is like butter.
Smiles are like upside-down rainbows.
Tongues are like little tails, wagging.
Toenails are like little glass trays.

Lisi B.
Age $4\frac{1}{2}$

A Child's Original Expression   Lisi did not perform an unusual feat of mental agility. She simply did what all human beings do naturally at some time in their lives. She responded to her surroundings through language. Most children share her ability to express everyday observations and thoughts in fresh, untried words. Take time to talk with a group of preschoolers and you will be overwhelmed at the original expression of their ideas and observations. Go one step further. After you write down their words, read them back to the children and watch the delight and surprise in those small faces. Remember, children have a gift that many adults have lost—the ability to see the ordinary in an extraordinary way and to express it.

Shockindakeiday's Monster

Frankie Reed's story "Shockindakeiday's Monster" is dedicated to his younger brother, Steven, who loves monsters. It begins like this:

It was mysterious, I can admit. And it all started when in the night we heard a moaning and groaning. It was getting louder and louder and louder. It went Ooooooooooooo Ahhhhhhhhhh. I got up and got my shotgun. My wife was scared. We searched the house but there was no spook to be seen. I telephoned the police. The Lieutenant was munching strawberries.

"Slurp . . . What's wrong, Shockindakeiday?" said he.

I said, "Will you come and search my house? I have looked around my house but found nothing."

The Lieutenant said, "Slurp. Nope. I'm too busy munching strawberries, Slurp . . ."

"Well", you're some help," I hung up and went back to sleep.

Frankie wrote "Shockindakeiday's Monster" when he was in the third grade. It's a long story, full of adventures. But the story behind the story is a remarkable example of that unique, almost indefinable human phenomenon: the creative process. Frankie will tell you about it.

> When I was three and Steven was two, we made up pretend friends and did stories about them. Then me and Steven figured out this big, long word made up of words we couldn't pronounce right, and we came up with this word, Shockindakeiday, and we made him another friend. We made up a lot of stories for Shockindakeiday and played a lot of pretend games with him. Even though I couldn't read or write then, I *knew* that when I got bigger and could read and write, I'd write a story about Shockindakeiday. When I got bigger, I made sculptures, papier-mâché masks, and clay models of Shockindakeiday and the other characters. And then, when I was in third grade, I finally wrote the story. I wanted it to be a surprise for Steven. You know, I spent a lot of years thinking about that story and now that it's finished, I feel proud.

A Child's Imagination   The most fascinating part of this wonderful tale is that somehow Frankie, at age three, *knew* that sometime in the future he would learn how to read and write and that then he would write the story of Shockindakeiday and give it to his brother as a surprise. That kind of knowledge is rare, but the process of creation experienced by the two brothers is another of those amazing yet ordinary human activities: making believe, inventing characters, dreaming up places and plots—the stuff of the imagination. Mauree Applegate so wisely wrote, "The world does not need more talented children; it needs to release and develop the talents latent in all children."[2]

It is important for you to remember that when Frankie finally wrote his story, he had not yet learned the structures and rules of the language. His grammar, punctuation, usage, and penmanship were still very rudimentary. After the first draft, Frankie was motivated to go over the story and correct his mistakes because he wanted people to be able to read it. He knew that if he left all the errors uncorrected, his story would not be easily understood. His father helped him with the corrections, then Frankie rewrote and illustrated "Shockindakeiday's Monster."

A Time to Create and a Time to Correct   Had Frankie's father hovered around him as he wrote, interrupting his flow of words with advice on grammar and spelling, Frankie might have become snarled in the technical obstacles and just stopped writing. Kenneth Koch, speaking to a group of university students, compared the devastating effects of ill-timed criticism and correction on creative efforts to "pruning seeds." William M. Logan and Virgil G. Logan urge you to remember that "at every level, it is important to provide each child with freedom to invent before he becomes concerned with the conventions of the discipline."[3] According to Lois Lenski,

> Creative expression should never be confused with the teaching of the techniques of writing. These are two distinct procedures. It should always be remembered that creation is a flowing of ideas. Given a stimulus, ideas come pouring from the mind like water from a fountain. It is all too easy to stop this creative flow. Rules for punctuation, spelling, grammar and handwriting will stop it. Emphasis on rules is sure to stifle creative thinking.[4]

I was asked to present an in-service program on encouraging creative writing to the staff of a nearby school system. Before the event, some of the students in the system called me and begged me, "Please tell the teachers not to check our spelling and grammar *while* we're writing. It makes us nervous and stops us from writing."

Apparently, this was one of the ways some people interpreted the push to go "back to basics"!

At the program, I shared creative writing exercises with the teachers. Heads bent, pencils scratching on paper, the vast room was silent with creative efforts. I tiptoed my way around the room, looking over the shoulders of a teacher at a time, noting handwriting or spelling errors, then moving on. *You could HEAR the pencils stop. You could FEEL the cessation of activity.* My brief, whispered encounters with but a few teachers, correcting their work as they wrote, spread such alarm, such anxiety, that *everyone* froze. Now the discussion of "a time to create and a time to correct" had greater relevance. It was no longer just theoretical.

There's an old joke that ends with this punch line: "Eat first. You'll talk later." Let's apply that punch line to the following approach of encouraging writing in your room: "Write first. You'll correct-edit-evaluate later!"

Teachers committed to that premise have treasure chests packed with precious materials. One of my most cherished items is a story written by Marissa. I visited her third grade and we excitedly celebrated the possibilities of the word *once* as a story starter. With the group, we gathered and speedily wrote on the board at least 25 story ideas beginning with the word *once*. Then the kids were on their own: "We don't have much time left. Write your ideas down quickly. Don't worry about spelling now. We'll check all that later!" What a diverse and delightful collection of "once" stories emerged from those papers. Marissa's story, on page 322, was written in just a few moments.

What would have happened if the rules of spelling, punctuation, and grammar had dominated the activity? Marissa's "iceikcol" would have stayed frozen in her imagination, never falling on her head, the bear's, or anyone else's! Marissa will learn how to spell *icicle, actually,* and *found.* "All of a sundent" those "probalems" will be "salled" as she continues on the "little rode" to skill mastery.

Marissa

Once A Iceikcol fell
on my head

I was walking
down a little rode I had
fnoud. It was winter then.
But all of a sundent
("Owch"), I said a
iceikcol fell on my
head, And then I saw a
iceikcol on a bear
Ackshle everyonee had
a iceikcol on their
head, I looked around
iceikcol's were falling
down, Why? Of corse
it was geting warmer,
That salled that probalem.

The
End

But she may never again be able to tell about the "iceikcols" melting and falling down.

And how will Marissa grow in language competency and development? She will grow as all children grow, as we all are growing: "all in one piece, with spurts and plateaus, in tears and laughter, and above all, through interactions with friends, teachers, texts, family and with herself."[5]

All children have stories simmering inside, waiting to be told, waiting to be written and shared. They have imaginations that delight in language. They play with words, rhymes, and rhythms. They invent new words and sounds.

They mix a sense of wordplay with sharp observation, sensory awareness, and fantasy. With encouragement, appreciation, and help offered in the spirit of lovingness, they will gladly share their wealth.

"The Universe Amazes Me"

When Dan was eleven years old, he went on an airplane and flew through a clear, starry night. He and his mother looked at the night through the window and were moved by its beauty. She suggested that Dan write his thoughts in a notebook so that he would be sure to remember how he felt on that airplane ride. This is what he wrote.

> Flying over the highest
> the highest clouds in the sky.
> They look so gentle like dandelions
> in a field. If those are the highest
> and mightiest that are so gentle
> how can earth be so far?
> The clouds are so beautiful.
> There are no wars and hatred.
> Why is earth so far?
> The universe amazes me
> with all its stars and planets.
> There must be life on other planets.
> Maybe they are like the clouds
> peaceful, beautiful, gentle,
> but if they met the average human
> with hatred toward differences
> would he not run away in fear
> to his own gentle planet?

Children Always Write about Something

When Dan flew in an airplane, the universe amazed him. He expressed his experience in writing. The experience fed his imagination, and the writing marked the event. He will not forget that day when he reads his notes years later. Dan's notebook is especially significant. He is now a professional skydiver.

Children don't write about *nothing*. They need things to happen, they need to make things happen, they need to think about things happening. Logan and Logan believe that without experience children have little to communicate. It is when they experience something firsthand or vicariously that they write most vividly. Experiences form a reservoir from which children can draw in expressing themselves creatively. These experiences make an impression so deep, so vital, that children are not content until they have shared them.[6]

Direct, firsthand experiences are always the best. It is always better to see, touch, smell, and climb a tree than to turn a page with the word *tree* on it and limit the experience to the written word alone. *Unfortunately, we can't always provide firsthand experiences in the classroom. The challenge to teachers is to share with children vicarious experiences so rich in meaning, enjoyment,*

and imagination that they are as vivid as direct experiences. Through literature, music, art, movement, dramatics—all the myriad combinations of activities possible—children push out the walls of their worlds and widen their understanding, appreciation, and knowledge.

An old Chinese proverb speaks directly to this point:

> I hear and I forget
> I see and I remember
> I do and I understand

Dan's notes on his airplane flight are not evidence of outstanding creative talent. They are but another example of the ability of all human beings to extend their feelings about experiences into words, which James Moffett considers the "real business of school."[7]

An Important Pause

Before we continue our focus on writing, let's pause for a moment to renew our commitment to an *integrated language arts philosophy* that will stamp all of our activities and behavior. We need to renew those "vows" repeatedly in the face of constant pressure to teach language skills and components in isolation, in disconnected, amputated compartments. Remember that writing, reading, oral language, and listening are all strands of language learning that are inextricably connected. They are *naturally linked* parts of a complex, dynamic process. Writing is a reading activity. Reading is a writing activity. Oral language through both reading and writing helps children maintain focus and interest.[8] Discussing these components in separate chapters is artificial. Keep integrating them in your mind as you read. Remember that

> language learning is different from other school subjects. It is not a *new* subject, and it is not even a *subject*. It permeates every part of people's lives and itself constitutes a major way of abstracting. So learning language raises more clearly than other school courses the issue of integration.[9]

Why do I keep nudging you to "keep making connections" and to help your students do the same? Because, sadly, there are still many teachers who do *not* see those relationships. There are still countless children "learning" in silent classrooms, "reading" from ditto sheets, surrounded by limited inspirational materials. Challenging projects and assignments are hoarded by narrow-minded teachers and used as "rewards." Tragically, with all we know about the interdependence of the language arts strands, many kids are still "taught" creative writing by the "menstrual" method: They get one assignment a month accompanied by severe cramps. In those rooms, voices are muted, questions are closed, imaginations shrivel, and freedom of spirit is stifled.

So much is up to you! Do you come from the Culture of YES or the Culture of NO?

Mom's Story

Now let's focus on a true story demonstrating the life-affirming, life-sustaining powers of teachers who vote YES.

I work with numerous Young Author conferences around the country. At one such event, I was assigned to be one of the main stations of the program. My job was to celebrate a specific sampling of children and their books, sharing their works with a large audience. The first young author to read her book was Mom (pronounced "mum"), a fourth grader at the time. As she read her very long story, *My Life in Danger*, an eerie stillness fell on the large group of people who stood listening. Not a person moved, not a sound was heard, as Mom read her powerfully, clearly written story of her family's harrowing experiences in the Cambodian war and their daring escape to America. Some excerpts:

> When I was three months old the Khmer Rouge took over my city and took my family to a work camp in the country. My father was taken to a different camp and we did not see him for a long time. . . .
> The only thing we had to eat for one day was less than a handful of rice. My mother made me pants with very large pockets. I would go to work in the rice fields with my mother and while she picked, I would too and put the rice in the large pockets. . . .

When I was about four years old the Vietnamese came to the camp and drove the Khmer Rouge away. At this time we had a chance to sneak away from camp and go back to our home. Before we left my mother went to look for my father. She found him in the camp that he had been sent to. They had to sneak back as there were still many soldiers around the camps. Father had no hair and was very sick. . . . He stayed in the hospital about two months, was made well, and returned to us. He looked so different we did not know him. Our mother told us it was him. . . .

During the darkness of night we left for Thailand. The trip to Thailand was through the country where the grass was very much taller than me. I could not see where I was going, I could only hold onto my mother's skirt. Sometimes we had to lie very still because there were still many soldiers around. Sometimes they would come within a few steps from us, but we were never found. . . .

I was about five years old when we got to Thailand. . . .

Father found that a friend of his already lived in America and that they wanted to sponsor our family. They sent us money to help us live while in the camp. He then sent us the papers we needed to fill out so we could come to America. In about one month we were asked a lot of questions about our family. We were then moved to Lem Pe Ne where we got the airplane to come to America. . . . I miss my country very much but we had to leave because of the unhappy and unsafe way of life. We were now on our way to America where we had a chance to be happy and free.

How did this child, a refugee first grader with absolutely *no* English, develop in just a few years into a highly competent, talented writer?

Francie Nolan (not the Francie Nolan of *A Tree Grows in Brooklyn*), a language resource teacher, worked with Mom in third grade. Here are excerpts from an interview with Francie about Mom's language-learning story:

The family had absolutely no English when they came. By the time I worked with her in third grade, she had broken English; she couldn't write in whole sentences. Her writing was very fragmented. She knew her letters but didn't put things together very well. She stumbled, tried, got discouraged, cried when she made mistakes. . . . I always want to find children's interests, talents, special strengths. Mom was very artistic. We used art activities, games, mazes, brain teasers as our materials. No matter what we did, writing went with it in nonthreatening, nonjudgmental ways. If she drew a picture, we asked her what the title was—how she would describe it—and she wrote it. We worked in small groups. The kids helped each other, praised each other. We wrote in bits and pieces and chunks. In the small groups, the kids helped her with her written work and she helped them with illustrations. Her classroom teacher, Betty South, was fantastic, expanding the group experiences, patient and encouraging. As the weeks and months went on, Mom made jumps you wouldn't believe. She relaxed, even joked. Her oral language came behind the written. She could ponder over the written, but in oral language she had to make snap decisions and often clammed up. Her reading came along. Most of our reading was based on the children's interests. Her family was behind her 100 percent, supporting all her efforts. The other kids helped her the most, rooting for her the whole time. Never put her down if she answered something out of context or misunderstood a word. They never laughed at her. They were her cheering section!

There was constant interaction, constant involvement with language and with language activities. In third grade, she wrote a book about lions. It was her first "book." In fourth grade, she worked with Sally Trethewey and Camille Bates, two wonderful teachers who continued encouraging, providing many opportunities for interesting language experiences. She wrote the book about her family because . . . she had this story to tell and she had to tell it. And now she had the tools to do it! It's our job as teachers to help kids make that happen.[10]

QUESTION: How well would Mom have learned her language in classrooms of rigid silence; tight, closed structures; isolated lessons in separate skills; minimal exchanges and interchanges and rare involvement in enjoyable learning activities? Case closed.

The Spotlight Is Back on You

Here are a few things to remember as you direct your energies toward encouraging writing in your classroom. Each of them is important. They are *not* in a vertical order of priorities. They are all spokes on a wheel and the hub of the wheel is SUCCESS.

Safety First

Your students will write in your room if they feel safe. If they know that they will not be humiliated, put down, harshly criticized, or ignored, they will write. If they know that you, their teacher, care about and appreciate their creative efforts and feel that their ideas are of value, they will write. If your students trust you, know that you will not betray them, know that you will protect their dignity and spirit as fiercely as conservationists protect endangered species, they will write. Mauree Applegate warns, "A child will no sooner turn out the pockets of his mind to one he does not trust than a shy boy will turn out the treasures of his trousers pocket to a stranger. He has so many wonderings, questions, fears and dreams and so few adult friends with whom he can share them."[11]

Enjoy! Enjoy!

As Harry Golden said, "Enjoy, enjoy!" Writing is a uniquely human activity. All animals leave some kind of tracks or marks, but only people carve "*I love you*" on the backs of wooden benches or on the trunks of trees. Rejoice in that expression of the uniqueness of human beings. Be yourself. Be an honest, consistent, caring, trustworthy, responsive person.

A warm, caring, open relationship with your students and a positive, nourishing climate in the classroom where you learn together are the two most important requirements in guaranteeing the successful encouragement of writing. Lois Lenski echoes these beliefs: "It is such a simple thing to help children enter the creative life, to help them to think clearly and to communicate their ideas to others through the spoken or written word. Provide the opportunity. Let the child talk and let him write, enjoying both. Share his enthusiasm."[12]

Write with your students.   Don't sit back and grade papers or organize plan books while your students are writing poems. Share your words. As often as possible, provide time to read the material that you and your students write. Older children may be cautious; they have learned to be afraid and inhibited. But when they discover that no one will be laughed at, humiliated, or put down, they will *want* to share whatever they write. Sharing is an important part of the creative process, and I urge you not to minimize the valuable ideas and inspirations that come from listening to other people's words. When it's your turn, read your words! Vary the experience and have the children read each other's works out loud.

Write every day.   You don't need hours set aside for writing. A few minutes a day of writing is enough to develop an ease, freedom, and fluency that will become an integral part of your students' lives. The number of children who can't write grew because children didn't write very often in school, and when they did it was an *event*, not a natural, everyday activity. Assignments were accompanied by instructions, requirements, lectures about what was important, and warnings on how many points would be taken off for mistakes. In too many classrooms, writing time is not a time of enjoyment and delight in the process of creative expression but a time of tension. So minimize anxiety, maximize pleasure. Take the worry out of writing by writing every single day.

Write about everything!   If writing is part of all experiences, studies, subject areas, and events, it will become natural and flow easily. Writing about *everything* will enable your students to enrich their abilities with a diversity of styles, purposes, and subject matter.

Write FOR young children.   Our very young children have amazingly large speaking and understanding vocabularies but often are not yet able to write. Most of them know the difference between pictures and writing. Their scribbly attempts at letters, their constant playing at writing, demonstrates their interest in and motivation for learning how to write. Their own writing attempts should be encouraged at all times. Those squiggly little scribbles will soon be shaped into recognizable letters. Young children need to know that their spoken words have visual images as well, that there are written symbols for their spoken words. In addition to encouraging their own writing attempts, *write their words down*—on the board, on "language experience" pads, on bulletin boards. Young children need to have numerous experiences in *seeing* their spoken words turned into print, into written language, and then in celebrating it by having it read back to them. We have even coined an expression for such writing: "Talking written down." Be sure to include the children's own names as often as possible.

Writing and Spelling

Again, young children should be encouraged to write as well as dictate or tell their stories. They need practice and direct experience in the important process of learning to spell as they learn to write. Scholars such as Chomsky, Read, Temple, Nathan, and Burris have studied the various stages of young children's spelling acquisition as they move from being prephonemic spellers, who make letterlike shapes but *don't* connect the shapes to sounds, through the "invented spelling" period, in which they write letters to represent the sounds they hear and recognize (sometimes one or two letters may express a whole sentence), through all the transitions leading to standard spelling skills.

As children move through these stages, their activities raise many questions about language and thinking abilities. Do young children differentiate between sounds? Do they know that certain symbols (letters) correspond to specific sounds? Which sounds can they hear and name and express with a written symbol? Do they have clear concepts of words? Do they understand what words are? Are they consistent in how they express certain words and ideas?

Throughout the country, teachers are learning to read the "invented spelling" of young children. Susan Hall and Chris Hall described the story-writing attempts of two five-year-olds:

> The children stated the sentences they were going to write, announced the words they were using to represent the sentences and selected the letters to spell those words. Tanya wanted to write "She has ears" and chose to spell the word "ears." She wrote the *E*, then looked at it for a long time. She suddenly looked up and announced, "It takes a lot of letters to spell 'ears.' " She then repeated the word aloud twice. She wrote the *R* and then she wrote the Z.
>
> ERZ.[13]

The authors report that, a few hours later, the children were able to "read back" what they had written. Writing with the children and observing their composing processes revealed the systems they had developed, their various transitional stages on the way to skill acquisition. Help our young writers along the way by giving them many opportunities to write and by sharing the exciting experience with them.

The Stuff of Writing Is Words

Potters work with clay, painters work with paint, writers work with words. Consider for a minute the immensity of words. Leland B. Jacobs expresses their range: "Words certainly do have their ways. They grow out of human experience and are used as an invention of man to communicate experiences. They may be regarded as labels. They are used for walls or fences. They are intended to be vehicles for the conveyance of ideas—sometimes facts, sometimes opinions, sometimes sales talks, sometimes directions, and sometimes feelings."[14]

Enjoy Pablo Neruda's inspiring words about words:

You can say anything you want, yes sir, but it's the words that sing, they soar and descend. . . . I bow to them. . . . I love them, I cling to them, I run them down, I bite into them, I melt them down. . . . I love words so much. . . . The ones I wait for greedily or stalk until, suddenly, they drop. . . . Vowels I love. . . . They glitter like colored stones, they leap like silver fish, they are foam, thread, metal, dew. . . . I run after certain words. . . . They are so beautiful that I want to fit them all into my poem. . . . I catch them in midflight, as they buzz past, I trap them, clean them, peel them, I set myself in front of the dish, they have a crystalline texture to me, vibrant, ivory, vegetable, oily, like fruit, like algae, like agates, like olives. . . . And then I stir them, I shake them, I drink them, I gulp them down, I mash them, I garnish them, I let them go. . . . I leave them in my poem like stalactites, like slivers of polished wood, like coals, pickings from a shipwreck, gifts from the waves. . . . Everything exists in the word.[15]

Create a Language-Rich Environment

Spark the students' desire to write inspiring materials: a wide and diverse offering of literature, posters, pictures, magazines, pets, plants, shared hobbies, collections, projects. Turn your room into the WRITE place: make room for special writing places. Creative teachers transform large cardboard cartons into miniature writing rooms with space enough for several children to sit and write. Writing suggestions are tacked to walls or hung on mobiles. Creative teachers place tables and chairs behind a screen for a private, quiet creating space, write ideas on cards or light-bulb shapes taped to the wall. Shoeboxes, envelopes, felt pockets, and grab bags can be filled with starter suggestions so no child will ever say, "I have *nothing* to write about!" Remember, *nothing* is a word. It's a challenging topic for writing. Try it.

Adapt the "Conference" Approach

Donald H. Graves and Lucy McCormick Calkins urge teachers to consider conferences as extremely effective ways of helping children evaluate and improve their writing. Used throughout the evolution of the writing, they sustain and extend the life force of the writing. Donald Graves' book *Writing: Teachers and Children at Work* and Lucy McCormick Calkins' book *Lessons from a Child: On the Teaching and Learning of Writing* (both Heinemann Educational Books, 1983) offer detailed descriptions of the many ways conferences are used in classrooms around the country.

The subject of the conferences is the students' writing: the content, purpose, process, technical areas of the pieces they have written. The weather of the conference is warm and loving. The interaction between students and teacher, student and teacher, students among themselves, is positive. Conferences can

be one to one; small groups can work together with or without the teacher; or the entire class can "conference" as one group.

Lucy McCormick Calkins shares the questions some third-grade children said they wished others would ask them in conference. They titled them "Good Conference Questions":[16]

1. How do you like your story?
2. Does your title fit your story?
3. Do you have more than one story in your piece?
4. Can you add more feeling to it?
5. Is there more you could add?
6. Tell me in detail what happened.
7. Are there too many extra things in it that you don't really need?
8. Are you going to keep working on it?
9. Have you enjoyed writing it?

As you can see, conferences go far beyond the "correct your mistakes" approach into follow-up writing activities. These are helpful, enjoyable, success-oriented meetings in which children learn to connect ideas and questions, to stay on the subject, to think helpfully and practically, to explore ideas—to behave as writers, practicing and improving their craft.

The questions asked and modeled by the teacher are "questions that teach." Donald Graves suggests excellent questions that "provide surprises for both child and teacher." Teachers listen to children. They ask questions they think children can answer (safety first!). They ask questions about process, structure, development. They ask questions that help children focus and reflect.[17] The experience of bringing all this thought and caring to a piece of writing is exciting. And it conveys an important message to your students. It says "I value your work. I respect you as writers. Working together to look at your work in a fresh, helpful way will give you some ideas on improving it, so you will like it even more!"

As you will do with all ideas that YOU like, you will mix the idea of conferences with your own teaching style, personality, and unique group of kids to make it your own.

Remember that the focus of evaluation is the student. Logan and Logan remind you that "since the purpose of creative writing is artistic self-expression, evaluation must be based on the extent to which the child grows in his ability to express his ideas in a manner satisfactory to him at any given point in his development."[18]

Publish or Perish

And what to do with this gathering, this ongoing collection of writings? Obviously, share them, celebrate them, display them, mimeograph them, distribute them. When students are writing all the time across the curriculum, throughout the days, weeks, and months, excellent reading materials multiply. The walls of lively, dynamic classrooms are filled with students' writings, handbound books, classroom magazines and newspapers. When kids know their work is in demand, is going to be shared and read by others, their motivation for clarity and correct usage is high.

Different Kinds of Writing

Writing is writing, isn't it? Yes, it is, but many people think of two kinds of writing—creative and expository. They see major differences in the purpose and language of the two.

The division of writing into these two categories is an oversimplification, but for practical reasons we'll explore them individually. Keep making connections in your mind.

In creative writing the emphasis is on self-expression. Children share ideas, feelings, fantasies, responses to experiences and relationships in their own unique ways. Experimentation, delight in language, encouragement of the free flow of words are featured ingredients. The emphasis is on the process rather than the product. Mauree Applegate calls creative writing one of the many "chimneys" necessary to release inner steam and pressure.[19] The more "chimneys" people have open to them, the healthier they will be and the more coherence and meaning their lives will have.

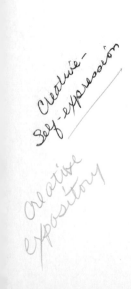

Creative Writing

In addition to providing a healthy outlet, creative writing, with its emphasis on observation, perception, and imagination, helps people achieve a higher level of awareness in their everyday lives, adding new dimensions to ordinary experiences and daily existence. Please note that these same powers of observation, awareness, perception, and imagination are high-priority qualities in scientific writing, research, journalism, and other areas which we label "expository." Keep making connections!

Helping children to write in language that is "clear, vigorous, honest, alive, sensuous, rhythmic without pretension, fresh, metaphorical, evocative in sound . . . surprising, memorable, and light"[20] is one of the most delightful jobs you will have as a teacher. Through shared creative writing experiences, you will discover "not only beauty but wisdom . . . and kindness, pity, mercy, a care for living things, love of the world, unprejudiced observation, instinctive insight, the joy of sharing, a reaching out to other peoples, the very core of humanitarianism. . . . It is there, and always has been there, in the guarded secrecy of child thinking and child feeling, an amazing potential power which could someday remake a troubled and distracted world."[21] Your commitment to the importance of creative writing in the classroom is essential. Ted Hughes affirms his belief that "the latent talent for self-expression in any child is immeasurable. . . . By showing to a pupil's imagination many opportunities and few restraints and instilling into him confidence and a natural motive for writing, the odds are that something—maybe not much, but something—of our common genius will begin to put a word in."[22]

A Special Look at Poetry

Because poetry is the one component of literature that has been most mistaught in our schools, I want to focus on it. To develop a positive approach to poetry and to be able to share it with your students, you will probably need to unlearn much of what you have been taught. Poems are not necessarily exercises in logic. Poems do not have to follow prescribed rules and regulations. Their special mystique confounds rigid, closed-minded people who are not happy unless everything in the universe is explained and answers are provided for all situations. The whole idea that a person can flunk a poem or be criticized for an interpretation of a poem is the antithesis of everything a poem is about. Perhaps you were lucky and never learned to dislike poetry. Your students will benefit from your good experiences. But you may be one of many, many people whose feelings about poetry are negative. For your own sake and the sake of your students, I urge you to begin to discover the wonder and power of poetry.

Children love poetry, with its originality, images, rhythms, and patterns, until something happens to make them dislike it. I consider this one of the disasters of our educational system. I hope that in your work with children you will never foster such a negative attitude. My favorite poets and poems may not be yours. You must find the ones that speak to you. Wallace Stevens considered poetry a "response to the daily necessity of getting the world right."[23] And you know that we all need something that helps us "get the world right"!

Two Poets Add Insight to Our Understanding of Creative Writing

Sometimes good poets are also good teachers who spend time in classrooms.

Michael J. Rosen[24] is an experience in himself as he prods, challenges, hurries, jokes, "disarms" students in his attempts to "leech them from the need to look for *correct* answers, to pull them from dependence on the familiar, common, accessible, easy answers. . . ." Michael and his students explore unfamiliar territory, enjoy the creative excitement of discovering more and more original ideas. They write quickly and in excess, generating many options. He gave a group of fourth graders two minutes to come up with about ten ideas on the notion of *alphabet books* ("I always ask for *more*. I don't want the kids to make simple, straightforward answers and be satisfied!"). What themes could they think of for alphabet books? Their lists began with the familiar: Animal ABCs, Fruit and Vegetable ABCs. But then, prodded by Michael, they reached further: Native American ABCs, Pioneer Day ABCs, Riddle ABCs, Things in My Closet ABCs. The hands-down class favorite was Mark's Things-That-Get-Me-in-Trouble ABCs. In Michael's approach, teachers share process with the students. They give up teachers' manuals and preset expectations and "ideal" responses. Michael asks teachers to be as responsive to the experience, as open and willing to risk, as the students are. Surprise and discovery are important ingredients of the creative process.

Michael puts high value on the children's experiences and knowledge:

> I always encourage kids to use what they know exclusively so they're using their experiences in their special provinces. I want them to be aware that what they have to write about is most *theirs*. They must never discount that which is most important to themselves—their own memories and experiences.[25]

Arnold Adoff,[26] popular children's poet, shared with fifth and sixth graders something of his experience as a writer and his love of poetry. His philosophy was expressed in every exchange with his fellow poets: freedom, experimentation, risk taking, flexibility, playfulness. He responded to each child with positive, thoughtful, helpful ideas. He continually encouraged them to see more, to see things in a slightly different way, to arrange and rearrange. He also encouraged them to make writing and rewriting a daily business.

As you are strengthening your own beliefs about creativity in the classroom, consider how Arnold's words below apply to all imaginative endeavors:

> There are so many things that you could do. The first thing to do with poetry after you're satisfied that you've written a poem that you like—if it were me or if you'd like to follow my advice—would be to then take that poem and to play with it some more, to break the first line as many ways as you possibly can do. If you have time, that's always a valuable way of learning to become a better writer. And also to play, to have fun with it—how many variations you

can do, just with the first line. You can take a whole week to do nothing but just the first line![27]

Expository Writing

When people think of expository writing, they usually associate it with more functional, more utilitarian purposes. The concern is with communicating information and facts for specific reasons. Letter writing, report writing, book reviews, and research assignments are familiar activities under the umbrella of expository writing. In our society, the ability to write easily for a variety of purposes opens many doors. The more opportunities your students are given to practice this kind of writing in an enjoyable way, the more competency and self-assurance they will develop. Here there is an emphasis on the skills of punctuation, penmanship, spelling, usage, and capitalization. Clarity and organization are essential in this kind of writing.

Before you place expository writing and creative writing in separate boxes in your mind, consider how arbitrary that separation can be. Some of the most powerful, poetic, original writing is found in letters. Vincent van Gogh's letters to his brother, Franz Kafka's letters to his father, and F. Scott Fitzgerald's letters to his daughter are examples of outstanding creative literature. Mary McCarthy and D. H. Lawrence wrote travel books about cities and countries in rich language. McCarthy's *Stones of Florence* and Lawrence's *Mornings in Mexico* are literary gems. *Beware of categorizing and compartmentalizing any aspect of the human spirit and intellect.*

The purposes of expository writing are practical, but that doesn't mean that you and your students can't enjoy the learning. The more fun you have while you practice these important thinking and writing skills, the more enthusiasm and confidence the children will respond with and the more meaning the lessons will take on. Expository writing will be easier for the children to learn when you have strengthened their confidence in their creative self-expression. As with all language activities, all human activities, the way to competency with confidence is *practice!* Think *many*, not few, opportunities. Think *daily*, not occasionally! Think *part of,* not separate from. Think *success!*

QUESTION: What do I want my students to learn?
ANSWER: I want my students to enjoy writing, be proud of their work, and develop a love for the process that will provide a source of enrichment for the rest of their lives.

Writing Activities (Take the Worry Out of Writing)

Cumulative Writing Projects

This type of activity is always popular and successful. Each individual contributes an original addition to a basic theme. For example, put up an I Am Proud chart: the children write their names on one half and something they are proud of on the other. Or create an I Can can—a can filled with statements that the children select and write responses to, such as "things I can do on the playground," or "things I can do at home." Instead of using only a chart, the class can create a Proud Chain. Everyone writes a statement about something that he or she is proud of on a strip of paper. The first strip is pasted together to form a circle and is attached to the ceiling. Subsequent links are formed from each child's strip of paper. More links are added as children add new things they are proud of. Don't forget to add your own links.[28]

Class Scrapbooks

These books are devoted to questions or topics of interest with room for original responses from everyone (including you). Third graders compiled a book called "Love Is" that featured definitions, feelings, and poems by everyone in the class. Fifth graders shared words and pictures in a special Thanksgiving book called "Thanksgiving Means."

Writing Collages

Thoughts about people, places, things, holidays, colors, events, or experiences are written on cardboard cut in shapes and hung from a clothesline stretched across the room. The shapes can be the outline of a child's body cut from a wide roll of paper. Each silhouette is filled in with color or design or whatever a child wishes. Words, poems, and stories are written on any or all parts of the shape. Then all the shapes are strung on the clothesline. Animal stories and poems can be written on animal shapes, decorated, and hung on the clothesline. Add clouds, clowns, cars, and stars! A.Y.O.

Spin-offs

a. A variation of this idea comes from Michael Rosen. Interested in whales, he shared ideas about them with a class of fourth graders. Then he drew a large outline of a whale on construction paper and cut it into sections—enough for each child to have a piece. The children wrote or illustrated their feelings and ideas about whales on their separate pieces of paper. Michael collected them all, fit them together into the original whale shape, and, with the children, mounted the paper whale on the corridor wall where it became a center of interest and stimulated further creative writing ideas.

b. Draw and cut out a cross-section of a thick tree trunk. Give everyone a ring of the trunk. Each ring represents a different year. (If the tree is very old, the first ring of the trunk could be from the year 1776.) Each child writes about the events of that year. When the rings are put back in order on the trunk, the history of the tree and the times it lived through are there for all to marvel at.

Crazy Questions

Innovative teachers are constantly on the lookout for any idea that sparks imagination and expression. A bright spot in their rooms is a clearly written question on chalkboard, bulletin board, or wall chart with room for all the students' responses. The question doesn't have to be crazy, but it should inspire original responses; for example, "How do you tell a snake 'I love you'?" or "What shall we do with the elephant in the room?"

Try one of Michael Rosen's favorite challenges: "What are some *impossible things to do*? Let's collect ideas." He follows that collection with "Now, choose one of those impossible things and write instructions for how to do it!"

What Do You See?

This is an example of the kind of writing exercise that sharpens powers of observation and helps children to learn to write quickly without tension. In one minute (two minutes for children in younger grades), everyone writes a list of all the things he or she observes in the classroom. When the time is up, share the lists. Two fourth graders' lists follow.

Jean	Bill
chalkboard	people writing
tables	eyeglasses
chairs	bead earrings
desks	Mr. Jones' mustache
door	batik shirts
supply closet	white and black sneakers

lights	red skirt
light switch	Amy's overalls
book shelves	Bob's headband
globe	curly hair
pencils	straight hair
pens	Monica's braids
workbooks	colorful socks
maps	Indian belt
fish tank	pictures of volcanoes
windows	trees outside windows
window shades	houses on the street
people	

No lecture on the phenomenon of human individuality is as effective in helping people to discover their uniqueness as this simple writing exercise. A variation is for everyone to *shift position* and then write everything seen from the new viewpoint. Just the change of position will bring a whole new world into focus. We all need to take a few minutes every day to rediscover the miracle of our powers of observation.

Spin-off This spin-off follows the activity described above very well. Instead of the wide-angle view used before, really zoom in on a specific object or area. Make up general categories, such as Something on the Wall, Something Colorful, Something on the Floor. Devote a minute to each category and allow the children to roam around the room getting close to the object under scrutiny. When the pieces are complete, tape them to the object described. So many parts of the room will take on new significance. The children will be able to "read" the room.

Catch the Spirit of a Poem*

Ideas for enriching the curriculum through poetry have been featured throughout this book. To demonstrate that ideas are limitless, enjoy the following activities that use poetry to inspire creative writing.

Upward Bound teens responded to Jed Garrick's poem by writing their own poems.

Answer in Bright Green

into their gray house I will not go
and when their lemon lips find me in the market-place
I shall laugh panurge at them
and when they polyp-shake my hand I shall prick them
with solomon and minarets . . .
and when they beam me holy in the street
my easter island face will rock against their eyes
and I will not go into their gray houses.

---

*Kenneth Koch's *Rose, Where Did You Get That Red?* (Random House, 1974) and Kenneth Koch and Kate Farrell's *Sleeping on the Wing* (Vintage Books, 1982) contain excellent suggestions for inspiring your students to write poetry.

and when they say me no in the bright morning
I shall give them breughel yes and falstaff
while they sip pekoe I shall pour rich burgundy
on the roots of a scarlet rose
and when they tell me sunday and stewed beef
my answer will be asteroids and nectar
and with two fingers I shall draw a sign in air
to exorcise the no they say on a bright morning.[29]

Their response to the poem was startling. Even though they did not at first know all of the words, they *loved* the spirit of the poem, the self-assertiveness of it, the rebelliousness of it, the way the poet "told them off!" The poem touched on very real feelings in the students, who were trying to work out their own identities and maintain their own integrity in an adult world that constantly defined them. The students wanted to try to write poems on that theme, using language as original and powerful as Garrick's. Here is an example from that writing session.

Don't Put Me Down Poem

I shall not run in your mellow orchid fields,
Or play in the gardens of your desires,
And when your tender eyes look low at me,
I shall not away, but rave like Rumpelstiltskin as if my
        heart and soul were in the depths of the fires.
And when we meet on some lonely uptown street,
My heart shall become Mt. Everest
And my tongue a whip lash of hail,
And should you whisper with those
        grape-colored pieces of moving meat,
I shall run my pride up a cactus
and slide it gently down the
banana stalk and feed it with bread and ale,
Till it grows like a seedling
to be huge, and strong, and made to fly high,
Till your Chicago's fire smothers and dies.

                                          Karen

Write about Poems

Ask your students to listen to poems and write what they feel and think as they listen. Here are Carl Sandburg's poem "Limited" and a sixth grader's response to it.

Limited

I am riding on a limited express, one of the crack trains of the nation.
Hurtling across the prairie into blue haze and dark air go fifteen all-
        steel coaches holding a thousand people.
(All the coaches shall be scrap and rust and all the men and women
        laughing in the diners and sleepers shall pass to ashes.)
I ask a man in the smoker where he is going and he answers:
        "Omaha."[30]

This is about a passenger on a train. He talks about life. He says the train will turn to rust and the people to ashes. He means everyone is on a train going to his destination. Which is nowhere!

David

CAREFUL

Teachers have the power of life and death over curriculum, materials, and the spirits of their kids. One high school student told how her teacher asked the class to bring in their responses to any example of poetic writing they liked. The day the assignments were due, one of the boys handed in a carefully written response to the lyrics of Bruce Springsteen's song "Born in the U.S.A." The teacher immediately tossed it back at him, saying, "This is not acceptable."

She tossed out the success of the day. The value of the experience was lost to *all* the students.

Questions as Poems

Questions are intriguing, challenging, and poetic. Many poems ask questions. "How do I love thee? Let me count the ways," asks Elizabeth Barrett Browning. "To be or not to be? That is the question," wonders William Shakespeare's Hamlet.

Children are the greatest question-askers. Talk about questions. Discuss their value. Read some poems together that feature questions; then ask your students to write a list of questions and share them.

A variation is to write the five Ws—Who? What? Where? When? Why? Ask your students to complete all of those Ws, some of them, or concentrate on any one of them. Another enjoyable variation is to write Big questions and Little questions. Children interpret that direction in many original ways.

> why does peanut butter stick?
> WHERE DO RABBITS GO IN WINTER?
> why does Mom sing when she does the dishes?
> HOW DO I DREAM?
> why do dogs wag their tails?
> WHEN WILL I BE ALL GROWN UP?

Grade 3

What else? (the magic words!)

In addition to Big/Little questions, I like to ask kids to write questions under such categories as these:

animals	ancestors
houses	mythological characters
objects	seasons
clothing	newborn babies
food	themselves
colors	teachers (be strong!)

Remind them to write the name of the person or thing to whom the question is being asked:

Fish, do you ever smile?
Grandmother, what was it like when you left Ireland to come to America?

A variety of questions makes fascinating reading. Hearing the students read aloud some samples of their questions is an exciting reading–listening–oral language combination plate!

Set aside one wall to decorate with question-full wall paper.

Choose any of the questions to "answer."

Second-grader Samantha wrote a very poignant question: *Mother, will you still be my mom when I grow up?*

Potpourri of Poetry-Inspiring Ideas

five-senses poems
memory poems
color poems
poems in nests, attics, igloos, and tenement houses
poems featuring *opposites*
alphabet poems
animal poems, flower poems, tree poems
poems inspired by a repeating line or phrase
poems that explore the universe of *one word*
journey poems
turn-yourself-into poems
poems that try to catch time
poems you can sing
playful, jingly poems
number poems
ocean poems, mountain poems, desert poems
poems written with a close-up lens (take a close look at something)
poems written from a wide-angle lens (take a wide look at something)
poems about pockets, places, people, planets
outside poems, inside poems
poems for the seasons, the weather, the different times of day
poems from another person's viewpoint—someone else's moccasins
read a variety of poetry and let poems inspire poems
A.Y.O.

Write to Music/with Music/about Music

Music can evoke pictures in the mind and the words that express those pictures are often powerful and original. If your room is filled with music, then you will have another marvelous source of inspiration for creative writing. Have the children listen to music and ponder the images evoked. Encourage them to express their feelings and ideas in words.

One of my most enjoyable and successful experiences of writing with music occurred when I asked my fifth and sixth graders to listen to music with all their might and write their feelings and ideas. I did not tell them the names or kinds of music.

After the session, the children *wanted* to know the names and types of music they had heard. I'm sure they will remember the music for a longer time than if the session had begun with the names and descriptions. That day I played Spanish flamenco music, scary music by Béla Bartok, joyful music by Jacques Offenbach, African tribal music, and mournful East European Chassidic chants. Here are some of the students' written responses.

> This music makes me feel like dancing and twirling. I want to run through sunlight fields and pick flowers and live to life's greatest extent. I want to do everything!
>
> Gail G.

> As I look up, the moon is tossed about storm clouds. The stars dance. A murderer is running through the jungle below the sky toward me. I am going to run, run, run. . . . The moon is covered with clouds. Cold sweat on my face. I found a cave. I am lost, lost, lost. . . .
>
> Yael Y.

There is a universe of music to listen to as you write. Combine the writing with improvisation, movement, art, and all subject areas. For example, in math, you might be studying the concept of *one* or in grammar the concept of *singular*. Play music featuring a solo instrument or voice. Ask the children to listen to the music, jot down as many ideas as they can, and then select *one* image to write about. Create solo movement using a singular pattern. Draw *one* image in response to the music.

If you want to concentrate on *words*, experiment with this approach: Think *words*. If you hear loud, action-filled music, write loud, action-filled words. If the music is calm and peaceful, write calm and peaceful words. If the music changes, catch the spirit of the music and write words that change their spirit with the music. It's a great way to free vocabulary!

Photos and Pictures

Sometimes writing about feelings can be very difficult. The closer something is to you, the more difficulty you may have writing about it with any originality. Pictures provide an avenue of self-expression. They enable people to respond truthfully and with depth. You will be surprised at your own and your students' insights after studying photographs and paintings.

Use one picture as the focus and inspiration for the entire class. Display a large picture so everyone can see it. Have each person write for a few minutes, then share the results of the picture's effect. Afterward, mount the picture on a wall and surround it with the individual writings.

Spin-offs

a. A different experience is to give each person a separate picture. Have everyone write for a few minutes about his or her picture, then pass it on. In a short time the children will have had the opportunity to write about five different pictures. When you share their responses, hold up the pictures and have those people who wrote about them read their pieces out loud. Be sure the kids write *titles* for their pictures.

b. Children love to share pictures from home that they especially like. As often as possible, encourage the children to write down their thoughts. Then display the pictures with the writings.

c. Set aside time for your students to sit down with scissors and piles of old magazines and cut out pictures that they think would be interesting to write about. A class picture file should be contributed to by everyone in the class.

d. Inexpensive postcards of famous paintings can be used to inspire creative writing as well as to introduce your students to the works of the great artists. Using paintings adds a different dimension to the writing. Questions, such as "Do paintings by Monet or Renoir evoke different words and feelings than works by Klee or Picasso? What kind?" will stimulate interesting responses.

e. Your presentation of pictures may guide the students to respond in new ways. Ask them to *take a slow walk into the canvas of a Monet garden*—smell it, touch it, listen to it—and then write about it. After the writing, the class will have definite ideas about whether their style, images, and feelings were affected by the swirl and dazzle of Monet's colors and shapes.

Here are additional suggestions that are helpful in triggering ideas to write about.

Write a title for the picture.

Write about what you see in the picture.

Write about what the images in the picture smell like.

Write about what you hear in the picture.

Imagine *yourself* in the picture. What are you doing?

Write what you think happened before this photograph was taken.

Write what you think happened after this photograph was taken.

Turn yourself into one of the people in the picture. Write your thoughts and feelings.

Write dialogue for the people in the picture.

Write a poem about the picture.

Write a story about the picture.

Write the picture as a memory or a dream.

Students' Pictures and Words

For many people, the way to free written and oral language is through their own art work. As we read in Mom's story, her written language improved as she described, titled, shared her feelings about her pictures.

Rick Johnston was initiating a creative writing activity with his sixth graders. Most of them were responding with enthusiasm, except for two recalcitrant doodlers, Tony and Ron. Instead of scolding the two for their nonparticipation, Rick voted YES and suggested that they work together on a story based on the cartoon characters they were doodling. Negative turned positive. The boys plunged into a long, complicated project that culminated in *The Crash Landing*, a science fiction film. The script for the story included dialogue, sound effect cues, technical instructions. The last page of the script tells *us* the other story:

The End

Written, Drawn, Voices and Sound Effects, Produced by
Ron Stewart, Grade 6   Tony D'Angelo, Grade 6
Director of Photography: Mr. Rick Johnston
A Hellen Keller School Production
Tinley Park, Illinois 1981

Not a bad accomplishment for two turned-off kids!

Journals

Journals are one of the best ways to mark your time, to record feelings, observations, and events. The most important thing to remember about a journal is that it is *for the writer*. For many children, journals may be the most significant and meaningful part of their school experience. Save a few minutes a day to write in journals (you write too). Sometimes a child will not know what to write about. If nothing else, write five sense images from the day: I saw, I heard, I smelled, I tasted, I touched.

One seventh-grade boy complained that he had nothing to write about in his journal. His clever teacher (from the Culture of YES) immediately suggested, "Well, just pick one word and keep writing it over and over until another word comes to mind." This is what the boy wrote:

boy
boy
boy
boy
boy
boy
man

Responsive, caring teachers build in success for their students every day. No child should end a school day without the memory of at least one (but many more, we hope) success experience.

My friend Don, who knows all the football teams, doesn't remember *one* moment of success in *all* his years of school. Sometimes we forget that "teaching is one of the few professions that permits love."[31]

Journals can go in any direction, from being totally open-ended—"write whatever you want"—to being more directed. I like the combination of both of these roads. My kids have loved having sections of their journals to jot down Memories or Sense Impressions or Interesting Names of People, Places, and Things or Ideas for Stories or Questions or Topics of Special Interest (like "My Street," "Mustaches," "Feeling Sick"). Especially when they decided on their own sections!

Word Categories

Different sections of journals can be devoted to different categories of words, such as *seasonal, food, colorful, ugly, loud, mysterious, silly,* and *beautiful*. Let the children choose their own categories. The words provide an added resource for further writings.

Spin-offs   Here are two ways to use word categories as a class activity.

a. Take several sheets of paper and write a different category at the top of each one. In addition to the categories mentioned above, I have used words that make me wonder, words that tickle my imagination, words that take me on an adventure, words that make me think, words of the earth, growing words, words that make me sad, and so on.

Give each person a paper. Ask the group to quickly write as many words as they can (spelling doesn't count) under that category in the few minutes before the stop signal. After the stop signal, the children pass their papers to the next person. Everyone now has a new category of words to write. After the papers have been passed a few times, read the categories so the children can discover that ugly words *sound* ugly and silly words *sound* silly. Fill a wall with the categories with extra papers for new words to be added. Use the categories for spin-off activities involving art, music, movement, choral reading, and drama.

b. Give each child an envelope with a category title printed on the outside. Cut construction paper into small pieces and give each child several to write words on for the category. Stuff the slips of paper inside and pass the envelopes around so each person has a few different categories to write about. Afterward, keep the envelopes visible and accessible so the children can continue to add words and pictures to them. Use them for other writing and art activities.

Existential Items

Earlier in the book we talked about how time keeps pulling us quickly along, and how we have to find ways to catch the moments. All our statistics changed as this book was being written. Our months, weeks, days, hours, and minutes are ticking away. This moment will never come again. How old are you now? Stop reading and look at the clock. What time is it? Record the exact time and date and then write for one full minute. Ask your students to do this as often as possible.

9:44 A.M. 8-4-69

Where am I?
I'll tell you—
making impressions on paper.
This is NOW—August 4, 1969
I'm doing my thing
in the morning

John
Upward Bound

2:02 P.M. Feb. 27, 1985

Finally, I'm done.
It's the end of the line.
It's over. I'm tired. Let's go.
Moving nevermore.
Summer, candies, nevermore.
Spring and A's
Birds and books,
Nevermore
I'm alive, nevermore.

Mark O.
Grade 5

Instants

You've probably noticed that many of the writing exercises suggested are written quickly and shared promptly. Because one of our major goals is to *free* writing, I urge you to write often, briefly, and quickly. Instants are quick word sketches that exercise the mind. They don't take a long time, just a few minutes, and yet they provide a necessary respite from the day's heavy schedule. They also provide a lively gathering of resource material to be developed into longer pieces. They are the numerous notes, word sketches, jottings that fill the notebooks of writers and may turn into stories, plays, and poems.

Instant topics can range from the sublime to the ridiculous, but never choose a topic that is unfamiliar to your students. Announce the topic and, for a minute or two, you and your students write your feelings, ideas, and impressions of that topic. The first time you do this, you may find your students a little stiff and inhibited. But you'll notice when you read the instants that the last few topics are more original, alive, and sharp than the first few. As people relax, their words flow more easily.

There's no limit to the topics for instants. Here are some I've used with people of all ages:

clouds	city	friend
ice cream	music	footprints
clocks	circus	America
goodbye	me	old
party	war	tornado
river	Native American	grandmother
pencil	banyan tree	whispers
noses	midnight	chair
teeth	rainbow	rain

Noses

Everybody has one. Some are small.
Some are long. It has two holes in it.
You can smell with it.

Carla
Grade 4

Rain

Rain is mean. It cancels baseball
games. It has lightning. It makes
floods. It gets things wet. It
ruins baseball gloves left outside.
It is scary and not understandable.
It falls on you when you are lying
in the sun and thinking it is going
to pass over.

Cliff
Grade 6

Word Fireworks! Word Explosions!

There's no such thing as *one* word when mixed with imagination. Words beget other words. They even explode in our minds, like colorful fireworks.

Here's an excerpt from a third-grade writing session that demonstrates this explosive theory. (Of course, it *followed* a lively discussion about the wonders of language and imagination. It didn't just pop up like a jack-in-the-box.)

I asked the kids to close their eyes. I wrote "rabbit" on the board. Then "Open your eyes. If you know the word on the board, tap your head."

Everyone tapped!

"Now, isn't that amazing in itself? We haven't said anything. No pictures or pantomimes. Just the scribbly letters on the board spelling a word that all of you know!" (Always take time out for amazement.)

"Well, right now all of you have a picture in your mind of a rabbit. But, do you each have the *same* rabbit in your mind? What kind of rabbit are YOU thinking about?"

We go around the room for suggestions. The chalk writes fast and furiously as ideas fly in the charged air. I write words everywhere on the board (this is not a structured, "web"-type approach). The more ideas we thought about, the more we thought about. Each new one launched others. It was virtually impossible to find our original word *rabbit* surrounded by the clutter of such words as

cute brown white black hoppy little peter rabbit peter cottontail easter bunny bugs bunny white hairy bald mean nice smart dumb funny silly serious thoughtful sensitive rude gross macho sexy athletic overweight gross musical sly shy insane sick perverted dead friendly

Well, what do you do when you have a headful and a boardful of rabbit ideas? You could go in hundreds of ways. In this instance, we chose any of the words on the board and turned them into titles. The children's stories, diverse and highly original, were accompanied by clever, lively illustrations. For example,

Pop, the Punk Rock Rabbit

How the Overweight Rabbit Learned to Jog

Hoppy, the Story of a Newborn Bunny That Turned into a Detective Rabbit

Any word will start it off. I used the word *ship* with a group of fifth graders. After the explosion activity, we closed in on one of the suggestions, "Treasure Ship," and wrote pages of logs, letters, and journals from the sunken ship.

Experiment. Be open for surprises. Remember: rabbits multiply, and so do words!

Letter Writing

Almost every straight assignment has its creative counterpart. Expand your views of letter writing to include letters to

seasons	mythological characters
animals	the Statue of Liberty
holidays	characters from stories and books
colors	A.Y.O.
objects	

During thirty years of sharing Halloween ideas with children, I have experimented with writing letters to Halloween among all grades and ages. The children love the idea, their imaginations are nourished, and their writing shows original thinking. Here's part of a sixth-grader's letter:

Dear Halloween,

Are you getting the characters ready for your big entrance? Where are you hiding until it's time? What do the cats, witches, skeletons, and zombies do all the other months?

I have my costume but I'm not telling you who I'll be. You'll have to guess. Maybe I'll scare you as much as you try to scare me. Oooooooooooooooooooo.

Spookly yours,
Shawn

Putting Words in Their Mouths—Dialogue Writing

We all have our own ways of speaking. We are not interchangeable. Our students need many opportunities to practice writing dialogue. It helps their awareness, listening, comprehension, vocabulary, reading, mastery of punctuation, and—it's FUN!

One of my favorite dialogue topics is the Seven Dwarfs. I have about a hundred different ways for kids of all ages to play with dialogue for the Dwarfs. A memorable experience happened during one fifth-grade's social studies/language arts session. The kids had been studying the American Revolution. I was into the Seven Dwarfs. Here come our magical words: "What if?"

"What if the Seven Dwarfs lived in Lexington and Concord during the time the Minutemen were trying to enlist support? What might they say when Paul Revere and the others approached them to join the struggle?" Here are some of the Dwarf responses. No need to write the names of the Dwarfs. Their responses identify them.

What time are you leaving? Too early. I need my sleep.

Ah ah choo! Sorry, I have a bad cold. Try me again sometime.

I don't get it—is it two if by night, one if by day? Or is it one if by night—never mind. It's too complicated!

I'm happy to join you. Count me in!

What's wrong with the British anyway? Bug off!

Try dialogue exercises with fairy tale characters; career education characters like nurses, engineers, teachers, lawyers; your own class characters! Add dialogue bubbles to pictures and bulletin boards.

Dialogue exercises are natural bridges to playwriting. The students' original plays are excellent language experiences.

"Things to Do When You're Six" and Other Examples of Serendipity

When my young neighbor Matt came to visit me, I told him how lucky I thought he was because he was six. He grumbled, "I hate being six!"

Shocked, I asked him why.

"Nothing to do," he complained. "Can't go anywhere, can't do anything!" At that instant, I decided to collect ideas from children of all grade levels for "Things to Do When You're Six." So far, I have about 300 items from kindergartners to high school students. At the end of this school term, I'm going to present Matt with the list. Here are a few examples:

clean your room

look at sticker books

tell jokes

ride a bike

take a walk

read

scare your parents

play with friends

wait till you're seven

Jump on the interesting situations presented to you every day that can encourage writing.

Another example comes to mind from a celebration of the Wizard of Oz. A fourth grade was creating movement for the different characters. When they got to Glenda, the Good Witch, they moved in a very floating way. One of the kids said, "It would be nice to have good powers." The teacher jumped on that: "What if you had *good powers, good magic*? What would you do with it?" The result was a huge class chart with every name printed next to some excellent use of positive magic!

Sense Charts

Sense charts sharpen powers of observation and awareness and help develop original, dynamic writing. When you think of life, you think of the senses. The senses convey the quality of life. The writers who have the ability to make you smell the damp, early morning woods, feel the rust of sharp, cold nails, or make your mouth water for the pot of corn soup simmering on an open fire are able to reach your senses. Actually, most words cut across the senses. They belong to more than one sense. Think of all the feelings and images you conjure up at the words *coffee and doughnuts* or *new-mown grass.*

I always launch sense charts as a class experience. Begin with a class discussion on the need for exercising minds and imaginations to keep them from getting flabby. Ask the students to choose a topic to describe in terms of the senses. The topic may be broad, such as spring, home, or war, or it may be more limited and more demanding, such as color, feelings, or even a single color or emotion. It is often difficult to write originally about your feelings, but sense charts enable children to express a variety of emotions. Writing the charts is one of the best ways to take the worry out of writing and to expand and enrich the mind. In addition, your students' appreciation for the power of language will be strengthened.

The charts are important in themselves as a storehouse of information about a topic. When you are on vacation, for example, write a sense chart on the experience in your notebook or journal. It will be as valuable to you as an album of snapshots.

If the class chooses spring as their topic, tell them to *fill their minds with spring.* First they might turn their minds into cameras taking pictures of spring. What pictures would they take that really showed spring? Write everything they say on the chalkboard under the column heading Sight. If there's a lull in ideas, be ready with thought-provoking questions, such as What are spring places? spring colors? spring clothing? spring shapes? Always ask for specifics. Write *flowers,* for example, but go beyond. What kind of flowers?

When you run out of room under the Sight column (never out of ideas), go on to the next column, Sounds, and encourage your students to think of the sounds they hear when they imagine spring. Remember, our sense of sight is the most depended on and most used. You'll find that words won't come so easily for touch, sound, and taste. Always be ready with helping questions, such as Is spring hard? solid? rough? What kind of musical instruments should play spring songs? As you do more sense charts with your students, you will feel your other senses develop. This is a tuning-up and tuning-in exercise.

When the board is full, admire all the words for a few minutes. Think of all that vocabulary! Think of all those ideas! Remember that this is an opportunity for students to share words they know, even if they may not be able to read and write them all.

Now move to another board. Write *Spring.* Ask the students to choose their favorite images from any of the sense columns. Have them cross columns and suggest combinations.

Following a "time machine" sense chart on the Westward Movement, Emily Manierre's fourth graders wrote a page from a diary kept by a person on the journey. The ideas were suggested by the group and written on the board.

April 2, 1847

Today it rained.
The wagon got stuck in the mud. The wheels screeched. The mud was as thick
as quicksand.
We were bored. We had to walk back to camp. We got wet.
We heard coyotes howl. We smelled wet fur and smoke.
We ate wet bread and salty stew.
Someone got sick but we still had fun when Tom played his banjo and we sang
and saw the stars come out.

Use sense charts as resources across the curriculum. They provide excellent vocabulary for cities, natural places (rivers, jungles), historical literature,
paintings, holidays, colors, feelings. The charts enrich the students' writing of
everything from informational reports to imaginative diaries, logs, journals,
letters, poems.

I first used sense charts in 1957 with my fifth graders after being introduced
to them by the poet George Abbé, my creative writing teacher in a graduate
course. My kids fell in love with them, wrote sense charts every day on numerous topics. One day we did a sense chart together on anger. After we stopped
the class chart, the kids wrote their own pieces about anger, using the chart for
ideas. To this day I remember Andrew's paper: "Anger is the smell of supper
burning."

Beginnings

Next time you have a few extra minutes, browse through some books and read
just the first two sentences of each. You'll probably find that you will want to
keep reading some of the works just because of the impact of the first two
sentences. Beginnings are wonderful ways to get writing started. Either read
just the first few lines of a number of pieces or pass around a book of short
stories and have each child read the first line or two of succeeding stories. Note
the different ways writers have of starting a story.

Try writing a variety of beginnings with your class. You don't need to write
more than one or two lines at the most. Children will enjoy the challenge of
experimenting with many ideas. Here are a few samples of beginnings suggestions.

Begin with a person.	Begin with a place.	Begin with the word *once*.
Begin with weather.	Begin with a date.	Begin with an object.
Begin with a question.	Begin with a sound.	Begin with a person's name.
Begin with action.	Begin with a color.	Begin with an article of clothing.

Tape the beginnings to a wall. Or drop them into a shoebox devoted to beginnings, where they will always be ready to help launch writing projects.

Encourage your students to choose any of the beginnings and follow it as
long as they can, see how far they can go with it. It's an exciting adventure, full
of surprises.

Children Write Books

There is a great literary revolution going on. Our kids are writing their own books. I have already mentioned the national program Young Authors, in which many schools participate. It is an excellent program of total school encouragement for student written books. Funds are provided for book-making materials, book-centered programs such as conferences and conventions, and often a special staff who work with classes in writing and producing books. Children respond with great enthusiasm. They write books on every subject, share their books with pride and confidence, and have the pleasure of seeing their books read and enjoyed by others.

CAREFUL

Some Young Authors Conferences are a substitute for a program of daily writing in the classroom. The writing then becomes too product-centered. The climate becomes competitive as only a few books from each classroom are chosen to be represented. Be sure your Young Authors program has ways to honor *all* of your Young Authors!

If you are not in a Young Authors school, you and your students can still write original books to be read and shared by others. You don't need to use a complicated construction for the book. Paper folded, stapled, and wrapped in construction paper or contact paper covers will serve nicely. Something magical happens when children see their names on original written materials. Let the children dictate or write their own stories and illustrate them, as well as helping to make the actual book. Celebrate the books with a party in which the children read and show their books to others. Add the books to your classroom and school library where they can be borrowed and enjoyed by many.

Donald Graves' *Writing: Teachers and Children at Work*[32] includes an easy to follow instructional section on bookbinding.

Be sure to keep the main purpose alive in this project—the encouragement of student writing. Don't let the technical procedures outweigh the value of the writing.

Taking Inventory

Given our need for finding ways to express some of the ideas, feelings, and observations bulging our knapsacks, inventory questions often yield material the writers didn't even realize was waiting to be written. Vary your approach. Write a list of inventory ideas on the board, including the children's suggestions. Or dictate inventory ideas, one at a time, and devote a few minutes to each one. Ditto an inventory sheet and hand it out for students to work on independently. Scatter inventory ideas around the room, in writing centers, on special boards, on free-time activity lists, so as to always prod the mind, stimulate the imagination, and free the writing. Here are a few inventory ideas.

The most beautiful sight I ever saw

The things that scare me the most

The best things to do on a rainy day

The best places in the world

The dullest times

The silliest I've ever been

The most powerful things I know

The loneliest time I've ever had

The cutest animals I know

The ugliest sight I ever saw

My earliest memory

Things I wonder about

My favorite words

Something ordinary

Turn Yourself Into

Human beings write books about fish, elephants, monkeys! *Babar* was not written by an elephant. *Curious George* was not written by a monkey. And *Swimmy* was not authored by a fish! Only human beings have the ability to pretend, to imagine.

Just as "Turn Yourself Into" is an excellent movement and drama starter, so it evokes exciting creative writing responses. Combine the suggestions with music, props, pictures, or objects—whatever is available. Often, the more unusual and challenging the assignment, the better the results.

Turn yourself into an inanimate object and write from that viewpoint.

Turn yourself into one part of your body and write from that viewpoint.

Turn yourself into a part of nature—mountain, river, valley, forest.

Turn yourself into an animal, a building, a color.

Turn yourself into a person very different from yourself and write about how you feel, what you see, what you do, and so on.

Correlate the writing with movement and drama. When writing follows such sessions, you will find unusually strong and dynamic language. With Kathy Liebfreund's fourth/fifth graders, we "turned ourselves into" fish and combined that metamorphosis with the idea of *dream*, a topic the children were exploring. This is part of the group writing that followed the movement drama/music session:

When I was a fish I had these dreams:

I dreamed that I could move my head without moving my body.

In my dream I had a plateful of worms.

I could breathe with lungs instead of gills.

I had imagination.

I lived happily ever after.

When I woke up, I was swimming. I was breathing with gills.

My imagination was gone.

Create Something New

It happened on Halloween. The third graders were telling about all the different costumed characters they had seen roaming the neighborhood on trick-or-treat night. We wrote each character on the board as it was mentioned. In a few minutes, the board was filled with colorful words like witch, robot, clown, garbage can. (Yes, someone was dressed as a garbage can!)

"What if we put two of these characters together and invented a new character?"

Ideas flourished. We were introduced to such new characters as Skelewitch, Batcat, Dracughost, and Darth Goblin. The children wrote about them, illustrated them, demonstrated their movement and sounds.

Try inventing new animals, flowers, superheroes, vehicles, food, colors, names of rock and roll bands, appliances. A.Y.O.

Word Series

This activity is 100 percent guaranteed to start children writing. In earlier chapters, we shared the idea of series of words using the senses and body parts. This idea started accidentally (as do many good ideas). My sixth graders and I were discussing pronouns: I, you, we, they, it. Just for fun, I wrote them on the board this way.

> I
> You
> We
> They
> It

and asked the kids to suggest ways to complete each line. In no time, ideas were written.

> I who stand alone
> You who watch
> We who care
> They who turn their heads
> It is lonely in the dark.

The class continued on their own, experimenting, sharing, and enjoying for the rest of the year. Since then, I have introduced this technique to children of all ages and have had immediate, imaginative responses. Here are a few of the most popular series we tried.

I saw or I see	One
I smelled or I smell	Two
I tasted or I taste	Three
I heard or I hear	Always
I touched or I touch	Never
I knew or I know	
(You may rearrange the order.)	Who
	What
My eyes	When
My ears	Where
My nose	Why
My hands	
My feet	
My heart	
(Change parts or omit *my*.)	

Have the children choose their own series. Experiment with word series based on colors, seasons, animals, places, and people.

> Here is close to me.
> There is way out—away.
> Far is where the North Pole is.
> Near is where my friends are sitting.
> Here is where I always am.
> There is a hard place to be.
> Far is away from home.
> Near is the clock on the wall.
> Everywhere is a great all round place.
>
> > Risa
> > Grade 4

> Hear my small cry from below
> See me reaching for your strength
> Smell the odor that spreads and stays
> Taste the sweetness of life
> Touch my hand and help.
>
> Hear the strength my words hold
> See that I want you to hear
> Smell the dew that life gives off
> Taste my bitterness, my love
> Touch my heart to free it.
>
> > Leslie
> > High school junior

Chick Moorman was trying to write an article. His mind blocked; he couldn't begin. He remembered the word-series exercise we had done in a workshop and tried some. Here is the introduction to his article, "The Flavor of Caring."

One man sat at the sewing machine
    destroying illusions with his presence.
Two large hands moved with precision,
    directing the effort.
A child looked on, receiving more than help.
Never underestimate the strength of gentleness.
Always appreciate the flavor of caring.[33]

Write Colorful Words

This is by no means the last creative writing idea; it's just the one I am going to stop with because time and space have run out. I stumbled on this idea through serendipity. I was sharing Michelangelo's theory of art with a group of fourth graders I was visiting. We talked of his unusual approach—that the idea of the sculpture, the shape of the statue, was already in the marble. Michelangelo's job was not to impose a shape on the marble but to free the already existing shape hidden deep in the block of stone, to chip and cut around it so it would define itself. In the room was a large box of brightly colored felt pens and on the spur of the moment, I thought of a marvelous idea. We translated Michelangelo's theory into a colorful, creative writing exercise.

We each picked a colored felt pen or crayon and pretended that we, like Michelangelo, could see beneath the surface of things. We imagined that the pen had special words that it wanted to write because of its color. A red pen probably wanted to write about certain kinds of red things and feelings. A blue pen would never want to write the same words as a yellow pen. We wrote for a minute or two. Then we traded pens and discovered what those colors wanted to write.

That day, the preschool-aged sister of one of the fourth graders was visiting. She listened to and understood the idea, fully participating in the activity, passing her color to the next person, writing vigorously on her paper with her new color and on through about three changes. Suddenly, she stopped. Blocked.

"What's wrong?" I asked in a worried whisper.

"I can't think of any words for Brown to write," she pouted.

"What about *dirt? Mud?*"

"OK!" her face brightened. She resumed writing with great enthusiasm.

At the end of the day, the children said goodbye and left. Suddenly, it hit me: "She's only four! She can't write yet!"

The classroom teacher and I rushed to find her paper. There, in the midst of the fourth-grade papers filled with color words, her sheet was rich with a four-year-old's hieroglyphs in sets of colors.

We looked at her page of markings and knew that each of them represented a real word in her mind. And there, in the section of Brown ideas, we understood what those two still unrecognizable symbols translated to: Dirt. Mud.

Where does writing begin? With papers? With pencils? With the knowledge of the written language?

None of the above.

Writing begins in the mind.

How Do I Know These Methods Are Working?

Your honest observations and perceptions are the best methods for measuring success. Stop. Look. Listen. Read the signals: *you are always evaluating!*

Checklist for Yourself

1. Are my students writing every day? In what ways?
2. Have I offered interesting, challenging, and diverse opportunities for writing? How?
3. Which were the most effective? Which bombed?
4. Am I continually helping students to express themselves, to respect each other, and to value their works? How?
5. In what ways are my students sharing their writing?
6. How are we celebrating the writing?
7. Are the conferences helpful? successful? Are we learning to be better at the craft as we offer each other helpful, practical suggestions about content, technical factors, process?
8. Are my students writing more easily and with more confidence?
9. Am I writing and sharing with them?
10. Am I learning more about my students? Are they learning more about me? Am I learning more about myself?

I don't know of any activity that more effectively contributes to a closer relationship between people than sharing their creative writing. Equally if not more important to the evaluation process is how your students feel about their writing. They are the real focus of the evaluation process. Self-searching questions shared with them as a group and individually will yield valuable information as well as provide further spurs for originality and freedom. Ask questions that evoke honest and open responses.

Some Questions for the Class

1. Did you enjoy writing this? Why?
2. How did you get the idea?
3. Which parts of the writing did you like the most? Starting off? Reworking your idea? Polishing it up?
4. Which parts were the most difficult? In what areas do you think you need more practice?
5. If you wrote this again, would you change it? How?
6. What other ideas are simmering in your mind?
7. What do you want to write about next?
8. How do you feel about the class discussions and conferences?

9. Any suggestions for more ways to share our writing?

10. Any suggestions for helpful and enjoyable writing exercises?

As we look at activities that help children improve their expository writing skills, remember that the suggestions in this chapter and the rest of the book can be molded to fit many purposes. Sense charts, word gatherings, word explosions, beginnings, inventories—all are excellent ways to enrich *any* writing.

Add the following ideas (those you like, of course!) to your growing cache of resources. Take the worry out of writing. *The only way to learn to write is to write and write and write.*

QUESTION: What do I want my students to learn?

ANSWER: I want my students to learn to enjoy organizing their thoughts, gathering information, and writing factual material to share with others.

Your Room as a Learning Lab

Your room is a dynamic place. Its many ongoing elements provide material and motivation for organizing information.

Pets

Don't miss the learning opportunities inherent in taking care of pets. Children can do so many valuable things with their pets. They can observe them and keep records, progress charts, sketches, daily logs, and background information on them. They can then summarize their findings on index cards or in a notebook displayed near the pet's tank or cage.

A second-grade class keeps daily records of the development of tadpoles into frogs. No chapter in the best science book can equal such firsthand observations.

Plants

As plants grow, so can children's awareness and powers of observation. Children enjoy caring for their plants and writing labels or booklets for each plant, complete with name, directions for care, and the plant's growth history.

Kindergartners fill egg crates with soil, plant different seeds in each section, label each, keep class charts on the growth of the plants, and rejoice as sunflowers grow tall, lima beans sprout, and sprays of sweet peas flower. They later replant them in larger pots or outdoors. Their information chart on their plants is filled with wonderful facts that they know to be true from their own eyes and hands.

Third graders set sweet potatoes and avocado pits in water and watch the roots and stems grow. Their reports on the project clearly express their excitement as well as convey important information.

Birds

If you have a tree outside your window, don't miss learning opportunities that may prove to be the most memorable of your year.

Frayda Turkel hung two bird feeders in the tree outside her window. Even though the number and variety of birds drawn to the feeder were a continuously fascinating subject, she and her students set aside a specific time for official observation, assigning responsibility for the "report" to different children each day. Using such resource books as *Peterson's Field Guide to the Birds*, the children kept a daily log of birdwatching that featured such birds as white-crowned sparrows, purple finches, downy woodpeckers, and black-capped chickadees. The kids flew high on vocabulary that year!

Book Nook

In the special place in your room that features books, set aside space for reviews and recommendations.

A fifth grade used index cards for brief summaries and opinions of books. They kept them in a file box in alphabetical order so they were always available for children to discover new reading adventures recommended by classmates. Book reviews are part of reading, and their purpose is sharing. Some fourth graders have a small loose-leaf notebook filled with book reviews they have written, kept always available for sharing. Sixth graders design book jackets for just-read books and write their book review on the jacket. Whenever possible, the book jackets are displayed on a table or the wall.

Daily Schedules

Even in the most open classrooms, there is some kind of organization for the day. Kids enjoy writing these programs and seeing their words take shape as activities and lessons.

In a third grade, a committee is chosen to help write the plans each day. They meet with the teacher for a few minutes and discuss the day. They decide how they want to write the plan—on the board, on a chart, or on ditto paper to be run off with copies for each member of the class. They enjoy organizing the information of the day into a coherent program that is easy to follow.

Weather Reports

Weather affects everyone. Observing firsthand, checking the daily newspaper, and listening to weather reports on the radio are common ways people find out about the weather.

Writing brief weather reports is a daily writing project in many classrooms. Each child has a turn as the Weather Reporter, writing a short, clear report that can be illustrated or diagrammed and presenting it to the class first thing in the morning. It can be added to the class log or to a weather report clipboard.

Sharing Hobbies, Experiments, and Projects

In classes where teachers teach in the "key of life," sharing is part of an ongoing process, a constant element in the everyday pattern, not relegated to a brief time slot once a week. Connect *sharing* with the idea of magic vocabularies. Each and every one of these sharings launches a written project.

Jamie shares his stamp collection with his sixth-grade classmates. He is encouraged to write a report about stamp-collecting for the class newspaper. Matthew builds a bird house, then shows it at school before putting it in the tree. He draws diagrams and writes directions for building the bird house. Two other boys use copies of the directions to build their own bird houses. After telling the class about her visit to Disneyland, Marcie organizes a committee that writes and illustrates a tour book about Disneyland, which is later presented to the children's ward of the hospital.

Some Thoughts on Reports

There's a direct link between children's interests and their high motivation for writing reports. Perhaps your report writing experiences in elementary school were similar to mine. The teacher alone assigned the topic for the report. Reports were *serious business* and could count for a large part of one's grade. We had perhaps four or five reports in a year and *each was a traumatic experience*. Too many children today are still writing these few anxiety-ridden reports on which much of their grade depends. Many times, they are still not given the opportunity to choose their own topics for the reports.

There is a better way to help students develop practical writing skills. Paul S. Anderson urges you to consider reports as natural outgrowths of children's interest in their environment. "When the material is pertinent, well-organized and interestingly presented, the report serves to enrich the ongoing experiences of the children."[34]

In creative classrooms, *report writing of every type is going on all the time*. It's a natural extension of interest, curiosity, and the desire to share information. It is far more relevant to the lives of the students than any assigned report topic could be, since the students choose topics that are important to them. Within the process of learning how to write expository language, it doesn't matter whether a child does a research report on the History of Rock and Roll or Professional Football in America. In classrooms where education is a shared adventure, children will gladly write reports on anything. Consequently, it is vitally important for you to be tuned in to your students' interests and feelings. It is also important for you to broaden their interests. The more experiences children have in writing on a variety of subjects with a variety of purposes, the more competent and confident they will grow daily.

Since reports are meant to convey information, clarity of language and style is very important. Your students will readily understand the importance of presenting facts in a clear way if you give an example of the consequences of misinformation, such as "What if you read a report about your favorite team and the writer didn't present the information accurately? What if he confused some of the facts and wrote *won* instead of *lost*, or mixed up the players?"

Reports come in all sizes and shapes: on index cards explaining a classroom project, in newspaper articles, in the form of a book, as a letter, as a diagram with explanations. Reports can range from one paragraph to one page to more complicated booklet-sized products handled in greater depth.

Help strengthen your students' skills in expository writing by giving them opportunities to write on many topics of varying length and depth.

Marking Reports   Nothing is sadder than to see a child who worked very hard on a writing project receive a D or a 65. Demolishing egos is not conducive to motivation and is the antithesis of encouraging and giving positive reinforcement. There are ways to ensure success to every person who attempts expository writing, while at the same time giving helpful technical direction. Two major ones come to mind.

Don't mark every single report. Consider many of the reports as extensions of sharing. Because communication is the purpose of the report, and because communication is blocked by sloppiness, misspellings, and mistakes in usage and punctuation, there must still be an emphasis on accuracy, clarity, and neatness. But all children who write sharing reports should be given extra credit in your records. Don't make the credit the major purpose for the reports; treat it as an acknowledgment of their contributions.

The few reports that are assigned can still be successful experiences for those who write them. *Two marks can be given*: one for the overall effort and spirit of the report, the other for the technical aspects of the report. With your students, work out a marking system that includes codes such as *SP* for spelling, *N* for neatness, *P* for punctuation.

Mary, a fifth grader, wrote about birds' nests for her monthly report. She received an A for effort and an interesting topic and a C for technical aspects of writing. She had eleven mistakes in spelling, paragraphing, usage, and punctuation. Within two days, she had corrected her paper and the technical mark was changed to an A. A wonderful story about marking reports comes from a fourth-grade teacher. She explained to her students that in order to give report card grades she needed to have papers to evaluate and grade. Since writing projects of all kinds were a daily activity in her class, she offered the students the opportunity to choose which of their papers they wanted graded. She had two boxes on her desk, one labelled Mark and another labelled Don't Mark. Materials for the Mark box included paragraphs of explanation, report on a specific topic, biography of a person, and letters of invitation, request for information, thank you, complaint, and opinion. It was the students' responsibility to provide her with enough material to evaluate and grade. At the end of the first marking quarter, she had very few examples of the students' work in the Mark box. The class was still inhibited and insecure about writing. By the second quarter, after a few months of writing all the time, both boxes were overflowing with the children's work.

Questions

We have talked about questions throughout this book. In too many classes only teachers ask questions. Many discourage their students' questions because they are afraid they will be unable to answer them. Yet questions are merely reflections of a healthy curiosity. They provide students with *direction in research, information gathering,* and *reporting. Questions expand the imagination and stretch the mind.* In creative classes, both teachers and students ask questions.

Questions can be used as the basis for report writing. List questions about a topic, grouping together those that deal with similar ideas. Your students can then choose the questions they wish to answer in their reports from these lists. They can work individually or in groups. Looking for answers to questions is the most basic learning of all.

Letter Writing Can Be Fun

Every standard language arts textbook devotes space to examples of the many different types of letters that children may need to know how to write. Use the following activities to make letter writing a natural part of your students' day.

Guests   When guests are invited to visit the class, invitations and thank-you notes are integral to the experience.

Research   Gather information by mailing postcards around the country. Ask your students to express their opinions on important current events by writing letters to members of Congress, mayors, governors, the president, the United Nations, or newspaper editors.

Classified Ads   Read the employment ads and then write letters of application. Tape ads to the top of each student's application and then pass it around the room. Classmates read the applications and write comments as if they were the person hiring the applicant.

Class Pen Pals   Have each student pick the name of a classmate out of a grab bag. For one week everyone writes different types of letters, such as complaint, thank you, invitations, greetings, requests for information, and expressions of sympathy. Each letter should be answered.

Teacher–Student Pen Pals   One year, Nancy Atwell and her eighth graders wrote more than 2,000 pages of letters to each other. At the beginning of the year, she introduced the letter writing activity with her own letter to her students inviting them to "write letters to me and I'll write letters back to you. In your letters to me, talk with me about what you've read. Tell me what you liked and didn't like and why. Tell me what these books meant to you and said to you."[35]

Class–to–Class Pen Pals   There are national and international programs that help bring classes of children together through correspondence. Many teachers arrange with friends who teach in other schools to have their students exchange letters during the school year.

Residents of Nursing Homes   Often forgotten, older people are most touched and responsive to the letters of children. In many cities, classes are encouraged to "adopt a grandparent" or participate in the Foster Grandparents program through letter writing.

Letters to Authors   (If you want *real* responses, be sure the authors are living. If not, turn the project into a creative writing activity!) Most authors of children's literature are very responsive to letters from their readers.

For an excellent reading resource, set aside a special place in your room to display or collect responses to your students' letters.

Newspapers and Magazines

Nothing encourages expository writing as effectively as a publication deadline—especially when readers are waiting impatiently for the next issue. Imaginative teachers can stimulate good writing through diverse approaches to newspaper and magazine publishing.

Hallow your time together with a newspaper reporting events, special projects, interviews with students, book reviews, field trips, classified ads—all the drama and doings of your class's days.

If you and your class have chosen a name for the year, a newspaper celebrating your uniqueness is a natural outcome. I received a copy of a sixth grade's class newspaper called *Space Cadets' Chronicle*. When you have a name, you don't have to search far for a newspaper title.

Time Machine Newspapers   One sixth grade wrote a newspaper for every culture they studied. Illustrations, maps, diagrams, cartoons, and sketches of famous people were included in the newspaper. After studying Ancient Rome, they divided into groups, each group writing about a different aspect of life in that time.

Good News Gazette   Tired of bad news? For a treat, write a Good News Gazette. Summarize with your students *all* the parts of a newspaper and write them on the board. Leave nothing out: editorials, comic strips, local–state–national–international news, classifieds, and so on. (Quite a vocabulary list!) Now, mix with our old friends "What if?"

"What if one day our newspaper had nothing in it but *good news?* Not one negative word. What would we read in all the columns, news stories, letters, reviews, weather, sports news—in *every* section of the paper?"

Pause for imagining.

"How about everyone in the class writing one kind of newspaper item—story, editorial, forecast, whatever—and write *only* good news!"

I give the group just a short time to do this writing activity while playing Anne Murray's song "A Little Good News" (*A Little Good News*, Capitol Records) as background.

In no time, we have produced a rich variety of materials. We read them all aloud (they are usually delightful) and, after basic editing and rewriting, paste and clip and run off our finished product.

Here is a news item from such a gazette dated January 13, 1984.

Teachers Cruising

Today was the last day of school for the 83–84 school year. The teachers are being rewarded for their fine efforts this year with a three-month Caribbean cruise.

Kirstin Kraft

Interviews: An Example of a School–Community Partnership

Ronni Hochman wanted to find a way to help her middle-school special ed students learn to gather information, sort it out, organize it, write it clearly, and meet success at every step.

Using career education as an initial focus, Ronni reached out to the large department store that had established a special partnership with her school. (Fortunately, programs like "Adopt a School" have gained great popularity in communities across the country!)

A "project" evolved that stretched through the entire school year; strengthened all subject areas, intergroup relations, every aspect of language; and yes, fulfilled the requirement of success at every step!

Most of the activities centered around interviews and the interviewing process. Ronni's kids

discussed, tested, role-played career ideas;

asked questions about various career options, organized questions into categories covering different aspects of vocational offerings;

watched videos of a local TV interviewer, invited him to the class, interviewed him, became the subjects of interviews *by* him;

with staff from the department store, learned of the many different kinds of jobs in the company;

were matched with specific employees from the store based on type of job interest each kid expressed an interest in;

prepared folders of highly organized questions covering every category of concern and interest regarding the specific job they were researching;

came to the store to meet their subjects for in-depth interviews (each student had a tape recorder);

were accompanied by a group of non–special ed students who photographed each of the department store employees during the interview process;

after the day at the store, began the long process of *transcribing the interviews*. With persistence, patience, and lots of group encouragement, all of the students finished transcribing their interviews.

completed the difficult job of outlining, selecting, organizing, and preparing the interviews for final form.

By the time the school celebrated its annual Spirit Day in May, Ronni's students' interviews were neatly organized, written or typed, and mounted next to the photographs and were enjoyed and appreciated by school, families, and community.[36]

To Ronni, *all* education is, as it should be, *special!*

As you may have noticed, none of these chapters *end*, they just *stop* due to the limitations of space and time. Before you look over the evaluation suggestions, enjoy this anecdote shared by a first-grade teacher at a recent NCTE conference.

She had been out sick for a few days. When she returned to school, her first graders smothered her with hugs and chatter. They had so much to tell her. She suggested that they sit right down and *write* her a letter or a note telling whatever they wanted. They were busily writing when one little boy whispered to her, "I forgot how to spell your name."

She whispered back, "It's right there on the wall near the door. You can copy it."

After the children left for the day, she read over their letters. She came to the paper of the child who didn't know how to spell her name and read,

I LOVE YOU, FIRE EXIT

Write? Of Course Write!

Write with your class every day because, like any other activity, writing needs to be practiced in order to be mastered. We cannot expect children to learn how to write with confidence and competency if they are given few opportunities to practice and if these opportunities are accompanied by tension. Think of writing as a *daily necessity*, a *natural and enjoyable habit*. If you do, your room will overflow with the wonderful words of your students. Writing will become an integral part of their lives—and of yours.

Checklist for Yourself

1. Am I listening to discussion, responses, questions, the sharing of students' writing and writing ideas?

2. Am I writing with my students? Am I sharing my work with them?

3. Are my written or spoken comments helpful, encouraging, and appreciative?

4. Am I doing all I can to foster creativity and excitement about writing? to encourage expansion of knowledge by having my students practice gathering and organizing information?

5. Am I providing opportunities for my students to write every day?

6. Am I in touch with my students' lives and interests so that I am aware of what subjects interest them? Am I matching their interests with expository writing activities?

7. What have I done to motivate those students who seem disinterested? What other approaches might I try?

8. Which students appear to be uncomfortable when asked to write? How can I put them at ease?

9. Am I offering enough resource materials?

10. Is my criticism or correction conveyed with warmth and care or does it seem harsh?

Checklist for the Class

1. Are all the students writing? Who isn't writing?

2. Are the students excited about what they are writing?

3. Are the writing experiences diverse enough for the students to learn flexibility and openness in expressing themselves on paper?

4. Are the students experiencing success at finding the answers to their questions? Are they growing more skilled at organizing information?

5. Which projects did they find the most difficult? the most interesting?

6. Are they communicating their ideas clearly to each other?

7. What improvements or changes would they recommend if they were to do the project over?

8. Do they feel more confident about expressing their ideas?

9. Do they feel more confident about their technical skills?

10. In what areas do they feel they need to improve?

11. Are they more aware of good writing?

More Excellent Resources

All of the teachers' magazines feature ideas for writing in every issue. The journals of the International Reading Association, National Council of Teachers of English, and National Association for the Education of Young Children offer a wide variety of materials.

Such diverse books as the following also offer many helpful suggestions.

Marjorie Franks, *If You're Trying to Teach Kids to Write, You've Gotta Have This Book!* (Nashville: Incentive, 1979).

Flora J. Arnstein, *Children Write Poetry* (New York: Dover, 1967).

Hugh Mearns, *Creative Power: The Education of Youth in the Creative Arts*, 2nd rev. ed. (New York: Dover, 1958).

Lucy McCormick Calkins, *The Art of Teaching Writing* (Portsmouth: Heinemann Educational, 1986).

For imaginative and innovative approaches to teaching writing, write to Teachers and Writers Collaborative, 5 Union Square West, New York, New York 10003.

Heinemann Educational Books offers excellent materials for language arts, especially writing. The address is Heinemann Educational Books, 70 Court Street, Portsmouth, New Hampshire 03801.

If you're *open* to ideas, they are all around you; if you're *closed*, they're nowhere to be found—even in the best of materials!

The books, poems, stories, plays, articles you are reading now have within them seeds of ideas for creative interpretations and expansions. For example, Maureen Reedy's fourth graders enjoyed their own original "One Inch Tall" stories and poems inspired by Shel Silverstein's poem "One Inch Tall" (from *Where the Sidewalk Ends*, Harper & Row, 1974). Children write their own "mitzi's" after sharing those written by Lore Segal in *Tell Me a Mitzi* (Scholastic Books, 1970). Read a book like *Guess Who My Favorite Person Is* by Byrd Ballor (Scribner's, 1977) and gather at least twenty-five writing ideas!

As with all creative teaching, be a person on whom "nothing is lost."

ENDNOTES

[1] James Moffett, *A Student-Centered Language Arts Curriculum, Grades K-12: A Handbook for Teachers* (Boston: Houghton, 1968) 23.

[2] Mauree Applegate, *Helping Children Write*, 3rd ed. (Evanston: Row, 1961) 1.

[3] William M. Logan and Virgil G. Logan, *A Dynamic Approach to Language Arts* (Toronto: McGraw, 1967) 339.

[4] Lois Lenski, "Helping Children to Create," *Childhood Education* 26 (Nov. 1949): 101–105.

[5] Lucy McCormick Calkins, *Lessons from a Child: On the Teaching and Learning of Writing* (Portsmouth: Heinemann Educational, 1983) 7.

[6] Logan and Logan, *A Dynamic Approach to Language Arts* 301–302.

[7] Moffett, *A Student-Centered Language Arts Curriculum* 11.

[8] See Betty Jane Wagner, "Integrating the Language Arts," *Language Arts* 62.5 (Sept. 1985): 557–60.

[9] James Moffett and Betty Jane Wagner, *Student-Centered Language Arts and Reading, K-12*, 3rd ed. (Boston: Houghton, 1983) 38.

[10] Interview with the author.

[11] Applegate, *Helping Children Write* 1.

[12] Lenski, "Helping Children to Create."

[13] Susan Hall and Chris Hall, interview with the author.

[14] Leland B. Jacobs, "Teaching Children More about Words and Their Ways," *Elementary English* 41 (Jan. 1964): 30–34.

[15] Pablo Neruda, *Memoirs*, trans. Hardie St. Martin (New York: Farrar, 1977) 53–54. Ellipsis points are from original.

[16] Calkins, *Lessons from a Child* 125, 126.

[17] Donald H. Graves, *Writing: Teachers and Children at Work* (Portsmouth: Heinemann Educational, 1983) 107–117.

[18] Logan and Logan, *A Dynamic Approach to Language Arts* 310.

[19] Applegate, *Helping Children Write* 2–3.

[20] Ken Macrorie, *Telling Writing* (New York: Hayden, 1970) 22.

[21] Hugh Mearns, "Forward" to Flora Arnstein, *Children Write Poetry* (New York: Dover, 1967).

[22] Ted Hughes, *Poetry Is* (Garden City: Doubleday, 1970) xv, xvi.

[23] Wallace Stevens, "Adagia," *Opus Posthumous* (New York: Knopf, 1957) 176.

[24] Michael Rosen participates in the Ohio Arts Council's Poets in the Schools and in the Greater Columbus Arts Council's Artists in the Schools. His collections of poems, *A Drink at the Mirage,* was selected for the *Princeton Series of Contemporary Poets* (Princeton UP, 1984).

[25] Interview with the author.

[26] Arnold Adoff has written numerous collections of poetry for children, among them *EATS, Tornado, All the Colors of the Race, Today We Are Brother and Sister,* and *Outside/Inside Poems* (all, Lothrop, Lee and Shepard Books). His work with children at the Ridgemont School in Mount Victory, Ohio, was written about by Diane L. Chapman, "Poet to Poet: An Author Responds to Child-Writers," *Language Arts* 62.3 (Mar. 1985): 235–42.

[27] Interview with the author.

[28] See Dee Dishon and Chick Moorman's book *Our Classroom: We Can Learn Together* (Englewood Cliffs: Prentice, 1983) for numerous ideas on writing suggestions that encourage cooperation and success. Chick and Dee are national consultants in creative education. Write to them at their Institute for Personal Power, P.O. Box 68, Portage, Michigan 49081.

[29] Jed Garrick, "Answer in Bright Green," in *You and Contemporary Poetry,* ed. George Abbe (Dublin, NH: Bauhan, 1965).

[30] Carl Sandburg, "Limited," *The Complete Poems of Carl Sandburg,* rev. ed. (New York: Harcourt, 1970).

[31] Theodore Roethke, *Straw for the Fire* (Garden City: Doubleday, 1974).

[32] Graves, *Writing* 59–62.

[33] Chick Moorman, "The Flavor of Caring," *The Alternative* 3.3.

[34] Paul S. Anderson, *Language Skills in Elementary Education* (New York: Macmillan, 1968) 359.

[35] Nancy Atwell's work in language was written up by Fred Hechinger, "Teaching the Excitement of Reading, *The New York Times* 24 Apr. 1984.

[36] Ronni's project took place in 1984–85 in cooperation with Hastings Middle School, Upper Arlington, Ohio, and the Lazarus Company.

10

Make letters
with clay.
Roll it
Shape it A a

Love

Smile When You Say "Skills"

"You ought to write 'A HAPPY BIRTHDAY' on it."
"*That* was what I wanted to ask you," said Pooh. "Because my
spelling is Wobbly. It's good spelling but it Wobbles, and the letters
get in the wrong places. Would *you* write 'A Happy Birthday' on it for
me?"

A. A. MILNE[1]

Let's play a word game. Consider the word *skills*. If you take off the first letter, what do you have? *kills*. Now, *s* begins some important, positive words that will remind you to teach the skills the way I have suggested throughout this book. But *s* also begins some words that will destroy any chances for success in teaching the tools of the language. In one minute, list all the *s* words that will guarantee *skills* won't become *kills*. In one minute, list all the words that will guarantee *kills* instead of *skills*.

Here is my own list:

Skills	*Kills*
sacred	stale
spirit	scorn
safe	scowl
secure	strict
support	scare
success	scold
synthesize	suppress
share	strangle
self-directed	struggle
self-respect	stigmatize
spontaneity	sin
serendipity	silence
stimulate	shame
strengths	snobby
special	self-righteous

Let's play another game. Here is a portion of the first verse of Genesis as found in the Oxford Bible (King James version) but presented without punctuation or capital letters. Will you punctuate the passage?

in the beginning god created the heaven and the earth and the earth was without form and void and darkness was upon the face of the deep and the spirit of god moved upon the face of the waters and god said let there be light and there was light and god saw the light that it was good and god divided the light from the darkness and god called the light day and the darkness he called night and the evening and the morning were the first day

Are you satisfied with your punctuation? Compare your work with others'. Did everyone punctuate the passage in the same way? Were you able to easily read the passages that had different punctuation? Which do you consider *more important*, the words or the punctuation?

In 1948, a punctuation experiment was conducted with fifty-seven graduate students. They punctuated Hamlet's soliloquy in twenty-three different ways.

They punctuated the first twenty-four words of the Lord's Prayer in thirty-two different ways. The study also showed that the same individuals would have punctuated the same material differently a week later.[2]

An Approach to Teaching the Skills

Do you remember how you were taught the skills? Were those important language tools emphasized throughout your school days as part of all subject areas, or were they relegated to a specific time and treated as separate subjects? Did you consider a sentence a group of words that expressed a complete thought or a punishment inflicted on a convicted person?

Intensified pressure on schools to "get back to basics" often makes it difficult for educators to maintain their calm holding position in the eye of the storm. In the cross-currents of alarmist headlines and emotional hearings, many teachers succumb—forgetting that the first syllable in *fundamentals* is FUN, forgetting everything they believe about creativity, positive climate, reassurance, success, and enjoyment. The rules of language are the *real* thing! The rest is frills!

Most adults have loving patience and good instincts with young children as they learn to crawl, stand, walk, and talk. We reward them not only for being right but for being *close*. What happens when they start school? Andrea Butler and Jan Turbill describe the incongruity of our attitudes toward the teaching of skills:

> A toddler points to a cup on the table and says, "Dat Daddy cup."
>
> No parent ever responds by saying, "You stupid child. You left out the auxiliary (indicative mood) *is* and the possessive *'s* and you mispronounced *that*. Now, say after me: 'This is Daddy's cup.' "
>
> How many children would want to go on with the task of learning to talk if this is how we treated them? Yet, a common experience I have, as I talk with teachers and observe classroom activities, is that, with regard to the written mode of language, children are expected to display adult competence from the beginning.[3]

What do we get when we mix rigid attitudes toward the teaching of skills with feelings of failure and low self-image on the parts (and in the hearts) of children? We get thousands of young people who never discover or experience the wonders of language and who consequently "hate" English! I took an informal poll at a nearby high school, asking about fifty students to tell me their favorite and least favorite subjects. More than half of them immediately responded, in almost the same words each time, "I *hate* English! It's my worst subject!"

How do you think children could possibly be taught to hate their own language? I think children learn to fear their language when they are taught the skills in an isolated way, separate from all other classroom activities. When the skills of handwriting, spelling, punctuation, and usage are viewed as ends in themselves rather than as means to ends, an inflexible approach will often develop. Numerous studies have found that when grammatical terminology is

not connected with an activity regularly used by the children, it is easily confused and forgotten. No evidence has yet been found that the formal teaching of traditional grammar results in excellent writing and speaking. In fact, the reverse seems to be true. Where a great deal of grammar is taught at the expense of practice in writing and speaking, children make very poor gains in their English expression.[4]

James Moffett suggests three keys to improving the language arts curriculum:

1. *individualization* of learning tasks;
2. *interaction* among individuals for oral language development and the benefits of small-group dynamics in all the language arts;
3. *integration* of learning across subjects, media, and kinds of discourse, so that individuals may continuously synthesize their own thought structures.[5]

Imaginative and creative teachers combine those three factors all the time. Carol Gray's third graders work in groups of all sizes, helping each other, teaching each other, sharing ideas and suggestions. Carol has a quiet room, an orderly room, but "I don't like children to sit still all day."

Carol looks at her students and tries to find where their problems are: "That's where we start."

Each person is different.

Ten-year-old Mark—speaking no English, only Spanish—was very lucky to have Carol as his third-grade teacher when he arrived in the United States to be adopted by a new family. Her classroom was a room of *individualization, interaction,* and *integration!*

He has thirty teachers! The kids want him to succeed, constantly tell him how great he's doing. Even when he's frustrated, he won't give up and the kids won't let him give up. . . . We immediately told him any word he didn't know. We show him, telling it, reading it, writing it. We try to touch all bases. . . . We have a reading–writing class so language is going on all the time. In September, he couldn't say one word in English and he couldn't read one letter. Now (January), he's gone from not being able to speak to getting scolded in the halls and cafeteria for talking too much! He's reading on a first-grade level and can skim and find key words. He's very close, on the verge, of writing good answers!

Teaching the Skills*

Obviously, children must learn the basic tools of their language or they will be severely handicapped in activities involving written and verbal communication. In this chapter, the question is not what skills should be taught. Rather the important questions are How? When? Why?

What is the purpose of teaching the skills? When is the best time to teach them, and how should they be taught? In what context? In what spirit? Your answers to these questions will help shape your method and may even determine the success of your efforts. In getting your ideas together, it is helpful to find out what some of the scholars in the field of language arts have to contribute to your understanding. You may even be surprised to discover how simple and practical their conclusions are.

Ruth Strickland sees the teaching of the skills as a matter of courtesy, of being able to "speak and write in accepted form so that others will not be inconvenienced, confused or misled by an unfortunate choice of words, poor handwriting, unfamiliar spelling or misleading punctuation."[6] The purpose of teaching the skills is to help children learn to communicate more accurately and more confidently with a minimum of obstacles.

Paul S. Anderson says spelling starts when the child first seeks to produce a written word in order to tell something.[7] He urges you to remember that children work on problems of sentence structure, pronunciation, punctuation, and word meanings in nearly every period of the school day. These skills have value in the daily, functional use of language. Very limited results are produced when instruction on any aspect of language is isolated and taught without reason or understanding on the part of the students. Children should see the skills as being of immediate service to them. The skills should be practiced in many situations on an ongoing basis, not forgotten immediately because they have been taught in a boxed-in way, unconnected to any other activity.[8]

William M. Logan and Virgil G. Logan emphasize the importance of *using* the language: listening, speaking, reading, and writing. "Through practice in meaningful situations, mastery of language becomes an exciting adventure, not

*A book to help you keep your head together as you think about the skills in relation to language learning is Kenneth Goodman's *What's Whole in Whole Language?* (Portsmouth, N.H.: Heinemann Educational Books, 1986).

a set of rules which have long since lost their vitality." The skills are taught not through mechanical exercises but "through practice in the understanding expression and communication of meanings and purposes which grow out of or arise naturally in the life of the students."[9] Children learn the most about the language by speaking it and hearing it!

What I Believe

Communication between people is a beautiful achievement. Helping others learn to communicate with ease and confidence is a loving goal. In order to move in that direction, children must learn about the structure of the language and its usage. These skills are really matters of habit that can only improve through practice and experience. Memorizing rules is futile if children see no application of the rules to everyday situations. Punctuation should not be treated as an inflexible set of regulations. Punctuation is part of breathing, pausing, changing voice levels, and conveying meanings. It is like a system of signals keeping the traffic of words from piling up or colliding with each other. When young children play at writing, they also play at punctuation. The want to learn to make order out of their words.

I believe that the skills are part of all the language strands. Children are working on these skills through all activities and lessons during the day. They are practicing their language from the moment they wake in the morning until they close their eyes at night.

Two Learning Experiences

Read and reflect on these ideas, for they will help you to shape your own attitudes toward teaching skills. But remember, *if ideas are not reflected in behavior, they are of limited value*. No vicarious experience can equal the knowledge and understandings that result from the on-the-spot observations of teachers and children in classrooms. If I could, I would take you by the hand and introduce you to the many outstanding people who are at this very minute teaching creatively, originally, or humanistically (invent your own label). But we are confined to the printed page and so, for now, we must settle for secondhand experiences that need your imagination and your responsiveness to provide the immediacy of direct experience.

Visit a First Grade   Let's visit Bernice Dunn's first-grade class. Her room is alive with pictures, words, and projects. The children are working, both in small groups and individually, on a number of projects. Everyone is relaxed and comfortable in the room. Some of the children line up at Mrs. Dunn's desk and ask for words to use in stories. She writes each word they need on a card, and the children return to their desks to continue their writing. They keep the words in colorfully decorated boxes they have made. When they need a word, they can find it in their box or ask Mrs. Dunn to write it for them. They have learned to read and spell all the words in their boxes and share them with their classmates.

Bernice Dunn is considered a master teacher and conducts in-service workshops to introduce her colleagues to her successful approach to teaching skills. Listen carefully to her deeply felt beliefs.

> Young children are already indoctrinated to want everything right. It's a sin to be wrong. I want them to know that our language is inconsistent, that it's not an easy language. I don't want them to stop the creative flow of ideas because of not knowing how to spell a word. They *know* hundreds and hundreds of words and want to use them in their stories. If they have to wait for me to give them the right spelling word or interrupt what they're doing to go and look it up in the dictionary, the important idea mulling around in their imaginations won't come out. I just tell them to spell the word the way it sounds to them and we'll correct it later. Their original spellings of words are absolutely marvelous. I've collected them over the years. Would you like to see a list?

Mysterious Spellings

next stordaber	next door neighbor
alathawaup	all the way up
lecdrek	electric
rtst	artist
youmenbein	human being
wereed	worried
vakumklenr	vacuum cleaner
jimnozzme	Jim knows me
filisdiler	Phyllis Diller
plgavalegents	pledge of allegiance

You can learn many things from the children's attempts to spell words they know. Teachers like Bernice Dunn base the bulk of their phonics, spelling, pronunciation, and reading lessons on translating these words into acceptable forms. The children's spellings reveal *the way they hear sounds as well as what sounds they don't hear.*

> I never want the kids to think that their language is inferior in any way. I lean to their side. I really try to listen to what they are trying to say. When a child says, "I brung you some flowers, Mrs. Dunn" I say, "Thank you for the wonderful present." Later, we'll try to help develop more socially acceptable speech patterns. But gently, never putting down the children.

Dunn talks specifically about how she teaches the skills.

> First, you don't have to teach everything to everybody. You need to teach only what the children lack. Each child has special needs. If you are actively involved with the children, you pick up on their strengths and weaknesses. If two kids are pronouncing *f* for *th,* you'll get with those two people by themselves. No need for twenty-five people to drill over something they already understand.

When I see that the majority of the children need work in one area, I'll say, "Hold on. We need to learn something together," and it will be a group experience with a lot of checking up afterward, asking them individually, "Did you get that? Did you understand that?"

We have many informal spelling lists. All the lessons come from their own work and words—their own speech, writings, experiences. I read to them a lot. They read to each other. We do a great deal of sharing and each day yields new understandings. Take exclamation marks. When children read or tell stories and their voices rise excitedly, we talk about exclamation points. We call them "excitement marks," and we first discover them through oral language, then transfer our learning to their written work. The skills are taught as they are needed. They come naturally out of what we are doing and are taught as part of the doing—to help the doing!

How can you separate the skills from the total language experience? All this continuous input and output. Where does one component begin and the other end? I have to think of the language process as a totality.

If you press, Dunn will admit to you that her students' scores on standardized tests have soared. The children especially excel in the language arts areas of word usage and structural analysis. Of far greater importance than scores on standardized tests is the confidence, pride, and zest of all the children in the class. They love school. It is obvious that their inner selves are being strengthened daily. They are lucky to have Bernice Dunn for a teacher, and outstanding "youmenbein," who says the feeling is mutual.[10]

Visit a Fifth Grade   Fasten your seat belts. This field trip has one more stop. We are visiting Shirley Davis, who works under a Community Resources program, initiating special enrichment activities in language arts with intermediate classes. One of her favorite projects is to help students write their own books and present them to the library to be shared with their schoolmates. The children discuss books and discover the many kinds they enjoy, such as science fiction, travel, and mysteries. Creative writing exercises charge their imaginations and make them aware that they, too, can write interesting words that others would want to read. They have time to think about the kind of book they want to write. All kinds of books are welcome. As the children work on their rough drafts, they also learn how to make the books themselves. They cut the pages, sew the bindings, and choose contact-paper designs for the covers. To enhance the project, a local author is invited to share experiences and ideas.

Davis has been working with a large group of mischievous, active fifth graders. They have finally finished rough copies of their original books. Davis tells us about the special procedure that works so successfully.

The class forms small groups of four or five children that think of themselves as editorial committees. They go over each manuscript, make suggestions, give helpful ideas, and work together to help the writer produce the best possible story. The writer doesn't have to accept the suggestions or corrections, but usually does because they are obviously good ones and are given in a positive spirit. We never say, "You spelled that word wrong!" or "You said that in a dumb way!" but rather, "Let's read this part over. Is that the way you

want to say it? Does it sound right to you?" or "That word is misspelled. Let's check it." There is never hesitation. Children run to the dictionary, run to their English books to check on words and usage. The process involves reading, listening, talking together, cooperating, and helping. Each manuscript goes through this process, so by the time it is being typed, it has five good friends who really care about it and are involved in it.

Davis called on parents to volunteer to type the children's books into final copies. Today, Carol Lee is typing. Children are gathered around her. Except for occasional exchanges between Carol and the author of the manuscript she is typing, the children are very quiet.

I was very touched by the whole experience. You saw the kids hover over me as I typed. They watched every word. They wanted it typed exactly as they wrote it. They questioned every change. I didn't correct grammar or usage but the spelling and punctuation errors their Editorial Committee missed, yes. But I had to check each error with the author before I corrected it. I said, "This doesn't look right. Will you look it over?" and the child checked in the dictionary, wrote down the correct word, and gave me permission to change the original spelling. I couldn't believe how quiet and attentive the kids were. They waited very patiently for their turns. They were so anxious for me to do this. They were so afraid someone was going to change what they wrote. I was really struck by how much these books are part of them. They wanted to protect them. They wanted them to be just right![11]

Carol Lee typed the children's material in a spirit of respect and appreciation. She valued their work and they, in turn, appreciated her help and caring.

Anderson notes that improvement takes place largely because the child wants it. What better example of such an observation than these motivated, turned-on fifth graders?[12]

A Positive Attitude

Carol Gray, Bernice Dunn, Shirley Davis, Carol Lee, and the many sensitive, imaginative people working with people in classrooms across the land personify in their actions and relationships all the good *s* words that guarantee that *skills* won't become *kills*. So often the way people are corrected silences and inhibits them. Were you ever criticized harshly for errors? Skills cannot be taught in classes of silence, in rooms so tightly structured that students are tense and fearful of venturing beyond ordained assignments, in climates of competition where correct answers are stressed and children fear failure. When kids feel free to use the language in a relaxed atmosphere of encouragement, experimentation, exploration, and enthusiasm (four *E*'s), they will reach out, initiate ideas, and develop new interests, strengths, and skills. They cannot learn to improve their language unless they first feel free to use language.[13]

Experiment and Succeed

Creative ideas on teaching the skills are all around you. Check any month's yield of teachers' magazines and you will find pages devoted to innovative methods

of teaching the skills. The commercial manufacturers produce toys, games, and puzzles guaranteed to help teach the basic language skills. If anything, there is a plethora of such material. The resourceful teacher is aware of what is available but does not rely completely on outside ideas. We have already said that there is no technique in the universe equal to the technique of the human heart and mind. Each day, imaginative teachers and their students invent new materials and methods relevant to their own experiences and interests. You and your students are your best natural resources. As you read, correlate the material with the activities already covered. Synthesize as you survey the various skills and constantly watch for ways that they can be taught as naturally and relevantly as possible. Remember magic vocabularies and special interests. Keep making connections!

The spirit in which you teach is perhaps even more important than the subject you are teaching. In all the other chapters, you have been encouraged to develop an open, flexible, creative approach to teaching the language arts. It is essential that you bring that spirit of enjoyment, adventure, curiosity, and motivation to the teaching of those skills. That is what this chapter is about.

QUESTION: What do I want my students to learn?

ANSWER: I want my students to enjoy learning the basic mechanics of the language, such as handwriting, spelling, punctuation, and usage, in ways that are practical and immediately useful, that are relevant to the students' experiences, and that ensure the students' success.

What are good ways to accomplish these goals? Reread the suggested activities in the preceding chapters and see how easily and naturally skill exercises can be related to them. On every page of this book you have read ideas that strengthen the skills; in every chapter, the stress has been on the essential goals of using and enjoying language in a variety of interesting, stimulating, and enriching activities. In rooms where children learn to use language freely and joyfully the mechanics can be taught with ease and practicality. Every idea is an example of the countless possibilities available if you tap the resources around you and within you. The suggestions in this chapter, as in all the chapters, demonstrate how spirit and attitude can be translated into action. Do not read them as rigid instructions in creativity, but rather as shared experiences from dynamic classrooms.

Computers in the Classroom

One of the most dramatic developments in American education is the widespread use of computers and word processors in the classroom. Children, our best learners, have taken to the new technology with agility and enthusiasm. They are using the new tools in a variety of ways clustered under four main categories:

The Medium of Instruction These programs teach children the language and machinery of the computer itself (a whole new body of knowledge with its own vocabulary and directions).

Delivering Instruction Under this wide umbrella are four subcategories:

a. Instruction in Drill and Practice These programs reinforce concepts and lessons already introduced.

b. Simulation These programs challenge children to put themselves into different situations in which they experience different times, cultures, adventures (widely used to develop imagination and creative writing).

c. Problem-Solving Problems are presented and the children find solutions. These programs are widely used to develop thinking skills.

d. Tutorial Actual skills are taught and retaught, often illustrated by animated graphics.

Management Systems These programs are probably used more by teachers than by students, to keep records, grades, averages . . .

Applications Programs Under this important category are probably the most used and useful of all the tools in the language-learning process, especially for writing. Spreadsheets, graphics, spelling, grammar and punctuation checkers, filers, and outliners help children organize their thoughts, help them recognize punctuation and spelling principles, enhance research, and provide information.

Word processors belong in this category. Word processors ease the way for students to learn about rewriting, editing, all the steps in the writing process, in a relatively easy and nonthreatening way. For many children, rewriting becomes an enjoyable experience because the technological magic of it is fascinating.

Many children with physical handicaps have been freed to express their thoughts through the use of computers and word processors.

As a person who has taught creative writing to children of all ages for over thirty years and who is still steadfastly loyal to her portable manual typewriter, I must voice a little concern. There is an excitement to language in our heads, our ears, our tongues, our imaginations. There is a power in crayons, pencils, and pens in our hands and a challenge in blank paper. I have seen children skip by these older discoveries on their way to embrace the new technology. Let's not encourage our children to rely on computers and word processors as the be-all and end-all. Let's keep computers in their place—as excellent *tools*.

Hilda Edwards has extensive experience in consulting with teachers on the use of computers in their classrooms. She is constantly evaluating new programs, which differ widely in quality. Her advice for teachers who are searching for excellent software is to go through a step by step process:

Identify the instructional objective.

Identify, evaluate, and select software that best meets the objective. Hilda believes that the best programs are those that allow teachers to input their own data instead of using pre-set data: Every group of children has different needs and interests. She urges teachers to be sure children can use the program independently. And most important: is the program "user-friendly"? Is it programmed to be encouraging and supportive?

Schedule computer time and groups for instruction. Hilda finds it very effective to schedule ten- to fifteen-minute time blocks with two children working together at the computer so interaction is possible.

Carry out some sort of evaluation and follow-up. During a lengthy interview, Hilda stressed the "user-friendly" aspect of high-quality computer programs. As she talked, I was reminded of my friend Lisa, who had confided to me that she preferred the computer in her classroom over her teacher.

"The computer is warm," Lisa explained, "and my teacher is cold. The computer is comforting. It's encouraging. If you make a mistake, it says 'Try again.' If you get it right, it says 'Good job!' My teacher never says 'Good job.' No matter how great you do, she never tells you she's pleased."

I have to admit that, given the choice between a computer programmed to be encouraging and supportive and a teacher who has programmed herself to be discouraging and negative, I too would prefer the computer. Which would YOU prefer?[14]

Hilda offered explanations for the children's enthusiasm for the computer.

> They enjoy working on it because they get *immediate feedback*. That's so important and teachers can think about that factor in everyday classroom situations. Another important reason is that good programs can be *branched*. They proceed to more difficult stages after success is achieved in easier ones. Children move at their own rates. That's another lesson that teachers can carry over. Children need experiences that ensure success. And don't forget, computers have *infinite patience*.

When Hilda works with teachers, she encourages them to think of the computer as *part of*, not *all of*, the instructional program. How do they relate it to the rest of their activities? Just as film strips, art materials, and music activities are correlated with curriculum, so computers can be integrated in all phases—another educational tool.

When looking for software, she suggests to teachers that they purchase only those programs that take advantage of the capabilities of computers and cannot be replicated with paper and pencil. The major responsibility for introducing new concepts, explaining and demonstrating ideas, rests with teachers. Creative teachers use computers to reinforce ideas in different and challenging ways.

"Have fun with computers. Enjoy them," Hilda Edwards suggests. "Use them as helpers."[15]

Language Laughs

Cartoons can provide a jumping-off point for work in mastering specific skills. Children love Charles Schulz's *Peanuts* cartoons, many of which relate directly to the language arts curriculum. His characters often express amazement at the complexity and incongruities of the language. Cover your walls with such insightful humor. Children can draw their own cartoons and commentaries about the various characteristics and idiosyncracies of the language.

Books that make important language points, such as *The King Who Rained* by Fred Gwynne (Dutton, 1973) and Dr. Seuss' *On Beyond Zebra* (Hale, 1955), are dearly loved by children of all ages. They stimulate discussions and imaginative projects and reassure children who are confused by language. Poets such as Mary O'Neill have written delightful poems about the different parts of speech and the mechanics of language. These short poems entertain students as well as help them to remember specific skills.

Colon

A colon gives a sentence a chance
To call a halt and then advance.[16]

Children can write their own poems about parts of speech or make up stories about language characters, such as Billy Comma or Jill Question Mark.

Students' posters, cartoons, poems, stories, murals, and traffic signs related to language are constant features of creative rooms, enlivening the teaching of the mechanics.

Games for Fun and Learning

Children of all grade levels have remarkable talent for inventing games, puzzles, dances, and songs that can be used to strengthen language skills.

Board and Table Games   Provide scrounge material and encourage the children to create their own games or make up their own spin-offs to already existing games.

Crossword Puzzles and Other Word Games   Many books, newspapers, and magazines feature puzzles and word games that children find challenging. *Encourage your students to create their own word games*. You will find that they enjoy jumbling letters, scrambling sentences, or creating crosswords. They will often choose themes that are important to them. Mickey, who loves cars, had a wonderful time scrambling the names of automobiles. His paper was the neatest he had ever handed in, because he knew that his teacher was making copies of the scramble for his classmates. Always use the kids' puzzles and games to supplement your standardized materials.

Silly Sentences   Comprehension, knowledge, and intelligence are important factors in the quality of playfulness. You don't laugh at a joke unless you "get it." You can't "mess around" with material unless you have come to terms with it.

After Carl Janiak's sixth graders complete their regular spelling and vocabulary exercises, they are ready to have some fun inventing new meanings and usages for their words. Imagine following the howls of laughter down the hall to Carl's room, where his students are writing and reading aloud such silly sentences as these:

> We like to play endorse. (indoors)
> Mom made orange juice in the blunder.
>
> K.C.

> The duck who lives on this earthquakes a lot.
>
> Heather

> You usually wear throngs to the beach.
> I mustache you, where did you get that perfume?
>
> Sarah

> The centaur of the circle is weary put his compass point.
> David

Punctuation Dance

A group of second graders made up a dance to help them remember punctuation marks. The class divided into groups representing different punctuation marks, such as capital letters, periods, question marks, exclamation points, and commas. The children decided how they wanted to show their marks through movement, and each group worked out a dance pattern to express its idea.

The capital letters group stretched their bodies to their very tallest and reached out their arms as wide as they could. Periods stamped their feet and held out both hands in a stop movement. Question marks lifted both arms and twisted down in a hula dance spiral.

The teacher read a short story. At each point where certain punctuation was needed, the groups moved. The children had to listen intently to hear their word cues. At the end of the session one boy said, "I'll never forget my question marks again because I'll always think of those hula dance arms!"

Original Punctuation: The "Awk"

When Bill Palmer summarized all the punctuation marks with his first graders, he asked the kids if there were any more suggestions, any ideas left out. Six-year-old Bonnie raised her hand and told Bill, "You left out the *awk*."

Bill thought for a moment and then apologized, "Bonnie, I don't quite remember the *awk*. Can you tell us a little about it? When do you use it?"

"After you write a *mad* sentence," she explained.

Bill asked her to draw it on the board. It looked like this:

"In all my reading, I don't think I ever remember seeing an *awk*," Bill said.

Bonnie reprimanded him: "If you had read my journal more carefully, you would have observed that I used an occasional *awk!*"

He reread her journal. So she had.

Handwriting Dances

If anything involves movement, it is handwriting. Handwriting is a motor skill. Handwriting is concerned with spaces, slants, sizes, loops, and stems. Take a break from papers and pencils and enjoy practicing the elements of good handwriting by moving your body to music. The children can dance loops, make circles with their arms, hands, heads, feet. They can change the movement into straight lines, small, big, very big. They can make small shapes, large shapes, small circles, large circles, small lines, large lines. They can clap letter dances. Usually, when they return to their papers and pencils, the memory of their pleasant movement break will help them with their writing.

The Seven Dwarfs' Handwriting

Give your students the opportunity to practice small muscle movements as they meet this imaginative challenge:

"Would Grumpy's handwriting look the same as Bashful's? Would Happy's handwriting look exactly the same as Sleepy's?"

Challenge your class to choose one or more or all of the dwarfs and show samples of their writing in signatures, journal pages, letters, poems, or stories.

Worst to Best Handwriting

Thank goodness we aren't graded on our telephone pads, shopping lists, or reminder notes! Our handwriting usually improves when we address thank-you notes or invitations to parties.

Our kids have the same range of handwriting options. They can go from their sloppiest scribble to their neatest, beautiful writing. Give them a chance to write something *ten* times, beginning with their very worst writing and improving subsequent lines so that the tenth represents, as of that date and time, their best handwriting efforts.

If all ways fail to help students improve their handwriting abilities, you can always vote LIFE and ask them, as Brenda Sims asked her kids, to "translate their work from the original!"

Language Songs

Kids love to make up songs. Inspired by handwriting practice, a third grader composed this song and choreographed an original fingerplay to go with it.

Don't make your letters too loose, too loose.
Don't make your letters too tight, too tight.
Round and round, up and down,
All my letters go to town.

The class was enriched by the new material, which soon became as familiar as traditional nursery rhymes.

Words as Concrete Art Designs

Margaret Ross's sixth, seventh, and eighth graders' favorite activity is expressing the meaning of words through the elements of art. The word *hot* looks *hot; sharp* is full of pointy angles; *drip* drips down the paper. Encourage the kids to choose their own words to express.

Understanding Quotation Marks

After spending several frustrating days trying to explain the punctuation of dialogue, teacher Stan Roy stood at the board and asked the class what puzzled them. When the students responded, Stan wrote their conversation on the board. For the next few minutes, he transcribed the class's conversation. For their homework assignment, the children wrote dialogues based on conversations of their families and friends.

The children not only learned the mechanics, but they so enjoyed writing dialogues that the experience continued throughout the year and became part of almost all other language experiences. Some of their favorite exercises consisted of writing dialogues for a person and an animal, a person and an inanimate object, a hero and a villain.

Games with Parts of Speech

Here is one of the most successful and enjoyable ways to learn the parts of speech. After the children have been introduced to the basic parts of speech, divide the class into four groups: nouns, verbs, adjectives, and adverbs. Each group writes as many different words as they can, each word on a separate index

card. Correct spelling and legible handwriting are essential because the cards need to be read and understood. In ten minutes, there should be four stacks of cards with the headings Nouns, Verbs, Adjectives, and Adverbs. Now, here is a game a fourth grade played.

A child chose a noun card, *clown*. Every child turned into a statue of a clown. But what was the clown doing? They needed a verb card. Another child chose one, *jump*. What kind of a clown was it? A child chose an adjective card, *clumsy*. Have you ever seen a clumsy clown jump? It's a scene you would never forget.

After a few minutes, another question arose. How was the clumsy clown jumping? A child chose an adverb card, *angrily*. Imagine the added drama. Jumping angrily is very different from jumping joyfully or gracefully.

How easily the parts of speech can become important parts of the students' lives! They can see how dull their existence would be without nouns, verbs, adjectives, and adverbs.

Spin-offs
a. Write a story about a clumsy clown who jumps angrily.
b. Illustrate an idea made up from the four cards.
c. Improvise a scene in which a clumsy clown jumps angrily.
d. Make up a dance for a clumsy clown who jumps angrily. Then make up or find music to accompany the dance.

Clap for Proper Nouns

After some initial work with proper nouns, it's interesting to practice them in ways other than the usual drill sheets.

Read a list of words, some of which are nouns, verbs, adjectives, and adverbs and some of which are proper nouns. Ask your students to listen for the proper nouns. The moment they hear one, they should clap their hands (or stamp their feet, or tap their fingers on the desk, or A.Y.O.).

Opposites Attract: Teaching Antonyms

Start this opposites activity by asking your class to *show you with their bodies* what the word *up* means. Then ask the children to show you the opposite of *up*. This gives the children the opportunity to share something they know.

Older children enjoy breaking into pairs and deciding on two antonyms to show the rest of the class and see if their words can be guessed. A class of fifth graders astonished me with the variety of antonyms they shared through movement: tame/wild; old/young; dry/wet; awake/asleep; healthy/sick.

Playing with Prepositions

All through the book I have made you prepositions you could not refuse! Here are more ideas! Prepositions are great words to use to start word-series poems.

Beyond the stars,	On top of Old Smoky,
Above the houses,	Beside the Shenandoah,
Near the forest,	Across the Wide Prairie
Under the moon,	Over the mountains, over the sea,
lived a troll.	A handsome singer sings to me.
Mark	Anna
Grade 5	Grade 6

Prepositions Dance

Prepositions are wonderful movement words. Working individually, in small groups, or with the entire class, children can convey prepositions through body language.

In one fourth grade the children were divided into small groups, and each group chose a preposition card from a stack of word cards. They had only a few minutes to work out a way of expressing their prepositions through movement. The rest of the class was to guess the word. One group formed a circle. A boy stood outside the circle. He walked toward it in slow motion. The circle broke, let him enter, and closed around him. The word was *in*.

Preposition Mix-Up

Mix learning prepositions with playfulness. Sing, say, draw, move, improvise, write, or read rearranged nursery rhymes, songs, chants, and games that feature prepositions.

> Jack-Be-Nimble jumps *around* the candlestick!
> The cow jumps *behind* the moon!
> The mouse runs *away* from the clock!

Enjoy the variety of ideas launched from a playful session on prepositions!

We've Got You Under Our Spell: Keeping the FUN in Spelling Fundamentals!

Paul Hammock and his puppet who occasionally gives the spelling tests to his middle-grade students remind us that spelling, like all the skills, can be taught in the spirit of enjoyment, adventure, and imagination. It doesn't always have to be grim. Enjoy these few sample suggestions for teaching spelling in the "key of life."

Take to the Streets

Spelling correctly can save your life. It's absolutely necessary in many types of communication. Using the question "What if?" to stimulate creative thinking, consider this thought with your students. What if all the street signs outside were misspelled? Compile a list of misspelled street signs. Here is a sample from a fourth-grade list:

WUN WEIGH STREITT   YEELDT
SLIPREE WIN WIT   STOPP

On another portion of the board, write the correct spelling of the signs, or mix the correct words with the incorrect words. Have the children cross out the incorrect spellings and leave the correct ones or match the incorrect with the correct.

Public street signs are good resources for collages and creative movement. I saw a third-grade class mural featuring street signs. Their teacher said that not only were the signs fun for the children to make and to play with, but they also helped strengthen the children's visual perception and awareness of words.

Correctly Spelled Words

One fifth-grade teacher occasionally gives a spelling test that involves a page of misspelled words and a smattering of correctly spelled words. The assignment is to find the ten correctly spelled animals, circle the fifteen correctly spelled colors, or underline the twelve correctly spelled geographic terms on the page.

Correct the Room

Designate a special day when the entire room will be filled with spelling errors that need correcting. Misspell labels, words on charts, words on the chalkboard.

One teacher didn't tell her students that words in the room would be misspelled. When the class walked in, they were immediately aware of the spelling errors around the room. In the first ten or fifteen minutes, the children found thirty misspelled words displayed around the room. The activity sharpened their awareness of correct spelling. When the words in the room were corrected, the daily schedule resumed.

Name Dropping

Persistent teachers often resort to unconventional ways to promote learning. In the following episode, keep in mind that this particular teacher and her students enjoyed a warm, trusting relationship of mutuality sparked with generous doses of humor and joking.

Once upon a time, there was a group of fifth graders who didn't care about their spelling errors. No matter how their teacher tried to motivate them to improve in spelling accuracy, there was no response. One day while taking names for committee assignments, she wrote the following list on the board.

Peetr

Margiritt

Filip

A deadly silence pervaded the room. From the hush, a strained voice was heard. "You spelled my name wrong, you know." Two more voices echoed the same complaint.

"So what? What's the big deal? It doesn't make any difference," responded the teacher. An uproar ensued followed by a gush of relief as the names were corrected. Some things are sacred.

From then on, whenever words were misspelled, the teacher kidded the students about the hurt feelings of the owners of the misrepresented names. "Remember how awful you felt when *your* name was misspelled? Just think of how *continent* feels when you spell it *contenent*. I can hear it whimpering right now!"

Skills and Drills Come in Different Flavors

There's nothing more fun for a pencil to write than a list of delicious ice-cream flavors.

They provide excellent source material for reading matter as well as the basis for enjoyable skill exercises. With your students, write a list of ice-cream flavors. Use the list to follow these instructions or answer these questions.

1. Arrange the flavors in alphabetical order.
2. Divide each flavor into syllables.
3. Which flavors have double letters?
4. What different consonant blends blend into the flavors?
5. Which flavors have nonfattening, silent letters?
6. Write a sentence using all the flavors that begin with the same letter.
7. Write plurals for all the flavors.
8. In your best handwriting, write a menu of your favorite flavors.
9. Make up new flavors, such as nugget almond fudge and nutty nutty lemonberry.
10. Write five adjectives that describe your favorite flavor.
11. Write a paragraph about your favorite flavor.
12. Write a paragraph about your least favorite flavor.
13. A.Y.O.

Language skills are especially enjoyable and successful when your students create their own exercises based on personal-interest material. You, as a creative teacher, can make good suggestions if you know your students' hobbies, interests, and favorite things—their magic vocabularies. All those interests are *words*, and it is to *words* that every skill is directed.

Neal, a restless fifth grader, turned off by his reading and language textbooks, agonized over the drill work assigned. But he is a fanatic collector of baseball cards, which his teachers always took from him and kept in their desk until school was over for the summer. This year his teacher realized that Neal, who stumbled over words in his reading book, was able to read the names of every baseball player, no matter how ethnically complicated, and memorize all the information on the cards. Rather than take away this treasure, his teacher used it for as many skills as possible. Neal helped make up assignments using his cards and is now alert and motivated, especially in language arts.

Teachers Talk about Skills

A small group of teachers stayed for a while after a workshop ended. We sat on the floor and exchanged ideas. I asked them if they could remember their most significant experiences in teaching the skills. I think their comments are valuable and I want to share them with you.

Class Newspaper (Sixth Grade)   "Last year for career education, we invited different guests to our class to share their careers with us. A newspaper reporter made a tremendous hit with my students and got them very excited about the whole world of newspapers. That visit launched a newspaper project that lasted the whole year. Each month, we published a class newspaper to which everyone contributed. Some people wrote long, involved articles, others wrote captions and headlines. But everyone did write, illustrate, help lay out, and edit. In our school, we have a list of curriculum guidelines in language arts that we are all supposed to follow. In sixth grade, the list for language skills is extensive, such as learning sentences, identifying nouns, pronouns, verbs, and so on. Working with the newspaper project, we covered every item on our skills sheet. By the end of the year, the class scored well on the standardized exams, breezed through the exercises in the textbook, and showed real growth in all areas of language development. What impressed me was that all these skills were learned painlessly, because they were part of the newspaper game."

Supermarket of Task Sheets (Fourth Grade)   "Over the years, I came to realize that not everyone needs work in everything. If a child already understands sentence structure, it's boring to have to go over and over the same lessons because other children in the class still don't understand it. I also realized that the most important part of handwriting is legibility. I had spent so much time in past years struggling with handwriting exercises that resulted in worry and tension rather than universally great handwriting. I've come to a way of teaching that links people with the specific problems they have to solve. Once in a while, of course, I get everyone together to introduce a new idea or concept, but after that, those who need to work longer on it do. Those who don't need the extra time and practice go on to other things.

"The most successful skills teaching experience I had was the year we made a supermarket of task sheets. We set aside a few shelves in the closet for specific tasks like plurals, homonyms, or spelling. Into each box went exercise sheets designed to strengthen their understanding of a specific skill. I encouraged the children to make up practice sheets of their own so that they could be teachers. Once they had mastered a skill, they would immediately want to be teachers, making up an exercise sheet for the others. I like the idea of children helping each other. When one person understands a concept and another is still having trouble with it, a little visit together is often more effective than a formal class session."

Singing the Skills (Second Grade)
"When I was young I learned to spell many words through singing. To this day I hum the tunes in my head as I spell the words. When my second graders had trouble learning certain words, we made up songs about them using the letters for words. (That also taught them something about syllabification and accent.) We tapped out words on our desks to hear their rhythms, too. It's wonderful to see children light up when they realize that this isn't just a word they have to spell correctly, but one with rhythm, sound, and feeling. I try to make the words come alive in as many ways as I can so that the children will get used to hearing them and using them in special ways."

Newspaper Treasure Hunt (Fifth Grade)
"One of our favorite games is a newspaper treasure hunt. We enjoy finding and writing, say, ten adjectives, twenty-five proper nouns, five direct quotations, eight adverbs, three exciting sentences, and two questions."

Made for Success Dittos

Recognizing that children often feel anxious about completing drill sheets and dittos, Ronnie Hochman distributes fun, impossible-to-fail exercises. For exam-

ple, on one of her sheets is the question, "Which is BIGGER?" Also on the sheet are two drawings: Drawing A is a huge watermelon with the word written on it. Drawing B is a tiny seed with the word written above it. At the bottom of the paper the directions read "Mark the correct box below with your answer A or B."

These occasional shots of playful reassurance go a long way toward helping kids develop confidence.

How Do I Know These Methods Are Working?

There is no area of the language arts curriculum easier to evaluate than this one. A virtual flood of evaluation materials is tumbling over the schools. Each school has its own system of textbooks and testing programs. You will have ample material with which to test your students at any point in the school year. But remember that many children freeze on formal, standardized tests and invalidate the results because of those immeasurable emotional-psychological factors, such as fear and insecurity.

I am always dismayed when language learning is limited to only meager offerings. Unfortunately, many children are still assigned only one or two writing projects a year or one or two oral reports. In such undernourished classes, real evaluation is difficult because there is no way of knowing how deeply the knowledge has become part of the everyday, functional life of the child. In classes empty of rich and diverse language experiences, the practice pages of skills in workbooks and textbooks remain just that—exercises to complete, words to underline, cross out, or circle that have nothing to do with the children.

CAREFUL

If our students don't use the language, it is almost impossible for them to make the connection between the ideas on the worksheets and their own language usage. The greater the distance between the drills and the kids' actual needs and concerns, the less effective the drills will be. In classes where oral language is used and enjoyed on many levels for many purposes, where writing happens every day in a variety of ways and for many reasons, and where reading is not confined to limited times, teachers have numerous opportunities to evaluate the work of students and decide, with them, which areas need extra time and effort.

I remember an incident that holds great significance for this discussion on evaluation.

A third-grade teacher walked into the teachers' lounge. With shining eyes and a joyous smile, she looked like a celebration. What was the cause of such cheer?

"Just now, Charlie stopped at the door before leaving school and said, 'I seen you—I mean, I saw you riding your bike yesterday, Mrs. Murphy.' "

That doesn't seem like much of a reason to celebrate, does it?

The story was told in April. Since school started in September, Mrs. Murphy had been trying to help Charlie grow from being almost illiterate in oral speech toward using a more acceptable, informal standard. It hadn't been easy. Her major methods of approach—besides constant encouragement, packs of personal drill sheets, and a variety of talk games—had been to restate Charlie's more blatant errors.

"I seen the new Corvette!" (New cars are on Charlie's magic vocabulary list.)

"You saw the new Corvette? I saw it too. What did you think?"

It looked like the variety of approaches was beginning to pay off.

Even with the excellent testing and measuring devices available to you, there is no evaluation method that can substitute for your own observations and perceptions. Throughout the book, your own powers of awareness and sensitivity have been stressed. The underlying belief on every page is that you, the teacher, must have a vital, open, honest relationship with your students so that all the strands of the language arts will be woven together into a powerful pattern. With your students, you are listening, speaking, moving, playing, reading, and writing. Your eyes are open to the dynamics of the classroom. Your gaze reaches to the far corners of your room where one child may be struggling along without asking for help.

Checklist for Yourself

1. Do I listen to my students, speak with them, read their written work, and note the types of errors common to the group as well as to individuals?

2. Which errors have I been able to pinpoint for special attention and effort, and how can I work on correcting those errors?

3. How have I motivated the students to want to work on correcting the specific errors?

4. What diverse opportunities have I provided for practice in mastering those specific skills? What activities have been especially effective? What activities have been minimally effective in achieving their major purpose?

5. What ways haven't I tried yet to connect with those students who do not show improvement? What interests or hobbies can be used as material for helping each one to master the skill he or she is having trouble with?

6. Have I provided sufficient opportunities for students' input, concerns, and ideas in the creating of materials to help with specific skills? Do they feel free to share their feelings?

7. Have I provided a variety of opportunities for my students to work together (peer-teaching) in improving areas that need extra help? Have I encouraged conferences, editorial committees, small group workshops, one-to-one partners, and other interactive activities? Am I an active participant as well?

Checklist for the Class

1. In what areas do the students feel they need to improve? What skills are they having the most difficulty with?

2. Are the exercises and activities they are doing in this area helping them? Do they need more practice?

3. What new ways can the students suggest to learn this skill?

4. How do they feel when they have mastered one of the more difficult skills after working at it for a long time?

5. How can they help themselves and others to learn the skills?

Encourage your students to save their written work in special folders or notebooks. As often as possible, go over their folders with them. It's always exciting to see where you've been and where you're going. Take time to talk with your students one by one, two by two, and as a whole group. Because you are not condemning or being critical, but are being caring and encouraging, your students will probably be glad to share their feelings and ideas.

A colleague of mine was working at his desk after school when one of his first graders shyly came back into the room.

"Mr. Sandberg," she almost-whispered.

"Yes, Julie?"

"I love you," she said simply.

"I love you, too, Julie," he warmly responded.

"Know why I love you?" the little girl asked.

"Why?"

"Because you love me even though I don't know all my vowels yet!"

ENDNOTES

[1] A. A. Milne, "Eeyore Has a Birthday," *The World of Pooh* (New York: Dutton, 1957) 78.

[2] E. L. Thorndike, "Punctuation," *Teachers College Record* (May 1948): 533.

[3] Andrea Butler and Jan Turbill, *Toward a Reading-Writing Classroom* (Portsmouth: Heinemann Educational, 1984) 9.

[4] Robert C. Pooley, *Teaching English Grammar* (New York: Appleton, 1957) 126–28.

[5] James Moffett, "Hidden Impediments to Improving English Teaching," *Phi Delta Kappan* (Sept. 1985): 50–56.

[6] Ruth Strickland, *Language Arts in the Elementary School* (Boston: Heath, 1957) 345.

[7] Paul S. Anderson, *Language Skills in Elementary Education* (New York: Macmillan, 1968) 164.

[8] Anderson, *Language Skills* 32–33.

[9] William M. Logan and Virgil G. Logan, *A Dynamic Approach to Language Arts* (Toronto: McGraw, 1967) 381–82.

[10] All Bernice Dunn's comments under "Visit a First Grade" are taken from an interview with the author.

[11] All Shirley Davis' and Carol Lee's comments under "Visit a Fifth Grade" are taken from an interview with the author.

[12] Anderson, *Language Skills* 418.

[13] Anderson, *Language Skills* 391.

[14] This incident was highlighted in Mimi Brodsky Chenfeld, "Words of Praise: Honey on the Page," *Language Arts* 62.3 (Mar. 1985): 266–68.

[15] All Hilda Edwards' (Ohio State Education Department) comments on computers in the classroom are taken from an interview with the author.

[16] Mary O'Neill, "Colon," *Words Words Words* (Garden City: Doubleday, 1966) 30.

EPILOGUE

the World
is bydful and the
world is nise.

JENNY

Just the Beginning

At the edge of the world
It is growing light.
The trees stand shining.
I like it.
It is growing light.

PAPAGO INDIANS[1]

You have focused your attention on the various components of the language arts curriculum, and now you have returned to your very first focus, yourself. There is no getting away from your vital role in the continuous process we call education. The curriculum is waiting for you among the pages of textbooks and manuals. It is waiting for a special spirit to bring it to life. It needs you to make the difference between *stop* and *go*, between *shrink* and *grow*, between *life* and *death*.

How many times have you *really* listened while the safety rules of an airplane were explained? Professor Herb Sandberg shared a delightful experience from a recent flight. The flight attendant spoke to the passengers with a mischievous twinkle in her eyes: "I want you to sit up and pay attention or you won't get any refreshments. Above you are the oxygen masks. You certainly want to know where they are, don't you? Can you guess where the safety exits are? If you can tell me, your bathroom privileges will be returned. How many of you see the No Smoking signs? No dinner until you show me." She continued with her message, covering all the points in her "curriculum." She held the attention of the passengers, many of whom had heard the announcements countless times before but had never really listened. They not only listened but enjoyed the change from the usual dull routine.

Getting the Best Directions

Have you ever become lost while trying to find an unfamiliar place? If you stopped at a service station to ask directions, you might have received a variety of answers.

Possible response one: Mumbo, jumbo, mumble, jumble.

You: Thanks very much. (Drive away with sinking feeling that you are still lost and should find another service station.)

Possible response two (spoken quickly): Three lights, pass blinking light, next right, over the hill, dead end, first left. You can't miss it.

You: Thanks very much. (Drive away with sinking feeling that you cannot recall whether it was three blinking lights and the next left or . . .)

Possible response three: Same as two but spoken more slowly and accompanied by body gestures, then repeated.

Possible response four: Same as three but with city map used as a learning supplement.

Possible response five: Same as four but with extra resource of a handmade map showing exactly where you are and where you are going.

Possible response six: Same as five but with person suggesting, "I'm headed that way, why don't you just follow me."

Do you see the simple parallels between this story and American education? How often do lost and searching students receive directions from teachers who *think* they are helping but who have limited their assistance to response number one? The children don't understand, and few will ask to have the explanation repeated because they don't want to sound stupid. How many try to find another service station to ask again? How many children ride through our classes and say, "Thank you very much" but are still lost and may, in fact, stop searching?

Effective teachers work zealously to guarantee that there are enough avenues of experiences for *all* students to have a way of learning. How many opportunities will you provide your students as they search for the meaning of the curriculum, as they learn to ask questions, as they look for answers to their questions?

Teaching as Renewal

My friend Professor Robert S. Herman, an educator and political advisor who is devoted to the idea of renewal in education, said this to me:

> When you come to my house, I don't offer you a meal composed of yesterday's leftovers no matter how delicious they are. I cook a special meal for you. Maybe I'll use a recipe I've used before, but I'll try something new with it— a different approach, a different twist! We can't keep serving leftover lectures to our students, no matter how effective they were!

Exciting teachers reflect Professor Herman's concern with discovering fresh ideas and approaches. No matter how successful last year's jungle program or solar system unit were, they will not repeat the exact experience with this year's classes. Alice Miel thinks of teaching as a "nonrepetitive process. No two groups of learners are ever the same, nor is one class the same from day to day. The world around the classroom changes constantly. The teacher changes."[2]

When I share with teachers and university students at workshops and conferences, I like to challenge them, prod them:

Your students are *not* taking fifth-grade or seventh-grade language arts! They are taking YOU, and YOU are a new and unique experience for them. YOU are not interchangeable! What is in store for them in their time spent with YOU?

Will this be a year of beginnings or of endings? Of everything or of nothing?

A year of making connections or a year of severing relationships?

Will this time with YOU be a time of addition and multiplication for your students? Or a time of subtraction and division?

A time of growing or shrinking?

Will your book this year be "Chicken Little, the Sky is Falling"? or "The Little Engine that Could"?

A year of rainbows or of quicksand?

Will your journey together be one of "No Frills" "No Stops" "No Detours" "Stick to the Straightaway"? Or will you take the scenic route?

Do you brake for animals, barns, autumn colors, ideas, surprises, poetry, serendipity?

What will you and your kids make happen this year? This is your time. How will you shape it together?

These are questions only YOU can answer!

It All Comes Together: More Examples of Creative Teaching

Black Elk, the great Oglala Sioux holy man, said,

Anywhere is the center of the world.[3]

When we teach in a holistic way, pulling together threads from all our strands, correlating and integrating, *whatever subject we teach* is enriched with multi-faceted learning experiences. Whatever we choose to hallow with imagination, wonder, attention, alternative ways of looking becomes the center of the world and for a little while the magic of education transforms into a reality.

Read the following examples that demonstrate this kind of spirit. Imagine the life, sounds, sights, interactions in the classrooms. Discover how many ideas are combined, how many moments children and teachers enjoy together!

Apples and Sunflowers

Marilyn Cohen loves apples. She shares that love with her kindergartners. Here are some excerpts from her notes:

A is for Apple.

Learned the word *apple*.

Ate apples.

Shared feelings about apples.

Asked questions about apples.

Read books about apples.

Learned an apple fingerplay.

Visited an apple orchard.

Picked apples.

Saw apples washed, sorted, packed, and crated.

Watched apple cider being pressed.

Drank apple cider.

Wrote thank-you notes to farmer and his family.

Dictated stories about the trip.

Drew picture of apple orchard.

Wrote an apple book with original stories, poems, and pictures.

Compiled cookbook of apple recipes with original illustrations.

Followed recipes for making applesauce, pie, and jelly.

Marked places on map where apple trees grow.

Read about Johnny Appleseed.

Dramatized story of Johnny Appleseed.

Used apple shapes for counting.

Made apple dolls and puppets.

Created original apple posters.

Made up riddles about apples.

A is for Apple.

Marilyn brought in a fully grown sunflower. For the next few weeks, she and her kindergartners celebrated the sunflower by

measuring its height and comparing the measurements to those of the custodian, principal, teachers, and themselves

tracing around it on brown butcher paper, painting it, measuring it again on the paper

cutting off the pod, looking in awe at the tiny seeds that could each grow into such a gigantic flower

"guesstimating" the number of seeds in the pod, recording each child's guess on a chart

removing the seeds, grouping them in tens, counting them—they totaled 1,040

Some of the things they did with the seeds:

distributed them to the children to replant in the spring

fed them to the gerbils (class pets) and the birds outside

toasted them for nutritious snacks

created seed collages, counting cards, pictures

They also wrote original poems and painted pictures featuring sunflowers. They read many books about sunflowers. One of their favorites was Janice Udry's *Sunflower Garden* (Harvey House, 1969). They enjoyed van Gogh's glorious painting, *Sunflowers*.

Both apples and sunflowers were celebrations that continued for weeks, with each idea evolving into another.

So many activities overlap. So many subject areas are linked. Where does listening end and oral speaking begin? Is this word recognition or following directions or both? Is this comprehension or small group activity? All of the above!

The Marvelous Medieval Happening

Nancy Herzog loves teaching sixth grade. One of her favorite areas of study is the medieval period. One of her dreams was to create a medieval festival with her students. She went to her principal, David Neustadt, with her idea. His only requirement was that the entire student body and school community become involved. What happened, from the first encounter between David and Nancy to the enormous school–communitywide "peak experience" that culminated the school year, could fill a book in itself. Catch the flavor of the events in excerpts from Nancy's letters describing some of the activities that she and Tom Healy, her fellow sixth-grade teacher, helped organize.

All three sixth-grade classes worked together on this. The materials they already had featured aspects of medieval culture so we constantly thought in groups: village life, castle life, religious life . . . and occupations: those who worked with their hands, those who fought, those who taught and prayed. . . .

We immersed ourselves in the medieval world, researching the period. We used books, pictures, film strips, films, models. We practiced caligraphy. We listened to and learned medieval music. Volunteers came from the community and taught the kids maypole dances and musicians practiced with the kids so they could be "strolling players."

We compiled lists of medieval activities, starring those that could be used with the rest of the school. Activities such as bread making, shield making, tilting the quintain, stilt walking, weaving, stained glass, puppetry, hat making . . . the list grew. . . .

We charted and coordinated group activities, posted schedules, handed out check lists, tests, assignments. Students worked individually, in small groups, in larger groups. Materials multiplied. Notes, study guides, vocabulary lists, biographies, instructions. . . . Hat makers cut out hat shapes and feathers. . . . Weavers learned spinning and weaving on drop spindles and prepared looms. . . . Booths were constructed. Shields designed. Bread baked.

A large gym is an enormous area to fill. Everyone made banners. Everyone made shields. Each group was responsible for a guild sign and a symbol of a trade or occupation. The castle had sponge-painted brick walls on long sheets of butcher paper. The monastery had stained glass windows (colored cellophane) taped to the gym windows. The walls of the gym featured hundreds of silhouettes of medieval people: guards, monks, potters, blacksmiths . . .

On the last day, lines were hung across the gym and while the children hung flags, banners, and shields the custodians and principal sawed wood and made stilts. The gym volleyball pole became our maypole, decorated with flowers and streamers. . . .

The sixth graders studying medieval history spent seven weeks learning, from the beginning of their "unit" to the unforgettable festival that involved teachers, staff, all students, families, and community friends. Not one aspect of the language arts curriculum was neglected. Learning ran across all subject areas. Intergroup relations, self-image, cooperation, enthusiasm flourished. Nancy ends her letter,

Will I do it again? Of course. This year will have its own flavor. . . . The children will do more writing—medieval journals. A third grader already has a magnificent dragon costume from Halloween. We'll use him somehow. The music teacher has a medieval musical we'll put on. The musicians will have more tunes. And perhaps we can have our feast. I'm eagerly looking forward to the whole affair. And what did the children learn? Lots of things—out of confusion and chaos came our exciting Happening. They had good feelings about what they accomplished, as well they should have. It was stupendous. A splendid way to end a year.[4]

I missed the event but caught the spirit from listening to kids and teachers, looking at slides, reading biographies and descriptions of people and occupations, enjoying the medieval music.

The Amazing Annual Multicultural Festival

Kay Noble is a principal with a passion! Catch the excitement in her explanation of how things happen in her school:

> Ours is a school where the arts—where all subject areas—are related throughout the year. Teachers work together: we integrate across curriculum areas and grade levels. . . . All of our classes focus on our city—as an ongoing study. Our city is a microcosm for the rest of the world. Everything comes from that core:
>
> Who settled our city?
>
> Where did they come from? When?
>
> Who were they? What did they bring?
>
> Why did they come here?
>
> How did their customs, traditions, languages become part of the greater community?
>
> What streets, what sections tell stories?
>
> What houses have poems and portraits in their closets?
>
> What cellars were once part of the Underground Railroad?
>
> Out of wonderings and questions like these, all other subjects and disciplines connect. By spring, every class is bursting with information, with history and geography, with books and records, with family stories and memories. We culminate with a huge multicultural festival—kids, families, community members, food, costumes, plays, songs—it's amazing! We all break bread together! . . . I think that at the end of the year every person in our school has a healthy reverence for diversity in harmony! Our common experiences and our individuality, our uniqueness![5]

Over and over again, creative teachers demonstrate that

Anywhere is the center of the world!

The Key to It All

Helping make things come together is something creative teachers do naturally. It's a way of thinking: How does this relate to that? How can we connect A to B, this song to that story, this word to that event? Enrichment comes through interrelationships.

Creative teachers link, blend, and synthesize subject areas, correlating classroom experiences as naturally as life fuses its many aspects.

Imaginative teachers view the language arts as inextricably bound to all subject areas. If necessary they could dissect their programs, but they are too busy *living them,* too involved with their students in the knowing and the growing.

They are gathering unusual materials and ideas to help enliven their curriculum, delving into their own and their students' knapsacks of experiences for resources. They reach out—to community, to other classes and teachers. They are open to old and new ways that will weave the many strands of their curriculum into exciting patterns. They experiment with tried and untried approaches, arranging, rearranging, mixing and matching, connecting the dots of seeds. They take risks. They believe.

I often think that we teachers walk around with a jangling bunch of keys. Sometimes we find the right key immediately and presto—the door opens! Sometimes we have to try a few keys until we find the one that works. Many times none of our keys fits. The door stays locked. We have to toss the ones we have, find others, persist until we get that door open!

Though we may have at our disposal the very best keys money can buy—test-proven materials, workbooks, cassettes, filmstrips, computer software, basal reading systems, learning games, electronic boards—we may find that none of these opens the doors to the minds of some children.

At that point some of us give up, saying "That child is unreachable, unteachable!"

At that point some of us begin to search for ways to reach that child. Often those ways are the most simple, natural, accessible, the ordinary waiting to be transformed into the extraordinary by our hallowing.

One of the sacred formulas of the Cherokee nation proclaims: "Let the paths from every direction recognize each other."

Creative teachers bring together paths from every direction in their journey with their students to the place where minds and hearts grow.

Share Your Light

Some time ago, I participated in a memorial candlelight procession. Our candles brightened the darkness as we moved slowly through the city. Observing the march from a distance, you would have seen just the flickering lights continue their path down the streets. Inside the march, when my candle blew out someone nearby rekindled it. When other candles blew out and mine was still lit, I would rekindle them. The procession was really a moving body of lights, some lit, some unlit, but all rekindled when the wind blew them out.

I think of all teachers as walking in a procession of moving light. When my imagination, inner resources, and original ideas grow dim or flicker out, I need other teachers, students, friends, materials to spark my light. I will give my flame to others when my light is burning and theirs is not. We, participants in the great educational process, have an interdependence and a responsibility toward each other.

Share Your Love

Theodore Roethke believed that teaching is one of the few professions that permits love.

What do you love? What are your commitments? Are the spirits of your students at the center of your focus? What are you enthusiastic about that will become part of your program? What will you share? How will your room become a haven of safety for all of your students? So the sweet smell of success permeates the air?

Language connects speaker to listener, reader to writer, thoughts and feelings to words. Be aware of the pervasive power of the language arts from the minute your students enter your room until the minute they leave, be aware of how language continues even before the entering and after the exiting.

The curriculum is waiting, like the dry bones, for you to infuse it with life. More important, the kids are waiting for you. They are so eager, so ready for something special to happen to them. Be someone they will remember for the rest of their lives. Bring to this great adventure of learning "all the sweetness of spirit you possess."

Believe that "all of your children are prodigies"[6] and they will surprise you. They will amaze you. They will be prodigies![7]

As you are, so you teach.

As you believe, so you teach.

I hope you construct a house of beliefs as strong as the house made of bricks so that, long after the wolves have disappeared, it will stand and withstand, its lights shining from within, its rooms warm.

The Nootka Indians have a prayer that I want to share with you as you walk toward the children waiting for you in the classroom

> You, whose day it is,
> Make it beautiful.
> Get out your rainbow colors,
> So it will be beautiful.[8]

Have you come to the end of this book? No, just to another beginning . . .

ENDNOTES

[1]Ruth Underhill, ed., "At the Edge of the World," *Singing for Power: The Song Magic of the Papago Indians of Southern Arizona* (Berkeley: U of California P, 1938).

[2]Alice S. Miel, *Creativity in Teaching: Invitations and Instances* (Belmont: Wadsworth, 1961) 8.

[3]Hugh C. Neihardt, *Black Elk Speaks* (New York: Simon, 1972).

[4]All Nancy Herzog's comments under "The Marvelous Medieval Happening" are taken from her letters to the author.

[5]Interview with the author.

[6]Yiddish proverb.

[7]See Robert Rosenthal and Lenore Jacobson, *Pygmalion in the Classroom: Teacher Expectation and Pupils' Intellectual Development,* enl. ed. (New York: Irvington, 1984).

[8]Hettie Johnson, ed., "You, whose day it is," *The Trees Stand Shining: Poetry of the North American Indians* (New York: Dial, 1971).

Special Acknowledgments

This book has been enriched by the ideas and experiences of numerous educators and caring citizens. Their contributions to the book are deeply appreciated. To the best of my ability, I have given their correct affiliations.

Rosemary Anderson, *Bexley Public Library, Bexley, Ohio;* **Camille Bates,** *W. Broad Elementary School, Columbus, Ohio;* **Libby Blaho,** *Avery Elementary School, Hilliard, Ohio;* **Louise Bogart,** *Montessori Program, Honolulu, Hawaii;* **Jay Brand,** *Sherwood Middle School, Columbus, Ohio;* **Kay Callander,** *Shady Lane Elementary School, Columbus, Ohio;* **Ellen Clark,** *Upper Arlington Public Schools, Upper Arlington, Ohio;* **Marilyn Cohen,** *Bet Shraga Hebrew Academy of the Capitol District, Albany, New York;* **John Davis,** *Purdue University, Calumet, Hammond, Indiana;* **Molly Davis;** *Cassingham School, Bexley, Ohio;* **Shirley Davis,** *Early Childhood Education Program, Jewish Center, West Bloomfield, Michigan;* **Tom Dill,** *Cassingham School, Bexley, Ohio;* **Bernice Dunn,** *Toledo, Ohio, Public Schools;* **Brian Edmiston,** *Ohio State University, Columbus, Ohio;* **Pat Edmiston,** *Ohio State University, Columbus, Ohio;* **Hilda Edwards,** *State of Ohio, Education Department;* **Marysue Garlinger,** *"Artists in the Schools," Columbus, Ohio;* **Roger Gerhardstein,** *Los Angeles, California;* **Anna Grace,** *Columbus, Ohio;* **Carol Gray,** *Alpine Elementary School, Columbus, Ohio;* **Tom Griffin,** *Cassingham Elementary School, Bexley, Ohio;* **Bess "Chee Chee" Haile,** *Schenectady, New York;* **Jan Hammock,** *Duxberry Park Alternative School, Columbus, Ohio;* **Paul Hammock,** *Duxberry Park Alternative School, Columbus, Ohio;* **Tom Healy,** *McKenzie Elementary School, Wilmette, Illinois;* **Robert S. Herman,** *Albany, New York;* **Nancy Herzog,** *McKenzie Elementary School, Wilmette, Illinois;* **Dawn Heyman,** *McGuffey Elementary School, Columbus, Ohio;* **Ronni Hochman,** *Hastings Middle School, Upper Arlington, Ohio;* **Carl Janiak,** *Hanby Elementary School, Westerville, New York, and "Days of Creation," Columbus, Ohio;* **Louise Johnson,** *Avery Elementary School, Hilliard, Ohio;* **Rick Johnston,** *Helen Keller School, Tinley Park, Illinois;* **Mom Kaun,** *Columbus, Ohio;* **Roger Klein,** *Wesleyan University, Middletown, Connecticut;* **Carol Lee,** *Columbus, Ohio;* **Kathy Liebfreund,** *Deshler Elementary School, Columbus, Ohio;* **Emily Manierre,** *Deshler Elementary School, Columbus, Ohio;* **Candace Mazur,** *"Days of Creation" and "Artists in the Schools," Columbus, Ohio;* **Chick Moorman,** *Portage, Michigan;* **David Neustadt,** *McKenzie Elementary School, Wilmette, Illinois;* **Kay Noble,** *Douglas Alternative School, Columbus, Ohio;* **Francie Nolan,** *"Gifted and Talented" Program, Columbus, Ohio;* **Linda Ohlinger,** *Ridgewood School, Scioto Darby School System, Ohio;* **Bill Palmer,** *Bellingham, Washington, Public Schools;* **Gay Su Pinnell,** *Ohio State University, Columbus, Ohio;* **Ella Rappaport,** *Del Ray Beach, Florida;* **Maureen Reedy,** *Barrington Elementary School, Upper Arlington, Ohio;* **Dusky Reider,** *"Artists in the Schools," Columbus, Ohio;* **Marlene Robbins,** *"Artists in the Schools," and "Days of Creation," Columbus, Ohio;* **Jean F. Robinson,** *Annehurst School, Upper Arlington, Ohio;* **Michael J. Rosen,** *Thurber House, Columbus, Ohio;* **Margaret Ross,** *Johnson Park Middle School, Columbus, Ohio;* **Herb Sandberg,** *University of Toledo, Toledo, Ohio;* **Penny Sanecki,** *Hamilton*

Elementary School, Columbus, Ohio; **Peg Schnittke,** *Strongsville, Ohio, Public Schools;* **Jeannette Shotter,** *Toledo, Ohio, Public Schools;* **Greg Siegler,** *Miami, Florida;* **Brenda Sims,** *Glendening Elementary School, Groveport-Madison School System, Ohio;* **The late Jack Snyder,** *Community Resources Program, Columbus, Ohio;* **Betty South,** *Houston, Texas, Public Schools;* **Sister Iona Taylor,** *New Orleans, Louisiana;* **Sally Tretheway,** *Knox County, Ohio, Public Schools;* **The late Frayda Turkel,** *Agudas Achim Religious School, Columbus, Ohio;* **Janis Wilson,** *Bexley Public Library, Bexley, Ohio*

Copyright and Acknowledgments

The author wishes to thank the following publishers and copyright holders for permission to reprint the material listed.

WILLIAM L. BAUHAN, PUBLISHER   For "Answer in Bright Green" by Jed Garrick. From *You and Contemporary Poetry* by George Abbe. Copyright © 1965 by William L. Bauhan, Publisher. Reprinted by permission.

DOUBLEDAY & COMPANY   For "Colon" from *Words Words Words* by Mary O'Neill. Copyright © 1966 by Mary O'Neill. Reprinted by permission of Doubleday & Company, Inc.

E. P. DUTTON   For excerpt from *Winnie the Pooh* by A. A. Milne. Copyright 1926 by E. P. Dutton, renewed 1954 by A. A. Milne; for excerpts from *The House at Pooh Corner* by A. A. Milne. Copyright 1928 by E. P. Dutton, renewed 1956 by A. A. Milne. All reprinted by permission of the publisher, E. P. Dutton, a division of New American Library.

ANNE FRANK STICHTING   For diagram from the Anne Frank House exhibit.

TOM GRIFFIN   For "Would You Like to Live Forever?" by Tom Griffin. Reprinted by permission of the author.

HARCOURT BRACE JOVANOVICH   For "Limited" from *Chicago Poems* by Carl Sandburg, copyright 1916 by Holt, Rinehart and Winston, Inc.; renewed 1944 by Carl Sandburg. Reprinted by permission of Harcourt Brace Jovanovich.

HARLIN QUIST BOOKS   For selections from *The Geranium on the Windowsill Just Died But Teacher You Went Right On* by Albert Cullum. Copyright © 1971 by Harlin Quist Books.

WILLIAM S. VINCENT   For "Key Concepts of Interpersonal Regard in the Classroom" from *Signs of Good Teaching* by William S. Vincent.

MOM KAUN   For excerpts from *My Life in Danger* by Mom Kaun. Reprinted by permission of the author.

THE KIDS' CONNECTION   For poem by Clarissa Boiarski from *The Kids' Connection* Magazine, Spring 1983; for "Spider Mountain" by Robin Howard, Erin Klingbeil, Karen Levy, et al. from *The Kids' Connection* Magazine, Fall 1985. Both reprinted by permission of the publisher, *The Kids' Connection.*

KATHLEEN MARKHAM   For poem from *Poems* by Edwin Markham (AMS Press, 1950). Reprinted by permission of Kathleen Markham.

THOMAS R. McDANIEL   For table, "How Good a Motivator Are You?" from Thomas R. McDaniel, "A Primer on Motivation: Principles Old and New," *Phi Delta Kappan,* September 1984. Reprinted by permission of Thomas R. McDaniel and *Phi Delta Kappan.*

CHICK MOORMAN   For "The Flavor of Caring" by Chick Moorman from *The Alternative*, Vol. 3, No. 3. Reprinted by permission of the author.

SMITHSONIAN INSTITUTION PRESS   For "You, whose day it is" by permission of Smithsonian Institution Press from *Nootka and Quileute Music* by Frances Densmore. Bureau of American Ethnology Bulletin 124. Smithsonian Institution, Washington, D.C., 1939.

UNIVERSITY OF CALIFORNIA PRESS   For "At the edge of the world" from *Singing for Power: Song Magic of the Papago Indians* by Ruth Murray Underhill. Copyright © 1938, 1966 Ruth Murray Underhill. Reprinted by permission of the University of California Press.

WILLIAM S. VINCENT   For "Key Concepts of Interpersonal Regard in the Classroom" from *Sign of Good Teaching* by William S. Vincent.

Picture Credits

2 Elihu Blotnick/*BBM Associates*;5 Fredrik D. Bodin/*Stock, Boston*; 19 Larry Hamill; 29 Enos Austin; 31 Ellen C. Eisenman; 36 Strickler/*Monkmeyer*; 41 Ellen C. Eisenman; 47 Mark Hovind; 52 Elizabeth Crews; 58 Ken Drenton; 63 Dawn Heyman; 69 Larry Hamill; 73 Elizabeth Crews; 80 Allen Zak; 82 David Powers/*Stock, Boston*; 87 *Peace on Earth Anonymous*; 91 Mark Hovind; 94 Elizabeth Crews; 103 Kopstein/*Monkmeyer*; 108 Larry Jacobson; 116 Larry Hamill; 122 Marion Bernstein; 128 Alan Mercer/*Stock, Boston*; 134 Alan Zak; 139 Larry Hamill; 146 Chick Moorman; 154 Mimi Forsyth/*Monkmeyer*; 161 Marcia Weinstein; 168 Paul Conklin/*Monkmeyer*; 181 Elizabeth Crews; 183 Enos Austin; 188 Elizabeth Crews; 197 Allen Zak; 203 Larry Hamill; 206 Elizabeth Crews/*Stock, Boston*; 208 Shirley Zeiberg/*Taurus*: 212 Larry Hamill; 221 Courtesy of Louise E. McKenzie Elementary School; 228 Larry Hamill; 229 Marjorie Pickens; 239 Mike Case; 245 Elizabeth Crews; 252 Elizabeth Crews; 258 Elizabeth Crews; 265 Elizabeth Crews/*Stock, Boston*; 267 Mike Case; 269 Craig Holman; 277 Elizabeth Crews; 279 Rick Turkel; 285 George Malave/*Stock, Boston*; 297 Chick Moorman & Dee Dishon; 301 Cara Chenfeld; 304 Peter Menzel/*Stock, Boston*; 309 Elizabeth Crews; 312 Elizabeth Crews; 316 Larry Hamill; 318 Chick Moorman & Dee Dishon; 324 George Bellerose/*Stock, Boston*; 331 Chick Moorman & Dee Dishon; 335 Chick Moorman & Dee Dishon; 349 Cara Chenfeld; 370 Chick Moorman & Dee Dishon; 373 Chick Moorman & Dee Dishon; 378 Jack Corn/*Image, Inc.*; 379 Chick Moorman & Dee Dishon; 386 Larry Hamill; 392 Elizabeth Crews; 397 Christopher Brown/*Stock, Boston*; 401 Chick Moorman & Dee Dishon.

Front cover: Drawing by Colin Young

Back cover: Larry Hamill

Index

creative
    characteristics of, 45–50
    examples of, 38–42
    and individual expression,
        42–44
    instincts, 41, 51
    magic of, 37–42
    philosophy of, 26, 27
    seeds of ideas, 38
    who is, 42–50
and enthusiasm, 49, 50
examples of skills, 391–93
and favoritism, 48
and humility, 92
ideal, 44, 45
importance of, 50–53
motivation, 164–66
as role model, 244, 245
sharing, 63, 66, 405, 406
vs. computers, 382
Teaching
    and change, 42, 43
    creative, 36–71
    effectiveness, 131, 132, 147,
        148, 152, 160, 192, 193,
        235, 236, 272, 310, 311,
        358, 359, 393–95
    five factors, 160
    goals, 94, 95
    Indicators of Quality, 45–49
    key to it all, 404, 405
    making promises, 167
    philosophy, 375, 376, 406
    questionnaire, 55–57
    as renewal, 399, 400
    share your light, 405
    share your love, 405, 406
    skills, 372–74, 388, 391–93
    spelling, 376, 377
    and student involvement, 192
    two examples of, 375–79
Teacher–pupil identification, 49
Television, influence of, 23
Testing ideas, 47
Texts, 100
Thinking skills, 48
Thoreau, Henry David, 14, 242

Tiedt, Iris, 285
Tolkien, J. R. R., 271
Tolstoy, Leo, 33
Torrance, E. Paul, 13, 66, 94
Trethewey, Sally, 327
Turbill, Jan, 372
Turkel, Frayda, 93, 360
Turner, Tina, 190

Udry, Janice, 402
Unusual ideas, 47
Uris, Leon, 244

Van Gogh, Vincent, 335, 402
Verdi, Guiseppe, 125
Viorst, Judith, 239
Voltaire, François, 234
Volunteers and reading, 289, 290
Vonnegut, Kurt, 29
Voting for life or death, 18, 20, 41,
        50, 60, 65, 111, 151, 155,
        156, 161, 385

Warm and safe
    activities, 67–71
    climate, 64–71, 326, 327
Weather. *See* Climate
Weissman, Cynthia, 169
Weitzman, David, 250
Welty, Eudora, 127
White, E. B., 83
White, T. H., 242
Whitman, Walt, 12, 99, 152
Whorf, Benjamin Lee, 84
Wilder, Laura Ingalls, 271, 279
Wildsmith, Brian, 271
Willert, Mary K., 16
Williams, Barbara, 169
Wilson, Janis, 270, 271
Wilt, Miriam, 104
Winn, Marie, 15
Witkin, Kate, 203
Wolkstein, Diane, 253
Word processors in classrooms,
        380, 381
Writing. *See also* Activities,
    writing

ABC ideas, 334
about something vs. nothing,
        323, 324
activities, 301, 336–66
beginnings of, 357
children writing their own
        books, 377–79
and a child's imagination, 320
and chimneys, 332
a collage, 8–10
conference approach, 330–32
creatively, 6–11, 24, 26, 27
daily, 328
dialogues, 386
different kinds of, 332–36
eagerness of children, 317–24
encouraging, 8
enjoy, 327, 328
expository, 335, 336
feeling safe, 326, 327
ideas by poets, 334, 335
"menstrual" method, 325
Mom's story, 325–27, 344
newspaper, 364, 365, 391
"once" as a story starter, 321
original expression, 319
poetry, 333–35
reports, 361, 362
and self-discovery, 8–10
and sharing, 326–28, 332
Shockindakeiday's monster, 319,
        320
and spelling, 329
students' examples, 126, 129,
        173, 174, 183, 210, 211,
        214, 319, 322, 323, 325,
        326, 329, 337–42, 344,
        346, 347, 349, 352,
        354–56, 365, 384, 385, 388
talking written down, 328
and words, 329, 330

Yes or No, culture of, 18–20, 41,
        111, 325, 344
Young author conference, 325, 353

Zeitlin, Patty, 190